Eigh

OLD EN

Poems

Eight
OLD ENGLISH
POEMS

CÆDMON'S HYMN

THE BATTLE OF BRUNANBURH

THE DREAM OF THE ROOD

THE BATTLE OF MALDON

THE WANDERER

THE SEAFARER

DEOR

THE WIFE'S LAMENT

Edited with Commentary and Glossary

by JOHN C. POPE

THIRD EDITION

Prepared by R. D. FULK

W·W· Norton & Company · New York · London

Composition by R. D. Fulk.
Manufacturing by Maple-Vail Book Groups

Library of Congress Cataloging-in-Publication Data
Eight Old English poems / edited with commentary and glossary by John C. Pope.—
3rd ed., rev. / by R. D. Fulk.
    p. cm.
    Rev. ed. of: Seven Old English poems. 2nd ed. c1981.
    Includes bibliographical references.
    Contents: Cædmon's hymn—The Battle of Brunanburh—The dream of the rood—The Battle of Maldon—The wanderer—The seafarer—Deor—The wife's lament.

    ISBN 0-393-97605-X (pbk.)

    1. English poetry—Old English, ca. 450–1100.   2. Anglo Saxons—Poetry.
I. Pope, John Collins, 1904–   II. Fulk, R. D. (Robert Dennis)   III. Seven Old English poems.

PR1505 .E36 2000
829'.108—dc21

                           00-060572

W. W. Norton & Company, Inc., 500 Fifth Avenue, New York, N. Y. 10110
www.wwnorton.com

W. W. Norton & Company Ltd., Castle House, 75/76 Wells Street, London W1T 3QT

3 4 5 6 7 8 9 0

CONTENTS

Preface

This edition has grown out of my needs as the teacher of an elementary course in Old English for graduate students. The poems are those I have found it most profitable to read early in the year, as a preliminary to the study of *Beowulf.* They are arranged in the order in which I usually take them up with the class. There is nothing sacred about this order, except that *The Wanderer* and *The Seafarer* offer difficulties of interpretation beyond the rest, since they exhibit a more richly metaphorical and connotative use of language in accordance with their intellectually complicated themes; while *Deor,* with its allusions to heroic legends, stands in that respect closer than the others to the world of *Beowulf.*

The text and glossary have been my principal concern. The text is normalized very much according to the system of Professor F. P. Magoun, Jr., whose normalized text, *The Anglo-Saxon Poems in Bright's Anglo-Saxon Reader* (Department of English, Harvard University, 1960), has been a staple of my course for several years; and I might have rested content with this if I had not wished to include the whole of *The Dream of the Rood* and *The Seafarer,* and to treat all seven poems somewhat more intensively than his edition allowed. I have decided to adopt as my norm a somewhat less archaic version of Early West Saxon than Magoun's, which follows the spellings of Holthausen's *Altenglisches etymologisches Wörterbuch.* These spellings are excellent for the student of etymology and phonology, but in certain respects (notably the rounded *œ,* long and short, and the distinction between *io* and *eo*) they go beyond the spellings most frequently encountered in the literary manuscripts, especially those of the poetry, and beyond the spellings adopted as standard by the leading grammars. I have retained the *e* of the poetical manuscripts for the *i*-mutation of *o,* and have included what was historically *io* under the generalized *eo* of many, though by no means all, of the manuscripts. The most conspicuous mark of Early West Saxon, the *ie,* long and short, though it became archaic during the tenth century and was obsolete by the time of *The Battle of Maldon,* is too helpful to the student to be abandoned.

In a few other particulars I have departed from Holthausen and Magoun, generally in favor of less drastic alteration of the manuscript records and in accord with the forms given precedence in the grammars of Sievers-Brunner and Campbell. Here and there (like Magoun) I have allowed variant forms to stand for fear of disturbing the meter, and at least once (*sleaht* in *The Wanderer* for *slieht* in *Brunanburh*) for fear of too drastic an alteration of the phonetic pattern—though in this matter we must generally resign ourselves to the probability that our inherited texts are very far from faithful to the dialectal forms and other details of the poet's own speech. At all events the full record and cross-references of the glossary should render my few inconsistencies harmless. I have deliberately refrained from normalizing the pronominal forms *mē, þē, ūs, ēow,* so that the reader must decide whether they are dative or accusative, or consult my guesses in the glossary. Similarly, I have not normalized the endings in the manuscripts for the nominative and accusative plural of adjectives. The generalized ending *-e* is very common and is allowed to stand even if the noun modified is feminine or neuter. Consequently there is no instance in the ensuing texts of the specifically feminine *-a,* and only two of the neuter *-u* (*Wanderer* 85, *idlu* and 100, *wæl-ġifru*).

Partly to let the reader know precisely how I have modified these texts, and partly to keep the student aware of the irregularities he will encounter as soon as he turns to our standard editions of Old English poetry, I have put at the foot of the page the full record of the manuscript readings insofar as they differ from the normalized text. Outright emendations (most of which are the work of previous editors) are distinguished from mere variations in spelling—though sometimes a grammatical ending in the manuscript is susceptible of more than one interpretation, and the normalizer must make an editorial choice.

The glossary has been an even greater concern than the text. It is planned for a double purpose. On the one hand, it enables the beginner to make considerable progress toward gaining a general control of the poetic vocabulary. All nominal and adjectival compounds, if distinctly recognizable as such, are separated into their two components by hyphens in the text of the poems, and each component is separately defined in its alphabetical place in the glossary. In this way the student, following a plan recommended by Professor Magoun, can learn a relatively small number of simple words out of which a rather large number of compounds are formed by the poets, and can usually understand the compounds for himself, as the poets themselves, freely compounding words as they wished, expected their audiences or readers to do. On the other hand, the student of poetry wants not only to increase his general command of the vocabulary but to understand the subtleties of his text. For this reason I have defined the compounds as well as their components, and tried as far as possible to give, for all words, the meanings most applicable to their particular occurrences.

My own practice is to return to the standard editions, with their unnormalized texts, as soon as the student has acquired a grounding in the grammar and has begun to build a substantial vocabulary. Those who wish to continue the use of normalized texts can with very slight adjustment proceed to those of Professor Magoun, which are published by the Department of English at Harvard. Besides the poems in Bright's *Reader,* he has normalized *Beowulf* and *Judith* in one volume (1959) and the poems of the Vercelli Book in another (1960). His own device for building vocabulary is the *Grouped Frequency Word-List* of *Anglo-Saxon Poetry,* prepared jointly with John F. Madden, C.S.B. (second corrected printing, 1960). An almost essential companion to these texts is Jess B. Bessinger, Jr., *A Short Dictionary of Anglo-Saxon Poetry* (Toronto: University of Toronto Press, 1960).

NOTE TO THE REVISED EDITION: The first edition of this book was reproduced photographically from typescript for the use of my own students. In preparing it for general use I have corrected many small errors and omissions, rewritten several portions of the commentary, augmented others, and added a section on versification. The bibliographical suggestions in the commentary have been extended but remain highly selective. The older bibliography is amply represented in the special editions to which I have referred. I must rely upon teacher and student to make further exploration and to add fresh items year by year.

I am grateful to many of my present and former students for call-ing attention to inconsistencies and oversights. To Dr. Robert B. Burlin I am indebted for valuable bibliographical suggestions and for generously given assistance in editorial tasks. To Dr. Frances Randall Lipp, who tried out the first edition with her classes, I owe searching criticism on several matters pertaining to the interpreta-tion of the texts and further help on bibliography.

J. C. P.

New Haven, Connecticut
1966

Preface to the Second Edition

The present edition is an exact photographic reproduction of the seventh printing of the first edition, except that it has been possible to correct a number of minor errors that had escaped notice in ear-lier printings. Most of these have to do with vowel length, pronun-ciation of palatal *c* and *g,* punctuation, and style of type. A few cor-rections of the glossary could not so easily be entered. They have been reserved for the Supplement, which attempts to add major bib-liographical information up to 1980 and to reconsider certain mat-ters of interpretation in the light of recent opinion. I am grateful to the Norton editors for undertaking publication of this new edition, and to Bobbs-Merrill for turning over the copyright to me and con-senting to the reproduction, with minor revision, of the first edition.

J. C. P.

New Haven, Connecticut
February, 1981

Preface to the Third Edition

Although a supplement of a self-described limited scope was added to this book in 1981, aside from some minor corrections it remained otherwise unchanged after 1966. It is no doubt a measure of the meticulousness of John Pope's work and of Anglo-Saxonists' esteem for his fair-minded and humane scholarship that the book has continued in use both in the classroom and as a source of serious scholarship on the seven poems he edited, even though the considerable advances in the study of these texts over the past thirty years went largely unaddressed in the commentary. Accordingly, my first concern in revising this volume has been to bring it up to date while preserving the features that have made it so useful to me and to others who continue to rely on it in the classroom.

One improvement in conditions for the study of these poems in the past thirty years is that the manuscripts, or surviving transcripts of them, are all now readily available in facsimile. The texts have been checked against the reproductions and the critical apparatus corrected on that basis. Some fine editions have appeared, and they have proved invaluable to revision of the commentary, which is much indebted both to them and to the considerable body of literature that has been devoted to these poems since 1966. Nonetheless, no attempt has been made to provide comprehensive coverage of the critical literature. The bibliography of the seven poems is by now quite large, and it goes without saying that many very fine studies have of necessity gone unremarked here. This is particularly true of analyses of primarily literary interest, since the commentary is devoted above all to the textual problems that beset these works. As a result, the literary studies that are mentioned are chiefly those of some relevance to the establishment of the text. It should be said that in this edition a more concerted effort has been made to explain the bases for textual choices and to outline the proposed alternatives. This is a consequence of the sensitivity that has come to be attached to questions of editorial practice among Anglo-Saxonists. The aim is not so much to justify the readings adopted as to engage students in questions of editorial practice and to facilitate study of the various and complex issues that attend textual criticism in Old English.

The chief alteration to this third edition is the addition of *The Wife's Lament*. The poem has in the past twenty years become so important to the Old English curriculum that it required very little persuasion on the part of Julia Reidhead at W. W. Norton to induce me to add it to the book. As for the other seven poems, despite the aim of conserving the most widely appreciated features of the book, I have ventured to alter readings in the texts themselves when recent studies have offered more attractive alternatives, or even, occasionally, when my own sense of the textual possibilities demanded it. On the whole, though, users of this volume will find that alterations to the texts are relatively minor. Aside from a few emended readings, the changes are in matters of phonological detail, such as the distribution of palatal and affricate consonants and of **þ** and **ð**. John Pope and I discussed the need for some of these changes before his death in 1997. The distribution of palatal and affricate consonants is particularly difficult to determine, since there is disagreement or uncertainty about the conditions for change, the extent of analogical disruption within paradigms, and the treatment of such consonants at points of morpheme juncture. I have attempted to make the phonological representation conform to the *original* distribution of sounds (except in some unstressed syllables, as in **cyning** and **æðeling**), even though this sometimes conflicts with what the standard handbooks prescribe on the basis of later disruptions to the patterns. This is in accordance with Pope's practice, since he preserved many paradigm irregularities—for example, nominative **cearu** together with accusative **ćeare**.

Among other changes, the method of citation has been converted to a parenthetical one and a new translation of Bede's account of Cædmon's miraculous gift of song has been supplied. The extent of the changes to the commentary varies from poem to poem, but in all cases it is substantial. The supplement to the second edition has been eliminated and its commentary, where retained, integrated with the rest. In addition, the essay on versification has been almost entirely rewritten. This was felt necessary because of the considerable advances of recent years in early Germanic metrics, and because the isochronous approach to which much of Pope's 1981 essay was devoted is now little used, as Sieversian metrics have dominated recent studies. Students will find that the fuller attention to Sievers' principles in this edition furnishes a more direct entrée to the issues that prevail in contemporary metrical scholarship.

This edition owes its existence to the support of several extraordinarily generous souls, to whose kindnesses my thanks are incommensurate. Joseph Harris provided timely offprints when the Indiana University Libraries for once were at an impasse. The help of Christopher M. Cain was indispensable, as he digitally scanned nearly the entire second edition of the book, and he corrected countless errors and offered invaluable suggestions when he proofread the early drafts. Chief responsibility for this edition's existence belongs to Julia Reidhead at W. W. Norton, whose enthusiasm for the project brought it into being, and who guided it with a sure hand from start to finish. To Diane O'Connor and Sue Carlson thanks are due for expert advice on production. The task of copyediting a manuscript that includes a glossary and a metrical treatise on poems in an unfamiliar language is surely any reasonable reader's nightmare; Alice Falk, far from being daunted, brought immense skill and penetrating insights to the task. Lucinda Miller at Indiana University provided technical assistance with the recordings mentioned on p. xiv, and Julie Tedoff and Steve Hoge at Norton made them available on the World Wide Web. Brian Baker and Kurt Wildermuth checked the manuscript, and Toni Krass designed a new title page. For more varied kinds of help at Norton, thanks are due to Christina Grenawalt and Marian Johnson. The Dean and Chapter of Exeter Cathedral kindly lent permission to reproduce the image on the cover of the book. I also owe much to friends and colleagues in Bloomington for their support, particularly to Al and Linda David; and, as always, to Brian Powell.

R. D. F.

Bloomington, Indiana
May, 2000

Aids to Pronunciation

Recordings of the eight poems read by Mary E. Blockley and by the present editor may be found on the World Wide Web at ‹http://www.wwnorton.com/nael/noa›.

ð   in normalized readings in this book represents the voiced *th* in *this*. It is used internally after a stressed vowel except in contiguity with a voiceless consonant. The uppercase form is **Ð**. Under the same conditions **f** is like *v* in *rave* and **s** is like *z* in *raze*.[1]

þ   comparably represents the voiceless *th* in *thin*. It is used initially (as in **þæt**) and finally (as in **sēaþ**), as well as internally after an unstressed vowel (as in **earfoþa**; also **mǣrþa** from ***mǣriþa**) or next to a voiceless consonant (as in **ġesihþe**).[2] The uppercase form is **Þ**. In Old English manuscripts the symbols ð and þ are used indifferently. Under the same conditions under which þ appears in this book, **f** is pronounced as in *fit* and **s** as in *sit*.

ċ   is an affricate pronounced like *ch* in *chin*. The rules for distinguishing **c** and **ċ** are intricate, and they are complicated by paradigm regularization. In general, though, the sound is deaffricated before consonants and when in prehistoric times it preceded a back vowel. Deaffrication does not occur, however, before juncture in compounds (as in **ġeswinċ-dagum**).

---

[1] The treatment of fricative consonants (*f, þ, s*) at the place of juncture in compounds has been insufficiently studied. In quasi-compounds with tertiary stress (as defined below, p. 139–40)—that is, in older, lexicalized compounds and words with derivational suffixes—it seems that these fricatives, when they appear finally in the first constituent of a complex word, are voiced before voiced sounds. Thus the fricative is voiced in names such as **Ælfwine** and **Wulfmǣr** and in words such as **wisdōm** and **weorðlice**. Despite reasonable expectations to the contrary, the evidence of Old English compounds contained in modern place-names shows that we should also assume voiced fricatives in genuine (primary) compounds like **Norð-menn** and **forð-ġesceaft**. The fricative **g** is devoiced finally in words such as **burg** and **bēag**, and it is often written **h** in the manuscripts; but to minimize spelling variation it is written **g** in this book. Hence the spelling **Brūnanburg**, though all the MSS have -*burh,* the traditional spelling retained here in the title only.

[2] Despite the apparent exceptions (see Campbell 1959: §445 n. 1), the nonvoicing of fricatives after unstressed vowels (as in **earfoþa**, **hæleþa**, etc.; also **for-þon**, **sēþe**, and **nemþe**, unstressed words) seems a necessary assumption. These matters are treated in a pair of forthcoming articles by the present editor.

ċċ is the same sound prolonged or doubled.

cg in the eight poems is always like *dge* in *edge*.

ng is like *ng* in *finger,* never as in *ring.*

nġ is pronounced like *nge* in *hinge* (but not if *n* belongs to a separable element, as in **an-ġinn** or **on-ġinnan**).

ġ when not preceded by *n* is like *y* in *year.*

g at the start of a stressed syllable is like *g* in *go.* At the end of a word (except in the combination **ng**, as above) it is like *ch* in Scottish *loch* or German *Nacht* (see note 1). Medially, **g** is the voiced equivalent of this *ch* sound, a voiced velar fricative, like the *g* in Danish *kage* or the γ in Greek γράφω.

h at the beginning of a stressed syllable is like *h* in *hat.* Everywhere else it is like *ch* in German *Nacht* or *nicht.*

sc is generally like *sh* in *shall, English.* It may also have the value of *sk* in *ask.* The two pronunciations are not distinguished diacritically here because there are just two Old English words in this book in which **sc** has the value of *sk,* and they are **æsca** (*Wanderer* 99b) and **ġe-āscodon** (*Deor* 21a). The pronunciation *sk* is used finally after all back vowels and medially before original back vowels if the preceding vowel has not undergone front mutation (or "*i*-umlaut"). Everywhere else, **sc** has the value of *sh.*

ę is not pronounced as a vowel. It represents an *e* that is written in the manuscripts with some consistency but that is merely a diacritic, indicating that the preceding consonant is palatal, as in **ġ̇eōmor** and **ġ̇eong**.

TEXTS

Cædmon's Hymn

The Northumbrian Version of MS M, *Eighth Century*
(The Moore MS, *University Library, Cambridge,*
Kk. 5. 16, f. 128ᵛ)

    Nu scylun hergan   hefaenricaes uard,
    metudæs maecti   end his modgidanc,
    uerc uuldurfadur,   sue he uundra gihuaes,
    eci dryctin,   or astelidæ.
5   He aerist scop   aelda barnum
    heben til hrofe,   haleg scepen;
    tha middungeard   moncynnæs uard,
    eci dryctin,   æfter tiadæ,
    firum foldu,   frea allmectig.

Variants in MS P (St. Petersburg, M.E. Saltykov-Schedrin Public Library, MS lat. Q. v. i. 18, f. 107, dated to the eighth century): **1** scilun. herga. hefenricæs. **2** mehti. and. modgithanc. **3** gihuæs. **5** ærist. aeldu. **6** hefen to hrofæ halig sceppend. **7** middingard. **9** allmehtig.

3

Cædmon's Hymn

The Hymn Normalized in West Saxon Spelling
Based on the Northumbrian Version of MSS M *and* P

Nū sculon herian   heofon-rīċes weard,
metodes meahta   and his mōd-ġeþanc,
weorc wuldor-fæder,   swā hē wundra ġehwæs,
ēċe dryhten,   ōr astealde.
5 Hē ǣrest scōp   ielda bearnum
heofon tō hrōfe,   hāliġ scieppend;
þā middan-ġeard   mann-cynnes weard,
ēċe dryhten,   æfter tēode—
fīrum foldan   frēa ælmihtiġ.

Substantive variants in MS T (Bodleian Library, Tanner 10, f. 100ʳ), the best of the West Saxon texts, included in the Old English version of Bede's *Historia ecclesiastica:* **4** onstealde.   **5** eorðan *for* ielda.

Spelling variants in T compared with the normalized text: **1** herigean. **2** meotodes. meahte.   **4** drihten.   **5** sceop.   **6** scyppend.   **7** moncynnes. **8** drihten.

Among variants in some of the later copies are the following: **1** we *before* sculon. **4** ord *for* or.   **5** gesceop *for* scop.

4

The Battle of Brunanburh

(The Anglo-Saxon Chronicle)

    Hēr Æðelstān cyning,   eorla dryhten,
    beorna bēag-ġiefa,   and his brōðor ēac,
    Ēadmund æðeling,   ealdor-langne tīr
    ġeslōgon æt sæċċe   sweorda ecgum
5   ymbe Brūnanburg.   Bord-weall clufon,
    hēowon heaðu-linda   hamora lāfum
    eaforan Ēadweardes,   swā him ġe-æðele wæs
    fram cnēo-māgum   þæt hīe æt campe oft
    wiþ lāðra ġehwone   land ealgoden,
10   hord and hāmas.   Hettend crungon,
    Scotta lēode   and scip-flotan,
    fǣġe fēollon.   Feld dennode
    secga swāte   siþþan sunne upp
    on morgen-tīd,   mǣre tungol,
15   glād ofer grundas,   Godes candel beorht,

A = Corpus Christi College, Cambridge, MS 173 (The Parker Chronicle),
ff. 26ʳ–27ʳ. B = British Library, MS Cotton Tiberius A. vi, ff. 31ʳ–32ʳ. C = British
Library, MS Cotton Tiberius B. i, f. 141ʳ⁻ᵛ. D = British Library, MS Cotton Tiberius
B. iv, ff. 49ʳ–50ʳ. A was copied at Winchester soon after 955; B and C are copies of a
MS at Abingdon, now lost; B after 977, C eleventh century. D was copied from a
northern MS after 1016.

1 B æþestan.   BC cing.   BCD drihten.   **2** ACD beah.   ABD gifa; C gyfa.
3 C ealdorlagne.   D tyr.   **4** B geslogan.   B sake; D secce.   C swurda.
B ecggum.   **5** BC embe.   BC brunnan (AD brunan, *but* A *corrected to* brunnan).
-burg] ABCD burh.   bord-] D heord.   AD weal.   ABD clufan.   **6** ABD heowan.
ABCD heaþo.   A linde; B lina; D linga *altered to* linda.   D hamera.   A lafan.
7 A afaran; C aforan; D eoforan *altered to* eaforan.   D eadweardæs.   **8** A from.
ACD mægum.   ACD hi.   **9** ACD gehwæne; B gehwane.   AC ealgodon;
B ealgodan; D gealgodon.   **10** D heted.   A crungun.   **11** A sceotta.   A leoda.
C scyp.   **12** ABC feollan.   A dænede *corrected to* dænnede; BC dennade.
13 A secgas hwate.   AD up.   **15** A condel.

ēċes dryhtnes,   oþ sēo æðele ġesceaft
sāg tō setle.   Þǣr læġ secg maniġ
gārum aġīeted,   guma norðerna
ofer scield scoten,   swelċe Scyttisc ēac,
20   wēriġ, wīġes sæd.   West-Seaxe forþ
andlangne dæġ   ēorod-cystum
on lāst leġdon   lāðum þēodum,
hēowon here-flīeman   hindan þearle
mēċum mylen-scearpum.   Mierċe ne wierndon
25   heardes hand-plegan   hæleþa nānum
þāra-þe mid Anlāfe   ofer ēar-ġebland
on lides bōsme   land ġesōhton,
fǣġe tō ġefeohte.   Fīfe lāgon
on þām camp-stede   cyningas ġeonge
30   sweordum aswefede,   swelċe seofone ēac
eorlas Anlāfes,   unrīm herġes,
flotena and Scotta.   Þǣr ġeflīemed wearþ
Norð-manna bregu,   nīede ġebǣded,
tō lides stefne   lȳtle weorode;
35   crēad cnearr on flot,   cyning ūt ġewāt
on fealone flōd,   feorh ġenerede.
Swelċe þǣr ēac sē frōda   mid flēame cōm
on his cȳþþe norþ,   Constantīnus,

---

16 ABCD drihtnes. oþ] B þæt. A sio; D se. **17** ABCD sah. D sætle.
A mænig; CD monig. **18** ACD ageted; B forgrunden. BCD guman.
BC norðerne; D norþærne. **19** A scild; BCD scyld. BD sceoten. AC swilce;
BD swylce. A scittisc. **20** BC wigges. D ræd. AD wesseaxe; B westsexe;
C and wessexe. **21** A ondlongne. BCD eored. A cistum. **22** A legdun;
D lægdon. C ðeodon. **23** ABD heowan. A herefleman; B hereflyman;
C hereflymon; D heora flyman. **24** A mylenscearpan; D mycelscearpum.
ABCD myrce. ABCD wyrndon. **25** A heeardes. A hond. **26** þara-þe] A þæ;
D þæra þe. A æra. **27** C liþes. A gesohtun; B gesohtan. **28** D fage. D feohte.
A lægun. **29** B þæm. A cyninges; B ciningas; C cingas. A giunge; D iunga.
30 C aswefde. ABC swilce; D swylce. AD seofene; C vii. **31** unrim] C and
unrim. A heriges. **32** ABCD flotan. A sceotta. A geflemed; BCD geflymed.
33 BCD brego. AB nede; CD neade. A gebeded. **34** D stæfne. A litle.
C werode. **35** D creat. cnearr on] BCD cnear on; A cnearen. D flod. B cing;
C cining. D *omits 35b and 36a.* **36** A fealene. CD generode. **37** AC swilce;
B Swylce; D swylce. **38** A costontinus.

    hār hilde-rinċ. Hrēman ne þorfte
40 mēċa ġemānan; hē wæs his māga sceard,
    frēonda ġefielled on folc-stede,
    beslæġen æt sæċċe, and his sunu forlēt
    on wæl-stōwe wundum forgrunden,
    ġeongne æt gūðe. Ġielpan ne þorfte
45 beorn blanden-feax bill-ġesliehtes,
    eald inwitta, nē Anlāf þȳ mā;
    mid hira here-lāfum hliehhan ne þorfton
    þæt hīe beadu-weorca beteran wurdon
    on camp-stede cumbol-ġehnāstes,
50 gār-mittunge, gumena ġemōtes,
    wǣpen-ġewrixles, þæs hīe on wæl-felda
    wiþ Ēadweardes eaforan plegodon.
    Ġewiton him þā Norð-menn næġled-cnearrum,
    drēoriġ daroþa lāf, on Dinġes mere
55 ofer dēop wæter Dyflin sēċan,
    eft Īra land ǣwisc-mōde.
    Swelċe þā ġebrōðor bēġen ætsamne,
    cyning and æðeling, cȳþþe sōhton,
    West-Seaxna land, wīġes hrēmġe.
60 Lēton him behindan hrǣw bryttian

---

39 har] D hal. A hildering; D hylderinc. D hryman. **40** meca] A mæcan; B mecea; D mecga. he] BC her. AD mæga. **41** ABCD gefylled. on] C on his. **42** beslægen] A beslagen; C beslegen; B forslegen. B sace; D sæcge. D forlæt. **43** A wundun. A fergrunden. **44** A giungne. A gelpan; BCD gylpan. **45** BC fex. A bil. A geslehtes; B geslyhtes; CD geslihtes. **46** A inwidda; D inwuda. þy] BD þe. **47** AB heora; CD hyra. D leafum. A hlehhan; BC hlihhan; D hlybban. AC þorftun; BD þorftan. **48** A heo; CD hi. BCD beado. A wurdun; B wurdan. **49** A culbod, cumbel *over line.* A gehnades. **50** ABC mittinge. **51** þæs] D þæs þe. ACD hi. **52** AD afaran; C aforan. AB plegodan. **53** AB gewitan. C hym. A normen *altered to* norþmen; D norðmen. C negledcnearrum; D dæg gled on garum. **54** C dreori. A daraða; C dareþa; D dareða. B dynges; D dyniges. **55** D deopne. A difelin; B dyflen; D dyflig. B secean. **56** eft] A and eft, *the* and *added later above the line.* Ira] A hira; CD yra. **57** AC swilce; B Swylce; D swylce. A gebroþer; C broðor. D bege. BC ætsomne; D æt runne. **58** BC cing. D eaðeling. B sohton. **59** A wesseaxena; C wessexena. BC wigges. A hramige *altered to* hremige; BCD hremige. **60** AB letan; D læton. C hym. C behindon. A hræ *with* w *added above the line;* B hraw; CD hra. B bryttigean; C brittigan; D bryttinga.

sealwiġ-pādan,   þone sweartan hræfn
hyrned-nebban,   and þone hasu-pādan,
earn æftan hwīt,   æses brūcan—
grǣdiġne gūþ-hafoc,   and þæt grǣġe dēor,
65   wulf on wealda.   Ne wearþ wæl māre
on þȳs īġ-lande   ǣfre ġīeta
folces ġefielled   beforan þissum
sweordes ecgum,   þæs-þe ūs secgaþ bēċ,
ealde ūðwitan,   siþþan ēastan hider
70   Engle and Seaxe   upp becōmon,
ofer brād brimu   Britene sōhton,
wlance wīġ-smiðas,   Wēalas ofercōmon,
eorlas ār-hwæte   eard beġēaton.

---

61 A saluwig; BCD salowig.   C hrefn.   **62** D hyrnet.   A þane.   A hasewan;
B haso.   D wadan.   **64** D cuðheafoc.   D grege.   **65** ABCD wealde.   **66** A þis;
D þisne.   A eiglande; B eglande.   A æfer.   BC gyta; D gita.   **67** ACD gefylled;
B afylled.   BCD þyssum.   **68** C swurdes.   B secggeaþ.   **69** B syþþan.
70 B sexan; C sexe.   AD up.   AB becoman.   **71** BCD brade.   AB brytene;
C bretene.   AB sohtan.   **72** A weealles.   AB ofercoman.   **73** ABC arhwate.
A begeatan.

The Dream of the Rood

(*Vercelli Book,* ff. 104ᵛ–106ʳ)

    Hwæt, iċ swefna cyst   secgan wille,
    hwæt mē ġemǣtte   tō midre nihte,
    siþþan reord-berend   reste wunodon.
    Þūhte mē þæt iċ ġesāwe   seldlicre trēo
5   on lyft lǣdan   lēohte bewunden,
    bēama beorhtost.   Eall þæt bēacen wæs
    begoten mid golde;   ġimmas stōdon
    fæġre æt foldan scēatum,   swelċe þǣr fīfe wǣron
    uppe on þām eaxl-ġespanne   —behēold on þām enġel
                                    dryhtnes—
10 fæġre þurh forð-ġesceaft.   Ne wæs þǣr hūru fracuðes ġealga,
    ac hine þǣr behēoldon   hālġe gāstas,
    menn ofer moldan   and eall þēos mǣre ġesceaft.
    Seldliċ wæs sē siġe-bēam,   and iċ synnum fāg,
    forwundod mid wammum.   Ġeseah iċ wuldres trēo
15 wǣdum ġeweorðod   wynnum scīnan,
    ġeġiered mid golde;   ġimmas hæfdon
    bewriġen weorðlīċe   wealdendes trēo.
    Hwæðre iċ þurh þæt gold   onġietan meahte
    earmra ǣr-ġewinn,   þæt hit ǣrest ongann

Emendations: **2** hwæt] MS hæt.   **9** eaxl] MS eaxle.   beheold on þam] MS be heoldon þær.   dryhtnes] MS dryht nes ealle.   **15** geweorðod] MS geweor ðode. **17** bewrigen] MS be wrigene.   wealdendes] MS wealdes.

Variant spellings in the MS: **1** wylle.   **3** syðþan. wunedon.   **4** syllicre. treow. **8** fægere. swylce.   **10** fægere. fracodes.   **11** halige.   **12** men.   **13** Syllic. fah. **14** forwunded. wommum. treow.   **16** ge gyred.   **17** treow.   **18** ongytan. **19** gewin. ongan.

20 swǣtan on þā swīðran healfe.   Eall iċ wæs mid sorgum
ġedrēfed;
forht iċ wæs for þǣre fǣġran ġesihþe.   Ġeseah iċ þæt
fūse bēacen
wendan wǣdum and blēoum: hwīlum hit wæs mid
wǣtan bestīemed,
beswiled mid swātes gange,   hwīlum mid sinċe ġeġierwed.
Hwæðre iċ þǣr licgende   lange hwīle
25 behēold hrēow-ċeariġ   hǣlendes trēo,
oþ-þæt iċ ġehīerde   þæt hit hlēoðrode;
ongann þā word sprecan   wudu sēlesta:
   "Þæt wæs ġeāra ġeō   —iċ þæt ġīeta ġeman—
þæt iċ wæs ahēawen   holtes on ende,
30 astyred of stefne mīnum.   Ġenāmon mē þǣr strange fēondas,
ġeworhton him þǣr tō wǣfer-sīene,   hēton mē hira
weargas hebban.
Bǣron mē þǣr beornas on eaxlum,   oþ-þæt hīe mē on
beorg asetton;
ġefæstnodon mē þǣr fēondas ġenōge.   Ġeseah iċ þā frēan
mann-cynnes
efstan elne micle   þæt hē mē wolde on ġestīgan.
35 Þǣr iċ þā ne dorste   ofer Dryhtnes word
būgan oþþe berstan   þā iċ bifian ġeseah
eorðan scēatas.   Ealle iċ meahte
fēondas ġefiellan,   hwæðre iċ fæste stōd.
Onġierede hine þā ġeong hæleþ   —þæt wæs God ælmihtiġ—
40 strang and stīð-mōd;   ġestāg hē on ġealgan hēanne,
mōdiġ on maniġra ġesihþe,   þā hē wolde mann-cynn līesan.
Bifode iċ þā mē sē beorn ymbclypte;   ne dorste iċ
hwæðre būgan tō eorðan,
feallan tō foldan scēatum,   ac iċ scolde fæste standan.

Emendation: **20** sorgum] MS surgum.

Variant spellings: **21** ge syhðe. **22** bleom. be stemed. **23** beswyled. ge gyrwed.
25 treow. **26** gehyrde. **27** ongan. **28** geo] iu. gyta. **30** genaman. **31** syne.
heora. wergas. **33** man. **34** mycle. **37** mihte. **38** gefyllan. **39** Ongyrede.
40 gestah. **41** ge syhðe. man cyn. lysan. **43** sceolde. **45** hyldan.

Rōd wæs iċ ærǣred;   ahōf iċ rīcne cyning,
45   heofona hlāford;   hieldan mē ne dorste.
Þurhdrifon hīe mē mid deorcum næġlum: on mē sindon
þā dolg ġesīene,
opene inwitt-hlemmas;   ne dorste iċ hira ǣnigum scieþþan.
Bismerodon hīe unc bū-tū ætgædere.   Eall iċ wæs mid
blōde bestīemed,
begoten of þæs guman sīdan   siþþan hē hæfde his gāst
onsended.
50   Fela iċ on þām beorge   ġebiden hæbbe
wrāðra wyrda.   Ġeseah iċ weoroda God
þearle þenian.   Þīestru hæfdon
bewriġen mid wolcnum   wealdendes hrǣw,
scīrne scīman;   scadu forþ ēode
55   wann under wolcnum.   Wēop eall ġesceaft,
cwīðdon cyninges fiell;   Crīst wæs on rōde.
"Hwæðre þǣr fūse   feorran cōmon
tō þām æðelinge.   Iċ þæt eall behēold.
Sāre iċ wæs mid sorgum ġedrēfed,   hnāg iċ hwæðre þām
secgum tō handa,
60   ēað-mōd, elne micle.   Ġenāmon hīe þǣr ælmihtiġne God,
ahōfon hine of þām hefigan wīte.   Forlēton mē þā hilde-rincas
standan stēame bedrifenne;   eall iċ wæs mid strǣlum
forwundod.
Aleġdon hīe þǣr lim-wēriġne;   ġestōdon him æt his
līċes hēafdum;
behēoldon hīe þǣr heofones dryhten,   and hē hine þǣr
hwīle reste,
65   mēðe æfter þām miclan ġewinne.   Ongunnon him þā
mold-ærn wyrċan
beornas on banan ġesihþe.   Curfon hīe þæt of beorhtan stāne;

ġesetton hīe þǣr-on sigora wealdend.   Ongunnon him þā

          sorg-lēoþ galan,

earme on þā ǣfen-tīde,   þā hīe woldon eft sīðian,

mēðe fram þām mǣran þēodne;   reste hē þǣr mǣte weorode.

70   Hwæðre wē þǣr grēotende   gōde hwīle

    stōdon on staðole.   Stefn upp ġewāt

    hilde-rinca.   Hrǣw cōlode,

    fǣġer feorh-bold.   Þā ūs man fiellan ongann

    ealle tō eorðan.   Þæt wæs eġesliċ wyrd!

75   Bedealf ūs man on dēopan sēaðe.   Hwæðre mē þǣr

          dryhtnes þeġnas,

frēondas ġefrugnon   *   *   *

    *   *   *   ġieredon mē   golde and seolfre.

   "Nū þū meaht ġehīeran,   hæleþ mīn sē lēofa,

    þæt iċ bealwa weorc   ġebiden hæbbe,

80   sārra sorga.   Is nū sǣl cumen

    þæt mē weorðiaþ   wīde and sīde

    menn ofer moldan   and eall þēos mǣre ġesceaft,

    ġebiddaþ him tō þissum bēacne.   On mē bearn Godes

    þrōwode hwīle;   for-þon iċ þrymfæst nū

85   hlīfie under heofonum,   and iċ hǣlan mæġ

    ǣġhwelcne ānra,   þāra-þe him biþ eġesa tō mē.

    Ġeō iċ wæs ġeworden   wīta heardost,

    lēodum lāðost,   ǣr-þon iċ him līfes weġ

    rihtne ġerȳmde,   reord-berendum.

90   Hwæt, mē þā ġeweorðode   wuldres ealdor

    ofer holt-wudu,   heofon-rīċes weard,

    swelċe swā hē his mōdor ēac,   Mārian selfe,

    ælmihtiġ God,   for ealle menn

    ġeweorðode   ofer eall wīfa cynn.

Emendations: **70** greotende] MS reotende.   **71** stefn] MS syððan.   **79** bealwa]
MS bealuwara.   **91** holt-] MS holm.

Variant spellings: **67** sorh.   **70** hwæðere.   **71** up.   **73** feorg. fyllan. ongan.
76 gefrunon.   **77** gyredon.   **78** miht. ge hyran.   **83** þyssum.   **84** forþan.
85 hlifige. heofenum.   **86** æghwylcne.   **87** Geo] iu.   **88** ærþan.   **92** swylce.
sylfe.

95 "Nū iċ þē hāte,   hæleþ mīn sē lēofa,
þæt þū þās ġesihþe   secge mannum;
onwrēoh wordum   þæt hit is wuldres bēam,
sē-þe ælmihtiġ God   on þrōwode
for mann-cynnes   manigum synnum
100 and Ādames   eald-ġewyrhtum.
Dēaþ hē þǣr bierġde;   hwæðre eft dryhten arās
mid his miclan meahte   mannum tō helpe.
Hē þā on heofonas astāg.   Hider eft fundaþ
on þisne middan-ġeard   mann-cynn sēċan
105 on dōm-dæġe   dryhten selfa,
ælmihtiġ God   and his englas mid,
þæt hē þonne wile dēman,   sē āg dōmes ġeweald,
ānra ġehwelcum,   swā hē him ǣror hēr
on þissum lǣnan   līfe ġe-earnaþ.
110 Ne mæġ þǣr ǣniġ   unforht wesan
for þām worde   þe sē wealdend cwiþ:
friġneþ hē for þǣre meniġe   hwǣr sē mann sīe,
sē-þe for dryhtnes naman   dēaðes wolde
bitres onbierġan,   swā hē ǣr on þām bēame dyde.
115 Ac hīe þonne forhtiaþ,   and fēa þenċaþ
hwæt hīe tō Crīste   cweðan onġinnen.
Ne þearf þǣr þonne ǣniġ   unforht wesan
þe him ǣr on brēostum bereþ   bēacna sēlest.
Ac þurh þā rōde sceal   rīċe ġesēċan
120 of eorð-weġe   ǣghwelċ sāwol,
sēo-þe mid wealdende   wunian þenċeþ."
      Ġebæd iċ mē þā tō þām bēame   blīðe mōde,
elne micle,   þǣr iċ āna wæs
mǣte weorode;   wæs mōd-sefa
125 afȳsed on forð-weġe;   fela ealra ġebād
langung-hwīla.   Is mē nū līfes hyht

Variant spellings: **96** ge syhðe. **99** man. manegum. **100** adomes. **101** byrigde.
hwæðere. **102** mihte. **103** heofenas. **104** þysne. man. **105** sylfa. **107** ah.
108 ge hwylcum. ærur. **109** þyssum. lænum. **111** cwyð. **112** frineð. mænige.
man. **114** biteres. onbyrigan. **118** on] in. **120** æghwylc. sawl. **122** þan.
123 mycle. **124** werede.

þæt iċ þone siġe-bēam   sēċan mōte,
āna oftor   þonne ealle menn
wēl weorðian;   mē is willa tō þām
130   miċel on mōde,   and mīn mund-byrd is
ġeriht tō þǣre rōde.   Nāg iċ rīcra fela
frēonda on foldan.   Ac hīe forþ heonan
ġewiton of weorolde drēamum,   sōhton him wuldres cyning;
libbaþ nū on heofonum   mid hēah-fædere,
135   wuniaþ on wuldre;   and iċ wēne mē
daga ġehwelċe   hwonne mē dryhtnes rōd,
þe iċ hēr on eorðan   ǣr sċēawode,
on þissum lǣnan   līfe ġefeċċe,
and mē þonne ġebrinġe   þǣr is bliss miċel,
140   drēam on heofonum,   þǣr is dryhtnes folc
ġeseted tō symble,   þǣr is singal bliss;
and mē þonne asette   þǣr iċ siþþan mōt
wunian on wuldre,   wēl mid þām hālgum
drēames brūcan.   Sīe mē dryhten frēond,
145   sē-þe hēr on eorðan   ǣr þrōwode
on þām ġealg-trēowe   for guman synnum:
hē ūs onlīesde,   and ūs līf forġeaf,
heofonlicne hām.   Hyht wæs ġenīewod
mid blǣdum and mid blisse,   þām-þe þǣr bryne þolodon.
150   Sē sunu wæs sigorfæst   on þām sīþ-fæte,
mihtiġ and spēdiġ,   þā hē mid meniġe cōm,
gāsta weorode,   on Godes rīċe,
anwealda ælmihtiġ,   englum tō blisse,
and eallum þām hālgum   þām-þe on heofonum ǣr
155   wunodon on wuldre,   þā hira wealdend cōm,
ælmihtiġ God,   þǣr his ēðel wæs.

Emendation: **142** me] MS he.

Variant spellings: **128** men.   **129** well.   **130** mycel.   **131** Nah. feala.
132 heonon.   **133** worulde.   **134** lifiaþ. heofenum.   **136** ge hwylce. hwænne.
138 þysson. ge fetige.   **139** blis. mycel.   **141** symle. blis.   **142** syþþan.
143 well.   **144** si.   **147** onlysde.   **148** hiht. ge niwad.   **149** bledum. þolodan.
150 fate.   **151** manigeo.   **155** wunedon. heora. cwom.

The Battle of Maldon

(*Bodleian Library*, MS *Rawlinson* B. 203, ff. 7ʳ–12ᵛ,
a Transcript Made between 1718 and 1724 by David Casley
from the Incomplete Eleventh-Century Manuscript,
Cotton Otho A. xii, Burned in 1731.)

      *   *   *   brocen wurde.
Hēt þā hyssa hwone   hors forlǣtan,
feorr afȳsan   and forþ gangan,
hycgan tō handum   and tō hyġe gōdum.

5   Þā þæt Offan mǣġ   ǣrest onfunde,
þæt sē eorl nolde   iergþe ġeþolian,
hē lēt him þā of handum   lēofne flēogan
hafoc wiþ þæs holtes   and tō þǣre hilde stōp;
be þām man meahte oncnāwan   þæt sē cniht nolde

10   wācian æt þām wīġe   þā hē tō wǣpnum fēng.
Ēac him wolde Ēadrīċ   his ealdre ġelǣstan,
frēan tō ġefeohte,   ongann þā forþ beran
gār tō gūðe.   Hē hæfde gōd ġeþanc
þā hwīle þe hē mid handum   healdan meahte

15   bord and brād sweord;   bēot hē ġelǣste
þā hē ætforan his frēan   feohtan scolde.

    Þā þǣr Byrhtnōþ ongann   beornas trymian,
rād and rǣdde,   rincum tǣhte
hū hīe scoldon standan   and þone stede healdan,

20   and bæd þæt hira randas   rihte hēolden

Emendations and restorations (C = Casley's transcript): **4b** to] C t.
5 Þa] C þ.   **10** wige] C w . . . ge.   **20** randas] C randan.

Variant spellings: **2** hwæne.   **3** feor.   **4** hicgan. hige.   **6** yrhðo.
7 handon.   **9** mihte.   **12** ongan.   **14** mihte.   **15** swurd.   **16** sceolde.
17 ongan.   **19** sceoldon.   **20** hyra. heoldon.

fæste mid folmum   and ne forhtoden nā.

Þā hē hæfde þæt folc   fæġre ġetrymmed,

hē līehte þā mid lēodum   þǣr him lēofost wæs,

þǣr hē his heorð-weorod   holdost wisse.

25   Þā stōd on stæðe,   stīðlīċe clipode

wīċinga ār,   wordum mǣlde,

sē on bēot abēad   brim-līðendra

ǣrende tō þām eorle   þǣr hē on ōfre stōd:

"Mē sendon tō þē   sǣ-menn snelle,

30   hēton þē secgan   þæt þū mōst sendan hræðe

bēagas wiþ ġebeorge;   and ēow betere is

þæt ġē þisne gār-rǣs   mid gafole forġielden

þonne wē swā hearde   hilde dǣlen.

Ne þurfe wē ūs spillan   ġif ġē spēdaþ tō þām;

35   wē willaþ wiþ þām golde   griþ fæstnian.

Ġif þū þæt ġerǣdest,   þe hēr rīċost eart,

þæt þū þīne lēode   līesan wille,

sellan sǣ-mannum   on hira selfra dōm

feoh wiþ frēode   and niman friþ æt ūs,

40   wē willaþ mid þām sceattum ūs   tō scipe gangan,

on flot fēran,   and ēow friðes healdan."

Byrhtnōþ maðelode,   bord hafenode,

wand wācne æsc,   wordum mǣlde

ierre and ān-rǣd,   aġeaf him andsware:

45   "Ġehīerst þū, sǣ-lida,   hwæt þis folc sæġeþ?

Hīe willaþ ēow tō gafole   gāras sellan,

ǣtrenne ord   and ealde sweord,

þā here-ġeatwe   þe ēow æt hilde ne dēag.

Brim-manna boda,   abēod eft onġēan,

50   sæġe þīnum lēodum   micle lāðre spell,

Emendations and restorations: **33** þonne] C þon.   hilde] C . . ulde.
36 þæt] C þat.

Variant spellings: **21** folman. forhtedon.   **22** fægere.   **23** lihte. leodon.
24 werod. wiste.   **25** clypode.   **28** ærænde.   **29** men.   **30** raðe.   **32** forgyldon.
33 dælon.   **36** gyf.   **37** leoda. lysan.   **38** syllan. hyra. sylfra.   **40** scype.
44 yrre.   **45** gehyrst. segeð.   **46** hi. syllan.   **47** ættrynne. swurd.   **48** geatu.
deah.   **50** sege. miccle.

þæt hēr stent unforcūþ   eorl mid his weorode,
þe wile ealgian   ēðel þisne,
Æðelrēdes eard   ealdres mīnes,
folc and foldan.   Feallan sculon
55   hæðne æt hilde.   Tō hēanlič mē þynčeþ
þæt ġē mid ūrum sceattum   tō scipe gangen
unbefohtne,   nū ġē þus feorr hider
on ūrne eard   inn becōmon.
Ne scule ġē swā sōfte   sinč ġegangan;
60   ūs sceal ord and ecg   ǣr ġesēman,
grimm gūþ-plega,   ǣr wē gafol sellen."
    Hēt þā bord beran,   beornas gangan
þæt hīe on þām ēa-stæðe   ealle stōden.
Ne meahte þǣr for wætere   weorod tō þām ōðrum;
65   þǣr cōm flōwende   flōd æfter ebban,
lucon lagu-strēamas.   Tō lang hit him þūhte
hwonne hīe togædere   gāras bǣren.
Hīe þǣr Pantan strēam   mid prasse bestōdon,
Ēast-Seaxna ord   and sē æsc-here.
70   Ne meahte hira ǣniġ   ōðrum derian
būtan hwā þurh flānes flyht   fiell ġenāme.
    Sē flōd ūt ġewāt.   Þā flotan stōdon ġearwe,
wīčinga fela,   wīġes ġeorne.
    Hēt þā hæleþa hlēo   healdan þā brycge
75   wigan wīġ-heardne   —sē wæs hāten Wulfstān—
cāfne mid his cynne;   þæt wæs Čeolan sunu,
þe þone forman mann   mid his francan ofscēat
þe þǣr bealdlicost   on þā brycge stōp.
Þǣr stōdon mid Wulfstāne   wigan unforhte,
80   Ælfhere and Maccus,   mōdġe twēġen;

Emendation: **61** we] C þe.

Variant spellings: **51** stynt. werode.   **52** gealgean. þysne.   **54** sceolon.
55 hæþene. þinceð.   **56** scype. gangon.   **57** unbefohtene. feor.   **58** in.
59 sceole.   **61** grim. gofol. syllon.   **63** hi. steðe. stodon.   **64** mihte. werod.
67 hwænne. hi. beron.   **68** Hi.   **69** seaxena.   **70** mihte. hyra.   **71** buton. fyl.
72 gearowe.   **74** bricge.   **77** man.   **78** baldlicost. bricge.   **80** ælfere. modige.

þā noldon æt þām forda   flēam ġewyrċan,
ac hīe fæstlīċe   wiþ þā fīend weredon
þā hwīle þe hīe wǣpna   wealdan mōston.

    Þā hīe þæt onġēaton   and ġeorne ġesāwon
85   þæt hīe þǣr brycg-weardas   bitre fundon,
ongunnon lytigian þā   lāðe ġiestas,
bǣdon þæt hīe upp-gangan   āgan mōsten,
ofer þone ford faran,   fēðan lǣdan.

    Þā sē eorl ongann   for his ofermōde
90   alīefan landes tō fela   lāðre þēode.
Ongann ċeallian þā   ofer ċeald wæter
Byrhthelmes bearn;   beornas ġehlyston:
"Nū ēow is ġerȳmed;   gāþ recene tō ūs,
guman tō gūðe.   God āna wāt
95   hwā þǣre wæl-stōwe   wealdan mōte."

    Wōdon þā wæl-wulfas   —for wætere ne murnon—
wīċinga weorod,   west ofer Pantan,
ofer scīr wæter   scieldas wǣgon,
lid-menn tō lande   linda bǣron.

100   Þǣr onġēan gramum   ġearwe stōdon
Byrhtnōþ mid beornum;   hē mid bordum hēt
wyrċan þone wīġ-hagan   and þæt weorod healdan
fæste wiþ fēondum.   Þā wæs feohte nēah,
tīr æt ġetohte.   Wæs sēo tīd cumen
105   þæt þǣr fǣġe menn   feallan scoldon.
Þǣr wearþ hrēam ahafen,   hræfnas wundon,
earn ǣses ġeorn.   Wæs on eorðan ċierm.

    Hīe lēton þā of folmum   fēol-hearde speru,
ġegrundene   gāras flēogan.
110   Bogan wǣron bisiġe,   bord ord onfēng.

Emendation: **103** feohte] C fohte.

Variant spellings: **82** hi. fynd. **83** hi. **84** hi. **85** hi. bricg. bitere. **86** lytegian. gystas. **87** hi. up. moston. **89** ongan. **90** alyfan. laþere. **91** ongan. cald. **92** byrhtelmes. **93** ricene. **97** werod. **98** scyldas. wegon. **99** men. linde. **100** gearowe. **102** wi. werod. **103** neh. **105** men. sceoldon. **106** hremmas. **107** cyrm. **108** Hi. folman. **110** bysige.

Biter wæs sē beadu-ræs, beornas fēollon
on ġehwæðere hand, hyssas lāgon.
Wund wearþ Wulfmǣr, wæl-reste ġeċēas,
Byrhtnōðes mǣġ; hē mid billum wearþ,
115 his sweostor sunu, swīðe forhēawen.
Þǣr wearþ wīċingum wiðerlēan aġiefen.
Ġehīerde iċ þæt Ēadweard ānne slōge
swīðe mid his sweorde, swenġes ne wiernde,
þæt him æt fōtum fēoll fǣġe cempa;
120 þæs him his þēoden þanc ġesǣġde,
þām būr-þeġne, þā hē byre hæfde.
Swā stefnetton stīþ-hyċgende
hyssas æt hilde, hogodon ġeorne
hwā þǣr mid orde ǣrest meahte
125 on fǣġan menn feorh ġewinnan,
wigan mid wǣpnum; wæl fēoll on eorðan.
Stōdon stedefæste; stihte hīe Byrhtnōþ,
bæd þæt hyssa ġehwelċ hogode tō wīġe,
þe on Denum wolde dōm ġefeohtan.
130 Wōd þā wīġes heard, wǣpen upp ahōf,
bord tō ġebeorge, and wiþ þæs beornes stōp.
Ēode swā ān-rǣd eorl tō þām ċeorle,
ǣġðer hira ōðrum yfeles hogode.
Sende þā sē sǣ-rinċ sūðerne gār,
135 þæt ġewundod wearþ wigena hlāford.
Hē scēaf þā mid þām scielde þæt sē sceaft tobærst
and þæt spere sprengde þæt hit sprang onġēan.
Ġegremed wearþ sē gūð-rinċ; hē mid gāre stang
wlancne wīċing þe him þā wunde forġeaf.
140 Frōd wæs sē fierd-rinċ; hē lēt his francan wadan
þurh þæs hysses heals, hand wīsode

Emendations: 113 wearþ] C weard. 116 wearþ] C wærd.

Variant spellings: 113 ræste. 115 swuster. 116 agyfen. 117 gehyrde.
118 swurde. wyrnde. 120 gesæde. 121 þene. 122 stemnetton. hicgende.
123 hysas. 124 ærost. mihte. 125 fægean. men. 126 feol. 127 stæde. hi.
128 gehwylc. 129 denon. 130 up. 133 hyra. 136 scylde. 138 Gegremod.
140 fyrd. 141 hals.

þæt hē on þām fǣr-scaðan   feorh ġerǣhte.

Þā hē ōðerne   ofostlīċe scēat
þæt sēo byrne tobærst;   hē wæs on brēostum wund
145 þurh þā hring-locan,   him æt heortan stōd
ǣterne ord.   Sē eorl wæs þȳ blīðra,
hlōg þā mōdiġ mann,   sæġde metode þanc
þæs dæġ-weorces   þe him dryhten forġeaf.

Forlēt þā drenga sum   daroþ of handa
150 flēogan of folman,   þæt sē tō forþ ġewāt
þurh þone æðelan   Æðelrēdes þeġn.

Him be healfe stōd   hyse unweaxen,
cniht on ġecampe,   sē full cāflīċe
bræġd of þām beorne   blōdiġne gār,
155 Wulfstānes bearn,   Wulfmǣr sē ġeonga
forlēt forheardne   faran eft onġēan;
ord inn ġewōd   þæt sē on eorðan læġ
þe his þēoden ǣr   þearle ġerǣhte.

Ēode þā ġesierwed   secg tō þām eorle;
160 hē wolde þæs beornes   bēagas ġefeċċan,
rēaf and hringas   and ġereġnod sweord.
Þā Byrhtnōþ bræġd   bill of scēaðe,
brād and brūn-ecg,   and on þā byrnan slōg.
Tō hræðe hine ġelette   lid-manna sum
165 þā hē þæs eorles   earm amierde.
Fēoll þā tō foldan   fealu-hilte sweord,
ne meahte hē ġehealdan   heardne mēċe,
wǣpnes wealdan.   Þā-ġīet þæt word ġecwæþ
hār hilde-rinċ,   hyssas bielde,
170 bæd gangan forþ   gōde ġefēran;
ne meahte þā on fōtum lenġ   fæste ġestandan.
Hē tō heofonum wlāt:

Emendation: **171** gestandan] C ge stundan.

Variant spellings: **142** sceaðan.   **143** ofstlice.   **146** ætterne. þe.   **147** Hloh.
modi. man. sæde.   **148** drihten.   **151** þegen.   **154** bræd.   **157** in.   **159** gesyrwed.
160 gefecgan.   **161** gerenod. swurd.   **162** bræd. sceðe.   **163** eccg. sloh.
164 raþe.   **165** amyrde.   **166** fealo. swurd.   **167** mihte.   **168** gyt.   **169** bylde.
171 mihte.   **172** heofenum.

"Iċ ġeþancie þē,   þēoda wealdend,
ealra þāra wynna   þe iċ on weorolde ġebād.

175 Nū iċ āg, milde metod,   mǣste þearfe
þæt þū mīnum gāste   gōdes ġe-unne,
þæt mīn sāwol tō þē   sīðian mōte
on þīn ġeweald,   þēoden engla,
mid friðe ferian.   Iċ eom frymdiġ tō þē
180 þæt hīe hell-scaðan   hīenan ne mōten."
Þā hine hēowon   hǣðne scealcas,
and bēġen þā beornas   þe him bī stōdon,
Ælfnōþ and Wulfmǣr   bēġen lāgon,
þā on-efen hira frēan   feorh ġesealdon.

185 Hīe bugon þā fram beadwe   þe þǣr bēon noldon.
Þǣr wearþ Oddan bearn   ǣrest on flēame,
Godrīċ fram gūðe,   and þone gōdan forlēt
þe him maniġne oft   mearh ġesealde;
hē ġehlēop þone eoh   þe āhte his hlāford,
190 on þām ġerǣdum   þe hit riht ne wæs,
and his brōðru mid him   bēġen ærndon,
Godwine and Godwīġ,   gūðe ne ġīemdon,
ac wendon fram þām wīġe   and þone wudu sōhton,
flugon on þæt fæsten   and hira feore burgon,
195 and manna mā   þonne hit æniġ mǣþ wǣre,
ġif hīe þā ġe-earnunga   ealle ġemunden
þe hē him tō duguþe   ġedōn hæfde.
Swā him Offa on dæġ   ǣr asæġde
on þām mæðel-stede   þā hē ġemōt hæfde,
200 þæt þǣr mōdiġlīce   maniġe sprǣcon
þe eft æt þearfe   þolian nolden.

Emendations: **173** Ic geþancie] C ge þance (*but there is probably more lost here*).
186 wearþ] C wurdon.   **191** ærndon] C ærdon.   **192** Godwine] C godrine.   **201**
þearfe] C þære.

Variant spellings: **173** waldend.   **174** þæra. worulde.   **175** ah.   **177** sawul.
179 frymdi.   **180** hi. helsceaðan. hynan. moton.   **181** hæðene.   **182** big.
183 wulmær.   **184** onemn. hyra.   **185** Hi. beaduwe.   **188** mænigne. mear.
192 gymdon.   **194** hyra.   **196** gyf. hi. gemundon.   **198** asæde.   **199** meþel.
200 modelice. manega.

Þā wearþ afeallen   þæs folces ealdor,
Æðelrēdes eorl;   ealle ġesāwon
heorð-ġenēatas   þæt hira hearra læġ.

205 Þā þǣr wendon forþ   wlance þeġnas,
unearge menn   efston ġeorne;
hīe woldon þā ealle   ōðer twēġa:
līf forlǣtan   oþþe lēofne ġewrecan.

Swā hīe bielde forþ   bearn Ælfrīċes,
210 wiga wintrum ġẹong,   wordum mælde.

Ælfwine þā cwæþ,   hē on ellen spræc:
"Ġemunaþ nū þā mǣla   þe wē oft æt medu sprǣcon,
þonne wē on benċe   bēot ahōfon,
hæleþ on healle,   ymbe heard ġewinn;
215 nū mæġ cunnian   hwā cēne sīe.

Iċ wille mīne æðelu   eallum ġecȳðan,
þæt iċ wæs on Mierċum   micles cynnes;
wæs mīn ealda fæder   Ealhhelm hāten,
wīs ealdor-mann   weorold-ġesǣliġ.
220 Ne sculon mē on þǣre þēode   þeġnas ætwītan
þæt iċ of þisse fierde   fēran wille,
eard ġesēċan,   nū mīn ealdor liġeþ
forhēawen æt hilde.   Mē is þæt hearma mǣst;
hē wæs ǣġðer mīn mæġ   and mīn hlāford."

225 Þā hē forþ ēode,   fǣhþe ġemunde,
þæt hē mid orde   ānne ġerǣhte
flotan on þām folce,   þæt sē on foldan læġ
forweġen mid his wǣpne.   Ongann þā winas manian,
frīend and ġefēran,   þæt hīe forþ ēoden.
230 Offa ġemǣlde,   æsc-holt ascōc:
"Hwæt þū, Ælfwine, hafast   ealle ġemanode

Emendations: **208** forlætan] C for lætun.   **212** Gemunaþ nu] C ge munu.
224 ægðer] C ægder.

Variant spellings: **201** noldon. **204** hyra. heorra. **205** þegenas. **206** men.
207 hi. **209** hi. bylde. **212** meodo. **215** sy. **216** wylle. æþelo. **217** myrcon.
miccles. **218** ealhelm. **219** man. woruld. **220** sceolon. þegenas. **221** fyrde.
228 ongan. **229** frynd. hi. eodon. **230** asceoc.

þeġnas tō þearfe.   Nū ūre þēoden liġeþ,
eorl on eorðan,   ūs is eallum þearf
þæt ūre æġhwelċ   ōðerne bielde
235   wigan tō wīġe,   þā hwīle þe hē wǣpen mǣġe
habban and healdan,   heardne mēċe,
gār and gōd sweord.   Ūs Godrīċ hafaþ,
earg Oddan bearn,   ealle beswicene.
Wēnde þæs formaniġ mann,   þā hē on mēare rād,
240   on wlancan þām wicge,   þæt wǣre hit ūre hlāford.
For-þon wearþ hēr on felda   folc totwǣmed,
scield-burg tobrocen.   Abrēoðe his anġinn,
þæt hē hēr swā maniġne   mann aflīemde!"
Lēofsunu ġemǣlde   and his linde ahōf,
245   bord tō ġebeorge;   hē þām beorne oncwæþ:
"Iċ þæt ġehāte,   þæt iċ heonan nylle
flēon fōtes trym,   ac wille furðor gān,
wrecan on ġewinne   mīnne wine-dryhten.
Ne þurfon mē ymbe Stūr-mere   stedefæste hæleþ
250   wordum ætwītan,   nū mīn wine ġecrang,
þæt iċ hlāfordlēas   hām sīðie,
wende fram wīġe;   ac mē sceal wǣpen niman,
ord and īren."   Hē full ierre wōd,
feaht fæstlīċe,   flēam hē forhogode.
255   Dunhere þā cwæþ,   daroþ acweahte,
unorne ċeorl,   ofer eall clipode,
bæd þæt beorna ġehwelċ   Byrhtnōþ wrǣce:
"Ne mæġ nā wandian   sē-þe wrecan þenċeþ
frēan on folce,   nē for feore murnan."
260   Þā hīe forþ ēodon,   feores hīe ne rōhton;
ongunnon þā hīred-menn   heardlīċe feohtan,
grame gār-berend,   and God bǣdon

Variant spellings: **232** þegenas. lið.   **234** æghwylc. bylde.   **237** swurd. hæfð.
238 earh.   **239** formoni. man.   **241** þan.   **242** scyldburh. angin.   **243** man.
aflymde.   **246** heonon. nelle.   **248** drihten.   **249** embe. hælæð.   **250** gecranc.
253 ful. yrre.   **255** dunnere. acwehte.   **256** clypode.   **257** gehwylc.   **260** hi.
hi.   **261** men.

þæt hīe mōsten ġewrecan   hira wine-dryhten
and on hira fēondum   fiell ġewyrċan.

265   Him sē ġīsel ongann   ġeornlīċe fylstan;
hē wæs on Norþ-Hymbrum   heardes cynnes,
Ecglāfes bearn;   him wæs Æscferþ nama.
Hē ne wandode nā   æt þām wīġ-plegan,
ac hē fȳsde forþ   flān ġeneahhe.

270   Hwīlum hē on bord scēat,   hwīlum beorn tǣsde;
æfre ymbe stunde   hē sealde sume wunde
þā hwīle þe hē wǣpna   wealdan mōste.

Þā-ġīet on orde stōd   Ēadweard sē langa,
ġearu and ġeornfull,   ġielp-wordum spræc

275   þæt hē nolde flēogan   fōt-mǣl landes,
ofer bæc būgan,   þā his betera læġ.
Hē bræc þone bord-weall   and wiþ þā beornas feaht
oþ-þæt hē his sinċ-ġiefan   on þām sǣ-mannum
weorðlīċe wræc   ǣr hē on wæle lǣġe.

280   Swā dyde Æðelrīċ,   æðele ġefēra,
fūs and forð-ġeorn   feaht eornoste;
Siġebyrhtes brōðor   and swīðe maniġ ōðer
clufon cellod bord,   cēne hīe weredon.

*   *   *   *

Bærst bordes lǣriġ,   and sēo byrne sang

285   gryre-lēoða sum.   Þā æt gūðe slōg
Offa þone sǣ-lidan   þæt hē on eorðan fēoll,
and þǣr Gaddes mǣġ   grund ġesōhte.
Hræðe wearþ æt hilde   Offa forhēawen;
hē hæfde þēah ġeforðod   þæt hē his frēan ġehēt,

290   swā hē bēotode ǣr   wiþ his bēag-ġiefan,
þæt hīe scolden bēġen   on burg rīdan
hāle tō hāme   oþþe on here cringan,

Emendation: **292** cringan] C crintgan (*for* crincgan).

Variant spellings: **263** hi. moston. hyra. drihten.   **264** hyra. fyl.   **265** gysel.
ongan.   **266** norð hymbron.   **269** genehe.   **270** hwilon. hwilon.   **271** embe.
273 gyt.   **274** gearo. geornful. gylp.   **276** leg.   **278** gyfan.   **279** wurðlice.
wrec.   **282** sibyrhtes. mænig.   **283** hi.   **285** sloh.   **288** raðe.   **290** beah gifan.
291 hi. sceoldon. burh.

on wæl-stōwe   wundum sweltan;
hē læġ þeġnlīċe   þēodne ġehende.
295   Þā wearþ borda ġebræc.   Brim-menn wōdon,
gūðe ġegremede;   gār oft þurhwōd
fæġes feorh-hūs.   Forþ þā ēode Wīstān,
Þurstānes sunu,   wiþ þās secgas feaht;
hē wæs on ġeþrange   hira þrēora bana
300   ǣr him Wīġhelmes bearn   on þām wæle lǣġe.
Þǣr wæs stīþ ġemōt;   stōdon fæste
wigan on ġewinne,   wīġend crungon
wundum wērġe.   Wæl fēoll on eorðan.
Ōswold and Ēadwold   ealle hwīle,
305   bēġen þā ġebrōðru,   beornas trymedon,
hira wine-māgas   wordum bǣdon
þæt hīe þǣr æt þearfe   þolian scolden,
unwāclīċe   wǣpna nēotan.
Byrhtwold maðelode,   bord hafenode—
310   sē wæs eald ġenēat—   æsc acweahte;
hē full bealdlīċe   beornas lǣrde:
"Hyġe sceal þȳ heardra,   heorte þȳ cēnre,
mōd sceal þȳ māre   þȳ ūre mæġen lȳtlaþ.
Hēr liġeþ ūre ealdor   eall forhēawen,
315   gōd on grēote.   Ā mæġ gnornian
sē-þe nū fram þȳs wīġ-plegan   wendan þenċeþ.
Iċ eom frōd feores;   fram iċ ne wille,
ac iċ mē be healfe   mīnum hlāforde,
be swā lēofum menn   licgan þenċe."
320   Swā hīe Æðelgāres bearn   ealle bielde,
Godrīċ tō gūðe.   Oft hē gār forlēt
wæl-spere windan   on þā wīċingas;

Emendations: **297** Forþ þa] C forða.   **299** geþrange] C geþrang.
300 Wighelmes] C wigelines.

Variant spellings: **294** ðegenlice.   **295** men.   **296** gegremode.   **298** suna.
299 hyra.   **302** cruncon.   **303** werige. feol.   **306** hyra. wordon.   **307** hi.
sceoldon.   **310** acwehte.   **311** ful. baldlice.   **312** hige. þe. þe.   **313** þe. þe.
314 lið.   **316** þis.   **319** leofan. men.   **320** hi. bylde.

swā hē on þām folce   fyrmest ēode,
hēow and hīende,   oþ-þæt hē on hilde ġecrang.
325   Næs þæt nā sē Godrīċ   þe þā gūðe forbēag

     *   *   *   *

Emendations: **324** oþ-] C od.   **325** guðe] C gude.

Variant spellings: **324** hynde. gecranc.   **325** forbeah.

The Wanderer

(*Exeter Book,* ff. 76ᵛ–78ʳ)

Oft him ān-haga　āre ġebīdeþ,
metodes mildse,　þēah-þe hē mōd-ċeariġ
ġeond lagu-lāde　lange scolde
hrēran mid handum　hrīm-ċealde sǣ,
5　wadan wræc-lāstas.　Wyrd biþ full arǣdd.
　Swā cwæþ eard-stapa　earfoþa ġemyndiġ,
wrāðra wæl-sleahta,　wine-māga hryres.
　Oft iċ scolde āna　ūhtna ġehwelċe
mīne ċeare cwīðan;　nis nū cwicra nān
10　þe iċ him mōd-sefan　mīnne durre
sweotule asecgan.　Iċ tō sōðe wāt
þæt biþ on eorle　indryhten þēaw
þæt hē his ferhþ-locan　fæste binde,
healde his hord-cofan,　hycge swā hē wille.
15　Ne mæġ wēriġ mōd　wyrde wiþstandan
nē sē hrēo hyġe　helpe ġefremman.
For-þon dōm-ġeorne　drēoriġne oft
on hira brēost-cofan　bindaþ fæste.
　Swā iċ mōd-sefan　mīnne scolde,
20　oft earm-ċeariġ,　ēðle bedǣled,
frēo-māgum feorr,　feterum sǣlan,
siþþan ġēara ġēo　gold-wine mīnne
hrūsan heolstre bewrāh,　and iċ hēan þonan

Emendations: 7 hryres] MS hryre.　14 healde] MS healdne.　22 minne] MS mine.
Variant spellings in the MS: 2 metudes. miltse.　3 longe. sceolde.　4 hondum.
5 ful. arǣd.　6 earfeþa.　7 mæga.　8 sceolde. gehwylce.　12 in.　13 ferð.
15 stondan.　18 in. hyra.　19 sceolde.　20 bidæled.　21 mægum. feor.
22 geo] iu.　23 biwrah.

wōd winter-ċeariġ   ofer waðuma ġebind,
25 sōhte sele-drēoriġ   sinċes bryttan,
hwǣr iċ feorr oþþe nēah   findan meahte
þone-þe on medu-healle   mīne wisse
oþþe meċ frēondlēasne   frēfran wolde,
wēman mid wynnum.   Wāt sē-þe cunnaþ
30 hū slīðen biþ   sorg tō ġefēran
þām-þe him lȳt hafaþ   lēofra ġeholena.
Waraþ hine wrǣc-lāst,   nealles wunden gold,
ferhþ-loca frēoriġ,   nealles foldan blǣd.
Ġeman hē sele-secgas   and sinċ-þeġe,
35 hū hine on ġeoguþe   his gold-wine
wenede tō wiste.   Wynn eall ġedrēas.
    For-þon wāt sē-þe sceal   his wine-dryhtnes
lēofes lār-cwidum   lange forþolian.
Þonne sorg and slǣp   samod ætgædere
40 earmne ān-hagan   oft ġebindaþ,
þynċeþ him on mōde   þæt hē his mann-dryhten
clyppe and cysse   and on cnēo lecge
handa and hēafod,   swā hē hwīlum ǣr
on ġeār-dagum   ġief-stōles brēac.
45 Þonne onwæcneþ eft   winelēas guma,
ġesiehþ him beforan   fealwe wǣgas,
baðian brim-fuglas,   brǣdan feðra,
hrēosan hrīm and snāw   hæġle ġemenġed.
Þonne bēoþ þȳ hefiġran   heortan benna,
50 sāre æfter swǣsne.   Sorg biþ ġenīewod.
Þonne māga ġemynd   mōd ġeondhweorfeþ—
grēteþ glēo-stafum,   ġeorne ġeondscēawaþ—
secga ġeseldan   swimmaþ oft on-weġ,
flēotendra ferhþ.   Nā þǣr fela brinġeþ

Emendations: **24** waðuma] MS waþena.   **28** -leasne] MS lease.

Variant spellings: **26** feor.   **27** in. meodu.   **32** nales.   **33** ferð. nalæs.
34 gemon.   **36** wyn. eal.   **38** longe.   **39** somod. æt gædre.   **40** an hogan.
41 þinceð. mon.   **43** honda.   **44** in. stolas.   **46** gesihð. bi foran. wegas.
48 hagle.   **49** benne.   **50** geniwad.   **52** gliw.

55 cūðra cwide-ġiedda   —cearu biþ ġenīewod—
    þām-þe sendan sceal   swīðe ġeneahhe
    ofer waðuma ġebind   wēriġne sefan.
    For-þon iċ ġeþenċan ne mæġ   ġeond þās weorold
    for-hwon mōd-sefa   mīn ne ġesweorce
60 þonne iċ eorla līf   eall ġeondþenċe,
    hū hīe fǣrlīċe   flett ofġēafon,
    mōdġe magu-þeġnas.   Swā þēs middan-ġeard
    ealra dōgra ġehwǣm   drēoseþ and fealleþ;
    for-þon ne mæġ weorðan wīs wer   ǣr hē āge wintra dǣl
65 on weorold-rīċe.   Wita sceal ġeþyldiġ,
    nē sceal nā tō hāt-heort   nē tō hrǣd-wyrde
    nē tō wāc wīga   nē tō wan-hyġdiġ
    nē tō forht nē tō fǣgen   nē tō feoh-ġīfre
    nē nǣfre ġielpes tō ġeorn   ǣr hē ġeare cunne.
70 Beorn sceal ġebīdan,   þonne hē bēot spriċeþ,
    oþ-þæt collen-ferhþ   cunne ġearwe
    hwider hreðra ġehyġd   hweorfan wille.
    Onġietan sceal glēaw hæle   hū gǣstliċ biþ
    þonne eall þisse weorolde wela   wēste standeþ,
75 swā nū missenlīċe   ġeond þisne middan-ġeard
    winde bewāwne   weallas standaþ,
    hrīme behrorene,   hrīðġe þā eodoras.
    Weorniaþ þā wīn-salu,   wealdend licgaþ
    drēame bedrorene,   duguþ eall ġecrang
80 wlanc be wealle.   Sume wīġ fornam,
    ferede on forð-weġe;   sumne fugol oþbær
    ofer hēanne holm,   sumne sē hāra wulf
    dēaðe ġedǣlde,   sumne drēoriġ-hlēor
    on eorþ-scræfe   eorl ġehȳdde.

Emendations: 59 mod-sefa min ne] MS modsefan minne.   74 eall] MS ealle.
78 Weorniaþ] MS w oriað (see note).

Variant spellings: 54 ferð. no.   55 cearo. geniwad.   57 waþema.   58 woruld.
59 forhwan.   60 eal.   61 hi. flet.   63 gehwam.   64 wearþan.   65 in. woruld.
66 no.   67 hydig.   71 ferð.   74 worulde. stondeð.   76 biwaune. stondaþ.
77 bihrorene. hryðge. ederas.   78 salo. waldend.   79 bidrorene. eal. ge crong.
80 wlonc. bi. for nom.   81 in. fugel.

85 Ieðde swā þisne eard-ġeard ielda scieppend,
oþ-þæt burgwara breahtma lēase,
eald enta ġeweorc īdlu stōdon.
Sē þonne þisne weall-steall wīse ġeþōhte
and þis deorce līf dēope ġeondþenċeþ,
90 frōd on ferhþe, feorr oft ġeman
wæl-sleahta worn and þās word acwiþ:
Hwǣr cōm mearh? Hwǣr cōm magu? Hwǣr
cōm māðum-ġiefa?
Hwǣr cōm symbla ġesetu? Hwǣr sindon sele-drēamas?
Ēa-lā beorht bune! Ēa-lā byrn-wiga!
95 Ēa-lā þēodnes þrymm! Hū sēo þrāg ġewāt,
ġenāp under niht-helm, swā hēo nā wǣre!
Standeþ nū on lāste lēofre duguþe
weall wundrum hēah, wyrm-līcum fāg.
Eorlas fornāmon æsca þrȳðe,
100 wǣpen wæl-ġīfru, wyrd sēo mǣre,
and þās stān-hliðu stormas cnyssaþ,
hrīþ hrēosende hrūsan bindeþ,
wintres wōma, þonne wann cymeþ,
nīpeþ niht-scua, norðan onsendeþ
105 hrēo hæġl-fære, hæleþum on andan.
Eall is earfoþlīċ eorðan rīċe,
onwendeþ wyrda ġesceaft weorold under heofonum.
Hēr biþ feoh lǣne, hēr biþ frēond lǣne,
hēr biþ mann lǣne, hēr biþ mǣġ lǣne.
110 Eall þis eorðan ġesteall īdel weorðeþ.
Swā cwæþ snottor on mōde, ġesæt him sundor æt rūne.
Til biþ sē-þe his trēowe ġehealdeþ, nē sceal nǣfre his
torn tō recene
beorn of his brēostum acȳðan, nemþe hē ǣr þā bōte cunne,

Emendations: **89** deorce] MS deornce. **102** hrusan] MS hruse.

Variant spellings: **84** in. **85** yþde. ælda. scyppend. **88** weal steal. **90** in.
ferðe. feor. gemon. **92** cwom. mearg. cwom. mago. cwom. maþþum gyfa.
93 cwom. **95** þrym. **96** no. **97** Stondeð. **98** weal. fah. **99** fornoman. asca.
101 hleoþu. **103** won. **105** fare. **107** weoruld. **109** mon. **110** eal. gesteal.
112 rycene.

eorl, mid elne ġefremman. Wēl biþ þām-þe him āre sēċeþ,

115 frōfre tō fæder on heofonum, þǣr ūs eall sēo fæstnung

standeþ.

Variant spellings: **115** eal. stondeð.

The Seafarer

(*Exeter Book,* ff. 81ᵛ–83ʳ)

Mæġ iċ be mē selfum   sōð-ġiedd wrecan,
sīðas secgan,   hū iċ ġeswinċ-dagum
earfoþ-hwīle   oft þrōwode,
bitre brēost-ċeare   ġebiden hæbbe,
5   ġecunnod on ċēole   ċear-selda fela,
atol ȳða ġewealc,   þǣr meċ oft beġeat
nearu niht-wacu   æt nacan stefnan,
þonne hē be clifum cnossaþ.   Ċealde ġeþrungen
fruron mīne fēt,   forste ġebunden,
10   ċealdum clammum,   þǣr þā ceara seofodon
hāt' ymb heortan;   hungor innan slāt
mere-wērġes mōd.   Þæt sē mann ne wāt
þe him on foldan   fæġrost limpeþ,
hū iċ earm-ċearig   īs-ċealdne sǣ
15   †   winter wunode   wreċċan lāstum,
wine-māgum bedroren,
behangen hrīm-ġiclum;   hæġl scūrum flēag.
Þǣr iċ ne ġehīerde   būtan hlimman sǣ,
īs-ċealdne wǣġ,   hwīlum ielfete sang.
20   Dyde iċ mē tō gamene   ganotes hlēoðor,
and hwilpan swēġ   fore hleahtor wera,

An obelus (†) indicates a corrupt passage that the editors hesitate to emend. For suggestions see the commentary.

Emendation: **9** fruron] MS wǣron.

Variant spellings in the MS: **1** sylfum. gied.   **3** þrowade.   **5** gecunnad. in. **6** bigeat.   **7** nearo. waco.   **8** calde.   **10** caldum. clommum. ceare. seofedun. **11** hat.   **12** mon.   **15** wunade. wræccan.   **16** mægum. bidroren.   **17** bihongen. gicelum.   **18** ge hyrde.   **19** caldne. ylfete. song.   **20** gomene. ganetes. **21** huilpan.

mǣw singende   fore medu-drince.

Stormas þǣr stān-clifu bēoton,   þǣr him stearn oncwæþ,
īsiġ-feðra;   full oft þæt earn beġeall,
ūriġ-feðra;   nǣniġ hlēo-māga
fēa-sceaftiġ ferhþ   frēfran meahte.

For-þon him ġelīefeþ lȳt,   sē-þe āg līfes wynn
ġebiden on burgum,   bealu-sīða hwōn,
wlanc and wīn-gāl,   hū iċ wēriġ oft
on brim-lāde   bīdan scolde.

Nāp niht-scua,   norðan snīwde,
hrīm hrūsan band,   hæġl fēoll on eorðan,
corna ċealdost.

For-þon cnyssaþ nū
heortan ġeþōhtas   þæt iċ hēan strēamas,
sealt-ȳða ġelāc   self cunnie;
manaþ mōdes lust   mǣla ġehwelċe
ferhþ tō fēran,   þæt iċ feorr heonan
el-þēodiġra   eard ġesēċe.

For-þon nis þæs mōd-wlanc   mann ofer eorðan,
nē his ġiefena þæs gōd,   nē on ġeoguþe tō þæs hwæt,
nē on his dǣdum tō þæs dēor,   nē him his dryhten
tō þæs hold,
þæt hē ā his sǣ-fōre   sorge næbbe,
tō hwon hine dryhten   ġedōn wille.

Nē biþ him tō hearpan hyġe   nē tō hring-þeġe—
nē tō wīfe wynn   nē tō weorolde hyht—
nē ymbe āwiht elles   nefne ymb ȳða ġewealc;
ac ā hafaþ langunge   sē-þe on lagu fundaþ.

Bearwas blōstmum nimaþ,   byriġ fæġriaþ,
wangas wlitigiaþ;   weorold ōnetteþ;

Emendation: **26** frefran] MS feran.

Variant spellings: **22** medo.   **23** beotan.   **24** feþera. ful. bigeal.   **25** mæga.
26 ferð.   **27** gelyfeð. ah. wyn.   **28** in. bealo.   **29** wlonc.   **30** in. sceolde.
32 bond. feol.   **33** caldast.   **35** sylf. cunnige.   **36** monað. gehwylce.   **37** ferð.
feor.   **39** wlonc. mon.   **40** gifena. in.   **41** in.   **45** wyn. worulde.   **46** owiht.
47 longunge.   **49** wongas. wlitigað. woruld.

25 †

30

35

40

45

50   ealle þā ġemaniaþ   mōdes fūsne
        sefan tō sīðe   þām-þe swā þenċeþ
        on flōd-wegas   feorr ġewītan.
        Swelċe ġēac manaþ   ġeōmran reorde;
        sinġeþ sumores weard,   sorge bēodeþ

55   bitre on brēost-hord.   Þæt sē beorn ne wāt,
        sēft-ēadiġ secg,   hwæt þā sume drēogaþ
        þe þā wræc-lāstas   wīdost lecgaþ.
          For-þon nū mīn hyġe hweorfeþ   ofer hreðer-locan,
        mīn mōd-sefa   mid mere-flōde,

60   ofer hwæles ēðel   hweorfeþ wīde,
        eorðan scēatas,   cymeþ eft tō mē
        ġīfre and grǣdiġ;   ġielleþ ān-floga,
        hweteþ on hwæl-weġ   hreðer unwearnum
        ofer holma ġelagu.   For-þon mē hātran sind

65   dryhtnes drēamas   þonne þis dēade līf,
        lǣne on lande.   Iċ ġelīefe nā
        þæt him eorð-welan   ēċe standaþ.
        Simle þrēora sum   þinga ġehwelċe
        ǣr his tīde ġegang   tō twēon weorðeþ:

70   ādl oþþe ieldu   oþþe ecg-hete
        fǣgum framweardum   feorh oþ-þringeþ.
        For-þon þæt biþ eorla ġehwǣm   æfter-cweðendra,
        lof libbendra,   lāst-worda betst,
        þæt hē ġewyrċe,   ǣr hē on-weġ scyle,

75   fremum on foldan   wiþ fēonda nīþ,
        dēorum dǣdum   dēofle toġēanes,
        þæt hine ielda bearn   æfter herien,
        and his lof siþþan   libbe mid englum
        āwa tō ealdre,   ēċan līfes blǣd,

Emendations: **52** gewitan] MS gewitað.   **56** seft-eadig] MS eft eadig.   **63** hwæl-weg] MS wælweg.   **67** standaþ] MS stondeð.   **69** gegang] MS ge.   **72** biþ] *not in* MS.   **75** fremum] MS fremman.   **79** blæd] MS blæð.

Variant spellings: **50** ge monað.   **52** feor.   **53** swylce. monað.   **54** sumeres.   **55** bitter (*perhaps an elided form of* bittere). in.   **66** londe. gelyfe. no.   **68** gehwylce.   **70** yldo.   **71** from.   **72** gehwam.   **73** lifgendra.   **77** ælda. hergen.   **78** lifge.

80 drēam mid duguþum. Dagas sind ġewitene,
ealle anmēdlan eorðan rīċes;
nearon nū cyningas nē cāseras
nē gold-ġiefan swelċe ġeō wǣron,
þonne hīe mǣst mid him mǣrþa ġefremedon
85 and on dryhtlicostum dōme lifdon.
Ġedroren is þēos duguþ eall, drēamas sind ġewitene;
wuniaþ þā wācran and þās weorold healdaþ,
brūcaþ þurh bisgu. Blǣd is ġehnǣġed,
eorðan indryhtu ealdaþ and sēaraþ,
90 swā nū manna ġehwelċ ġeond middan-ġeard.
Ieldu him on fareþ, ansīen blācaþ,
gamol-feax gnornaþ, wāt his ġeō-wine,
æðelinga bearn eorðan forġiefene.
Ne mæġ him þonne sē flǣsc-hama, þonne him þæt
feorh losaþ,
95 nē swēte forswelgan nē sār ġefēlan
nē hand onhrēran nē mid hyġe þenċan.
Þēah-þe græf wille golde strēgan
brōðor his ġeborenum —byrġan be dēadum,
māðmum mislicum, þæt hine mid wille—
100 ne mæġ þǣre sāwle þe biþ synna full
gold tō ġeoce for Godes eġesan,
þonne hē hit ǣr hȳdeþ þenden hē hēr leofaþ.
Miċel biþ sē metodes eġesa, for þon hīe sēo molde onċierreþ;
sē ġestaðolode stīðe grundas,
105 eorðan sċēatas and upp-rodor.
Dol biþ sē-þe him his dryhten ne ondrǣdeþ: cymeþ him
sē dēaþ unþinġed.
Ēadiġ biþ sē-þe ēað-mōd leofaþ; cymeþ him sēo ār
of heofonum.

Emendation: **82** nearon] MS nǣron.

Variant spellings: **80** dugeþum. **81** on medlan. **83** swylce. iu. **84** hi.
85 dryht licestum. **86** eal. **87** woruld. **88** bisgo. **89** indryhto. **90** monna.
gehwylc. **91** yldo. onsyn. **92** gomel. iuwine. **94** homa. feorg. **96** hond.
100 ful. **101** egsan. **103** meotudes. egsa. hi. oncyrreð. **104** ge staþelade.
105 up.

Metod him þæt mōd ġestaðolaþ,   for-þon hē on his
                           meahte ġelīefeþ.
Stīeran man sceal strangum mōde,   and þæt on
                        staðolum healdan,
110   and ġewiss wǣrum,   wīsum clǣne.
Scyle manna ġehwelċ   mid ġemete healdan
wiþ lēofne lufan   and wiþ lāðne bealu,
þēah-þe hē hine wille fȳres   fulne habban,
oþþe on bǣle   forbærnedne
115   his ġeworhtne wine: wyrd biþ swīðre,
metod mihtiġra,   þonne ǣnġes mannes ġehyġd.
Wuton wē hycgan   hwǣr wē hām āgen,
and þonne ġeþenċan   hū wē þider cumen;
and wē þonne ēac tilien   þæt wē tō mōten
120   on þā ēċan   ēadiġnesse
þǣr is līf ġelang   on lufan dryhtnes,
hyht on heofonum.   Þæs sīe þām hālgan þanc,
þæt hē ūsiċ ġeweorðode,   wuldres ealdor,
ēċe dryhten,   on ealle tīd.
                          Amen.

Emendations: **109** man] MS mod (*for* mon).   **112** lufan] *not in* MS.
113 habban] *not in* MS.   **115** swiðre] MS swire.   **117** hwær we] MS hwær se.

Variant spellings: **108** meotod. gestaþelað. in. gelyfeð.   **109** strongum.
staþelum.   **110** gewis. werum.   **111** monna. gehwylc.   **112** bealo.
116 meotud. meahtigra. monnes.   **117** Uton.   **120** in.   **121** gelong. in.
122 in. sy. þonc.   **123** geweorþade.   **124** in.

Deor

(*Exeter Book,* f. 100^{r–v})

Wēland him be wurman   wræces cunnode,
ān-hyġdiġ eorl,   earfoþu drēag;
hæfde him tō ġesīþþe   sorge and langoþ,
winter-ċealde wræce;   wēan oft onfand
5   siþþan hine Nīþhād on   nīeda leġde,
swancre sinu-benda,   on sēlran mann.
    Þæs oferēode;   þisses swā mæġ.

Beaduhilde ne wæs   hire brōðra dēaþ
on sefan swā sār   swā hire selfre þinġ,
10   þæt hēo ġearulīċe   onġieten hæfde
þæt hēo ēacen wæs;   æfre ne meahte
þrīste ġeþenċan   hū ymb þæt scolde.
    Þæs oferēode;   þisses swā mæġ.

Wē þæt Mæþhilde   maniġe ġefrugnon:
15   wurdon grundlēase   Ġēates frīġe,
þæt hīe sēo sorg-lufu   slæp' ealle benam.
    Þæs oferēode;   þisses swā mæġ.

Þēodrīċ āhte   þrītiġ wintra
Mæringa burg;   þæt wæs manigum cūþ.
20   Þæs oferēode;   þisses swā mæġ.

Variant spellings in the MS: **1** Welund. cunnade.   **2** an hydig. earfoþa.
3 longaþ.   **4** onfond.   **5** nede.   **6** swoncre. seono bende. syllan. monn.
8 Beado. hyre.   **9** hyre. sylfre.   **10** gearo.   **12** sceolde.   **14** monge.   **16** hi.
slæp. binom.   **19** monegum.

Wē ġe-āscodon   Eormanrīċes
wylfenne ġeþōht;   āhte wīde folc
Gotena rīċes;   þæt was grimm cyning.
Sæt secg maniġ   sorgum ġebunden,
25   wēan on wēnum,   wȳscte ġeneahhe
þæt þæs cyne-rīċes   ofercumen wǣre.
Þæs oferēode;   þisses swā mæġ.

Siteþ sorg-ċeariġ,   sǣlum bedǣled,
on sefan sweorceþ,   selfum þynċeþ
30   þæt sīe endelēas   earfoþa dǣl;
mæġ þonne ġeþenċan   þæt ġeond þās weorold
wītiġ dryhten   wendeþ ġeneahhe,
eorle manigum   āre ġescēawaþ,
wislicne blǣd,   sumum wēana dǣl.

35   Þæt iċ be mē selfum   secgan wille,
þæt iċ hwīle wæs   Hedeninga scop,
dryhtne dīere;   mē wæs Dēor nama.
Āhte iċ fela wintra   folgoþ tilne,
holdne hlāford,   oþ-þæt Heorrenda nū,
40   lēoþ-cræftiġ mann,   land-riht ġeþeah
þæt mē eorla hlēo   ǣr ġesealde.
Þæs oferēode;   þisses swā mæġ.

Emendations: **25** wenum] MS wenan (*leveled ending or error*).   **30** earfoþa]
MS earfoda.

Variant spellings: **21** ge ascodan.   **23** grim.   **24** monig.   **28** bidæled.
29 sylfum. þinceð.   **30** sy.   **31** woruld.   **33** monegum.   **35** bi. sylfum.
36 heodeninga.   **37** dyre. noma.   **38** folgað.   **40** monn. londryht. geþah.

The Wife's Lament

(*Exeter Book,* f. 115ʳ⁻ᵛ)

Iċ þis ġiedd wrece   be mē full ġēomorre,
mīnre selfre sīþ.   Iċ þæt secgan mæġ
hwæt iċ iermþa ġebād   siþþan iċ upp awēox,
nīewes oþþe ealdes,   nā mā þonne nū.
5   Ā iċ wīte wann   mīnra wræc-sīða.
  Ǣrest mīn hlāford ġewāt   heonan of lēodum
ofer ȳða ġelāc;   hæfde iċ ūht-ċeare
hwǣr mīn lēod-fruma   landes wǣre.
  Þā iċ mē fēran ġewāt   folgoþ sēċan,
10   winelēas wreċċa,   for mīnre wēa-þearfe,
ongunnon þæt þæs mannes   māgas hycgan,
þurh dierne ġeþōht,   þæt hīe todǣlden unc,
þæt wit ġewīdost   on weorold-rīċe
lifdon lāðlicost,   and meċ langode.
15   Hēt meċ hlāford mīn   hēr hīred niman;
āhte iċ lēofra lȳt   on þissum land-stede,
holdra frēonda.   For-þon is mīn hyġe ġēomor.
  Þā iċ mē full ġemæcne   mannan funde—
heard-sǣliġne,   hyġe-ġēomorne,
20   mōd-mīðendne,   morðor-hycgendne—
blīðe ġebǣru   full oft wit bēotodon
þæt unc ne ġedǣlde   nefne dēaþ āna
āwiht elles.   Eft is þæt onhworfen;

Emendations: **3** aweox] MS weox.   **15** hired] MS heard (*for* heord: *see note*).
20 -hycgendne] MS hycgende.

Variant spellings: **1** bi. ful.   **2** sylfre.   **3** yrmþa. up.   **4** niwes. no.   **5** wonn.
8 londes.   **9** folgað.   **10** wreċċa.   **11** monnes.   **12** dyrne. hy.   **13** woruld.
14 longade.   **16** lond.   **18** ful. monnan.   **21** gebæro. ful. beotedan.
22 nemne.   **23** owiht.

is nū sēo nēawest   swā hit nā wǣre,

25   frēondscipe uncer.   Sceal iċ feorr ġe nēah

mīnes fela-lēofan   fǣhþu drēogan.

Hēt meċ man wunian   on wudu-bearwe

under āc-trēo   on þām eorþ-scræfe.

Eald is þēs eorþ-sele;   eall iċ eom oflangod.

30   Sindon dena dimme,   dūna upp-hēa,

bitre burg-tūnas   brērum beweaxne,

wīċ wynna lēas.   Full oft meċ hēr wrāðe beġeat

fram-sīþ frēan.   Frīend sind on eorðan,

lēofe libbende,   leġer weardiaþ,

35   þonne iċ on ūhtan   āna gange

under āc-trēo   ġeond þās eorþ-scrafu.

Þǣr iċ sittan mōt   sumor-langne dæġ,

þǣr iċ wēpan mæġ   mīne wræc-sīðas,

earfoþa fela,   for-þon iċ ǣfre ne mæġ

40   þǣre mōd-ċeare   mīnre ġerestan,

nē ealles þæs langoþes   þe meċ on þissum līfe beġeat.

Ā scyle ġeong mann   wesan ġeōmor-mōd,

heard heortan ġeþōht,   swelċe habban sceal

blīðe ġebǣru,   ēac þon brēost-ċeare,

45   sin-sorgna ġedrēag—   sīe æt him selfum ġelang

eall his weorolde wynn,   sīe full wīde fāh

feorres folc-landes—   þæt mīn frēond siteþ

under stān-hliðe   storme behrīmed,

wine wēriġ-mōd,   wætere beflōwen

50   on drēor-sele.   Drēogeþ sē mīn wine

micle mōd-ċeare;   hē ġeman tō oft

wynlicran wīċ.   Wā biþ þām-þe sceal

of langoþe   lēofes abīdan.

Emendations: **24** seo neawest] *not in* MS.   **25** Sceal] MS seal.   **37** sittan] MS sittam.

Variant spellings: **24** no.   **25** feor.   **27** heht. mon. wuda.   **28** in.   **29** eal. oflongad.   **30** up.   **32** ful.   **33** from. frynd.   **34** lifgende.   **35** gonge. **41** longaþes.   **42** mon.   **43** swylce.   **44** gebæro.   **45** sy. sylfum. gelong. **46** eal. worulde. wyn. sy. ful.   **47** londes.   **49** wætre.   **51** gemon. **53** langoþe.

COMMENTARY

Introduction

Some thirty thousand lines of Old English poetry have come down to us from Anglo-Saxon times.[1] Their alliterative form, descended from a preliterate stock once common to the Germanic tribes of the European continent, appears with minor modifications in the oldest poetic remains of some other early Germanic languages, High German, Saxon, and, most important, Scandinavian, chiefly in Old Icelandic. Certain features of its diction, even verse formulas, besides many of its themes and stories, are similarly shared and betray a common inheritance supplemented now and then by early borrowing. In England itself the earliest poetry of the Anglo-Saxon settlers was necessarily composed orally, like that of their ancestors; and Bede's account of Cædmon indicates that even in his time, unlike Scandinavian verse, it was often, if not always, sung or chanted to the accompaniment of a stringed instrument, a harp or lyre (see Boenig 1996). Without a doubt, oral composition was practiced throughout the period in spite of the introduction of writing; for writing was an art restricted to a relatively small portion of the population. How much of the output of unlettered singers may have found its way into books by dictation or by memorial reconstruction we have no reliable means of discovering; but it is evident from the style of the surviving poetry, with its use of a common verse form and its ready acceptance of a host of verse formulas, that even the most literate productions are steeped in oral tradition.[2]

Writing as a literary art, in contrast to the old half-magical runic writing—confined to brief inscriptions—of the early Germanic peoples, was introduced among the Anglo-Saxons in the seventh century by missionaries from the Mediterranean world as well as from Ireland. Englishmen were engaged in literary pursuits, writing in Latin or English, prose or verse, very soon after the Conversion, starting with the composition of the laws of King Æthelberht of

---

[1] The standard collective edition is that of Krapp and Dobbie (1931–53), in six volumes, each with its own title. Two poems missing from the standard edition are *William the Conqueror* (ed. Fowler 1966: 14) and *The Grave* (ed. Schröer 1882).

[2] For a fine and concise discussion of the dangers inherent in classifying Old English verse as solely oral or literate, see Foley 1991.

Kent at the beginning of the seventh century, though they are pre-
served only in a manuscript of the twelfth. Thus we have some four
and a half centuries of writings in Old English to reckon with before
the Norman Conquest brought about the subversion of the old aris-
tocracy and the beginnings of a new era. Culturally these were
centuries marked by astonishing intellectual advances and sudden
retrogressions; by sharp contrasts between the learned few, chiefly
though not exclusively clerics, and the rest of society; but also in
some quarters by a fruitful blending and assimilation. Old English
poetry shows at times the collision, but often the harmonious fu-
sion, of Mediterranean and native Germanic ideas and traditions.

One difference between classical and early Germanic poetry is
that while metaphors of various sorts constitute the chief poetic ef-
fect of Greek and Latin poetry, explicit metaphors are rare in Ger-
manic. Rather, poetic discourse in Old English is most directly
marked by the use of poetic vocabulary.[3] Many Old English words
are found only in verse, and it is clear that they were regarded as in-
appropriate to prose. Everything in Old English verse seems de-
signed to promote the use of a wide variety of poetic terms. It is no
doubt the need to multiply poetic diction that prompts the wide-
spread and sustained use of apposition as a rhetorical device—or
VARIATION, as it is called. This may be defined more precisely as the
deliberate dwelling on different aspects of an important subject by
partially synonymous repetition. It is the feature that lends Old
English poetry something of a foreign, halting quality in translation,
since extended apposition is not a prominent feature of contempo-
rary diction.[4] There is very often an aggregative rhetorical strategy
to variation, each synonym or quasi-synonym lending greater
specificity and clarity to the concept expressed, the whole forming a
dramatic sequence leading to a particular insight. For example, in
the variation in lines 20–21a of *The Wanderer* we are first told that

[3] For general introductions to the native rhetoric of Old English poetry, see Leslie
1959; Scragg 1991c; and Fulk 1996b.
[4] The most thorough study of variation in early Germanic poetry is by Paetzel
(1913). The variations in *Beowulf* have been studied in detail by Brodeur (1959: 39–
70; rpt. in Fulk 1991: 66–87) and Robinson (1985).

the speaker is **earm-ċeariġ** 'wretched and sorrowful'; then the source of his misery is revealed when he calls himself **ēðle bedǣled** 'separated from his native land'; and finally the specific aspect of life in that land of which he feels the most urgent lack is revealed: he is **frēo-māgum feorr** 'far from noble kin'.

No doubt much of the appeal of poetic vocabulary to the Anglo-Saxons derived from its traditional nature: poetic words are mostly archaic or dialectal terms that have passed out of general nonliterary use; thus in the conservative, tradition-bound medium of oral poetry they evoke the better world of days gone by that is so often contrasted in verse with the present, decadent state of human affairs. But the poets also continually coined new poetic terms by the method of COMPOUNDING, or the combining of words to express new or complex concepts.[5] This is a vital process of word formation in all the Germanic languages to this day—English examples are *blackbird, battleship,* and *barefoot*—and as anyone who has studied German knows, speakers of that language freely create new compounds at will, just as Old English poets did. Some compounds in these eight poems that are found nowhere else are **brim-mann**, **hrim-ċeald**, and **lēoþ-cræftiġ**. A particular type of compound is characteristic of the traditional diction of heroic verse: neither element of the compound refers literally to the thing denoted, but meaning is derived from the juxtaposition of terms in a metaphoric or metonymic process of poetic circumlocution. For example, **feorh-hūs** is literally 'life-house', the dwelling place of the spirit, and thus the body. Compounds of this sort are more prominent in Scandinavian verse than in Old English, and thus they are known as KENNINGS, or *kenningar*, an Icelandic term that is derived from the verb *kenna*, which can bear many meanings, the most relevant of which in this context is 'to paraphrase'.[6] Kennings need not be

---

[5] On Old English poetic diction see Wyld 1925, and for noun compounds in particular see Storch 1886. The poetic diction of *Beowulf*, both simplices and compounds, is studied by Brodeur (1959: 1–38); for Germanic compounds in general, Carr 1939 is best consulted.

[6] There are several studies of kennings in Old English and in relation to other Germanic languages: see Bode 1886; Krause 1930; Mohr 1933; Marquardt 1938; and Collins 1959; see also Gardner 1969, 1972.

genuine compounds: although in Old Icelandic there is terminology to distinguish a compound like **feorh-hūs** from a quasi-compound comprising a noun plus a modifying genitive—for example, **Godes candel** in reference to the sun—both types are subsumed under the term *kenning*.

The other chief guiding principle in the construction of verse, in addition to the use of poetic vocabulary, is CONTRAST, which is observable at various levels of analysis. It may be a local phenomenon, as when the *Maldon* poet says that Ælfhere and Maccus would *not* flee from the ford, *but* they defended themselves while they could (lines 81–83); or it may be of a conceptual or thematic nature, as when the speaking Rood is alternately covered with gems and blood to signify its dual role as instrument of torture and means to salvation (lines 14–23); or it may be an organizing principle, as in *Beowulf,* where the contrast between the hero's youth and age provides a structure to the poem; or in *The Seafarer,* where the larger meaning of the poem derives from the contrast between the hardships of this world and security in the next; or in *Deor,* the structure of which is predicated on a series of comparisons.[7] The ironic tendency that pervades Old English poetry, as in Byrhtnoth's response to the viking messenger, is also a type of fondness for contrast, pitting a set of false expectations—like Grendel's confidence that he will find yet another meal at Heorot—against an opposing representation of the facts.[8] Even LITOTES (or meiosis), the device of ironic understatement so characteristic of Old English verse, may be seen as largely a product of contrast: in many instances it is simply a local contrast with the positive element left unstated, as at *Maldon* 220–23 and 258–59.[9]

Beginning with the reign of Æthelstan in 924/925, the kings of Wessex claimed sovereignty over all parts of England not controlled by the vikings. With the rise of their political fortunes their native West Saxon variety of Old English came to serve as a standard literary language, as a consequence of which it was written in

[7] On contrast as a poetic principle see Mandel 1971.

[8] Irony in Old English verse is treated by Timmer (1942).

[9] For a study of litotes, see Bracher 1937.

scriptoria from one end of the island to the other, and records sur-
viving in other dialects are few. Nearly all the extant verse is also
written in a language variety that resembles West Saxon, but it
contains features that derive ultimately from the Anglian dialects—
those spoken in the Midlands and the North, where political power
and cultural ascendancy were for the most part concentrated before
the viking invasions. Many of these Anglian features are entirely
conventional: they are used even by the West Saxon King Alfred
the Great, and so they are to be regarded as part of a traditional and
artificial literary language reserved for verse. Some other Anglian
(Mercian and Northumbrian) features of poetry, though, are not so
traditional, and they confirm the long-standing belief of most
Anglo-Saxonists that the greater part of the surviving Old English
verse was composed not in Wessex but north of the Thames—a be-
lief that derives support from examples such as *Cædmon's Hymn*
and *The Dream of the Rood,* since Northumbrian versions of these
poems, or parts of them, attest to the practice of the Saxonization of
Anglian verse (see the commentary on these poems). Certainty is
difficult to attain in respect to short texts, but of the eight poems in
this book, *The Battle of Brunanburh* is likely to be a West Saxon
composition, and *The Battle of Maldon* may have been composed
by a speaker of an eastern dialect, perhaps of Essex (see Scragg
1981: 24–25 and Griffith 1998); the remainder seem to be of
Anglian origin.[10] The evidence, though, is slender. In this book
most of the purely conventional Anglian features of verse have
been eliminated by the normalization of the spelling to early West
Saxon standards. Certain of the less conventional Anglianisms,
however, remain, and some are pointed out in the commentary and
the glossary.

So conservative are the traditions of Old English verse composi-
tion that the formal properties of *Cædmon's Hymn,* composed in the
second half of the seventh century, between 657 and 680, are vir-
tually indistinguishable from those of *The Battle of Brunanburh,*

---

[10] The Anglian features of verse, and the dialect features specifically of some of
these poems, are surveyed by Fulk (1992: 269–347, 415–18).

which can have been composed no later than about 955 and no earlier than the year of the battle itself, 937. Of the eight poems edited in this book, only *The Battle of Maldon,* which dates to 991 or later, shows marked divergences from the formal features of earlier verse. As a consequence of this compositional uniformity, in conjunction with the usual Anglo-Saxon practice of anonymous authorship, most Old English poems cannot be dated even to a particular century or two with much confidence. Longer poems such as *Genesis A* and *Andreas* yield enough linguistic evidence to suggest earliness or lateness within the Old English period, but *The Wanderer, The Seafarer, Deor,* and *The Wife's Lament* are too short to afford even such limited conclusions.

Most Old English poetry is preserved in manuscripts datable to the second half of the tenth century, the time of the Benedictine reform, when monastic life was revitalized throughout England. *Cædmon's Hymn* and *The Battle of Brunanburh* are extraordinary in that they are preserved in multiple copies; to nearly all other verse texts there is a single witness. As the textual apparatus to these two poems illustrates, in those few instances in which multiple texts may be compared there is often substantive variation. It has been shown that some of this variation is intentional: scribes did not always treat vernacular texts in verse the way they did texts in Latin, but, being familiar with poetic traditions, they sometimes recomposed the poems as they copied (see in particular O'Brien O'Keeffe 1990). Yet even poems that they did not obviously attempt to rewrite show the natural effects of recopying, which almost invariably produces unintended changes in the transmitted text. The result of the combination of unique preservation and the inevitability of copyists' errors is the virtual assurance that the Old English poetic texts known to us, by and large, must contain many manuscript readings that were never intended by those who first set them down. One might therefore expect Anglo-Saxonists to show little respect for what the manuscripts say. Paradoxically, the case is the opposite, and for about a century the prevailing view has been that emendation, if it is justifiable at all, should be applied only in cases of extreme unintelligibility. Emendation is relatively sparing in the texts in this book as well, though fidelity to the manuscripts, naturally, is not a pressing need in a set of normalized texts. But as one unravels the intricacies of difficult passages it is best not to grow too attached to particular interpretations of them, keeping in mind that many of the obscurities of these poems may simply be copyists' errors.

Among the numerous guides to Old English literature, the most authoritative and useful are Greenfield and Calder 1986 and Godden and Lapidge 1991. Recent critical trends that reemphasize examining Old English literature in its cultural and historical contexts reinforce the value and importance of Whitelock 1979 for the study of these and other poems. That volume contains a broad selection of documents, from laws and charters to letters, histories, sermons, and poems, admirably translated into Modern English from Latin, Old English, and occasionally Old Icelandic. The introductions, notes, and bibliographies are of the highest quality.

The bibliography of the eight poems is by now quite large. The essential bibliographical tool to 1972 is Greenfield and Robinson 1980, a superb resource. The most comprehensive annual bibliographies of Old English poetry are to be found in *Old English Newsletter* and *Anglo-Saxon England;* the former also is home to a collaborative annual review of scholarship that is often quite useful, "The Year's Work in Old English Studies."

Cædmon's Hymn

This hymn has a peculiar importance within the corpus of Old English poetry, an importance by no means limited to its literary merit or its purportedly miraculous origin. It has come down to us as the initial effort of the first English poet to treat the major themes of the Christian religion, and although he is described as the author of a great many poems, this is the only surviving composition that can with assurance be ascribed to him. Even the copies of it are notable, since the two oldest are our earliest manuscript records of Old

English poetry and of the Northumbrian dialect. The occurrence of the poem in twenty-one known manuscripts is in contrast to the preservation of all but a minuscule number of Old English poems in unique copies, and it has thus served as an important source for the study of the textual transmission of Old English verse, particularly in O'Brien O'Keeffe 1990. The hymn itself has a further interest: as the work of a man who had never learned to read and write, it affords an indisputable example of that orally composed poetry, largely unrecorded, by which the written poems were preceded and in all probability surrounded.

All the oldest copies of the hymn have been preserved in the manuscripts of Bede's *Ecclesiastical History of the English Nation,* either in its original Latin form[11] or in the Old English version that was produced a bit more than a century and a half later;[12] and our knowledge of Cædmon himself depends entirely on a single chapter of that work. Bede completed the history about 731, some four years before his death. Cædmon had died long before, probably while Bede was still a boy, and there is nothing in Bede's account to suggest that the two had ever met; but they were both Northumbrians, and Cædmon's monastery at *Streoneshealh* (the modern Whitby) was just sixty or seventy miles to the south of Bede's at Jarrow. Bede, who was assiduous in gathering information for his history and received some of it from much more distant regions, would have had ready access to the records of Cædmon's monastery, and it is entirely possible that he should have talked with persons acquainted with the poet.

According to Bede, the beginning of Cædmon's poetic career and the greater part at least of his subsequent achievement belonged to the period between 657 and 680, when Hild, having built the monastery, governed it as abbess. This remarkable woman, whom Bede celebrates in the previous chapter of the history, was a grandniece

---

[11] *Historia ecclesiastica gentis Anglorum,* most recently edited by Colgrave and Mynors (1969).

[12] Edited with translation by Miller (1890–99). This version has sometimes been attributed, though mistakenly, to King Alfred. It was probably produced in or about his time, if not at his instigation.

of Edwin, the first Christian king of Northumbria, with whom she was converted in her youth. Having taken the veil in middle life and acquired some experience as abbess at another foundation, she presided at Streoneshealh with wisdom and vigor. The monastery, which was of the double type not uncommon at this period, with separate houses for men and women, soon became renowned for learning as well as devotion. It was chosen as the meeting place of the great synod of 663, where Roman authority prevailed over Irish. Several of its monks were afterward bishops; but Cædmon, an unassuming herdsman on the monastic estate at the time of the miracle, was to become the best known of all its inmates. Bede's account of him is too rich and too skillfully wrought to be summarized without loss. The greater part of it, which is to be found in its entirety in book IV, chapter 24 of the history, runs as follows:

In the monastery of this abbess there was a certain brother specially marked by divine grace, since he was accustomed to composing songs appropriate to religion and piety, in such manner that whatever he learned out of divine Scripture through interpreters he would render again after a short while in poetic language composed with the greatest sweetness and feeling. By means of his songs the spirits of many were often moved to contempt of this world and hunger for heavenly life. And indeed, others after him among the nation of the English tried to compose religious poems, but none was able to equal his skill, because he did not learn the art of singing from being instructed either by men or through a man, but he received the gift of song freely, with divine help.[13] For that reason he could never compose a frivolous or idle poem, but only those that pertain to religion were fit for his devout tongue. Since he had never learned any songs while settled in his secular state, up until the time that he was well advanced in age,[14] for that reason now and again at a dinner, when it was decided for the purpose of entertainment that everyone should sing in turn, when he saw the harp approaching him he would rise in the middle of the meal and leave, returning to his house.

[13] This echoes St. Paul's reference to his calling as an apostle in Galatians 1.1.

[14] The Latin, *usque ad tempora provectioris aetatis,* might suggest any time past the prime of life, perhaps no more than forty, though the Old English translator seems to think of a greater age.

When he did this on a certain occasion and had left the house of the dinner and gone to the outbuilding where the watch over the live-stock had been allotted to him that night, and there at the appropriate hour he had laid himself out in slumber, someone stood by him in a dream, and greeting him and calling him by name, said, "Cædmon, sing something for me." And responding he said, "I don't know how to sing, and that's why I came out here from the dinner: I couldn't sing." "Still," he said, "you have to sing for me."[15] "What should I sing?" he said. "Sing," the other said, "about the beginning of created things." When he received that answer, at once he began to sing verses in praise of God the Creator, verses that he had never heard, of which the sense is this: "Now let us praise the Maker of the heavenly kingdom, the power of the Creator, and his plan, the acts of the Father of Glory; how he, being eternal God, was the Maker of all miracles; who, almighty Guardian of the human race, first created for the sons of men the sky as a roof for their home, then the earth."[16] This is the sense but not the precise order of the words that he sang while sleeping, since songs, however well composed, cannot be translated verbatim from one language into another without detriment to their grace and worth. Arising, then, from his dream, he retained in his memory all that he had sung while sleeping, and to that he then added some words, in the same meter, of a song worthy of God. And coming the next day to the steward who had authority over him, he showed him what gift he had received; and when he was led to the abbess he was commanded in the presence of many rather learned men to recount his dream and sing the song, so that it might be put to the test by all what this thing was that he reported, and where it came from. And it seemed to all that a heavenly favor had been granted him by the Lord. And they recited for him a certain reading from a holy story or a lesson, asking him, if he could, to put it into the meter of a song. And he, accepting the task, went away, and when he returned the next day he rendered what had been asked of him, made into a very good song. On that account the abbess, embracing the grace of God in the man, instructed him to give up the secular state and take the monastic vow; and when he had done so she made him a

[15] For alternative renderings of *mihi cantare habes,* see Mitchell 1969.
[16] Bede's exact words are worth having here: "Nunc laudare debemus auctorem regni caelestis, potentiam Creatoris, et consilium illius, facta Patris gloriae; quomodo ille, cum sit aeternus Deus, omnium miraculorum auctor exstitit; qui primo filiis hominum caelum pro culmine tecti, dehinc terram custos humani generis omnipotens creavit."

member of the company of brothers who were with her in the monastery, and she ordered him to be taught the course of sacred history. And he, ruminating to himself on all that he could understand of what he heard, the way a clean animal chews the cud,[17] would convert it into the sweetest song; and very pleasantly singing it back to them, he made his teachers in turn his audience.[18]

Now, he sang about the creation of the world, and the origin of the human race, and the whole story of Genesis, about the departure of Israel from Egypt and entry into the Promised Land, about a great many other stories from Holy Writ, about the incarnation of the Lord, his passion, resurrection, and ascension into heaven, about the coming of the Holy Spirit, and the teaching of the apostles. Likewise he composed many songs about the terror of Judgment Day, and the frightfulness of punishment in hell, and the sweetness of the heavenly kingdom; but also very many others about divine favors and judgments, in all of which it was his aim to wean men from the love of sin and to arouse in them a delight in, and indeed an aptitude for, good works. For he was a very devout man and obedient to the discipline of the rules—indeed, one inflamed with a spirit of great fervor against those who wished to do otherwise. Thus he concluded his life with a fine end.[19]

Although Bede did not include the hymn itself in his account of Cædmon, the scribes of the original Latin version of his history frequently added it in the margin, and the author of the Old English version substituted it for the Latin paraphrase. In this way all the surviving copies of the hymn came into being. Because there are substantive variations in these copies, there have been differences of opinion about the best readings. It has seemed best to select the

[17] This image derives from Leviticus 11.3.

[18] The Old English translator says that they wrote at his dictation. Was this simply the translator's notion of the proper way to learn, or was he familiar with written poems that were thought to be Cædmon's? Bede's description suggests the possibility that many poems were recorded by dictation, though this cannot be proved by the surviving records. Still, certain peculiar manuscript readings (e.g., *secga swate* in the Parker Chronicle for **secgas hwate** at *Brunanburh* 13) do suggest an oral element in the recording of some poems, and it is known that some extant prose texts were copied from dictation (see, for example, Bately 1966).

[19] The remainder of Bede's chapter tells the ʿstory of Cædmon's last hours. Whether he died before or after Hild is not known.

oldest Northumbrian version for the base text, since this is the one
with which Bede's paraphrase most nearly agrees, and to present it
first with its original Northumbrian spellings as they appear in the
two oldest copies, then in the normalized West Saxon spellings
adopted for the other poems in this volume. A sampling of the ac-
tual West Saxon versions is given at the foot of the page below the
normalized text.[20]

The manuscripts containing the two oldest copies cannot be far
removed from Bede's own time. The Moore manuscript was once
thought to be firmly datable to the year 737, but now all that can be
said with assurance is that it belongs to the eighth century.[21] It con-
tains the Northumbrian version at the top of the last page rather
than where one would expect it, in the margin near Bede's para-
phrase. It is followed by the identifying statement, *primo cantauit
caedmon istud carmen* 'Cædmon first sang this song', and by three
glosses, alphabetically arranged, of Latin words that appear in the
history. Apparently the scribe of the manuscript was gathering to-
gether at this spot certain items from the margins of his exemplar
that he had passed over while he was copying the text. In the St.
Petersburg manuscript, which is also to be dated to the eighth cen-
tury, the Northumbrian version of the hymn is at the foot of the
page that contains Bede's paraphrase of it.[22] An old argument re-
vived some years ago by Kiernan (1990; see also Dumville 1981:
148; Frantzen 1990: 146; and Isaac 1997) would regard the Old
English hymn preserved in these early manuscripts as a translation
of Bede's Latin translation, rather than the reverse, meaning that
Cædmon's original hymn is nowhere preserved. But this view faces
some difficulties, chief of which is that the accident would be a pe-
culiar one if Bede's Latin version of the hymn happened to furnish
precisely the words required to produce a poem with perfectly

---

[20] The fullest study of the text and its manuscripts is by Dobbie (1937). His later
edition of it (Krapp and Dobbie 1931–53: 6.105–6) presents the Northumbrian and
West Saxon versions with very full collations of other manuscripts.

[21] For a summary of the controversy over the dating of the Moore and St. Peters-
burg MSS, see Fulk 1992: 426–28.

[22] For facsimiles of the Moore and St. Petersburg MSS, see, respectively, Blair
1959 and Arngart 1952.

regular meter and alliteration in a word-for-word translation of it, with a few variations added, unless of course the Old English version we have is Cædmon's own.[23]

In spite of Cædmon's supposed incompetence as a singer before the moment when this hymn came into being, it exhibits the characteristic meter and style of Old English poetry under skillful control. The individual half-lines or verses have the typical range in number of syllables and stress patterns, the alliteration linking each pair of verses is placed according to the rules—no easy task for the novice—and the sequence of verses has, for so short and simple a piece, a surprisingly varied yet expressive movement. This is an accomplished piece of versification. Conspicuous also is the familiar stylistic device of variation: in these nine lines there are seven different epithets for God, just one of them repeated. Magoun (1955) accordingly is not alone in finding it impossible to believe that this poem is actually the first piece of Old English verse devoted to religious themes. Cædmon, he argues, must have been drawing on a preexistent corpus of religious formulas. But Magoun's disbelief illustrates why the poem was regarded as a miracle. Malone (1961) explains that to Anglo-Saxons who were accustomed to hearing songs only on heroic themes, the novelty and aptness of expressions like **heofonrīċes weard** and **frēa ælmihtiġ** must have seemed products of divine inspiration, especially in the mouth of a peasant employed in looking after herds. This explanation seems more straightforward than the argument of Wrenn (1946) that it was Cædmon's mastery of an aristocratic genre rather than a popular one that so amazed his contemporaries, or the argument of Magoun that Cædmon had formerly been able to sing when alone but simply could not conquer his fear of public performance. In any case it seems not to be simply Cædmon's ability to sing at all that is miraculous, since the passing of the harp at dinner shows that the ability to perform was by no means rare. There is nonetheless a certain literary quality to the miracle and the account of it, as the gift of

---

23 For responses to Kiernan's argument, see James Hall 1992; Biggs 1997; and Fulk 1992: 427–28.

poetic song conferred in a vision seems to have been a medieval commonplace (see Shepherd 1954)—indeed, divine inspiration for verse is a literary convention of late antiquity and the medieval period (Fritz 1969)—and Bede's translation of the hymn shows some Latinate poetic features (Orchard 1996: 413). The Old English hymn itself, it should be added, is constructed of language reminiscent of various of the Psalms, as documented by Orchard (414).

The hymn and Bede's account of its composition have proved fertile ground for cultural critique. Lerer (1991: 42–48) reads Cædmon's story as a narrative of the appropriation of an entire poetic tradition for a new, Christian purpose by converting it from an oral to a literate medium. The varied uses to which the hymn has been put since its time of composition—serving particularly Bede's historical vision of the triumph of Christianity and later scholarship's promotion of Bede's aim—have been subjected to a penetrating critique by Frantzen (1990: 130–67). Building on Frantzen's findings, Lees and Overing (1994; see also Earl 1994: 85–86) add that the ideology informing representation of the hymn's composition as an originary moment in English literature is a gendered one, promoting a male model of authorship. These and some other studies of the past decade aim to subvert complacent credence in the framework that Bede's account constructs for the poem. They instead promote engagement with some issues that have preoccupied literary scholarship in recent years—issues that include literacy, historical agency, and the politics of gender.

The most authoritative edition is that of Dobbie (1937), based on seventeen manuscripts. Twenty-one medieval copies are now known, and though two of the manuscripts have been destroyed, copies of them survive. All of these are reproduced in the collection of facsimiles edited by Robinson and Stanley (1991: 2.1–21). The Northumbrian versions have been edited with particular care by Smith (1933). For recent studies of Cædmon and his hymn, see the annual bibliographies cited above (p. 49); for earlier scholarship the cumulative bibliographies of Whitbread (1942) and Caie (1979) are best consulted.

Notes

1. Mitchell (1985a), pursuing a suggestion of Sir Christopher Ball (1985), argues that the intended subject of **sculon** cannot be anything but **weorc wuldor-fæder**. The idea is so clever that one would like to be able to approve it without reservation, as in fact many have. But the far remove of the proposed subject from the verb, in conjunction with the immediate shift of focus in 3b away from the subject after it is finally introduced, makes an awkward puzzle of the syntax. Even Bede took the subject to be *wē* (whether it was understood or, as Robinson 1993a assumes, it was actually in the version Bede knew), as shown by his *debemus;* and *wē* has actually been inserted after **nū** in all the West Saxon versions in the Latin manuscripts of Bede's history and in some of those in the English ones. Clearly more than one Anglo-Saxon believed *wē* to be the intended subject. Despite the slender evidence, in hortative use, and at least in early verse or verse of this dialect, some auxiliaries (like **[w]uton**) may reasonably be supposed to lack an overt subject. The closest parallel is at *Andreas* 1487, an instance Ball finds sufficiently convincing (though not Mitchell 1985b: §1515). But *wē* may simply have been omitted, through the inadvertence of a scribe, from the source text of the Northumbrian versions, whence the error passed to the West Saxon ones.

2. **meahta** 'powers'. The distinctive plural ending **-a** of the feminine *ō*-stem nouns has been chosen for the normalized text in view of the **maecti** of the Moore MS and the **mehti** of the St. Petersburg MS. The word *meaht* or *miht* was originally a feminine *i*-stem with no ending in the accusative singular and *-i* in the accusative plural, but in West Saxon it came to be declined like the *ō*-stems, with *-e* in the accusative singular and *-a* in the accusative plural. The spelling *meahte* in the West Saxon Tanner MS may represent either the old plural or the new singular. Bede's choice of the singular *potentiam* in his paraphrase may be due to his sense of Latin usage.

3, 4. **swā hē wundra ġehwæs, / ēċe dryhten, ōr astealde**. The expression **wundra ġehwæs** 'of each of wonders' goes together as if it were a compound, and the genitive **ġehwæs** depends on **ōr**, the direct object of **astealde**: 'as he, eternal Lord, established the beginning of every wondrous thing'. The word **swā** could be an adverb here (Mitchell 1985b: §3269), though that is not how Bede renders it.

7. By putting the object, **middangeard**, ahead of the subject, **weard**, the poet not only solves a metrical problem but produces a syntactic contrast to his parallel clauses. Unlike Bede, Blockley (1998) regards **þā** as a conjunction rather than an adverb, lending **scōp** (5) pluperfect aspect.

9. Either **foldan** and **frēa ælmihtiġ** are in variation individually with **middanġeard** and **ēċe dryhten**, respectively, or this entire line is a variant of the preceding two, with the verb **tēode** understood as repeated from the previous line. Bede's translation suggests the former interpretation.

The Battle of Brunanburh

The victory of the English forces at Brunanburh under the command of Athelstan and his brother Edmund was the climax of a movement by which Alfred the Great and his immediate successors, having first freed their hereditary West Saxon kingdom from the threat of Danish conquest, gradually gained power over the whole of England and made themselves secure against their enemies abroad.[24] The poem describing the battle was early put on record as chief English witness to the event. Accordingly it has survived in four manuscripts of the Anglo-Saxon Chronicle, appearing in each of them as the sole entry for the year 937.[25]

---

[24] See Stenton 1971: chap. X, esp. 342–43, for a careful assessment of the historic significance of the battle

[25] The manuscripts are listed above, at the head of the critical apparatus below the text of the poem. The readings of a fifth manuscript, destroyed by fire in 1731, have been reconstructed by Lutz (1981) from earlier transcripts, but they bear no independent witness to the text of the poem, since the manuscript was a direct copy of MS A. The entirety of MS A is available in facsimile (Flower and Smith 1941). The

In spite of this association, the exact time and circumstances of
the composition of the poem are uncertain. In our earliest manu-
script (A) the poem is included in a series of entries that were not
transcribed till about 955. We cannot tell how long before that it
might have been composed, though the poem itself offers no reason
to suspect historical distance from the event. Neither do we know
for certain that it was composed specifically for inclusion in the
Chronicle, though this is the most probable interpretation, for met-
rical reasons.[26] Moreover, its perspective and its concerns are not
far removed from those that govern the Chronicle as it had taken
shape under Alfred and Edward.

Although this is one of the better known Old English poems,
made familiar by Tennyson's translation, with its "clash of the war-
glaive" and "garbaging war-hawk," it is not altogether easy to eval-
uate in its tenth-century form and setting. Comparison with earlier
Old English poetry has shown that it is conventional in meter and
diction. What is likely to escape us is its no less remarkable origi-
nality in design and vision. Nothing quite like it in genre has sur-
vived from earlier periods, nor are there close parallels in poetry in
other Germanic languages. It does indeed have partial parallels, and
it probably had antecedents, insofar as it can be classified as a royal
panegyric; but it is more than a panegyric by reason of its peculiar
nationalism. This strong national feeling depends in part, doubtless,

various versions of the Chronicle are published, with translations in a second vol-
ume, by Thorpe (1861) in the Rolls Series. Still of importance for its annotations is
the edition of Plummer (1892–99); but modern critical editions of the separate chron-
icles are currently appearing in an ongoing series (Dumville and Keynes 1983–) in
which editions of MSS A, B, and D have already come to hand. Of the many trans-
lations that have been made, Whitelock's (1961) is the most authoritative.

[26] The meter of the first verse is of a common sort only if the word **hēr** is an or-
ganic part of the poem. This is the way **hēr** must be treated in another Chronicle
poem, *The Coronation of Edgar;* and although an alternative scansion is possible
whereby the word here at the beginning of *Brunanburh* might be regarded as ex-
trametrical, the result would be an unusual metrical variety. Two other Chronicle
poems (*The Capture of the Five Boroughs* and *The Death of Edward*) would then
open with the same infrequent verse type, and this scansion in *Brunanburh* thus
seems improbable. The problem is that although type A2k is common enough, the
second metrical position usually takes secondary stress. Exceptions (like **æðeling
maniġ**, *Beowulf* 1112b) are infrequent.

on the long antecedent years of adversity caused by Scandinavian ravagers and invaders and in part on the consolidation of England that had been achieved under West Saxon leadership. Likewise original, though now it seems a matter of course, is the author's historical perspective—not quite the same thing as the knowledge of heroic tradition of which Norse panegyrists made use. He has been reading Bede and the Chronicle, and he knows the conventions of battle poetry. He places the battle historically within a firmer frame of reference than an unbookish author might be expected to supply, and even in treating the conflict itself he maintains a distant view, surveying the scene as from a height and noting armies and battalions rather than individuals. There are some analogues to this in the battle scenes of Cynewulf and the biblical poets, but a more conventional way of describing a battle in poetry is to be seen in *The Battle of Maldon,* where the originality lies in a different sphere.

A thorough edition of the poem from all the manuscripts, with full historical introduction and notes, has been produced by Campbell (1938). See also the edition of Dobbie (Krapp and Dobbie 1931–53: 6.16–20), whose full presentation of the text is followed by that of the other conventionally composed poems of the Chronicle, which celebrate later events and are of particular historical interest. All the manuscript copies are reproduced in facsimile in Robinson and Stanley 1991: 14.1. On these facsimiles depends the report, slightly abridged, of the manuscript readings.

The main facts about the battle as presented in the poem are confirmed by a number of later accounts, partially or wholly independent. Among those cited in Campbell's edition are Irish and Scottish annals, a Norse saga, and Latin histories produced in England. Yet the location of Brunanburh is still uncertain, and even the correct form of the name of the place is in doubt (see the glossary of proper names). Of the various sites proposed, those that seem most probable lie near the west coast of England between Chester and southern Scotland. According to the poem, the opposing army consisted of two main forces: Scots under their king **Constantinus** (Constantine III, king of the combined Picts and Scots) and Norse vikings, the **scip-flotan** of line 11, who had come by sea from

Ireland under the command of a certain **Anlaf**. Other reports make it clear that this Anlaf, a son of Guthfrith,[27] ruled a viking settlement in and around Dublin. His uncle Sihtric had held sway in York, but Guthfrith, claiming the succession after Sihtric's death, had been driven out of England by Athelstan and had ruled for a few years in Ireland before he died and left his kingdom there to Anlaf. The Scottish forces were apparently supported by their neighbors and allies, the Welsh of Strathclyde, who held the coastal region west of Northumbria.

Brief treatments of some of the puzzling details, such as the spelling **Brūnanburg** and the identity of the body of water called **Dinġes mere** in line 54, will be found in the glossary of proper names, where also are offered identifications of the chief persons. For full discussion of such matters the reader must be guided by the notes and bibliographies of Campbell and Dobbie.

Notes

1. The word **Hēr** 'Here' introduces each annal in the *Anglo-Saxon Chronicle* directly after the number of the year. Hence it takes on the temporal meaning 'In this year'.

5. **bord-weall**. This expression refers to a defensive position in which the men hold their shields so that the edges overlap. For illustrations of this formation from the Bayeux Tapestry, see Abels 1991: 152.

6. The expression **hamora lāfum** 'with swords', literally 'with leavings of hammers', is a typical kenning as this device is described above (pp. 45–46). The term is often applied to any periphrasis consisting of two or more words, or to a compound even if the meaning is obvious, but there is frequently something metaphorical or recondite about a kenning. Here, although a sword is in fact what is left on the anvil after a smith's hammer has forged it, perhaps

---

[27] This Anlaf, the later form of whose name is *Ólάfr* (*Olaf*), appears in a seventeenth-century English version of some Irish annals (quoted by Campbell 1938: 159) as *Awley McGodfrey*.

comparison is intended to a human warrior as the survivor of a battle. In line 54 we find the expression **daroða lāf** 'what was left by the spears' applied to the bedraggled remnant of Anlaf's army.

7–9. **swā ... ealgoden** 'as befitted the nobility they got from their ancestors, that they should often defend the land in battle against every foe'. Instead of the distinctively subjunctive ending **-en** of the normalized **ealgoden** the manuscripts have *-on* or *-an,* which at this period can be either indicative or subjunctive. Campbell recommends the subjunctive, which yields a more plausible meaning and firmer syntax.

12. **dennode**. The meaning of the word is unknown. This spelling, that of MS D, is also the normalized form of *dennade,* found in B and C; and *dænnede* in A (corrected in the MS from *dænede*) is a typical spelling for the same word, since *æ* for *e* before nasal consonants is very frequent outside of later Northumbrian texts, and unstressed *-e-* for *-o-* in these preterites is common in the tenth century (see Campbell 1959: §§193[d], 385). The word may be related to Sanskrit *dhánvati* 'flows', as Holthausen (1932–34) suggests. But this could be only a very distant connection, as the Sanskrit verb has no known cognates in the Germanic languages; and because **denn-** must be assumed to show front mutation, *dennian* is probably best explained as denominative. If **dennode** is thus related to the noun *denn,* as would appear most likely, then it is worth noting that the Old English meaning 'den, lair, cave' is likely to be a relatively late semantic development, since the Germanic cognates indicate that the original meaning was perhaps 'clearing trodden in the grass' (Pokorny 1959: 2.249). In that event **dennode** might mean 'lay flattened'. The treatment of this word most favored in recent years—emendation to *dynode* or *dynede* 'resounded'—has not been adopted here not just because emendation may not be necessary but because it produces an unmetrical verse. Harris (1986), however, has demonstrated the semantic plausibility of this reading, citing remarkable parallels in skaldic verse and showing the image to be elliptical rather than strictly synaesthetic. The substantial note on the word furnished by Campbell (1938: 98–102) summarizes the emendations that have been proposed.

22. **on lāst leġdon lāðum þēodum** 'pursued the hostile peoples'. Since **lecgan** 'to lay' is normally transitive, the expression **on lāst leġdon** is evidently elliptical: probably, as Campbell has suggested, for *on lāst leġdon lāstas lāðum þēodum* 'they laid tracks behind the hostile peoples', where *on lāst* is an idiom for 'behind', literally 'on the track (of)', with the dative, which then has possessive force. The possessive dative is customary with nouns closely associated with parts of the body, as **lāst** 'footprint, track' was evidently felt to be.

35. **cnearr**. This is the most probable example of Norse influence on the diction of the poem (see the glossary), though other possibilities have been suggested by Hofmann (1955) and Niles (1987), including **gūþ-hafoc** (64) as a kenning for 'eagle' and **Īra land** (56) rather than *Scotta land* to designate Ireland, among others. As Niles points out, the very genre of the poem, so unlike anything else in Old English, may be a sign of Scandinavian influence.

51. Possibly the demonstrative **þæs** is here used as a relative 'which', agreeing with the last of its series of antecedents, each of which is in the genitive singular, and serving also as object of **plegodon**, which normally takes the accusative (Campbell's explanation). But more likely **þæs** is used as a conjunction 'after, when' or 'because' (Mitchell 1985b: §2302). The scribe of MS D has substituted the more usual form of the conjunctive phrase, *þæs þe*. Cf. 68b below.

54. **drēoriġ**. Campbell (cf. Gendre 1988–89) maintains that the meaning 'bloody' attributed to this word in addition to 'dejected' cannot be substantiated from its use in Old or Middle English; but since *drēor,* as he admits, means 'blood', it is not implausible that **drēoriġ** should have suggested 'bloody' in the context of a battle. That is not its usual meaning, however, and it need not be dominant even here.

60–65. In this enumeration of the creatures that prey on corpses after a battle—a familiar motif in Old English poetry, often referred to as the "beasts of battle" typescene (on which see Griffith 1993 and Honegger 1998)—one may choose to combine the words in several ways. One might take **sealwiġ-pādan** as a noun, 'dark-coated ones', applicable to all the creatures enumerated, each being credited with a slightly different shade of the common darkness: 'the black raven with horny beak, and the dusky-coated one, the eagle white from behind—greedy war hawk—and that grey beast, the wolf in the forest'. Campbell suggests that **gūþ-hafoc** is not the name of some unknown kind of hawk but a kenning for the white-tailed eagle previously mentioned. Raven, eagle, and wolf are the usual trio. It is true that the **earn** is separated from the **gūþ-hafoc** by the verse **æses brūcan**, but this is only a variation of **hrǣw bryttian** above and may well be followed by a variation of **earn æftan hwīt**. The uninflected **hwīt** is metrically necessary and may, as Campbell suggests, be excused if the verse is felt to be parenthetical.

65b–68a. 'No greater number of people was ever yet slain in this island before this by sword's edges'. Campbell points out that **wæl**, in its frequent sense 'number of slain', governs the genitive **folces**, and that **wearþ** goes with **ġefielled** to form the preterite passive of **ġefiellan**. On the historical significance of the appeal in this passage to the Anglo-Saxon invasion of Britain, see Howe 1989: 30–31.

68b. Here **þæs-þe** is used as a conjunction, 'according to what, as'. This use is found in other poems—for instance, in *Beowulf* 1341, *þæs þe þinċean mæġ þeġne monegum,* 'as it may seem to many a thane'.

The Dream of the Rood

This poem stands on ff. 104ᵛ–106ʳ of the Vercelli Book, a manuscript of the late tenth century, being the fifth of six items of religious verse interspersed in the volume among twenty-three homilies. The best and most recent facsimile of the manuscript is edited by C. Sisam (1976). There are several fine editions of the poem available, the most comprehensive being those of Cook (1905), Dickins and Ross (1966), and Swanton (1970).

Two sections of the poem (39–49, 56–64) correspond to verses, somewhat abridged and in some places obliterated, inscribed in runes on a monumental Northumbrian cross preserved at Ruthwell in Dumfriesshire, southwestern Scotland. For the most comprehensive treatment of the cross, with fine illustrations and bibliography, see B. Cassidy 1992; and for the text of the inscription see Dickins and Ross, or Dobbie's edition (Krapp and Dobbie 1931–53: 6.114–15), and especially the reconstruction by Howlett (1992: 83). The verses on the cross are almost certainly excerpted from a longer composition, but whether that composition was in most essentials identical with *The Dream of the Rood* is impossible to say. Since the cross is generally dated on art-historical grounds to about 750, or perhaps a bit earlier, most have dated the poem to about that time; but it has been pointed out that the inscription is very likely a later addition to the cross (for references and discussion see Fulk 1992: §372 n. 155), and so although the poem could be that old, the language does not forbid a date as late as the ninth century.

Despite its Marian interest (92–94) and its form of a dream vision, this earliest vernacular example of the genre to emerge from Western Europe actually has little in common with dream visions of the later Middle Ages. The late antique and early medieval cult of the cross is the proper context in which to understand the poem (a context briefly sketched by McEntire 1986), since it finds frequent expression in Anglo-Saxon art and literature. The conception of the cross as jeweled invites comparison with preciously adorned early medieval crosses, many of them made to house fragments of the True Cross—particularly with the splendid relic known as the Brussels Cross, which bears a poetic inscription in Old English.[28] Although the form of the poem is highly original, with its alternating hypermetric and normal verses, the dream vision itself is not unique in the Anglo-Saxon period, since several others are recorded (those of Fursa, Adamnan, and Dryhthelm (all in Bede), of Leofric, of Eadwine, and of St. Paul are among the most familiar; see also the commentary on *Cædmon's Hymn*, pp. 55–56). Yet it differs from late medieval dream visions, particularly in its emphasis on the

[28] This inscription is to be found in various of the editions of the *Dream;* for a fine photograph of the Brussels Cross, and of some other Anglo-Saxon crosses, see Backhouse et al. 1984, esp. plate 75.

aftermath of the dream (as pointed out by Galloway 1994). What is most remarkable about this vision, especially given its status as the premier example, is, on the one hand, the depth and subtlety of its understanding; on the other, the art and imagination with which the speeches of dreamer and cross are invented, complexities of meaning and emotion are conveyed, order is maintained, and a significant progression is unfolded from beginning to end.

Some have surmised that the sequence of normal verses forming the second half of the poem is a later addition to a shorter original composition. Yet if that is the case, it is remarkable how this addition lends the poem a structure similar to that of some other Old English lyrics. Just as with *The Wanderer,* the narrator opens the poem only to introduce a second speaker, who first describes the hardships he has faced and then generalizes from his experience, applying the wisdom he has gained to a more expansive view of human history. At the close the narrator returns, relating the second speaker's acquired wisdom to the fate of the individual in God's plan and affirming the security to be found in the heavenly home that awaits those who have suffered. Unity is also implicit in the poem's didactic method: adopting a reader-centered strategy, Irving (1986) has shown how the dreamer and the rood itself are confronted with fearful mysteries that are resolved as the poem unfolds, and how the reader achieves similar resolution through the experience that the poem offers.

The presentation of the cross as an individual able to address the dreamer—a device that gives the poet opportunity for his highly original account of the crucifixion—may owe less to the talking trees of classical poetry than to the technique illustrated in many of the riddles of the Exeter Book (as argued by Orton 1980 and Bennett 1982). It should be added, however, that there was a broad basis for the device in classical and postclassical Latin poetry and rhetoric (see Schlauch 1940). Equally important in the background of the poem is the devotional and doctrinal literature accorded to the cross. Its discovery by St. Helena, the mother of Constantine the Great, was commemorated on the feast of the Invention of the Cross, celebrated on the third of May, and it is the subject of the longest composition signed by Cynewulf, the poem *Elene*. Two Latin hymns on the cross composed by Venantius Fortunatus—an Italian who spent most of his life in Merovingian Gaul, became bishop of Poitiers in 599, and died about 610—show an equal fervor and some of the same concepts. They are reprinted conveniently in Raby 1959: 74–75. On the liturgical background of the poem, see, besides the editions mentioned, Patch 1919; and for an explanation of how the poet navigates his way between opposing dangers in the early medieval Christological debates, see Woolf 1958.

For bibliographic guidance to the study of the poem, see Pasternack 1984, the 1996 revised reprint of Swanton 1970, and, for more recent work, the annual bibliographies cited above (p. 49).

Notes

1. **hwæt**. As usual, this word is metrically unstressed, so emphatic (and archaic) glosses like 'Lo!' and 'Hark!' seem misapplied. The closest equivalent may be something resembling 'well' or 'now', as the word is often a mild connective. Heaney (1999: xxvii) in a like context plausibly renders the word 'so'.

4. **seldlicre**, 'exceedingly rare', an absolute use of the comparative, perhaps in imitation of similar Latin constructions. See Mitchell 1985b: §§183, 186.

5. **on lyft lædan**. It is unnecessary to assume confusion with the rare verb *lēodan* 'spring up, grow', since **lædan** may have the same meaning (cf. *Resignation* 106).

8. **æt foldan scēatum** 'at the surface of the earth'—that is, at the base of the cross—a natural conception if the poet was thinking in part of ornamental crosses he had seen, and if the gems are to be associated with Christ's blood, as they are in lines 7 and 23. Dickins and Ross favor the very different notion of Patch (1919: 246; see also Huppé 1970: 75): "*Foldan sceatas* are the corners of the earth, to which the cross reaches as it spreads over the sky." They compare the tree in the dream of Nebuchadnezzar as described in the Old English *Daniel* 497–503. This interpretation of *sceatas* is

entirely legitimate (cf. *Christ III* 878–79), but the meaning 'surface' fits better at 37 and is imperative at 43.

9. **behēold on þām enġel drhytnes**. A much-discussed crux, to which no entirely satisfactory solution has been found. Many would defend the reading *beheoldon* (MS *be heoldon*) on the assumption that **enġel**, referring metaphorically to Christ, is the object of this verb. However, to this point in the poem there has been no mention of anyone affixed to the cross—indeed, there is never any indication that Christ hangs from the rood that the dreamer sees, even though a considerable degree of attention is devoted to the rood's appearance—and **hine** (11a) must then refer to **ġealga** (10b), not to Christ. To apply **enġel** to the rood itself also strains sense. Emendation thus seems to be required, and in that event the likeliest site of corruption is the word *ealle* that appears in the manuscript (*be heoldon þær engel dryht nes ealle*), since it disrupts the meter and/or the alliteration regardless of whether it is thought to belong to verse 9b or 10a.[29] The solution of Pope (1942: 101; endorsed by Cavill 1992, after a thorough consideration of other readings proposed), which was adopted in earlier editions of this book, prescribed emendation to *behēoldon þær enġel-dryhta fela* 'many hosts of angels looked on there'. This renders transparent sense and at least plausible meter. (For metrical parallels consult Fulk 1992: §95.) The reading adopted here instead furnishes a motive for the scribal insertion of *ealle:* after *be heold on* was mistaken for *beheoldon,* a subject was required for the plural verb, and *ealle* was therefore supplied. The incorporation of *on* into the verb left *þæm* (here normalized to **þām**) without a syntactic motive, resulting in its alteration to *þær.* The idiom *behealdan on* means 'watch (over)' or 'attend to', and so the reconstructed passage may be regarded as parenthetical and translated 'an angel of the Lord watched them

---

[29] The discussion of Bolton (1968), on whose authority Swanton pronounces the unemended verse 9b sound, leaves some metrical matters unresolved. The cadence *engel dryhtnes ealle* cannot be scanned as a normal verse, even with the unique underdotting of the second *e* in *engel* suggested by Pope, though, as Bolton recognizes, the cadence of a hypermetric verse ought to resemble a full normal verse (see below, pp. 151–52). Alliteratively the verse is also faulty, since alliteration is prohibited after the first lift of the off-verse.

[i.e., the **fife**]'. **fæġre** (10) then is used to refer back also to the **fife**; or, with the same referent, perhaps it is an anaphoric pleonasm, taking us back to **fæġre** in line 8, if it is not simply an adverb meaning 'tenderly'.

10. **þurh forð-ġesceaft**, 'by eternal decree'. The word **forð-ġesceaft** occurs in five other poems (never in prose) with two apparently diverse meanings: the nature of things or the created world on the one hand, future destiny or the future state or condition on the other. These meanings can be reconciled by taking **ġesceaft** in its basic sense 'that which has been created or ordained' and **forþ** 'forth, onward' as indicating the created thing's perpetuation if it is already present or its prospective existence if it is not. Thus the combination means 'that which has been created or ordained to be', either for all time (the nature of things, the created world, or some preordained condition) or in the future. This explanation slightly modifies the interpretations of Cook and of Dickins and Ross without changing the basic concept.

15. **wǣdum ġeweorðod**, literally 'worthily adorned with garments', but perhaps the phrase means no more than 'splendidly appareled'. Cook suggested that the *wǣda* were some kind of streamers such as those that decorated processional crosses, and this is no doubt possible. Yet when **wǣdum** is repeated at 22, it seems primarily to refer to the contrasted costumes, gold and jewels on the one hand, blood on the other. In that context streamers are either superfluous or positively distracting.

19. **earmra ǣr-ġewinn**. The word **ǣr-ġewinn** is not elsewhere recorded, but it clearly is constituted of the elements **ǣr** 'former, of old' and **ġewinn** 'labor, struggle'. The latter normally denotes not suffering but active exertion, and **earmra** most likely refers to Christ's tormenters rather than to the many who suffered this form of punishment. Swanton compares *fyrngeflit* (*Elene* 903, *Panther* 34) and argues that God's struggle with his primeval adversaries here devolves upon the Son—naturally enough, since throughout this poem the crucifixion is portrayed as a variety of battle (cf. the note on **ġewinn** 65). Under this interpretation the verse leads directly to the precisely significant vision of the bleeding on the right

side. Hermann (1978) similarly attributes to **ǣr-ġewinn** a larger typological reference to spiritual warfare on a cosmic scale.

20. The cross bleeds **on þā swīðran healfe** 'on the right side' because, according to postbiblical tradition, it was Christ's right side that was opened by the centurion's lance (John 19.34). This tradition is mentioned by the modern authorities cited in Cook's note, and also by Bede in his treatise on the temple of Solomon. He interprets a certain door on the right of the temple (I Kings 6.8) as a type of the wound in Christ's side, "because," he says, "holy Church believes it was his right side that was opened by the soldier" (*quia dextrum ei latus a milite apertum sancta credit ecclesia,* cited from *De templo libri II,* ed. Hurst 1969: 166).

22. **blēoum**. The uncontracted form is metrically desirable.

31, 32. **þǣr**. Dickins and Ross urge that the word here means 'at that juncture; at that; on that occasion; then', a meaning otherwise unrecorded until about 1400.

34. **þæt**. Rather than as a conjunction 'so that', this word may be best regarded as a complementizer introducing a substantive clause, a direct object in variation with the first object of **ġeseah** (33). On the difficulty of translating it as a conjunction, see Mitchell 1985b: §2980.

36–37. The earth quaked at the crucifixion (Matthew 27.51).

39–49, 56–64. These are the lines partially preserved and somewhat abridged on the Ruthwell Cross. For the full text of the inscription, see the editions cited above. At lines 39–40 the corresponding passage on the Cross consists of a single pair of hypermetric verses, running as follows in normalized spelling:

Onġierede hine God ælmihtiġ   þā hē wolde on ġealgan ġestīgan.

The greater regularity of the form suggests that the inscription at this point gives us an earlier reading rather than an abridgment. The greater economy of the inscription (a feature prized in verse of the classical sort) also makes for a superior reading, especially as the added material is mostly rather conventional; but **ġeong hæleþ** is certainly a welcome addition, reinforcing the heroic aspect of the action, an aspect that the poet is all along at pains to emphasize as proper to Christ in his divine nature. Cook cites classical parallels to the notion that Christ here strips himself as for battle, and Woolf (1958: 146) quotes Ambrose, who makes the stripping voluntary and heroic, saying, *Pulchre ascensurus crucem regalia uestimenta deposuit* ("Most rightly, when he was about to ascend the cross, he laid aside his royal garments," cited from *Expositio evangelii secundum Lucam,* ed. Adriaen 1957: 376). The next few words of the inscription, corresponding to lines 41–42 of our text, are partially defaced, but the reconstructed verses look like an unmetrical abridgment. All the other remnants of the inscription show verse-by-verse correspondence with our text, with only minor verbal variations.

55. **wēop eall ġesceaft** 'all creation wept'. The sympathy of inanimate nature, familiar in classical elegy, lies close at hand in Matthew's account of the crucifixion, and the theme was developed by some of the church fathers. Swanton highlights convincing examples of the theme in Old English literature. The weeping of all creatures, animate and inanimate, for the dead Baldr is a notable analogue, though it is generally believed to have been inspired by the crucifixion story. See the note in Dickins and Ross's edition.

62. **stēame bedrifenne**. Glanz (1997) rightly observes that both these words are here used in unique senses. But the reading is supported by **blōde bestiemed** (48), in which the participle belongs to a causative verb derived from the noun **stēam**, and so there is insufficient cause to abandon the long-held assumption that the noun here refers in some way to blood, probably in the form of droplets.

63. **ġestōdon him æt his līċes hēafdum**. Here **him** is probably a reflexive or ethic dative plural, suggesting deliberate action on the part of the subject: 'they took their stand' or 'they came and stood'. For what may be a comparable instance see *Maldon* 300.

65. The word **ġewinn** here refers most directly to Christ's agony on the cross, but the word reinforces the military context into which the Passion is placed. In his divine nature Christ has waged war against the devil and all the forces of evil.

66. **banan**, probably the cross itself as the agent of death; the word *bana* is applied to one who has killed another even if the act

was unintended. Possibly, however, this is an error for, or a Late West Saxon leveled form of, the genitive plural *banena,* as Cook and others have thought. The reference would then be to the human agents of the crucifixion.

69. **mǣte weorode**, literally 'with limited company', meaning 'alone'—a characteristic example of litotes, or ironic understatement (see p. 46). The meiotic import of the expression is more obvious in line 124.

71. **stefn**. Most editors, noting the lack of sense and alliteration, have followed Kluge (1888) in inserting this word; but Kluge substituted it for the *syððan* of the manuscript, as did Sweet in his *Reader* (see Whitelock 1967) and Craigie (1926) after him, whereas Cook, Krapp, Dickins and Ross, Huppé, and Swanton retain *syððan* and add **stefn** after it. The sense thus produced is good, but the meter is defective, for *syððan* then would extraordinarily serve the metrical function of anacrusis before a verse of the type Sievers called D, which does not ordinarily admit even one such preliminary syllable in the second half of the line. Since there is no real need for the conjunction here it seems better to follow Kluge.

76–77. The reference here to St. Helena's discovery of the cross and its adornment under her direction is surprisingly brief, and since the meter is defective we may reasonably suppose that some material has been omitted through the inadvertence of a scribe.

79. **bealwa weorc**. The manuscript reads *bealuwara weorc,* which George Stephens (1866) and many subsequent scholars have thought to mean 'the work (or deeds) of dwellers in iniquity (wicked men)'. This is not impossible: though *-ware* is usually joined to a word designating a place, cf. Northumbrian *hālig-ware* 'saints' and probably *āþol-warum* 'dwellers in pestilence' (*Maxims I* 198b, as explained by Pope 1995). Yet the syntax of the passage is odd: it would seem that **sārra sorga** in the next line must depend directly on **ġebiden hæbbe**, even though this means that the verb, which usually governs the accusative, must govern two different cases in sequence (cf. Mitchell 1985b: §1240). This license might be excused on the ground that **sārra sorga** is almost partitive in feeling, and it might be rendered '(a number of) sore sorrows'; but

the construction is nonetheless unusual. (To construe **weorc** in apposition to **iċ**, as recommended by Britton 1967, seems uncharacteristic of Old English poetic diction.) The meter of 79a is also irregular, as **-wara** is heavy, verses of Sievers' type B not usually bearing so heavy an element in this position. These difficulties may be resolved under the assumption, recommended by Cook, that *bealuwara* is a scribal alteration of *bealuwa*, a common spelling of **bealwa** (as at *Beowulf* 281). Then both **bealwa** and **sārra** may be said to depend on **weorc**, probably best interpreted as one of the many examples in verse of this word substituted for Anglian *wærc* 'pain' (as at *Beowulf* 1721 and elsewhere: see Fulk 1992: §366).

91. **ofer holt-wudu**. There have been repeated attempts to justify the scribe's *ofer holm wudu* (where *ofer holm* ends a manuscript line). Ingenious exegetical interpretations of *holm-wudu* cannot be reconciled with the logic of the superlative assertion and the parallel it affords to the superlative exaltation of Mary. The scribe could very well have absentmindedly substituted the phrase *ofer holm* (in itself intelligible) without attending to its impropriety in conjunction with **wudu** and the logic of the passage.

93. **for**. This word, like Anglian *fore* (for which West Saxon scribes regularly substitute *for:* see Fulk 1992: §353.14) can have the sense 'before' as well as 'for the sake of' when it takes the accusative case. Thus its meaning in the present context is open to more than one interpretation.

101b–106. Grasso (1991: 32) identifies the source of this passage in the Nicene Creed: *Et resurrexit tertia die, secundum Scripturas. Et ascendit in caelum: sedet ad dexteram Patris. Et iterum venturus est cum gloria, judicare vivos et mortuos* ("And on the third day He arose again, according to the scriptures. And He ascended into heaven, and is seated at the right hand of the Father. He will come again with glory to judge the living and the dead"; Grasso's trans.).

112. The word **sie** has the metrical value here of two short syllables, and it may be pronounced accordingly (*si-e*). This decontracted scansion is to be found even in verse as late as Alfred's and Cynewulf's: cf. *Meters of Boethius* 16.8b and *Elene* 675b. For discussion see Fulk 1992: §115.

125. **on forð-weġe**. Possibly the accusative -*weġ* should be substituted for the dative here and at *Wanderer* 81 on the analogy of several parallels: *on forð-weg* at *Beowulf* 2625, *Exodus* 129, *Menologium* 218, *Guthlac* 801 and 945; *on forð-wegas* at *Exodus* 32, 350; and *[on] forð-wegas* at *Genesis* 2814. In all these instances, as here, motion is implicit, and *on* (or Anglian *in* in *The Wanderer*) would be expected to govern the accusative case. The resulting metrical type here and at *Wanderer* 81 would be an improvement, but the metrical need is not exigent.

125. **ealra**. Swanton, in agreement with Dickins and Ross, glosses this 'in all', a meaning well attested when *ealles* or *eallra* accompanies a numeral. Here the idiom seems to be extended to the indefinite **fela**, which then governs **langung-hwila** separately. Huppé (1970: 73) translates **fela ealra** with judicious freedom as 'full many'.

146. **guman**. Dickins and Ross defend this as a generic singular, 'man's' in the sense 'humankind's', and it has been allowed to stand on that assumption, though this usage is exceedingly rare (paralleled, dubitably, just once), and so it is suspect. Cook's emendation to *gumena,* genitive plural, may be right. Wrenn (1936: 106), wishing to interpret the word *wyrsan* at *Beowulf* 525 as genitive plural of the comparative, cites both **guman** here and **banan** at 66 as examples of a late West Saxon genitive plural in -*an*. If this is the right explanation we ought to normalize the words as *gumena* and *banena,* since this is not a late West Saxon poem; but neither *wyrsan* in *Beowulf* (as Klaeber [1950: 150] explains) nor these words here are necessarily to be interpreted as, or emended to, genitive plurals. Late West Saxon -*an* for -*ena* certainly is genuine, though it is not frequent: see Brunner 1965: §276 Anm. 5, and Hoad 1994.

148–51a. The allusion in these lines is to the harrowing of hell: Christ's descent into hell, his effortless victory over Satan, and his redemption (in some versions of the story from limbo, but here from hellfire itself) of all the virtuous people of old, from Adam onward. The adverb **þǣr** in 149 points to hell, as implied by **bryne** and the context as a whole. Dickins and Ross locate a full stop after **spēdiġ** (151) in order to make **þām sīþ-fæte** 'that expedition' (150) refer exclusively to the harrowing; but Cook's punctuation has been adopted here because it seems essential to maintain a parallel between the two clauses introduced by þā in 151b and 155b. With this punctuation, **þām sīþ-fæte** must refer not simply to the harrowing but also to the subsequent entry into heaven, even though this was delayed for forty days until the Ascension. Both Bede's hymn on the Ascension and the poem on the subject in the Exeter Book associate the harrowing with the Ascension in the same way. The procession that advances toward the gates of heaven includes an escort of angels and a vast throng of the redeemed led by Christ.

154–55a. **and eallum þām hālgum þām-þe on heofonum ǣr / wunodon on wuldre.** Since no human souls should have entered heaven before the harrowing, the identification of these saints has been a matter of some small controversy. Finnegan (1983) would identify them as the good thief, Enoch, and Elijah, while James Hall (1986) explains that the term **englum** (153) may refer only to the first of the ten orders of angels, allowing **hālgum** to refer to the rest.

The Battle of Maldon

In the entry for 991 in most versions of the Anglo-Saxon Chronicle, the battle at Maldon figures as a comparatively small though ill-starred engagement between Byrhtnoþ, *ealdormann* of Essex, at the head of what was probably the local levy, and a band of vikings, part of a large Scandinavian—mainly Norwegian—army under the general direction of Anlaf (Óláfr, Olaf) Tryggvason, later king of Norway. The series of harryings and invasions that began in 991, after half a century of comparative tranquillity, continued with occasional intermission under several different Scandinavian leaders, some Norwegian, some Danish, until 1016, when the throne of England passed to a Danish king, Cnut (Knútr, Canute), who eventually ruled an empire that included Denmark and Norway as well. In the course of this onslaught the English were obliged to buy peace with the invaders year after year at ever-increasing sums: 10,000 pounds of silver in 991, mounting to a staggering 48,000 in 1012.

For a grasp of the action it is useful to accept the hypothesis first advanced by Laborde (1925) that the vikings had sailed up the estuary of the river Blackwater, then called the *Pante,* in Essex, to an island of about a mile square called Northey, two miles below the village of Maldon. They evidently planned to use the island as their base for raids on the neighboring countryside. This island was cut off from the mainland at high tide, but at low tide a ford gave access to the shore on the Maldon side of the river. The poet observes in line 97 that the vikings bore their shields **west ofer Pantan**, and this approximates the direction of the causeway, exposed only at low tide, that today extends from the island to the shore. The expression **lucon lagu-strēamas** (66), Laborde argues, describes the way that the two arms of the tide rising about the island meet not far from the causeway. For photographs and maps of the site, see Dodgson 1991.

The poem presents the battle on that August day in greater detail than we find in any other account of it, but not in historical perspective. Indeed, as a historical source the poem is a poor one, telling us little about strategy or even the course of the battle, since the poet is instead concerned to render this self-contained tragedy in the conventions of heroic verse, in which the things that matter are courage and cowardice, the veneration of kin, individual grand gestures, and fine, if implausible, monologues. Thus it resembles such legendary encounters as we read of in the fragmentary Old English lay *The Fight at Finnsburg* or, on a greater scale, the unavailing last stand of the Burgundians in the hall of Attila the Hun. But it is the poet's distinction to have made us feel the contrast between those carefully shaped, heroic old stories and this vividly actual battle, enacted by everyday men who find themselves put to a test as absolute as any that the heroes of legend encountered. In his poetic style, as in his basic conception, he holds the ideal and the actual in balance, letting us see the imperfect, sometimes haphazard quality that belongs to most events as we experience them, and nevertheless the emergence of a pattern, the partial reenactment of something long familiar to the imagination but larger than life. The result is a document a good deal less reliable for its fact than a sober journalistic report, as several studies of the poem have emphasized.[30] A particular respect in which the historicity of the poem has been brought into question is its assumption that battle to the death is the only honorable choice when one's lord has fallen on the field. Several studies have argued persuasively that no matter how similar this ethic may seem to what Tacitus, the Anglo-Saxon Chronicle (in its account of Cynewulf and Cyneheard s.a. 755), and Saxo Grammaticus (in his Latin rendering of the Old Norse *Bjarkamál*) tell us about the obligations of the thegn in early Germanic societies, it does not reflect actual tenth-century Anglo-Saxon practice and seems rather one more convention of the genre of heroic verse.[31] But no matter what other fictions may haunt the poet's account, we must suppose that the general setting, still more the named persons, are altogether actual, for without this kind of local fidelity the poet could not have persuaded his contemporaries to take him seriously. Indeed, his own inspiration clearly depended in great measure on his belief in these men and their sudden emergence into tragic splendor.

The central figure in this tragedy is Byrhtnoþ. Of a wealthy and influential family, he was a benefactor of Ely, where he was eventually interred, as well as of other religious houses. He was in fact one of the leading members of the Anglo-Saxon aristocracy, in 991 perhaps the foremost *ealdormann* in England, governing Essex (which included what are now surrounding regions) as the king's representative for thirty-five years before the battle.[32] A later account of the battle describes him as a tall, white-haired man. It has

[30] The body of literature on the historicity of the poem is considerable. For a bibliographic overview of this aspect of scholarship on the poem, see Andersen 1991: 99–120. A subsequent study of some importance is that of G. Clark (1992), who reaffirms his view that the poet was more concerned with art than with facts.

[31] Of the many studies that touch on this issue, the two that treat it most directly are those of Woolf (1976) and Gneuss (1976b). Toswell (1996) deals with the reliability of Tacitus' account itself. John Hill (1991) maintains that the ethic of dying by one's lord is a disturbing tenth-century development. Harris (1993) furnishes important correctives to Woolf's argument.

[32] Scragg (1981: 14–20) offers an enlightening account of Byrhtnoth's career and his importance.

always been difficult to assess the exact blend of feelings with which the poet regards him. Although at most points his admiration is unequivocal, he makes Byrhtnoþ fully responsible for the decision that constitutes the turning point of the action and costs both his own life and the lives of his loyal retainers. Allowing the vikings safe passage across the causeway may indeed have been the only course open to him;[33] but though we cannot be certain what the precise error was—allowing them too much space in which to maneuver? not attacking before their ranks were formed? accepting their challenge at all?—the poet clearly locates the fault in the leader's **ofermōd**. Much study has been devoted to determining the extent of Byrhtnoþ's culpability, on which see the commentary on lines 84–90. Yet however grave or trivial his fault may have been, it is clear that the poet mingles his blame with reverence and admiration for the man.[34]

Whether the poem was composed soon after the battle or after a lapse of several years is a matter of dispute. The editors of this book incline to the former view: for discussion and bibliography see Scragg 1993 and Fulk 1992: 415–18.

The formal properties of the verse reflect the poem's late composition. There are frequent departures from the standards of classical Old English verse in respect to meter and alliteration, and the verse construction is less economical, so that more unstressed words, particularly demonstratives, are employed than in compositions of an earlier date. The diction is less original than that of *Brunanburh*, and more than a few verses are repeated entire or altered slightly. Scragg (1981: 28–35) provides an admirable analysis of the style.

In manuscript the poem was already at an early date a book fragment that was bound together with other Old English material in the seventeenth century. This fragment was destroyed in the fire

---

[33] Samouce (1963) argues that the historical Byrhtnoþ had good reason to accept the challenge of the vikings, since he may have thought there was no other way to prevent them from evading the battle and attacking some other undefended part of the coast. This idea has subsequently been approved by many. For discussion see North 1991.

[34] For a sensitive discussion of these and other issues in the interpretation of the poem, see O'Brien O'Keeffe 1991: 117–23.

of 1731 at Ashburnham House, Westminster, that also damaged the *Beowulf* manuscript and so many other irreplaceable medieval books. Fortunately, a transcript of the fragment had been made before the fire, and though this was formerly attributed to John Elphinston(e), under-keeper of the Cottonian Library, it has since been shown beyond doubt by Rogers (1985) to have been made by his successor David Casley. For facsimiles of the transcript see Scragg 1991a and Robinson and Stanley 1991. There may at one time have existed another transcript for which there is some small evidence (see Robinson 1993b), but if that is the case, its present whereabouts are unknown.

An indispensable guide to the poem is the edition of Scragg (1981), which owes much to that of E. V. Gordon (1937); and for the text and some helpful notes, Dobbie's edition should be consulted (Krapp and Dobbie 1931–53: 6.7–16, 142–46). Several other very good editions are also available. The millennial volume edited by Scragg (1991a) is a superb introduction to the documentary, military, and historical contexts of the poem. Other collections containing some fine articles are those edited by Niles (1991) and Cooper (1993). Szarmach (1993) discusses Continental analogues and Frank (1991) more far-flung ones. For scholarly bibliography consult Collier (1991), in both print and electronic form, along with the annual publications cited above (p. 49).

Notes

2. **hēt**. The understood subject is Byrhtnoþ, **sē eorl** of line 6.

4. **hycgan to handum** 'be intent on (the work of) hands', that is 'on deeds of arms' (Gordon).

5. The pronoun **þæt** is to be construed as the object of **onfunde**, and it anticipates the clause in line 6. It need not be translated. The same construction appears in lines 36, 84, and 246.

7. **hē lēt him þā of handum**. Donoghue (1987: 196) points out that in addition to violating the alliterative rule of precedence

(explained below, p. 134), this verse does not conform to Kuhn's first law (as defined on pp. 137–38). The verse is not emended here because there are so many metrical and syntactic peculiarities to *Maldon* that textual corruption does not seem sufficient explanation, and we ought to assume that this poem, composed so late in the Anglo-Saxon period, does not conform to the same formal principles that govern earlier compositions.

23. **þǣr him lēofost wæs**, literally 'where it was most pleasing to him'—that is, 'where he was most pleased to be' (Gordon).

29–41. See Robinson 1976 for evidence that the speech of the viking messenger is colored by Scandinavian vocabulary and idiom. As demonstrated by Gordon and by Robinson, the poem contains several other Scandinavianisms—for example, **drenga** (149)—and some men on the English side bear Scandinavian names (see C. Clark 1983). If the poet composed in an Eastern dialect it is conceivable that Scandinavianisms should have been common in his own speech, though the record of Eastern dialects in Old English is too slender to render reliable evidence.

34. **ġif ġē spēdaþ tō þām**, perhaps 'if you are prosperous to that extent', i.e., 'if you are wealthy enough to meet our demand'. (Gordon's tentative explanation; the expression occurs only here.)

40. **ūs**. The excellent expedient of placing this word in the on-verse to avoid a violation of Kuhn's first law (see pp. 137–38) is recommended by Donoghue (1987: 198).

45. **sǣ-lida**. If this word is correct, the alliteration of the second half-line is irregular, falling on **sæġeþ**, which should yield alliterative precedence to **folc**. The line runs too smoothly to invite rearrangement, but it seems possible that **sǣ-lida** is a scribal substitution for a less familiar compound with the same meaning, such as *flot-lida,* which would alliterate in orthodox fashion with **folc**.

48. **here-ġeatwe**. The general meaning 'war-equipment' makes good sense, as Dobbie maintains, though most agree with Gordon in accepting the richer meaning 'heriot' first proposed by Brett (1927). See the glossary. Most editors have retained the manuscript reading, *-geatu,* interpreting it as accusative singular even though other feminine *wō*-stem nouns form the accusative singular in *-we.*

Retention of -*geatu* in an unnormalized text is defensible, especially since the recorded instances of the compound show somewhat irregular endings and a tendency to use the plural rather than the singular; but for the purpose of normalization it has seemed best to follow Kluge's *Lesebuch* (1888, to which Dobbie draws attention) in reading -**geatwe**. ·

75. **sē wæs hāten Wulfstān**. This parenthesis has a prosaic look, though it may be intentional. The orthodox verse formula here would be simply *Wulfstān hāten,* with alliteration where it belongs, on the first lift.

84–90. The controversy over the meaning of this passage has grown large and is not done justice by the following bare summary. The debate centers on the word **ofermōde** (89), which many take to imply that Byrhtnoþ was not just headstrong, daring, or reckless, but something worse. Gneuss (1976a) has shown that *ofermōd* (noun and adjective) is never used with positive connotations, that it means 'pride' or 'proud' in its more than 120 attestations, and that as an adjective in many instances it translates Latin *superbus* 'proud'. Some have taken this to mean that the hero is a lost soul, worthy of the worst opprobrium, or that the poem is a critique of the heroic ethos; others remain unconvinced that the religious contexts in which the word is found are a reliable guide to its meaning here. Yet there is no direct evidence that the word could be used in a positive sense,[35] the way Mod.E. *pride* can be, and two other phrases in this passage also seem to imply opprobrium for Byrhtnoþ: **lytigian** (86), some insist, suggests that he was too easily

[35] There is a significant piece of indirect evidence, however. G. Clark (1979: 274) points out that in King Alfred's Boethius (ed. Sedgefield 1899: 62), without warrant from the Latin there is an addition to the definition of a hypothetical wise (and therefore worthy) man, in that he is said to have *swīðe gooda oferhȳda* (where the plural *oferhȳda* might perhaps be rendered 'high-spirited thoughts'). Since *oferhygd* is a dialect equivalent of *ofermōd* (see Schabram 1965 and Hofstetter 1987), in similar manner usually signifying pride in a bad sense—and is so used by Alfred himself in his translation of Gregory's *Pastoral Care* (ed. Sweet 1871: 1.111.22), where the reference is to the pride of Lucifer himself—it is clear that Alfred's qualification *swīðe gooda* 'very good' shows his awareness of an admirable kind of pride or high-mindedness. Scragg regards the question of a possible positive meaning for **ofermōd** as closed, but dissent continues to be heard—e.g., in T. Hill 1997: 8.

deceived by the vikings;[36] and **landes tō fela**, as argued by Tolkien (1953), more clearly accuses him of irresponsibility, regardless of whether it is taken at face value or as meiosis—that is, implying that he should not have let the vikings cross the ford at all. Szarmach (1993: 58-59; see also Cain 1997) suggests that the blame placed on the hero is a product of the need for Christians somehow to comprehend a triumph of vice as bewildering as the vikings' victory. Cavill (1995) offers a well-ordered summary of the controversy, with full bibliography.

102. **wiġ-hagan**. This term is equivalent to **bord-weall** (277) and to **scield-burg** (242). The formation is explained in the note to *Brunanburh* 5.

109. **ġegrundene**. Most modern editors emend, inserting *grimme* 'grimly, cruelly' before this word, as at *The Ruin* 14a, for the sake of the meter: **ġegrundene** is a late spelling for *ġegrundne,* and in verse that conforms to classical standards it would have to be scanned as three syllables—that is, the unetymological syllable would be treated like the extra one in *hāliġe* as that word's scansion is explained below (pp. 143–44). But in late verse such excrescent syllables sometimes make metrical position (see Fulk 1992: §§216–20 for discussion), in this case producing an acceptable metrical type. Emendation of the verse thus is not warranted in a poem as late as this one. In order to indicate the metrical value assumed for the word, the spelling remains unnormalized here, as with **ġetrymmed** at line 22. The normalized, syncopated spelling expresses the correct prosodic pattern under normal metrical assumptions, however, in the case of **mōdġe** (80) and **hǣðne** (55, 181).

115. **sweostor sunu**. A sororal nephew was traditionally dear among the Germanic peoples, as in some other tribal societies. Gordon quotes Tacitus in illustration of the antiquity of the sentiment. The poet shows his consciousness of the tradition as well as his sense of design by opening his account of the slain with the death of the sister's son and the swift reprisal for it.

---

[36] For the latest word on this see Pulsiano 1997, arguing that the poet did not need to specify the nature of the Danes' guile because their duplicity was a medieval commonplace.

130. Robinson 1976 suggests that a line or two may have been lost before this, introducing the viking here described as **wiġes heard**.

136–37. As Gordon explains, Byrhtnoþ breaks the spear-shaft by thrusting the edge of his shield against it, and this action strains the fragment carrying the spearhead—springs it—so that it quivers and flies out of the wound. Note the play on transitive **sprengde** and intransitive **sprang**. The subject of **sprengde** can be either Byrhtnoþ or the shaft, which in bursting imparts a spring to the fragment.

143. **ōðerne**. Probably 'another (viking)'. The word could refer to another spear, since the accusative object of *scēotan* may be either the weapon or the target, and Scragg is right that an extended encounter with one viking would be stylistically more appealing. But since Byrhtnoþ's blow to the viking's neck has already been described as a mortal wound (142), a subsequent wound to the heart would be gratuitous. This interpretation is lent a certain degree of support by the capitalization of **Þā** (143) in Casley's transcript, marking a section division and thus more likely implying a second encounter than a second weapon.

170 ff. Dobbie's punctuation for 170 and 171 has been adopted here, which enables us to perceive lines 166–71 as a continuous sequence of events from Byrhtnoþ's dropping of his sword to his sinking to the ground. The half-line at 172 introducing the prayer is clearly in need of a mate, either before or after it, and there may be a greater loss; but in any event the prayer should be set apart from the exhortation to the retainers in 168–70, which is uttered by Byrhtnoþ as he makes a last effort not to fall.

183. This line is obviously faulty; **bēġen** is likely to be a copyist's repetition.

190. **þe hit riht ne wæs**. Scragg, on the authority of Bruce Mitchell, advises regarding this as a comparative construction and treating **þe** as a conjunction 'as'; but it is difficult to see the construction as a comparison in the normal grammatical sense of the word. Mitchell's later opinion (1985b: §3369) is more compelling: either the clause is elliptical, and **þe** is the object of an understood **on** (Gordon's view), or **þe hit** may be regarded as a periphrasis meaning 'which' with broad reference.

212. **ġemunaþ nū þā mǣla**. This verse poses more than one mor-
phological puzzle. The transcript reads *ge munu þa mæla*. Most
editors alter *ge munu* to **ġemunaþ**, as proposed by Grein (1857),
though other readings have been suggested. Dobbie reads *gemunan,*
calling this a first person plural imperative (which we should prefer
to call a hortatory subjunctive: see the note to *Caedmon's Hymn* 1).
He maintains that the loss of *n* is more likely than the loss of *þ*. But
since the next word begins with *þ,* paleographically the alternatives
seem equally probable. The letter *u* is written *a* also at 171 and 208.
Robinson (1976: 35–37) proposes that *ġemunu* is a first person
singular form; but the inflection *-u* is an Anglian one, and this poem
appears to have been composed in a Saxon dialect; the deliberate
omission of *iċ,* moreover, is dubitable. The solution chosen here
seems paleographically the most plausible, assuming that the scribe
inadvertently dropped three letters because the sequences *naþ* and
nu both begin with *n*—a very common scribal error called "eye-
skip," paralleled, for example, at *Dream of the Rood* 17, where the
scribe wrote *wealdes* for *wealdendes.* Then **nū** need not be stressed:
for the many parallels in *Beowulf* see Bliss 1967: §20, and cf. also
lines 55, 66, 72, and so forth. As for the direct object, the gender of
mǣla may be feminine, as Dobbie assumes, following the de-
duction made by Bosworth and Toller (1898) and Holthausen
(1932–34), among others, from this particular passage. But Old
Norse *mál* 'speech' is neuter, and so is Old English *mæðel,* which is
simply an alternative form of the same word *mǣl* (if in fact it does
mean 'speech' rather than 'occasion' here in this lone attestation).
Gordon, in agreement with some earlier editors, accordingly alters
þā to *þāra* (since **ġemunaþ** may take a genitive object), and there is
a close parallel in *Heliand* 4710a (ed. Behaghel 1984): *manon iu
thero mahlo* 'to remind you of the speeches'. However, little is
known about the East Saxon variety of Old English, and it is by no
means implausible that the word should have become feminine in
that dialect—especially if the word means 'speech', as the gender
change would then help to differentiate it from *mǣl* n. 'occasion'. In
the face of this uncertainty, the word has been left unemended,
though the reading is without conviction.

224. **hē wæs ǣġðer min mǣġ and min hlāford**. If the alliteration is on *m,* stress is required on the second **min**, though this word is usually unstressed when attributive. Stress on the first **min** then is also possible: although the metrical type comprising a string of unstressed syllables followed by two stressed monosyllables at the end of the verse is avoided in verse of the classical variety, it is not infrequent in later verse (see Fulk 1992: §291), and it is found in this poem at 239a and 270a. Accordingly, rhetorical emphasis might be intended on both instances of **min**, as proposed in earlier editions of this book: Ælfwine's affliction is the greatest possible, as he has said, because for him (but not for everyone among the retainers) the loss is double. But if **min** may be stressed in this unorthodox fashion, the objections to stressing **ǣġðer** and **and** instead may not be insurmountable. The former always alliterates in verse (five instances), as do *ǣġhwæðer* (from which **ǣġðer** is derived) and its inflected forms and variants (thirteen instances all told)— though, to be sure, elsewhere in verse it is a pronoun, here a conjunction. The word **and** is not elsewhere stressed in verse, but there are no other poetic instances of its correlative use with **ǣġðer**, and if **and** might ever be stressed, this is the construction in which stress might be expected. Since conjunctions may function as particles (Kuhn 1933: 5), this may be the best analysis.

230–43. Offa's approval of Ælfwine's exhortation, his use of the first person plural, his explanation of the disastrous mistake made by some who had followed Godric in flight, and the fact that unlike the other speakers he does not immediately go forth to die—all point to the widely shared assumption that he was one of Byrhtnoþ's chief lieutenants. The prolonged attention to his death, along with his promise to Byrhtnoþ, in 287–94 carries the same import. Very likely he was second in command to Byrhtnoþ and has now assumed the leadership. As he is never introduced as the other men are, though he is referred to familiarly in line 5, presumably he was introduced and identified in the lost opening to the poem.

239–40. Scragg points out that the horse mentioned here was the only one on the battlefield, since the rest had been driven away to safety, as related at the opening of the fragment. The poet earlier draws particular attention to the presence of Byrhtnoþ's horse in lines 18 and 23. This observation highlights the infamy of Godric's actions and the plausibility of the men's mistaking Godric for Byrhtnoþ. Also, Scragg would stress the first syllable of **formaniġ**, but the alliterative parallels cited do not lend support, as this word is an adjective and must alliterate, and in a verse of type B the second drop would be exceptionally heavy—doubtless heavier than in the other exceptional verses of this sort in the poem, as at 300a and 320a. The prefix is stressed in **forheardne** (156), as is the related prefix *fore-* when attached to adjectives; but not in *is sīn meaht forswīþ* (*Order of the World* 26b), where initial stress would place disallowed half-stress at the end of a verse of type C. There are no other alliteratively unambiguous examples of this intensive prefix on an adjective in verse, but examples of adverbs (*foroft, for-swīðe, forwel*) stress the root rather than the prefix. On the metrics see the commentary to line 224.

284. A brief passage, not above two or three lines, seems to have been omitted before this line. The antecedent implied by **þone** in 286 does not appear, and if we look more narrowly at the passage with this hint to guide us we see that the account of Offa's death is incomplete. There should have been mention of a viking's assault upon Offa, since it is the **lǣriġ** of Offa's shield that bursts and his corselet that sings a terrible song. He has been fatally wounded, and though he manages to kill his assailant, he falls in the very act of doing so and is cut to pieces at once by other vikings. For a thorough analysis of the passage, see Pope 1993.

299. **ġeþrange**. Scragg lets Casley's *geþrang* stand, but the emendation produces more conventional syntax and meter (see p. 145 below on Sievers' type B3).

300. Casley's *wigelines* almost certainly stands for *wigelmes* (normalized **Wiġhelmes**). With or without the emendation, Wistan would appear to have two fathers, Þurstan and Wighelm/Wigelin. Robinson's argument (1991; cf. Dobbie's note) that *wigelines* refers to the man's mother demands that we assume there existed an otherwise unrecorded feminine name-element *-lin(e)* and that the masculine possessive ending is a late substitution. One would prefer to

think of Wighelm as the actual father, rather than Þurstan, given the alliteration and possible identity of the first consistuent of father and son's names (see the glossary of proper names); but **bearn** (300) has greater semantic range than **sunu** (298), sometimes denoting a descendant rather than a literal son, as when the three young men in the fiery furnace are called *Abrahames bearn* in *Daniel* 193—though, to be sure, as an analogue this is hardly exact. Gordon's suggestion that **Wiġhelmes bearn** refers to Offa faces the difficulty that it breaks the poet's dramatic pattern in this section of the poem of ending each passage about an individual warrior with an allusion to his death. Scragg suggests that Wighelm is a by-name for Þurstan, but in his translation (1991b: 31) he instead chooses to render **bearn** as 'descendant'. There seems no entirely satisfactory solution to the problem. The reflexive datives **him** in this line and **mē** in 318 mark a distinction of meaning for the verb *licgan*. At all other places in the poem it refers to someone who is already lying prostrate or to an enemy who is caused to lie dead. At the two places mentioned, the person who is the subject of the verb is felt to be sacrificing himself voluntarily and so deliberately to be assuming a prostrate position. The sense indicated by the pronoun can be conveyed by translating the verb 'lie down'. See the note on *The Dream of the Rood* 63 for a possible parallel.

315. **Ā mæġ gnornian**. Not 'may he ever mourn': Gordon rightly observes that **mæġ** is not used in an optative sense in Old English. (See the note below on **mæġ** at *Deor* 7.) He translates 'he has cause to mourn ever'.

The Wanderer

The Exeter Book, a late tenth-century anthology of poems long and short—the only manuscript devoted exclusively to Old English poetry—is the unique source of most surviving Old English lyric verse, of which *The Wanderer* and *The Seafarer* are the most familiar examples. The two are often discussed together, since they treat of similar themes and have similar structures, and they are classified with other poems referred to as "elegies"—not in the classical sense of the word, but as lyrics on themes of worldly mutability infused with intense suffering in a mood of loneliness and isolation. The difficulty of defining very precisely the requisite features of an elegiac mode in Old English and of determining which poems belong to it reinforces the impression of many that Old English elegy as a concept obfuscates more than it explains.[37] This classification is a legacy of nineteenth-century scholarship on Old English, which tended to see mirrored in these lyrics the melancholy that infused the Romantic imagination and the oneness with the natural world toward which it yearned. For this reason also the religious sentiment of these poems was very often regarded as the intrusive meddling of monkish interpolators, and both poems were thought to be of composite origin. Even until fairly recently *The Seafarer* was sometimes edited to excise the moral content and leave only the imagined genuine expression of native (i.e., pagan) sensibilities.[38] Studies founded on the notion that Christian and non-Christian elements in these poems can and should be differentiated still appear perennially, but it is now more widely believed that the Anglo-Saxons who created and appreciated these poems would not have drawn any very clear distinction between what we call their heroic and their Christian elements. Whether or not the wanderer's relationship to his lord reflects actual social conditions at the time and place of the poem's composition—and that is a difficult proposition to prove or disprove—it may be viewed as expressive of the way that the conservative traditions of verse make all things conform to a heroic mold, rather than as evidence of composition in a pre-Christian or even a half-Christianized world.

[37] Yet this view is by no means universal. For a defense of Old English elegy as a genre, see Klinck 1992: 223–51; and for a concise history of elegy as a critical preoccupation among Anglo-Saxonists, see Green 1983.

[38] Klinck (1992: 118 et passim) provides a useful summary of views about interpolations in *The Wanderer*. Ironically, the ending of *The Seafarer* may indeed be foreign to the rest of the poem, but not because of any redactor's Christianizing tendencies, nor because its homiletic content is uncongenial to the poem's theme, but because of a possible loss in the manuscript: see below.

Scholarship of the second half of the twentieth century tended to reverse the earlier trend, identifying the primary inspiration for these poems not as a native tradition of elegy but as one or another mode of late Latin literature, such as complaint, consolation, meditation, penitential exercise, or allegory. The poet's method of interspersing elements of lament with philosophic meditation clearly can be seen as akin to the type of consolation developed on a grand scale in the *Consolatio philosophiae* of Boethius, one feature of such consolations being the effort to alleviate a personal sorrow by recognition of the instability of all earthly values and the necessity of seeking lasting satisfactions in another realm.[39] Attention is called in the notes to some particular Boethian imagery. Yet it is also clear that the poet was a good deal less interested in the possible therapeutic virtue of his discourse than he was in the imaginative realization of loss and loneliness in this unstable world.[40]

Accordingly, as Shippey (1994; see also 1972: 53–79) has argued persuasively, it may be that *The Wanderer* and *The Seafarer* are more nearly comparable to examples of so-called wisdom poetry, a type of verse that is extensively represented in Old English—there are several such poems in the Exeter Book—and has analogues in Old Icelandic. It is chiefly characterized by its aphoristic qualities, and these qualities are to be found not just in gnomic verse but in narratives, particularly in *Beowulf,* in which the narrator and characters alike tend to speak in maxims. Scholarship on *The Wanderer* and *The Seafarer* has paid scant attention to the proverbial content of the poems. They have been regarded chiefly as narratives of personal experience rather than as expressions of a sort of aphoristic cultural capital, one that obviously constituted for the Anglo-Saxons a significant component of their poetic production and played for them a prominent role in the process of rendering narrative material appropriate to verse. It is a measure of the difference of Anglo-Saxon sensibilities, and of our own continued allegiance

[39] Four particularly influential studies of this kind are Lumiansky 1950; Cross 1961; Erzgräber 1961; and Horgan 1987.

[40] Conner (1993: 158–59) hypothesizes that these qualities are adopted from late Carolingian compositions on which these poems are modeled.

to Romantic ones, that poems like these two, with their savor of bi-
ography—no matter how anonymous—exert a greater appeal than
the larger and more pervasive genre of wisdom poetry. Yet the
gnomic content of these poems is fundamental to their purpose,
constituting the tangible evidence that the experience of hardship
leads to the attainment of wisdom.

The structure of *The Wanderer* has provoked more than a little
discussion. In the first edition of this book the text was punctuated
in accordance with the argument of Pope 1965, reviving and re-
fining the views of some predecessors, that the poem is a dialogue,
an analysis inspired by similar but more widely credited views
about the structure of *The Seafarer*. In addition to the narrator who
opens the poem and provides closure, Pope argued, there are two
speakers, an **eard-stapa** (6) who relates his experience of exile and
a **snottor** man (see the note to line 111) who offers more general
reflections on the human condition and the mutability of mundane
existence, the division between their monologues occurring at the
end of line 57. This analysis gained some currency, but after an
exchange of views with Stanley B. Greenfield and a reconsideration
of the reasoning of Whitelock 1950 (on which see the commentary
on *The Seafarer* below), Pope retracted his argument in 1974. Al-
though even now the poem is occasionally analyzed as a dialogue,
there is at present a fairly broad consensus that it instead exem-
plifies what Bjork (1989) has referred to as an "envelope pattern": it
is something like a bildungsroman in miniature, setting before our
eyes one who acquires insight from his trials, evolving from an ig-
norant sufferer into the role of the man who is described as **snottor**.
It is still not possible to determine with certainty where speeches in
the poem begin and end. Do lines 1–5 belong to the wanderer or to
the narrator? Does line 111 refer back to lines 8–110 or just to 92–
110? or forward to lines 112–15? or both? Is the speaker in lines 92–
110 a wise person imagined by the wanderer, or has the narrator re-
turned before this to introduce another monologue by the wan-
derer?[41] As we lack definitive answers to such questions, no attempt

---

[41] Richman (1982) discusses the variety of critical views on such matters.

has been made in the text to delimit speeches with quotation marks. Still, the analogous structure of *The Dream of the Rood* (on which see the commentary above, p. 66) suggests that we should not expect too complex a series of changes of speaker.

Excellent guidance on these and other matters is to be found in the two editions devoted exclusively to the poem, Leslie 1966 and Dunning and Bliss 1969. Valuable for the text is Krapp and Dobbie 1931–53: 3.134–37, 288–90; and for the notes, Cassidy and Ringler 1971, Klinck 1992, Mitchell and Robinson 1992, and Muir 1994. Fowler (1966) and Whitelock (1967) furnish more concise notes. Muir's edition includes a textual apparatus indicating scribal corrections in the manuscript that have not previously been noted. The Exeter Book is reproduced in facsimile in Chambers, Förster, and Flower 1933; facsimiles of the relevant leaves will also be found in Klinck's edition. The most recent bibliography, but covering the whole of the Exeter Book, is Muir's; for more selective bibliographies see Klinck's edition, Conde Silvestre 1992, and the 1985 reprint of Leslie's edition.

Notes

1. **ān-haga** 'solitary one'. This word describes Beowulf when he has lost his uncle Hygelac and all his former comrades in the battle with the Franks and Frisians and is obliged to swim home alone. Thus it has no necessary connection with the religious recluse.

5. **wyrd biþ ful arædd**. For the meter see p. 144, n. 29. From an exhaustive study of this verse, Griffith (1996) draws the conclusion that it may mean either 'fate is wholly inexorable' (as most understand it) or 'one's lot is very settled'; and given the latter possibility it need not be the expression of profound fatalism that it is usually taken for.

7. **hryres**. MS *hryre* is unlikely to be the accusative object of **cwæþ** (6)—a suggestion offered by Fischer 1935 and adopted by Cassidy and Ringler—since examples of objects for *cweðan* that are not forms of speech or things spoken are not very convincing (see

the examples in the *Dictionary of Old English,* Cameron et al. 1986–), and they are usually attributable to literal translation from Latin. Mitchell (1985b: §1413) is doubtless right that the explanation of Kershaw (1922: 162), adopted by most editors—that the word is a causal or comitative instrumental—is improbable. Muir digests other analyses. Since we should expect a genitive parallel to **wæl-sleahta**, and since none of the explanations offered for *hryre* is entirely satisfactory, it has seemed best to emend.

15. **wēriġ mōd** is taken by a variety of editors, beginning with Thorpe (1842), as a compound adjective used substantively, meaning '(one who is) weary in spirit, dejected'. The reading selected here assumes close parallelism with **sē hrēo hyġe** (16), the contrast being between despair and anger.

17. The masculine noun **mōd-sefan**, which occurs in line 19, is apparently to be understood after **drēoriġne**: see the comment of Dunning and Bliss.

23. **heolstre**. This reading, that of the manuscript, seems better than emendation to the nominative *heolster,* as advocated by Bright (1891; no longer retained by Cassidy and Ringler), since it makes the wanderer the subject. He himself has buried his lord. In 83–84 a similar situation is imagined.

25. **sōhte sele-drēoriġ sinċes bryttan**. If, as some editors have assumed, **sele** and **drēoriġ** are separate words, the line means 'Dejected, I sought the hall of a giver of treasure.' But this interpretation conflicts with the order of words and the meter. The order is awkward because **drēoriġ**, modifying the subject of the verb, is wedged between the object, **sele**, and **sinċes bryttan**, which has to be taken as a genitive phrase limiting the object. The metrical pattern instead subordinates **drēoriġ** to the bearers of the alliteration, **sōhte** and **sele**. The difficulty is overcome by reading **sele-drēoriġ** and taking **sinċes bryttan** as the object of **sōhte**: 'sad for want of a hall, I sought a giver of treasure', a reading first suggested by Fischer (1935) and now very widely adopted. The clause beginning with **hwǣr** (26) may then be regarded as a second object of **sōhte**. The compound here postulated occurs nowhere else. It exhibits a rare but not unexampled relation between its two members, being

almost exactly paralleled by the modern *homesick* and by Old English **wine-ġēōmor** 'mournful for loss of friends', which occurs at *Beowulf* 2239.

27. **mine wisse.** There is no end of emendations proposed for this verse: for a detailed account see Muir's commentary, to which should be added Cassidy and Ringler's suggestion *mīnne wisse,* with *mīnne* referring to **sinċes bryttan** (25). An especially attractive reading is that of Dunning and Bliss: *mīnne myne wisse* 'would know my thought', as they translate, or perhaps better 'might understand my feeling', a reading inspired by an equally obscure passage in *Beowulf.* This has the dual advantage of being the result of a plausible scribal omission and of making excellent sense. It has the disadvantage of sounding modern and a bit banal. With much admitted doubt the reading of the manuscript and of earlier editions of this book has been retained here, **mine** referring elliptically to the wanderer's kin. (Note that a heavy initial syllable is required by the meter.) There are several parallels in Old English to this use of *mīn* without a specified noun, of which the closest in verse is *þæt þū mundbora mīnum wære* 'that you would be a protector to my (people, followers?)' (*Descent into Hell* 75; see also Beowulf 2737 and *Genesis A* 2253). One must take *wisse* as 'might know of', not 'might know, be acquainted with', which would presumably have been expressed by *cūðe.* This reading explains the use of **oþþe** (28): the contrast is between being comforted by a lord to whom one's kin are familiar and being comforted even as a complete stranger. Though the mention of kin might seem something of an irrelevance to modern readers, in Anglo-Saxon society it was of central importance to establishing one's status among strangers. Compare how Beowulf's first words to the coast warden are about his lord and his father, and how Hroþgar's immediate response when told of Beowulf's arrival in Denmark is that he is familiar with his kin.

29. **wēman.** A number of editors alter this to *wenian* 'accustom' (giving Mod.E. *wean*), noting that *m* and *ni* are nearly identical in insular scripts and are confused elsewhere by this scribe. To be sure, the meaning of **wēman** 'persuade, entice' does not seem fully apposite to the wanderer's situation; but *wenian* is awkward, as it

normally requires that the thing to which one is accustomed be ex-
pressed; yet there is no evidence that **mid** can be used in Old Eng-
lish to mark that thing (commonest in this function is *tō,* as below at
line 36). The closest parallel is in Old Saxon, at *Heliand* 2817 (ed.
Behaghel 1984): *uuennien mid uuilleon* 'attract in accordance with
their own desires'. Yet despite the significance attached to the par-
allel by Gollancz (1895) and Kershaw (1922), this furnishes no sup-
port for reading *wenian,* since the Old Saxon verb here has the same
meaning as OE **wēman**, though it is on a semantic basis alone that
wenian has sometimes been preferred. The usual form of the infin-
itive is *wennan;* the form *wenian* first appears in late prose.

37–48. The intransitive use of the verb **wāt** (37) without a quali-
fying adverb such as **ġearwe** is unusual. Accordingly, Leslie ana-
lyzes the verb as elliptically introducing the entire passage in lines
39–48, where the main clauses begin with **þynċeþ** (41) and **þonne**
(45). The sense then would be 'Indeed he who must long be de-
prived of his beloved lord's instruction[42] knows [that], as often as
sorrow and sleep joined together bind the wretched solitary, it
seems to him in his mind [i.e., he dreams]. . . . Then . . .'. But it is
dubitable whether this analysis can be admitted without a comple-
mentizer **þæt** to introduce the clausal object.[43]

50b–57. The syntax of these most interesting verses is tantaliz-
ingly ambiguous, and they have been edited any number of ways.
The most thorough analysis is that of Dunning and Bliss, but all the
editions should be consulted, as well as Mitchell 1968. There is still
no consensus. The interpretation offered here draws on various of
these explanations, but it begins with the assumption that verse 54b
opens a new clause. Otherwise it would be peculiar that **nā** and **þǣr**
(54b) are unstressed.[44] The subject of this clause beginning in 54
must be singular, and so **flēotendra ferhþ** from the preceding

---

[42] Perhaps **lār-cwidum** (38) might be rendered 'maxims', as suggested by Alfred
(1982: 33).

[43] Mitchell (1968) cites examples of clausal complements lacking a complement-
izer, but the parallels (esp. *Vainglory* 77 ff.) are not close enough to resolve conclu-
sively the problem of the intransitivity of **wāt**.

[44] See the discussion of particle stress below, pp. 137–38.

clause is most plausibly understood as the unstated subject.[45] If
flēotendra ferhþ is thus singular, the subject of **swimmaþ** (53) is
most likely to be **secga ġeseldan**, which then is not available to
serve as the object of the verbs **grēteþ** and **ġeondscēawaþ** (52),
both of which are transitive.[46] The most plausible object of these
verbs is then **māga ġemynd**, understood from the preceding clause,
and the subject accordingly may be the hypothesized sailor (i.e., *hē*
is understood). It might at first seem odd that the sailor is said to
greet the *memory* of kinsmen, but this is as it should be, as there are
no actual kinsmen to greet, and the use of **ġemynd** in such a con-
crete sense is not unparalleled. The clause beginning in line 51 is
most likely subordinate, to judge by the word order, and the edi-
tions uniformly subordinate it to a preceding clause. If it is made in-
stead to depend on what follows we may make sense of **oft** (53), a
word usually emended to *eft* by editors beginning with Thorpe
(1842). Mitchell (1968) renders **þonne . . . oft** in 39–40 'as often
as'—a translation adopted above—and if we proceed similarly
here[47] and assume some parentheses (in part suggested by Dunning
and Bliss) we may translate, 'Sorrow is renewed. As often as the
memory of kinsmen pervades his mind (he greets them gladly, ea-
gerly gazes at them), the companions of men swim away, the spirits
of floating ones. They never bring many familiar accents—care is

---

[45] Naturally, **ferhþ** may be either singular or plural. Dunning and Bliss (pp. 23–24)
explain that whereas Modern English uses a plural for both possessor and possessed
in constructions like *the deaths of kinsmen* (a usage in fact adopted relatively re-
cently), in Old English only the possessor is plural—though Mitchell (1985b: §87)
rightly characterizes this as a trend rather than an absolute rule. Thus we are justified
in translating both **flēotendra ferhþ** and **bringeþ** as plurals.

[46] It has been suggested more than once (see Mitchell 1985b: §3794) that **secga
ġeseldan** is used ἀπὸ κοινοῦ as both object of **ġeondscēawaþ** and subject of
swimmaþ. But Stanley (1993) rightly questions the validity of the concept of such
overlapping grammatical functions, which (though it is not Stanley's objection) is a
concept that conflicts with contemporary theories of language production. Of course,
one might assume, as it is assumed in earlier editions of this book, that the phrase is
the object of **ġeondscēawaþ** and that an understood *hīe* with the same referent is the
subject of **swimmaþ**.

[47] The constructions are not identical, as here **oft** is in a separate clause; but the
translation given furnishes the right idiom for what may be construed literally as
"when . . . (as) often."

renewed—to one who is accustomed to sending his weary spirit very often over the congregation of waves'. Of course **fela** is meiotic, like **lȳt** (31). Dunning and Bliss are most likely right that the **secga ġeseldan** are the sea-birds; but there is just enough ambiguity in the phrase—an ambiguity reinforced by the use of **ferhþ** in apposition to this—to recapitulate the way that the two sets of companions, the birds and the remembered kin, are juxtaposed and seem to coalesce in the sailor's dreamlike state. If one is willing to emend **oft**, the syntax may be simplified by reanalysis of the parentheses, but the passage makes good, if complex, sense without the emendation. On patristic analogues to the soul's converse with absent friends, see Clemoes 1969 (with Godden 1985); and on the relation of this passage to Anglo-Saxon beliefs about dreaming, see Galloway 1994.

64–65. All editions of the poem, beginning with the first (Thorpe 1842), divide these verses as follows:

> for-þon ne mæġ weorðan wīs   wer, ǣr hē āge
> wintra dǣl on weorold-rīċe.   Wita sceal ġeþyldiġ

However, this version of 65a is by any measure unmetrical as a normal verse and unparalleled as a hypermetric one. The verse division selected here remedies that problem, also improving the stilted syntax of 64b; and the consequent meter of 64a, though unusual, is not unparalleled: infinitives do sometimes lack stress (as at *Maldon* 39; *Wife's Lament* 42; *Genesis A* 2483, 2820; *Phoenix* 165; *Christ and Satan* 590; etc.); on the verse type see the note to *Maldon* 224.

66–72. Logically **tō** repeated in these verses ought to be meiotic, as pointed out by Mitchell (1968): the speaker should not advocate moderation but the complete avoidance of the listed vices. **fæġen** (68) would then necessarily designate an undesirable quality of mind, and this seems improbable: Dunning and Bliss's gloss 'servile' receives no support from other contexts. But the incursion of **fæġen** into an otherwise litotic passage should not be surprising in the context of the loose, associative logic of poems such as *The Wanderer* and *The Seafarer*.

78. **weorniaþ**. MS *w oriað,* interpreted as *wōriaþ* 'wander about', seems singularly inappropriate, though it is retained in most editions. Muir (1994) adopts the emendation *woniað* (which would be normalized as *waniaþ* 'decline') of Dunning and Bliss; but he also notes that in the space between *w* and *o* in the manuscript there is an erasure which was probably the letter *e*. Very possibly, then, the original reading *weoriað* was in error for *weorniað* 'decay', perhaps by inadvertent omission of a titulus (mark of suspension to indicate *n*), an error that prompted the nonsensical correction. The metrical type is unusual but not implausible: cf. *Beowulf* 1790a and *Exodus* 76a; and for the metrical treatment of -*iaþ* see Fulk 1992: §229.

80b–84. Anaphora on a form of *sum* is not infrequent in Old English verse—two other poems in the Exeter Book, *The Fortunes of Men* and *The Gifts of Men,* for example, are predicated entirely on this device—and it is not found only in passages translated from Latin: see Cross 1958–59 for discussion. The **sume** (80b) of the manuscript is probably correct, referring with understatement to *many* who fell in battle. The singulars that follow suggest the varying fate of individual corpses left on the battlefield, some made prey to the beasts of battle (on which see the note to lines 60–65 of *Brunanburh*). The word **forð-weġe** (81) should perhaps be emended to an accusative, but see the note to *Rood* 125. The bird of line 81 may be assumed to bear away the dead piecemeal (as pointed out by Cross 1958–59: 92–93 and Brown 1978), and it is therefore unnecessary to regard it as a metaphor for a ship or as a valkyrie, or to compare it to the eagle that bears away Loki at the beginning of *Skáldskaparmál.* As for the expression **dēaðe ġedælde** (83), Dunning and Bliss point out that versions of this formula occur twice in *Andreas,* indicating that it ought to mean 'handed over to death'. It may betray too literal a reading of the passage to wonder whether the wolf's victim has not already been killed in battle.

88. **Sē** may be equivalent to *sē-þe,* indefinite 'he who; whoever': see Mitchell 1985b: §§2206, 2216 for other examples.

92. **Hwǣr cōm** 'Where is; what has become of?' On the theme expressed by this formula and its relationship to the *ubi sunt* passages of Latin homiletic literature, see Cross 1956. The earliest

examples are in the Old Testament, but there the note of regret is less conspicuous than that of scorn or warning.

98. **wyrm-līcum fāg**. This seems to refer to some type of serpentine ornamentation, perhaps a frieze (Leslie), or herring-bone masonry in the shape of serpents such as can still be seen in the remains of Roman buildings in Britain and in some later imitations (Millns 1977). Muir summarizes other interpretations.

107. **onwendeþ wyrda ġesceaft**. In a passage in King Alfred's translation of Boethius' *Consolatio philosophiae* (ed. Sedgefield 1899: 11.22–32) to which there is no close Latin equivalent, Wisdom upbraids Boethius for having said that *wyrd* (Lat. *fortuna*) governs the world without God's consent, and the verb describing what *wyrd* does to the world is *wendan,* either 'change' or 'turn'. Wisdom is referring to an earlier passage (10.18) in which Boethius uses the verb *hwierfan* 'turn, change' to express what *wyrd* does to the world; and in the same place (10.2) the closely related verb *ymbhweorfan* is used to express God's might as he turns the heavens. The same polysemy attaches to Latin *vertere* 'turn, change', and indeed to English *turn,* and the relationship between the meanings 'turn (revolve)' and 'change' is captured in that iconographic staple of the antique and medieval world, Fortune's wheel. Usually, however, in Old English *wyrd* is not personified Fortuna (as it is above in line 100) but refers simply to what takes place (cf. *wyrd-wrītere* 'historian'). Here it is ambiguous whether **wyrda ġesceaft** refers to the decree of fate or simply to the course of events.

110. In earlier editions of this book, **mæ̈ġ** was read as *mæġ* 'maiden' (so also Klinck), assumed to be a nominative singular of the *þ*-stem *mæġþ* (though Campbell 1959: §637 n. 1 advises otherwise). Although *mæġ* could be used metonymically here to refer to women in general (compare how it refers poetically to a wife and mother at *Genesis A* 1053), the implied contrast with **mann** seems unlikely, since that word has no gender implications, being frequently applied to women. As suggested by Dunning and Bliss, possibly **mann** refers to a retainer; but more likely it refers to an individual as representative of humankind—or of oneself, a reading to which there is a remarkable parallel in *Hávamál* in the poetic

edda, stanzas 76 and 77, as pointed out by Leslie: *Deyr fé, deyja frǽndr, / deyr sjálfr it sama* 'livestock die, kinsmen die; one dies likewise oneself'. The transitory trio of goods, kindred, and friends persists in medieval literature to the time of *Everyman*.

111. **on mōde**. This has often been assumed to mean, somewhat redundantly, that the person referred to is wise 'in spirit'; but as Richman (1982) shows persuasively, the parallels indicate that the phrase should be construed with **cwæþ**, in support of the theme stated early on (lines 11–14) that gloomy thoughts should not be spoken aloud. The phrase **æt rūne** has no exact parallel; but as Leslie notes, along with **sundor** and reflexive **him** it would also seem to indicate that private reflection is what is referred to here.

The Seafarer

The unity of *The Seafarer* as a poem, even more than of *The Wanderer*, has often been doubted. After line 64 the sea fades entirely from view, and the speaker's ambivalent attitude toward travel on the sea, presenting it at once as a gruesome hardship and as a superior way of life, convinced Max Rieger (1869) that the poem does not offer a unitary point of view but is a dialogue between two men, old and young. Even very recently some have reverted to Rieger's view that there is more than one speaker (e.g., Smol 1994), though scholars have never agreed about the placement of speech boundaries. The poem was punctuated as a dramatic exchange in the first edition of this book, the change of speakers occurring in line 33; but as noted above, Pope subsequently retracted this analysis, and in the present edition no attempt is made to distinguish speakers. That a change of speakers should have been intended at line 33 indeed seems dubitable, given the formality with which speaking characters are introduced in Old English narrative poetry; but the absence of quotation marks in this edition is intended not to prevent a dialogic reading but to avoid imposing one.

The predilection of some earlier scholars, starting with Friedrich Kluge (1883), for regarding the conclusion of the poem as a later, moralizing addition to an essentially heroic poem—or indeed for regarding the poem as in other ways a composite text—proceeds from assumptions about heroic poetry that have little currency today. As noted above in the headnote to the commentary on *The Wanderer,* the motive for such analyses was the Romantic desire to uncover a realm of "pure" Germanic literature in its "original" state, free of the corrupting influence of Mediterranean learning. Changes in critical methods in the course of the twentieth century, and particularly the rise of New Criticism and related formalist approaches, made it more or less inevitable that such anatomizing readings would fall by the way and that value would instead be placed on demonstrating the poem's unity, balance, and intricacy of structure. The analysis that seemed to promise the soundest basis for uncovering such formalist virtues in the poem was that of Whitelock (1950), who explained the conflicting attitudes of the speaker toward seafaring not as an allegorical expression of the relationship between suffering in this world and the hope of eternal life, but as something quite a bit more literal. She identified the speaker as a *peregrinus,* a traveler who has chosen a life of seafaring and exile abroad as a means of mortifying the flesh and meriting the joys of the life to come. Whitelock provided ample documentation of pilgrimage and religious exile as actual Anglo-Saxon practices. The assumption that the speaker's exile is self-imposed does indeed explain much about his attitude toward the sea; yet surely the chief reason that Whitelock's analysis found such favor is that it afforded a means of reading the poem as a unified composition without resorting to allegorical interpretation. Whatever its excesses, the allegorical and exegetical, or so-called historical, criticism that played such a significant role in Anglo-Saxon literary studies in the years following the publication of Whitelock's analysis (examples pertaining to this poem are cited in the notes below) served the purpose of blunting opposition to an allegorical reading of the poem. This is as it should be, since for many readers the poem loses much of its imaginative appeal if it is interpreted only literally—if, in referring to **dryhten** (43, 65), the speaker is thought to mean just one thing, or if in disparaging **þis dēade lif, lǣne on lande**, he is thought not to be offering the alternative of seafaring as a transparent metaphor for the hardships and rewards of a life of spiritual devotion. Whitelock rejects allegorical interpretation on the ground that we should expect any intended metaphor to have been made as crudely obvious as it is made in some Old English homiletic prose. But it is perhaps the chief poetic virtue of *The Seafarer* that it moves almost imperceptibly from a literal account of hardships at sea to a philosophical meditation on mutability in this world and permanence in the next, continually suspending resolution of its ambiguities of reference, preserving its indeterminacies of meaning with a delicacy not to be expected in prose, and not often matched in Old English verse.

Yet despite the New Critical imperative of uncovering unity and intricate design in the poem, there is still something of value to be derived from the earlier views of those who would dissect the poem. Even those who in reaction rejected most arguments for a composite origin for the poem were often willing to believe that lines 103–24 are a later addition, and these lines are in fact set apart and labeled an epilogue in earlier editions of this book. If, as it is now generally agreed, the final, moralizing lines of *The Wanderer* are of the very essence of the poem, then there is no reason to regard the homiletic close of *The Seafarer* as extraneous in any way. Yet a variety of scholars, including Lawrence (1902: 471), Dunning and Bliss (1969: 2–3), and Pope (1978: 32–34), noting that line 103 begins a new quire in the manuscript, have remarked the possibility that one or more quires may have been lost before it, and that lines 103–24 therefore may belong to an entirely different, acephalous poem. Indeed, in its present state the manuscript cannot very accurately be described as a *micel englisc boc* (as remarked already by Humphrey Wanley in 1705 and reiterated by Dunning and Bliss, pp. 2–3),[48] as the entry that seems to be referring to the Exeter Book

---

[48] "Nam dum Codex esset perfectus & inviolatus, rectè diceretur liber Grandis; nunc autem, illi jam truncato Codici, tam initio quam in fine, ea quæ restant folia, una cum foliis septem aliis libro præmissis in Volumen mediocriter crassum à

describes it in the eleventh-century list of Bishop Leofric's dona-
tions to Exeter Cathedral. If the book was large in the eleventh
century, it must now be missing several quires. Although there is no
disruption of the sense, the syntax, or the meter at line 103, the shift
at this place from the specifics of a retainer's sad condition—the
approach of decrepitude, the loss of a lord, the futility of burying
gold with the dead—to a passage of mostly devotional generalities,
in conjunction with a sudden change to hypermetric form, raises the
possibility that *The Seafarer* is not one poem but fragments of two.
It is not necessary to read the text this way—there is, after all, men-
tion of **Godes eġesan** in line 101, which suggests naturally enough
the theme of lines 103–6—but unity of design is by no means as-
sured. Rather than to regard this uncertainty as a frustration, or as a
puzzle that must be solved conclusively before the text can be in-
terpreted, it may be best to recognize it as an example of the variety
of indeterminacies that lend particularity and a peculiar value to
Old English in the larger context of literary studies—indetermina-
cies above and beyond those that inhere in language itself and that
attracted intense critical interest in the last part of the twentieth cen-
tury—setting it apart from the literatures of more recent eras, and
particularly those of print cultures.

There is an excellent edition of the poem—which in addition to its
formal peculiarities has in some spots a badly corrupt text—by Ida
Gordon (1960), upon which the following commentary relies heav-
ily. Of the numerous editions in collections, the ones most worthy
of consultation for the notes are those of Krapp and Dobbie (1931–
53: 3.295–98), Cassidy and Ringler (1971), Klinck (1992), Mitchell
and Robinson (1992), and Muir (1994). Less extensive notes are
provided by Fowler (1966) and Whitelock (1967). O. S. Anderson
(1937–38) offers a study and notes, but no text. The Exeter Book
has been edited in facsimile by Chambers, Förster, and Flower

---

Bibliopego jam denuo rediguntur" ("For while the codex was complete and
undisturbed, it might rightly have been called a large book. Now, however, those
leaves which remain in this codex, which is truncated at both beginning and end,
together with seven other leaves prefixed to the book, are made anew by the
bookbinder into a moderately thick volume"; Wanley 1705: 279).

(1933); see also Klinck's edition for facsimiles of the relevant leaves. The most useful bibliography is that compiled by Mary Clayton for the 1996 reprint of Gordon's edition of the poem; Klinck also provides a bibliography; those of Muir (1994) and Conde Silvestre (1992) cover other material as well.

Notes

9. **fruron**. The manuscript instead has *wæron*, and if this is correct the sentence must not begin with **ċealde ġeþrungen** (8b), as then we should expect *wǽron* to be stressed, and the alliteration indicates otherwise. One might reasonably, with Orton (1982b), begin the sentence with *wǽron*, which then would not require alliteration (see pp. 137–38 for a discussion of the conditions under which finite verbs are stressed; also the note to line 19 below); but **ċealde ġeþrungen** less plausibly describes an inanimate object like the ship of line 6 than the seafarer's feet, and keeping this phrase in the latter sentence (the practice of all the editions cited above) also maintains the vigor of the contrast between the cold of lines 8b–10a and the heat of 10b–11a. Emendation to **fruron**, which remedies the alliterative problem, also produces a less dubitable metrical type (see p. 145, n. 33 below), and it is licensed by the obvious state of corruption of the text of this poem.

15. **wreċċan lāstum** 'on the paths (or with the steps) of an exile'. The theme is relevant, as shown by its proper occurrence at line 57; but the stock expression is so familiar that it is here devoid of its original metaphoric reference and seems something of a cliché in the context of a sea voyage. As line 16a lacks a mate, it may be assumed either that a verse is missing or that one has been carelessly added; and since the next verse alliterates on *w* and forms an excellent second half-line for 15a, flawless in meaning and in meter, it may be best to assume that **wreċċan lāstum** is a scribal addition.

19. **hwīlum ielfete sang**. Though it would seem preferable rhetorically to begin a new sentence with this phrase, as is done in all the editions listed above, Orton (1982b) rightly observes that doing

so disturbs line 20a, where we should then expect the particles to be stressed. The most authoritative description of the patterns of stress actually found on particles in verse is that of Hans Kuhn (described below, pp. 137–38).[49]

21. **hleahtor wera**. Magennis (1992) points out that laughter has rather different connotations in heroic and in homiletic literature—positive and negative ones, respectively—and the competing connotations should both be expected to be of relevance in *The Seafarer*.

24. **þæt** is a pronoun, object of **beġeall**, perhaps referring vaguely to the scene, perhaps (though with no explicit antecedent) to the call of the tern.

25. **ūriġ-feðra** does not alliterate and is too much like 24a to be right. For the sake of the alliteration, Grein (1857) alters **nǣniġ** to *ne ǣniġ,* in which he is followed by the majority of editors, and indeed it is possible to stress *ǣniġ* even in attributive position. But in addition to leaving the problem of the repetition unresolved, this produces a metrical type not to be expected in the off-verse on two counts, since it is a type that contains both a compound bearing secondary stress and an expansion syllable (see pp. 146–47). The emendation is thus not an improvement, sacrificing the meter for the sake of the alliteration. No obvious solution presents itself; guesswork has been avoided here.

27. **for-þon**. Particularly in connection with arguments for multiple speakers, uncertainty about the meaning of this word, which recurs so often in the poem, has provoked substantial controversy: for references see Jacobs 1989. Despite attempts to give the word a causative meaning in all its uses in the poem, Gordon's note on this verse may fairly be said to reflect the currently prevailing view: "The normal meaning of this conjunctive phrase is 'for that reason'

---

[49] Mitchell (1985b: §3947), on self-admittedly subjective grounds, questions the authority of Kuhn's findings in this instance; but in contexts in which the syntax is not in doubt, Kuhn's perceptions on the whole are a rather accurate report of what we find. Though neither is infallible, Kuhn's observations are almost certainly a more impartial and trustworthy guide to the syntax of verse than modern rhetorical preferences and suppositions.

(either adverbial 'therefore', or conjunctival 'because'), but in some contexts in OE poetry, as here, it appears to be used in a more colourless sense as an introductory adverb to mark a shift of thought, and may be translated 'truly', 'indeed'."

33b–35. 'Truly (or indeed), thoughts are even now beating against my heart, urging that I myself make trial of the high (or deep) seas, the tumult of the salt waves'. Gordon is probably right that **heortan** is the object of **cnyssaþ**; yet the possibility of taking **heortan** as a genitive with **ġeþōhtas**, and **cnyssaþ**, in the sense 'urge', as comparable to verbs of saying or commanding, governing the clause only as object, is not to be denied. The meaning of **self** (35) in this context is debated by Pope (1965, 1974) and Greenfield (1969, 1981), without a clear resolution: Klinck gives a concise summary of the controversy. Many editors and translators have passed over the word (forgivably and perhaps rightly) as untranslatable, a mere alliterating iteration of **iċ**, at most enforcing the idea of the speaker's bold confrontation of the high seas.

37. **tō fēran**. Uninflected infinitives after **tō** are not uncommon in verse. For a list see Grein 1912–14: 682 (s.v. *tō* IV).

38. **el-þēodiġra eard**. If we take this section of the poem to pertain to ordinary voyaging (and at least on the surface it should), these words mean simply 'the land of foreigners', those who are foreigners in relation to the speaker. To this point in the poem there has been no very clear suggestion of anything other than a literal meaning for the seafarer's wandering; but given the implications that arise later, this expression might mean 'the homeland of those who are strangers on earth', and if so, the speaker is intimating already that heaven is his destination. The notion that **el-þēodiġra eard** refers to heaven is supported with a number of pertinent quotations from Old English homilies and their patristic sources by Smithers (1957–59).

48–49. 'The groves burst into bloom, adorn the manors, make beautiful the meadows; the world hastens on'. The onset of summer recalls the onward rush of time, which warns the prospective voyager to set forth before it is too late. The second half of the poem invites extension of the meaning to include thoughts of the end of

the world. Cross (1959) has very interestingly connected the pas-
sage with Gregory the Great's interpretation of a saying of Jesus
about the fig tree and the end of the world. Gordon, in agreement
with Whitelock, argues that in MS *wlitigað,* "-*ig*- is a perfectly
defensible spelling for [*iji*]." But *g* here should be velar, since the
derivation is from **wlitig-ōjaþ,* and **wlitigiaþ**—which is the
normalized spelling, in any case—is thus required.

50–52. Mitchell 1985c outlines the wide variety of ways that the
syntax of these verses can be analyzed. It may be best to take **þām-
þe** (51) as a dative of possession (a possibility not considered by
Mitchell; see the note on *Brunanburh* 22) modifying **sefan**: trans-
late '(the mind) of him who thus thinks', etc.

53. In Old English poetry the cuckoo is a harbinger of sorrow
only here and in *The Husband's Message,* though this is also a mo-
tif of Welsh elegy: see the introduction to Gordon's edition, p. 17;
and Pheifer 1965.

56. **sēft-ēadiġ secg**. Sedgefield's reading *secg ēst-ēadiġ* (1922:
33) is formally unlikely, as verses of type D with secondary stress
normally alliterate on both full lifts. The emendation chosen here,
which is Grein's, and which has subsequently been adopted by
many editors, is the only other one proposed so far that renders a
normal pattern of alliteration. The compound made of two adjective
stems is extremely unusual, but as Gordon points out, there is a
parallel in *hwæt-ēadiġ* (*Elene* 1194).

58–64. In this extraordinarily intense and imaginative passage the
speaker's soul is likened to a bird that soars out over the waters,
sights the far country of its desire, and comes back, a lone flier, rav-
enous with hunger for what it has seen, to urge the man himself to
follow. Pope (1965) suggests that the imagery is appropriate to an
eagle, while Gordon (see also Orton 1982a) argues that the **ān-floga**
(62) is the cuckoo. Clemoes (1969) quotes two passages from
Alcuin's *De animae ratione* (one in prose, the other in verse) that
expatiate on the mind's power to travel, in imagination, far from the
body, and to fly, as the verse has it, "across sea, lands and lofty
sky," and he argues that they are likely to have provided a psycho-
logical basis for these lines.

65. þis dēade līf. The oxymoron has a counterpart in *līfgendra lond* 'land of the living' (*Christ I* 437), referring to heaven, as pointed out by Cassidy and Ringler.

69. tīde ġegang. The MS reads *tīde ge,* which some early editors interpreted as a compound, *tīd-eġe,* lit. 'time-fear' (fear of the time of death?), improbable as this may seem. Most accept the emendation of Grein (1857), *tīd-dæġe,* a word that has the virtue of being attested elsewhere, in the expression *his tīd-dæġe . . . rīm* 'the number of his day[s]', meaning 'his lifetime' (*Genesis A* 1165–66). The difficulty with this is that not on its own but only in conjunction with *rīm* does the word seem to refer to the *extent* of one's days. In addition, this reading leaves **his** (69) without an antecedent. The emendation adopted here, **tīde ġegang,** remedies both of these problems and assumes a more natural scribal error than the corruption of *tīd dæge* to *tīde ge,* since omission of a word or word element is common. Almost precisely the same expression translates Latin *tempus* in Wærferth's rendering of the *Dialogues* of Gregory the Great, in a passage describing Paulinus of Nola: *sē maniġe mæn þāra, þe iċ ġemunde, æġþer ġe on tīda ġegange ġe ēac on wundrum oferþēah* (ed. Hecht 1900–1907: 1.179), translating *qui multos quorum memini uirtute et tempore praecessit* (ed. Vogüé 1979: 256) 'who preceded many men, of those I remember, in time and surpassed them in miracles'. There is a similar expression *æfter þon tīda bigong* 'after the passing of (the proper amount of) time' at *Christ I* 235. Although *tīda* is plural in both of these passages, the singular may be used in the same way: see the examples in Bosworth and Toller's dictionary. The meter will not accommodate dat. *ġegange* with much plausibility, but **ġegang** is an acceptable reading.[50] Translate 'Always, in every case, one of three things becomes

---

[50] The example of *bigong* cited above shows that we may assume an endingless locative of this stem, a formation that is particularly common in temporal expressions (as, probably, at *Maldon* 198; see Dahl 1938: 48–55). Even were this not the case, **ġegang** could be regarded as correct, since the preposition **ǣr** occasionally takes an accusative object: see Wülfing 1894–1901: 2.668 and the supplement to Bosworth and Toller's dictionary, s.v. "Correction" of the word to *ge gange* in the Exeter scribe's exemplar would help to explain the error in the Exeter Book, since the word contains a homoeoteleuton (*ge . . . ge*), a common cause of scribal error.

uncertain before its time', or more literally 'before the passing of (the proper amount of) time', i.e., all too early.

72–80. Most recent editors, following Gordon, alter MS *þæt* to **biþ** (72); but as a scribal error this is less likely than the assumption, proposed by Holthausen, that **biþ** was inadvertently omitted after **þæt**. The interpretation of Cassidy and Ringler (1971: 335) makes fine sense: "The *þæt* not only anticipates *lof* in 73a ('that, i.e. the praise of after-speakers, of the living, [is] the best of posthumous reputations'), but is correlative with *þæt* in 74a ('that [is] the best of posthumous reputations for each man that he bring [it] about' etc.)." The emendation **fremum** (75) is K. Sisam's (1912–13), and it is preferable to the reading *fremme* of Kock (1918: 75–77), since it furnishes an attractive parallel between lines 75 and 76.

82. **nearon**. The form *næron* of the manuscript, a preterite, was doubtless prompted by West Saxon scribes' unfamiliarity with this Anglian form of the verb. See Klinck for examples of the same error in other texts—though her view that this is merely a variant spelling cannot be endorsed.

89–90. Cross (1962) details the numerous analogues in Latin and Old English to the comparison between the aging of the world and of an individual. One such analogue is to be found in Boethius (book II, poem 5).

97–99. Most editors assume a dual focus in this passage, on the inefficacy both of gold and of friends in the face of the Judgment to come (as argued explicitly by Gordon). Coherence with the following lines, however (100–102), is clearer if gold is the subject of the entire passage. Changing **wille** (99) to *nil(l)e* or *nyle* and translating, with K. Sisam (1945), 'that (i.e., the gold) will not go with him'—a double emendation, since in addition to the negativization an indicative form (with one *l*) must be substituted for the subjunctive (with two) of the manuscript—is almost certainly wrong, since *willan* in verse normally is a modal verb of volition rather than an auxiliary in the modern sense.[51] The entire passage may better be rendered

---

[51] As pointed out by Hamer 1992. The only indisputable exceptions that Ogawa finds (1989: 53) are in the prosaic Alfredian *Meters of Boethius;* cf. Gordon's note.

'Though a brother may wish to strew the grave with gold for his born (brother)—bury by the dead (one), with various treasures, that which he wishes (to go) with him—gold cannot', etc. This interpretation assumes that **dēadum** (98) is singular and that the object of **byrġan** (98) is not an understood *hine* (referring to the buried man) but **þæt** (99), referring to the gold, a relative pronoun containing its antecedent, as at *Maldon* 289.[52] Elements of this analysis have been favored in some other editions and studies: see the summary of adopted readings in Hamer 1992. Gordon's objection that "the sentence becomes awkward syntactically and logically in its blending of two separate ideas (though brother will strew the grave with gold . . . gold cannot help him when he hoarded it before)" assumes without cause that the gold and the future fate alluded to are not both the dead man's own. The focus is on him rather than his brother. Compare the passage in *Ynglinga saga* (chap. 8, cited by Kershaw 1922: 171) in which Óðinn is said to decree that *alla dauða menn skyldi brenna ok bera á bál með þeim eign þeira* ("all dead people should be burned and their possessions placed on the pyre with them"; ed. Bjarni Aðalbjarnarson 1941: 20). The use of **mid** with the accusative case is an Anglianism.

103. Gordon renders this very persuasively, 'Great is the terrible power of God, before which the earth will turn aside'. She aptly

[52] See Mitchell 1985b: §§2126–28. K. Sisam (1945) objects that **byrġan** is "restricted in early use to the burial of bodies"; it is in fact used exclusively of human remains throughout the Old English period. The etymology is not straightforward, but the most widely accepted explanation of the word is that it shows (as is usual for *ja*-stem causative formations) a different ablaut grade of the related strong verb, which is *beorgan* 'protect' (see the *OED*, s.v. *bury*): hence the etymon is **burg-jan*. But given the sense restriction in Old English it is more natural to assume that the stem shows the reduced grade not of a strong verb but of the noun reflected as OE *beorg* 'burial mound': compare OE *wyrċan* 'make' based on what would be the reduced grade of the noun *weorc* 'work'. The fundamental meaning, then, should be 'place in (lit. cause to be in) a burial mound (or, later, grave)', and that explains why all the direct objects in the approximately 45 recorded instances of the verb happen to be some form of human remains, and never treasure or other objects simply concealed in the earth. If this really is the meaning of **byrġan** there can be no objection to its use to describe the placement of gold in a grave. In modern parlance one might refer to gold that has been interred with the deceased, since this is a funerary context, though one would not normally say that a dragon's gold was interred in the earth if one means simply that it was hidden.

compares Revelation 20.11, *a cuius conspectu fugit terra* ("from whose face the earth fled away").

109–10. Accepting in general Gordon's interpretation, but assuming that **mōde**, to which **þæt** refers, is understood as the object modified by the adjectives in 110, we may translate these lines, "A man must govern a headstrong spirit and keep it steady, and unfailing in its pledges, pure in its ways." Consequently **mōde** must not be rendered 'temper'.

111–15. For a concise overview of the variety of emendations that have been proposed for this obviously corrupt passage, see Muir. The interpretation adopted here, which owes much to those proposals, assumes that the passage may be translated 'Everyone ought to keep in moderation affection for a friend and spite for an enemy, even if he (the enemy) may wish to have him steeped in fire, or (may wish to have) his (the hypothetical original person's?) fast friend consumed in fire'. Gordon objects that it is illogical to recommend practicing **bealu** even in moderation, but cf. the note to *Wanderer* 65–72. **lufan** is Holthausen's addition, and most editors accept it but place it at the head of the verse. This renders an appealing chiasmus, but paleographically the omission of the word is likelier if **lēofne** and **lufan** originally stood together. A more intrusive emendation would have to be adopted if the omission were assumed to be in the off-verse. Though the expression *fȳres full* is applied elsewhere to hell itself (*Christ III* 1625, and cf. *Genesis B* 333–34), once the expression *fȳres afylled* 'filled with fire' describes a sinner condemned to hell (*Christ III* 1562). Placing the caesura between **fȳres** and **fulne** is awkward syntactically, but such divisions do occur in the eight poems (see p. 131 below); and there is no way to put the two words into the same verse without altering the text more radically than has been done here. If the assumption is correct that a word is missing after **fulne**, it is almost certainly an infinitive (rather than, say, a phrase such as **on helle** 'in hell'), since **hine wille fȳres fulne** cannot be rendered 'wishes him full of fire' without straining the syntax and semantics of **wille**. For a construction parallel to **hine habban** 'have him, cause him to be' plus adjective, cf. *þonne magon wē ūs God ælmihtiġne mildne habban*

'then we can cause almighty God to be kind to us' (Blickling Hom.
x, ed. Morris 1874–80: 107); a parallel to the construction with a
participle is *þā hæfdon hīe hiera clūsan belocene* 'then they had
closed their passes' or 'then they had their passes closed' (Orosius,
ed. Bately 1980: 62.25; on the ambiguity raised by the original,
adjectival function of the participle in the periphrastic perfect con-
struction, see Mitchell 1985b: §§724 ff.). Invoking fire is apparently
the usual method of wishing someone or something destroyed, as in
a charter of the mid-tenth century (no. 1447 in the numeration of
Sawyer 1968) in which a litigant says that he would sooner that fire
or flood had possession of a disputed estate (*þæt hit tō fȳre oððe
flōde ġewurde*) than that his brother should have it. Instead of
habban a verb meaning 'see' might be inserted here—cf. *þæs þe hī
hyne ġesundne ġesēon mōston* 'that they might see him safe and
sound' (*Beowulf* 1628)—perhaps *behealdan,* though not (*ġe*)*sēon,*
since this, having a short root syllable when decontracted, would
produce an unusual metrical type.

Deor

Deor is one of the few poems in Old English devoted to the matter
of early Germanic legend. It resembles *Beowulf* and *Widsith* in its
allusiveness: the *scop* clearly expected his audience to be familiar
with an array of legendary figures, since he feels no need to recount
their stories, but only to allude to them in passing. Though our
knowledge of the legends is limited, the remaining fragments, pri-
marily from Scandinavia and the Continent, of what must once have
been a vast body of oral heroic literature are sufficient in scope to
confirm our understanding of the poet's theme as one of hardships
passed away.

And this *is* undeniably the theme. As a consequence, in the past
thirty years the prevailing view has been that *Deor* belongs to the
genre of consolation, and many would identify the poem as explic-
itly Boethian in its conception. Yet this view depends upon a

particular interpretation of the refrain as expressing an essentially optimistic attitude. This is not the only, or perhaps even the most plausible, interpretation (see the note on **mæġ** in line 7). Regardless, the refrain seems less to form the core of the poet's real interest than to serve as a unifying device, tying together the elliptical narrative strands designed to inspire his audience to recall one after another of the tales of fierce cruelty that dominated their secular literary heritage. In terms of sheer weight of reference, then, the *scop* directs our attention not to the change of fortune that provided consolation—a change that is never explicitly mentioned—but to the hardships themselves.

This focus on pitiful plights rather than their remedies is in actuality what should be expected of material derived from early Germanic heroic literature, a corpus that is pervaded by the theme of suffering and that shows little interest in happy endings. An instructive comparison is to the Old Icelandic *Guðrúnarhvǫt,* which begins with Guðrún summoning her sons to vengeance. When they have departed on their mission she sits alone and, lamenting, recounts the losses she has endured, allusively summoning up the stories of her three marriages and the tragedies they spawned. The poem ends with the following stanza (ed. Neckel and Kuhn 1983, here normalized):

> Jǫrlum ǫllum   óðal batni,
> snótum ǫllum   sorg at minni,
> at þetta tregróf   um talið væri.

This may be rendered, freely, 'May every lord's lot seem improved, every lady's sorrow lessened, for this lament's having been uttered'. Technically this might be called consolation, and undeniably, part of the appeal of tragedies recounted is the perspective they provide on one's own discontents. But to call the poem a consolation would be to misconstrue it entirely. It is not about the grim comfort that one may or may not derive from this depressive final strophe; it is about the tragic splendor of Guðrún's magnificent losses (including the imminent loss of her sons Hamðir and Sǫrli on the mission on which she has just sent them), to which the poem's twenty other strophes are devoted. So, too, with *Deor:* one at least hesitates to assume that legendary material has been adapted to a theme foreign to Germanic legendary literature, given that the poem may be read with at least equal cogency in the spirit of the surviving literature that is most closely related to it, such as the heroic poems of the poetic edda and the lament of the last survivor (*Beowulf* 2247–66).

The only edition devoted exclusively to *Deor* is that of Malone (1933, rev. 1977), but the poem is to be found in several edited collections of recent years, which are listed by Muir (1994: 2.567). Particularly useful are the commentary and bibliography of Klinck (1992). The poem appears in the Exeter Book, and it will be found on ff. 100$^{\text{r–v}}$ of the facsimile (Chambers, Förster, and Flower 1933), and also in the reproductions in Klinck's edition.

Notes

1. **Wēland**. The story of Weland the smith, maker of Beowulf's corselet and of many a famous sword, is told at some length in *Vǫlundarkviða* (from the ninth century?) in the poetic edda, and even more elaborately, but differently, in the twelfth- or thirteenth-century Norwegian saga of Dietrich von Bern, *Þiðreks saga*. From these two we can piece together an outline that fits the implications in the first two stanzas of *Deor*. Weland, as a young man, came to work for a certain king named Niþhad, who, greedy for his wonderful productions and wanting to prevent his escape, took him by surprise and cut his hamstrings. Weland, in revenge, lured the two sons of Niþhad to his smithy, killed them, and made bowls out of their skulls, gems out of their eyeballs, and brooches out of their teeth. He presented these objects to Niþhad as masterpieces of his art. Later he raped Niþhad's daughter, Beaduhild, impregnating her. Finally, having made a coat of feathers with the help of his brother Egill, he escaped, perching on the roof of Niþhad's palace long enough to tell him all he had done. Niþhad sickened and died. A son

was born to Beaduhild, and within a few years she was reconciled to Weland, with whom she went to live as his wife. Their son, named Widia, was to become a notable adventurer. Scenes from the story of Weland are also depicted on the Franks Casket, a splendid Anglo-Saxon box carved from whalebone. Harris (1987: 53) remarks the essential similarities between this poem and the casket as cultural artifacts, with their mixture of scenes from history and legend arranged in "panel structures." For photographs of all the panels on the casket, see Becker 1973; views of individual panels are also locatable at various sites on the World Wide Web with the help of a standard search engine.

1. **him be wurman**. OE *wurma* refers to purple dye or its source, and this is obviously not what is intended—though J. Anderson (1986) defends this interpretation as a metonymic reference to blood. Nor it is likely to refer to the inhabitants of Värmland in Sweden. Several emendations have been proposed, the most ingenious of which are *wornum* 'multitudes'; *wurnan* 'pain, sorrow' (otherwise unattested); *wearnum* 'hindrances' (in allusion to the hamstringing); *wīfmen* 'woman'; and *wyrmum* 'serpents', either literally or as a metonym for the damascened or otherwise decorated products of Weland's craft. But most of these emendations face explicit objections, and none carries sufficient conviction. If the word is a name, it is one that is not found in early Germanic myth.

5–6. Possibly a witty allusion to the hamstringing, as if the supple sinews, being cut, were equivalent to bonds. But in *Vǫlundarkviða* 11 (ed. Neckel and Kuhn 1983, here normalized), when the hero is first captured he is fettered, as pointed out by Ekwall (1934): when he awoke, *vissi sér á hǫndum hǫfgar nauðir, enn á fótum fjǫtur um spenntan* 'he became aware of a bond on his hands and a fetter clasped about his legs'.[53] The preposition **on** governs the accusative **hine**. The plural **nieda** (cognate with *nauðir* in the quotation above) is used concretely to mean physical restraints, fetters, though of course these may be figurative fetters.

---

[53] Jost (1961) argues on different grounds that the **sinu-benda** may be literal; see also Harris 1987: 50.

7. The genitives **þæs** and **þisses** have fueled much controversy: for a fine summary see Klinck's commentary. The usual assumption is that **oferēode** is used impersonally, and the genitives are in one way or another adverbial, perhaps as genitives of respect. One rather standard way of rendering the verses, then, fairly literally, is 'It passed away with respect to that; so can it with respect to this'. Still, there is no evidence for a genitive of respect in Old English: see Erickson 1975 and Mitchell 1985b: §§1404–7. Moreover, there is no parallel in Old English to the impersonal use of *ofergān;* and though the use of **ofercumen** (26) with an accompanying genitive is sometimes cited as a parallel, this case is different, as *ofercuman* is once attested with a genitive object.[54] A genitive subject in a passive construction, a pattern found both in Old English and in related Germanic languages, is thus unsurprising.[55] If *ofergān* could be used impersonally, as most assume, it would not be peculiar for the logical subject to be expressed in the genitive, much as in *him ðæs sceamode* 'that made them ashamed' (see Mitchell 1985b: §1028). Under this interpretation one could render the formula simply 'That passed away; so can this'. Despite the lack of supporting evidence, taking **þæs oferēode** for a true impersonal construction is probably a better solution than assuming that these genitives modify an unexpressed subject such as *wēa* 'sorrow', as Erickson and others have argued.

7. **mæġ.** This word, it should be noted, means 'can', not 'may'. Occasionally **mæġ** can plausibly be translated 'may', but only in the sense that something is licit, not in the optative sense that it is to be desired.[56] The solace offered by this formula is thus minimal; a

---

54 The text is *The Life of St. Christopher* in the Beowulf Manuscript (ed. Rypins 1924: 75): *Wuldorfæst ys and miċel cristenra manna God, þæs wuldorġe[wor]ces nāne mennisce searwa ofercuman ne magon* 'Glorious and great is the God of Christian folk, whose glorious work no human schemes can overcome'. The relative clause, it should be noted, is wide of the Latin, *qui facis voluntatem timentibus te* ("[you] who do the will of those who fear you").

55 Compare, e.g., Icelandic active *hún beið mín* 'she awaited me', where *mín* is genitive, and passive *mín var beðið* 'I was awaited'. For Old English examples see Mitchell 1985b: §849.

56 This holds true in spite of the ingenious arguments of Klinck: cf. Mitchell 1985b: §1013 and Bloomfield 1964: 536. The use of *magan* to express futurity in

more consolatory note would have been struck by *sceal*—though that word would have entailed its own ambiguities. Accordingly, there may be some truth to the argument of Frankis (1962: 171–72) that the refrain does not refer so much to the prospect of remedy as to the vicissitude inherent in existence. Harris (1987) is particularly persuasive in arguing that the refrain is an expression of the mutability of all things and thus not an indication of later restitution but a contributor to the poem's solemn and stoic mood. He also points out that the poem culminates in a sorry situation for the speaker for which legend is unlikely to have provided any remedy. If the refrain, as applied to Deor's own situation, is intended to be a promise of better things, it is singularly inappropriate. In offering the very interesting argument that the poem is a literary appropriation of the genre of blame poems known from Norse and Celtic literature, Biggs (1997: 310–11) also offers reasons to doubt the consolatory nature of the refrain.

14–17. The story to which this passage alludes is not recorded in any known medieval source. Malone has argued ingeniously that Mæþhild and Geat are the principals in a story told in differing versions in two ballads recorded in modern times, one Norwegian, the other Icelandic. In the Norwegian version, Gaute finds his bride Magnild (Icelandic Gauti and Magnhild) in tears because she foresees that she will drown in a certain river during her wedding journey. In spite of precautions she falls into this river at a bridge; but Gaute, calling for his harp, plays on it so effectively that Magnild rises up, still seated on her horse, escaping altogether from the power of the water-demon that had tried to capture her. In the Icelandic version, Gauti succeeds in recovering only her dead body. The names correspond more precisely in the case of Gaute than in that of Magnild: Scandinavian *Gaut-* is cognate with OE *Ġēat,* and in Old German the name-element *Māth-* (OE *Mæþ-*) 'honor' came to be confused with *maht* 'power', which corresponds in meaning to Scandinavian *magn.* The objections of Norman (1937, 1937–38)

---

renderings of the Gospels is surely irrelevant, as that appears to be a glossographic convention rather than native idiom.

raise telling questions about the plausibility of these parallels, particularly questions about the emendations necessary to bring the Old English poem into conformity with the outline of the account in the ballads. And if these ballads do reflect the tale to which the Old English poet alludes, they are so altered by oral tradition that they cannot be said to tell us more than *Deor* itself about the legend—they confirm only that the love of Mæþhild and Geat was great—and in some respects they tell us less, since the ballads do not suggest an obvious occasion for sleeplessness as the Old English poem does.[57]

14. **Mǣþhilde**. Although there is no unambiguous parallel to this usage with *ġefriġnan,* the word is probably best analyzed as a genitive akin to "the genitive which says that *x* is about *y*": see Mitchell 1985b: §§1285, 1288. Translate 'about (or of) Mæþhild'. Some find the syntax of this line implausible (e.g., Joyce Hill 1994: 30), and various emendations have been recommended. But the division of **maniġe** from **wē** is not an obstacle: the separation of quantifiers from their heads, sometimes to a considerable remove, is common in verse. Examples are *Hē þā maniġe fram him mānġewyrhtan yrre awende* (Psalm 77.38.1–2), *þǣr wē ymb hine ūtan ealle hōfan . . . lofsonga word* (*Christ and Satan* 153–54), and *ond hē him helpe ne mæġ, eald and infrod, ǣniġe ġefremman* (*Beowulf* 2448–49). See also *Dream of the Rood* 37–38. As to the very validity of the expression **wē . . . maniġe**, the modification of pronouns by *maniġ,* to be sure, is not idiomatic in prose, but it seems to be licensed in verse, perhaps because the words were felt to be in variation: cf. *ond hī onhnīgaþ tō mē / moniġe mid miltse* (*Riddle* 30a, 7b–8a); also *Psalms* 105.7.5.

15. **Ġēates**. Syntactic parallels suggest that this should be interpreted as a subjective rather than an objective genitive, referring to the love *of* Geat rather than Mæþhild's love *for* him. But as the latter meaning gives clearer sense, perhaps the distinction is too nice for Old English grammar.

---

[57] Malone suggests that the water-demon's love is what deprives Mæþhild of sleep—though of course under this interpretation the strophe loses much of its narrative appeal.

16. **hie sēo sorg-lufu slǣp' ealle benam**. Though there are no clear examples in Old English of *beniman* used with an accusative of person and an instrumental of thing (as pointed out by Krapp and Dobbie 1931–53), that is the best analysis of this phrase. **Hie** may technically be either plural (neuter in this case, referring to both sexes) or feminine singular, but the focus of the strophe seems to be on Mǣþhild.

18. **Þēodriċ**. The reference appears to be to Theodoric the Ostrogoth, who held sway in Italy from 493 to 526. And yet, even though various sources seem to mean that the *Mǣringas* were a Gothic tribe (see Klinck's note; they were Ostrogoths, according to Frankis 1962 and Kuhn 1963), it is unknown what place is meant here by the reference to their **burg**. Perhaps, as it has been supposed, it is Ravenna, Theodoric's capital. In later legend, in which he is known as Dietrich von Bern (i.e., from Verona), Theodoric is said to have been exiled thirty years among the Huns, and this may be the misfortune that the *Deor* poet has in mind.[58] Or possibly, as some have thought, Þeodric in this strophe is like Eormanric in the next—not a victim but an oppressor. Certainly, as the persecutor of Boethius, Symmachus, and Pope John I, Theodoric is portrayed as a brute in Old English ecclesiastical literature. But there is no evidence that in heroic literature he had a reputation like the cruel Eormanric's; and in the Old English *Waldere* fragment (II, 4–10) he is a victim rather than a tyrant, since Beaduhild and Weland's son Widia is there said to have released him from captivity, delivering him from the power of monsters. In his 1933 edition of the poem Malone argued with great subtlety that the person referred is a different Dietrich, the Wolfdietrich of Middle High German legend, whom he identified with the Frankish Theodric (Thierry) I, king of Austrasia (511–34) and son of Clovis I, first of the Merovingian kings. He later altered this view (see Malone 1939 and the 1977 revision of his edition), eventually identifying Wolfdietrich with another Frank, Sigiwald, a kinsman of Theodric I. Although the parallels reveal some notable

---

[58] Kuhn (1963) argues that *Deor* here shows a tradition in transition, the thirty years being in process of changing its reference from the period of Þeodric's reign to that of his exile.

correspondences, on the whole neither of the two versions of the hypothesis that the poet's reference is to a Frankish Þeodric now seems particularly persuasive.

21. **Eormanrīc** is the famous Ermanaric of history, long-reigning king of the Goths until his death about 375. He was the powerful ruler of a vast empire stretching from the Baltic to the Black Sea, but the stories of his tyrannical behavior—especially his savage treatment of his son, his wife, and several of his nephews, under the influence of a wicked counselor—appear to belong wholly to legend, and to have accumulated gradually until they emerge in Norse saga and Middle High German epic of the twelfth and thirteenth centuries. In *Þiðreks saga* Ermanaric has become king of Rome and uncle of Dietrich von Bern. Added to other crimes against his kin is his culpability in Dietrich's thirty-year exile among Attila's Huns. The Old Icelandic *Hamðismál,* in the poetic edda, and *Vǫlsunga saga* represent older and different traditions, as does *Deor.* The Old English *Widsith,* perhaps still older, lays stress on Eormanric's munificence and mentions almost parenthetically his dangerous temper. In *Beowulf* we have one brief allusion to his threatened vengeance against the outlaw Hama, who appears to have stolen from him a necklace of great value and run away from his *hete-nīðas.* Here in *Deor* his tyranny afflicts everyone in his realm.

26. **þæs cyne-rīces ofercumen wǣre**. On the use of a genitive subject in this passive construction, see the note on **oferēode** (7).

37. **Dēor**. This character may have been invented by the poet, since he is not otherwise known. Still, his name (an actual Old English one meaning 'bold') does not suggest an obvious fiction, the way the name *Wīd-sīþ* does, and he connects himself with persons who figure in a very ancient legend. A version of it in Middle High German, contained in the poem *Kudrun,* comes closer than the Icelandic versions to explaining the allusion to Heorrenda along with the Hedenings. King Heden laid plans to steal Hild, celebrated for her beauty, from the watchful care of her father, King Hagen. He took with him some helpers, including the giant Wate (still talked of as Wade in Middle English) and a wonderfully talented minstrel named Horant (the Heorrenda of *Deor*). This man so

captivated Hild by his singing and harping that she consented to elope with Heden. In the Scandinavian versions, which are older and differently descended, the result is a tragic pursuit and an endless battle between Heden and Hagen, over which Hild, true to her name, presides; but in *Kudrun* we have a more romantic version in which the lovers escape. We may surmise that in the fiction implied here, Heorrenda supplanted Deor in anticipation of his aid in the seduction, or else as reward for it. The main versions of the Hild story, including that related in *Kudrun,* are interestingly summarized by Chambers (1912: 100–109).

42. **þæs**. The exact reference of this word has been debated at length. Since we have no indication that Deor's fortunes ever improved after he was displaced by Heorrenda—indeed, **þisses** in all the refrains most likely refers to his present misfortune—**þæs** here would seem to mean something different in this final refrain. Perhaps it refers vaguely or generically to the adversities faced by all the previously mentioned legendary figures; perhaps, as Mandel (1977: 8) argues, it refers to Heorrenda's good fortune. Most are now agreed, however, that it turns the formula on its head, referring to Deor's prior state of contentment. Yet this last interpretation in particular renders the refrain exceedingly obscure; and if the poet intended just one of these interpretations to the exclusion of the others, his meaning is even now mysterious. Perhaps the intent of the refrain is vague here because the poet was less interested in its precise meaning than in the general sense of transitoriness that it conveys (see the note on **mæġ**, line 7). The precise meaning is worth debating only if the prospect of improvement in Deor's condition is of genuine importance, and not if the poet instead cares only about the sublime suffering of a great artistic forebear.

The Wife's Lament

This most difficult of poems is unique neither in its female speaker nor in the intensity of feeling it conveys, but it nonetheless projects an exceptional, and exceptionally engaging, narrative voice. It shares the allusiveness of *The Wanderer* and *The Seafarer,* reproducing in its indeterminacies the frustrated quality of the speaker's frame of mind, moving lightly over the less immediate specifics of her situation. Unlike those poems, this one narrates a sequence of events, and yet the details are too elusive to aid in unraveling the poem's syntax, which is even more ambiguous than that of most Old English lyrics.

Interpretations have in fact been exceptionally varied. Scholarship of the early twentieth century, predictably, tended to interpret the poem in the context of heroic literature, and various attempts were made to identify the events of the poem with those of one or another early Germanic legend, though without convincing results. This approach encouraged a tendency to understand the speaker's plight solely in the terms of the *comitatus* bond—the bond between lord and retainer in the early Germanic war-band—in which it is couched. As a consequence, even as late as the 1960s attempts were made to emend out of the text the evidence of the speaker's gender, the feminine inflections in the first two lines, in order to bring the poem into better conformity with scholarly notions of the heroic. The school of "historical" criticism that arose at midcentury (see above, p. 100) inspired Christian contextualizations of various sorts, reading the poem as typology (e.g., allegorizing the speaker as the Church, yearning for reunion with Christ) or as the product of women's experience as ascetics. Inspired by the speaker's residence in an *eorþ-scræf,* a remarkably persistent vein of scholarship has viewed the speaker as a disembodied soul or revenant speaking to us from the grave. Inevitably, the poem has also been identified as a riddle. These and other views are detailed in the admirable and concise overviews of literary scholarship on the poem by Mandel (1987: 149–55) and Klinck (1992: 49–54).

Given the strong vein of skepticism in recent Old English literary studies, it is not surprising that the poem's most recent editors have for the most part avoided hanging the poem's meaning on the uncertain details of the speaker's situation. They tend instead to disengage the poem from all such interpretive contexts, with the result that it is now widely treated simply as a love lyric of a particularly intense sort. The language of the bond between lord and retainer that pervades the poem is to be explained at least in part as normal to Anglo-Saxon gender relations: there is ample evidence that the male head of a household was referred to as *hlāford* and *frēa* by his wife and children (see the note on **hlāford**, line 6). This is not to say that there is nothing metaphorical about the poem's language of love, but that if the relationship analogizes the *comitatus* bond, it does so in a conventional manner. So, too, the hints of a setting for the speaker's banishment—the oak tree, the cavern, the steep hills, the fortifications overgrown with briars—are to be taken not as clues to the riddle of her identity but as objects conveying affective resonance (as argued by Jensen 1990), outwardly reifying an inward state of desolation, much as ruins and wintry weather do in *The Wanderer*.

In keeping with this less fraught approach, the tendency of late has been to avoid multiplying characters and events: whereas some earlier scholars perceived a second man in the speaker's affections, or a grand feud of the proportions encountered in the Icelandic sagas, there seems to be a growing consensus among the poem's editors that the tale is simpler than the syntax in which it is expressed. The poem is here edited in accordance with that view, assuming an uncomplicated sequence of events: for unstated reasons, the woman's husband travels abroad (line 6); she follows (9) but is prevented from being reunited with him by his scheming kin (12–14). Their meddling seems to have turned her husband against her, since it is he who commands her to live in a lonely place (15–17). Discounting the possibility of the introduction of another man in line 17, we may assume that here the speaker is returning us to the beginning of her tale, recalling an earlier time of happiness with her husband. The verse paragraph in lines 18–26 is thus not intended to further the action: it serves to contrast past happiness and present suffering—a common theme in Old English verse—and in doing so its purpose is to heighten and help to explain the intensity of the misery she has told us about in the preceding passage. This analysis obviates a certain awkward iteration of the action, enabling the assumption that lines 27–28 do not indicate that the woman was ordered to move to yet another place; they instead describe more fully her husband's demand mentioned earlier in lines 15–17.[59] It makes sense that they should do so, given the assumption that, starting in line 17, the woman has taken up her tale again from the beginning, this time filling in the affecting details left out in the earlier summary of events. On this reading the poem assumes a familiar shape, one that we have learned to recognize in other lyrics in this book: the speaker is formally introduced (lines 1–5); she outlines her situation (6–17); she details the causes of her anguish, focusing, however, more on her feelings than on the concrete particulars of her precarious existence (18–41); and finally she universalizes her experience, entering the gnomic mode (42–53), constructing a ġeong mann who must suffer as she has—one who, in fact, is hardly to be distinguished from the speaker herself.

The most significant editions (to which the one offered here is much indebted) include those of Krapp and Dobbie (1931–53: 3.295–98), Leslie (1961), Cassidy and Ringler (1971), Klinck (1992), Mitchell and Robinson (1992), and Muir (1994). For facsimiles of the poem in manuscript, see Chambers, Förster, and Flower 1933, and Klinck's edition. The most recent bibliography, but covering the whole of the Exeter Book, is Muir's; Klinck's bibliography is more directly focused on this poem.

Notes

3. **awēox**. The emendation, first proposed by Sievers (1885–87: 516), mends the meter and has parallels in verse. The proposal of Klinck to stress **iċ** and not **upp** cannot be endorsed, as **upp**, being a nondemonstrative adverb, is always stressed in verse.

6. **hlāford**. Technically the senior male member of a household, hence in this context best translated 'husband', its meaning in some

---

[59] Note **heonan** (6), which seems to imply that the speaker's lonely habitation is located near her husband's family.

charters (nos. 1064, 1200, 1495, 1497, etc., as numbered by Sawyer 1968). Perhaps a metaphor is intended—the reverse of the chivalric metaphor of a knight as his lady's vassal—since the imagery of a retainer's service is sustained in **lēod-fruma** (8), **folgoþ** (9), and **frēan** (33; cf. Toller's supplement to Bosworth and Toller 1898, s.v. *heord* III); but if so it is one that belongs to the culture rather than to the individual poet's imagination.

9. **þā** may be an adverb 'then', parallel to **ǣrest** (6); but it may with equal probability be a conjunction 'when', the interpretation adopted here. Note that **mē** is reflexive and need not be translated.

11. **þæt** antecedes the *þæt*-clause beginning in line 13.

15. **hīred.** Several ingenious explanations have been offered for *her heard niman* in the MS (with *her* at the end of a line). Grein (1865: 422) was the first to read *her heard* as *herh-eard,* interpreting this to mean 'habitation in the woods'—although actually *herh* (a plausible Anglian spelling for *hearg*) denotes a pagan shrine. Others have supposed *heard* 'hard' to describe the husband, or to serve as an adverb, though in either case the syntax would be unusual. Some early scholars even thought that *Herheard* was the husband's name. Recently Hough (1998) has associated *heard* with place-names in which it describes ground that is hard to plow; however, it seems never to be used substantively in this fashion. Most assume that *heard* stands for *eard*—and reasonably enough, since *eard niman* is an idiom 'make one's home'. This solution, though it renders the clearest sense, does not remedy the syntactic and metrical peculiarities of the verse, the way Grein's does: full stress on *hēr* with alliteration would be peculiar, since the immediately following noun must receive greater stress; yet **hēr** ought to be stressed, since it does not occupy the first drop of the verse clause (see pp. 137–38). The only close metrical parallel in verse, with a noun immediately following clause-internal **hēr**—which also appears to be a semantically close parallel—is *hēr bū nāmon* 'took up residence here' (*Psalms* 101.25.1b), where the alliteration is on *b.* Although the psalms of the Paris Psalter are, to be sure, metrically irregular, the parallel nonetheless lends sufficient conviction to the metrical requirement that it is not **hēr** but the word following it that

ought to alliterate—thus casting doubt on the emendation of MS *heard* to *eard*, as the *h* is required for alliteration. The reading selected for the text is based on a different assumption, that *heard* is a corruption of *hēord*, more commonly spelt *hēorod*, the chiefly Mercian equivalent of West Saxon **hīred** 'household'.[60] This reading is not far removed semantically from *eard niman* or *bū niman*, but it is more ironic in intent (like **lȳt** in the next line: cf. the note to *Dream of the Rood* 69), as the speaker seems to represent a household unto herself.

18. **þā**. Cassidy and Ringler take this word to head an independent clause, either introducing a second man or, less disturbingly, indicating that only afterward did the speaker discover her husband to be well suited to her—a brilliant solution. Yet the latter reading demands unusually compressed syntax. Klinck arrives independently at a similar interpretation, but she would subordinate the clause to the preceding one and render **þā** 'since'. The change in tense, however, along with the use of **þā** after a present-tense verb, is arresting. As these alternatives face uncertainties, it has seemed best to interpret this clause as dependent upon the one beginning in line 21.

20. **mōd-mīðendne, morðor-hycgendne**. These words have not usually been treated as compounds, but since the first constituents require no inflection, it is impossible to say for certain whether or not they should be treated as independent words. Modern orthographic practices compel a decision, and the construction *hycgan* with an accusative object other than a *þæt*-clause is unusual enough to suggest the likelihood that **morðor-hycgende** is a compound. The resultant parallelism with line 19 is agreeable, though perhaps only to modern sensibilities.

21. **blīðe ġebǣru**. It is debated whether this phrase belongs to the preceding or the following clause; both interpretations are entirely plausible. If with the following, it creates a violation of Kuhn's first law (pp. 137–38); but this is not a weighty objection, since there are instances elsewhere in the poem of abnormal stress patterns of this

---

60 The syncopated stem *hēord-* is found, however, in the glosses on the Junius and Lambeth Psalters, which are not Mercian texts. The alternation between *hēorod* and *hēord* precisely parallels the variation in West Saxon between *hīred* and *hīrd*.

sort (lines 1, 42; very likely 15). If the phrase adds an unexpected quality to the man's temperament, the shift of sense may seem abrupt to a modern ear, but it is wholly characteristic of the use of contrast in Old English poetry; and a contrast between gloomy thoughts and a cheerful demeanor is the explicit concern of another passage in the poem (see lines 42–45). The syntactic shift from accusative adjectivals in lines 19–20 to instrumental phrase in 21 is not implausible, either, though its uncommonness perhaps favors the interpretation adopted here, taking **blīðe ġebǣru** instead to describe the manner of the couple's former vows. On this analysis it is no longer the man's temperament and his manner that are contrasted but the high hopes of the couple and the actual course of events, expressed in lines 23 ff. This is a variety of irony (defeat of expectations) that seems more characteristic of OE poetry than a simple contrast of the man's thoughts and his manner: see, for example, Ringler 1966 for examples in *Beowulf*.

24. **sēo nēawest**. Though there is no gap in the manuscript, something is clearly wanting. The past participles of several verbs have been suggested (giving, e.g., *is nū ġeworden*), but nearly all demand stress on **nū,** which would be unparalleled; and the exception, Leslie's *fornumen,* produces a rare metrical type. The insertion selected here furnishes good form and sense, and the change of gender seen in **hit** is natural enough: see Mitchell 1985b: §§69–71, and cf. *Beowulf* 2806, *Widsith* 44, and *Riddles* 60.16.

26. **fǣhþu**. Leslie rightly observes that this word normally refers to a state of feud, from which he concludes that it cannot refer to the husband's hostility toward his wife. Still, if their relationship is implicitly compared to that between a lord and his retainer, **fǣhþu** may bear metaphorical significance. Compare the use of *fǣhðe* in the context of God's banishment of Cain at *Beowulf* 109.

27. **wudu-bearwe**. Given the widespread confusion, from an early date, of the endings *-u* and *-a* in the *u*-stems (as at *Maldon* 298; see Campbell 1959: §613), it is impossible to say whether MS *wuda* stands for a genitive or for the first constituent of this familiar compound, which is attested in both prose and verse. This ambiguity was recognized by the poem's first editor, Thorpe (1842).

28. **eorþ-scræfe**. The nature of this place (also called an **eorþ-sele** in 29) is in dispute, as it is variously identified as a cave, a burial chamber, and a sunken-featured building. Battles (1994) discusses the alternatives and concludes that it is a souterrain, "an artificial underground dwelling or chamber" (268), a structure large enough for the speaker to roam within (lines 35–36). Cassidy and Ringler compare an enigmatic passage spoken by Brynhildr in two manuscripts of the eddic *Helreið Brynhildar* (6.1–4, ed. Neckel and Kuhn 1983: 220, here normalized): *Lét mik af harmi hugfullr konungr, / Atla systur, undir eik búa* ("Out of grief that courageous king had me, the sister of Atli, live under an oak"). The setting under an oak thus possibly has some cultural significance that is lost to us.

31. **burg-tūnas**. Perhaps, as argued by Battles (1994: 286 n. 55), these are not literal fortifications but merely a metaphorical variation on **dūna** (30). But the word may also refer simply to manors, which were typically enclosed by an earthwork and a stockade.

42. **scyle**. There seems no clear distinction between subjunctive **scyle** and indicative **sceal** in such gnomic expressions: cf. *Seafarer* 111, *Christ II* 820, *Maxims I* 177, and so forth.

42–53. The syntax of the closing verse paragraph is exceptionally ambiguous and has provoked widely different interpretations. Do the subjunctives **sīe . . . sīe** of lines 45–46 represent a pair of wishes or an alternative 'whether . . . or'? Some of the poem's earliest editors favored the former view and saw in this a curse on the **ġeong mann** believed responsible for the husband's plight. But since such a reading entails the introduction of a previously unmentioned person, the latter view now prevails. Then does the pair of alternatives describe the possible conditions under which the husband is living, as most now seem to assume? The implication then would be that the speaker does not know which of the alternatives is correct, and yet she indicates in lines 50–52 that she knows him to be living in miserable circumstances. Hence the alternative conditions of lines 45–47 may be better applied to the **ġeong mann** of line 42, the sense being that regardless of whether a young person is living comfortably or in exile, it is necessary to bear both gloomy thoughts and a cheerful demeanor. As a generalization about how young people ought to bear themselves, this is not very compelling—why must they all have gloomy thoughts? And so it seems best to adopt the view first advanced by Schücking (1906: 445) that the **ġẹong mann** is to be equated with the speaker herself. This assumption has the further advantage of making it easier to assume that the unhappy person of lines 52–53 is the wife rather than the husband, since everything in the poem has led us to believe that it is she rather than he who awaits a loved one. This interpretation settles the chief remaining syntactic uncertainty, demanding the assumption that the *þæt*-clause beginning in line 47 does not elaborate upon the meaning of **fāh** (46) but instead explains why a young person's thoughts—that is, this young person's thoughts—must be gloomy. These are the assumptions that guide the present punctuation of the passage. Their overall effect is to make the speaker's hardships, rather than the husband's, the focus of the final verse paragraph, and this is surely a welcome conclusion, since the poem all along has been about her, not about her husband.

47. **feorres folclandes**. The genitive implies that he is exiled *to* rather than *from* a 'distant country' (as observed by Klinck, appealing to Mitchell 1985b: §1399).

49. **wætere beflōwen on drēor-sele**. Most interpret *beflōwan* to mean 'flow around', suggesting that the husband is surrounded by water. But it is dubitable whether the participle to such an intransitive verb can describe the husband if the prefix means 'around'. In the only other places in which the word occurs, in the compounds *tō-beflōwan* (Lambeth Psalter, glossing *affluant*) and *on-beflōwe* (in a gloss on a hymn, corresponding to *effluat*), the sense of the verb is 'move by flowing'. That is, rather than signifying 'around', *be-* has perfective force (or transitivizing force in a past participle), as it often does. Hence it may be best to translate 'conveyed by water to desolate lodgings', referring simply to the husband's sea journey.

52. **biþ** represents a verity rather than a wish.

Old English Versification

With Particular Attention to the Eight Poems

In Modern English, most traditional verse forms evince one or another pattern of stresses occurring at evenly spaced temporal or syllabic intervals, producing a regular beat, and the end of the verse line is often marked by rhyme. These formal properties are employed in some other European poetic traditions as well, such as German and Russian. But poetry in most other languages conforms to different compositional rules altogether, employing different formal properties. Thus Greek and Latin meters are based on feet and lines of predetermined syllable count and weight to which stress and rhyme are irrelevant; most Old Irish verse is based on a combination of syllable count, a fixed caesura, a restricted cadence, and rhyming classes of consonants; Classical Chinese verse makes use of rhyme, approximate uniformity of line length, and tonal balance; and Japanese verse is structured only by syllable count. Old English poetry also differs from Modern English in this respect: it clearly does not conform to any pattern like iambic pentameter or dactylic hexameter. The formal rules according to which Anglo-Saxon poets composed are not known, but even if scholarship has not succeeded in recovering those rules, or even in reaching a consensus about what linguistic properties the rules ought to take into account, nearly three centuries of study of alliterative meters in Old English and related languages have given us a good idea of what are and are not standard metrical patterns in this type of verse. It is possible to distinguish the standard and the nonstandard for two reasons: (1) The surviving corpus of Old English verse, at some 30,000 lines, is large enough to show that certain patterns of stressed and unstressed syllables are common or rare. For example, the pattern reflected in the words **rihtliċe lifie** is not uncommon in prose, but as a verse type it is vanishingly rare. (2) Poetry in Old Saxon, Old High

German, and Old Icelandic is obviously based on similar formal principles, and yet the different structures of these languages allow us to perceive commonalities that point to fundamental principles. In the case of Old Icelandic we also have an early thirteenth-century tract on verse composition, called *Háttatal,* by the Icelandic scholar Snorri Sturluson, a tract that, though tantalizingly vague at some crucial junctures, does lend some support to the conclusions of modern metrical study.[1]

The current, fairly broad consensus about standard and nonstandard verse types is largely the product of the metrical studies of Eduard Sievers (1885–87, 1893, 1905), who synthesized the work of some brilliant predecessors and worked out even more inspired ideas of his own to develop a comprehensive and memorable analysis of meters in all the early Germanic languages. Though today most metrists doubt the theoretical adequacy of Sievers' analysis, few dispute its descriptive accuracy. As a result, even scholars whose methods of scansion differ widely from Sievers' usually regard his basic metrical types as a touchstone, and the efficacy of alternative systems is generally gauged by their ability to account for the regularities uncovered by Sievers. Accordingly, the analysis of verse forms presented in the following pages is that of Sievers, modified slightly in the light of subsequent findings.

The metrical form is predicated on the binding together of two verses by a carefully controlled system of initial rhyme, loosely called ALLITERATION. Such a combination is often referred to as the ALLITERATIVE LONG LINE, or simply the line, because in modern editions the pair of verses is printed as a single line, usually with a space in the middle (sometimes called the CAESURA) to separate the first half-line from the second. The metrical form, however, was invented long before the literary period, and when poems came to be written down, the scribes copied them continuously across the page as if they were prose, marking the metrical form, if at all, merely by points between verses.[2] Hence, although it is convenient to speak of

---

[1] There is a dependable translation by Faulkes (1987: 165–220).

[2] Even Latin poetry at this period was usually written continuously across the page, the verses being marked by punctuation only. See, for example, the scribal treatment of Bede's alphabetic elegiacs in the Moore MS of his *Ecclesiastical History,* f. 86ᵛ

lines and half-lines, the poets themselves almost certainly thought rather of verses and verse pairs, as Snorri does in *Háttatal*. In what follows, the first half-line will sometimes be called the ON-VERSE, the second the OFF-VERSE.[3]

Each verse is typically marked by some degree of syntactic discreteness. The syntactic coherence of the single verse is rarely disturbed: the boundaries of words and phrases within the verse are usually less conspicuous than those between verses. Thus it is unusual, for example, to find an attributive adjective at the close of one verse modifying a noun at the opening of the next.[4]

In addition to being syntactically discrete, each verse conforms to one of several familiar patterns of stress. The patterns are fundamentally similar for the two halves of the verse line, but a slight imbalance in the line (examined below) results from a characteristic difference in weight between its two components: the on-verse is freer (and often heavier), permitting a wider variety of verse types. Some alliterative and syllabic patterns thus tend to be restricted to one or the other half of the line, and as a result, the majority of verse pairs employed are metrically irreversible. Occasionally a verse without a mate is encountered—there are examples at *Maldon* 172 and *Seafarer* 16—but these occur at about the rate at which one would expect them to be produced by scribal error, and accordingly most metrists do not regard them as intentional departures from the canonical form.[5] Although poetry in Old Icelandic is strophic, being organized into stanzas of a standard length, Old English verse is stichic, lacking any division into stanzas. *Deor* is one of the few

(ed. Blair 1959). The St. Petersburg MS, f. 100ᵛ (see Arngart 1952), is exceptional in starting each verse on a new line.

[3] German *Anvers* and *Abvers*. Some metrists prefer to speak of the "*a*-verse" and the "*b*-verse"; but in oral discussion this terminology can lead to confusion with the common shorthand designations of Sievers' verses of types A and B, which are discussed below.

[4] Some possible violations of the syntactic integrity of the verse are at *Maldon* 33 and 151.

[5] For bibliographical references to arguments in favor of regarding singlets as intentional, along with counterarguments, see Fulk 1996a: 4–5. There is one poem, however, the lyric *Wulf and Eadwacer* in the Exeter Book, in which the verses are arranged in three unequal groups of lines, each of which is closed in thought and form by an unpaired verse with double alliteration.

undoubted exceptions to the rule, being marked by a refrain, itself a rarity, that closes verse groups of unequal length.

1. Alliteration and Rhyme

Regardless of their syntactic relation, verse pairs are linked by a strictly regulated variety of initial rhyme, one that is limited to the initial sounds of stressed syllables. Snorri tells us that in the skaldic verse forms of Old Icelandic it is an error for alliteration to occur more or less often than the prescribed number of times in a pair of verses, though it is a license for unstressed words to participate in the alliteration; and so it is probably best to assume that in Old English, alliteration on unstressed syllables is not art but accident.[6] Among initial consonants, alliteration is usually exact: *b* alliterates only with *b*, *d* with *d*, and so forth. It is a sign of the conservatism of the poetic tradition, however, that the two varieties of *c*—that is, *c* and *ċ*, sounds that closely resembled the initials of *kin* and *chin*, respectively, if they were not in fact identical with them—were still treated as equivalent, even though the difference in pronunciation became quite marked long before the end of the Old English period.[7] The same is true of the different varieties of *g*, and here the examples are more numerous.[8] The poet of *Maldon* is exceptional in distinguishing the two forms of *g*, doubtless because this poem

[6] Thus in **secga swāte siþþan sunne upp** (*Brunanburh* 13) the word **siþþan** does not participate in the conventional alliterative scheme because, as a conjunction, it is subordinate to the noun **sunne** and the adverb **upp**.

[7] Examples, even in *Beowulf*, are not very common, partly because words of the substantive class beginning with *c* are not especially numerous in poetry, and most of those that do appear have the *k* sound in all dialects. Three examples in the normalized text of *The Seafarer* depend on **ċeald** 'cold', but the word took the form **cald**, with the *k* sound, in Anglian, the probable dialect of the poem's composition; and one in *The Wanderer* involves the dubitable palatal affricate of the accusative **ċeare**. There are just two persuasive instances in the eight poems: *Seafarer* 5, involving **ċēol** 'ship'; and *Maldon* 76, involving the proper name **Ċēola**.

[8] See *Brunanburh* 44; *Rood* 7, 16, 18, 39, 77, 146 (but with West Saxon **ġealg** instead of Anglian **galg**); *Wanderer* 22, 35, 52, 73; *Seafarer* 40, 62, 83, 92, 101; and *Deor* 15.

was composed so late in the period.[9] When a syllable begins with two or more consonants, all may alliterate (as do those beginning with *sw* at *Maldon* 118), but usually only the first is actually required to do so. Exceptional are the combinations *sc* (originally a consonant cluster), *sp,* and *st,* each of which normally alliterates only with itself.[10]

What is called VOCALIC ALLITERATION depends not on the likeness of initial vowels but the absence of initial consonants: any two stressed syllables beginning with vowels are considered sufficiently alike to alliterate with each other, no matter how similar or different the vowels may be. The poets in fact generally avoid the alliteration of identical vowels (Snorri tells us that in Old Icelandic verse this was considered inelegant) and make no distinction between vowels and diphthongs. Typical examples are *Cædmon's Hymn* 4, where ēċe alliterates with ōr, and *Brunanburh* 1, where Æðelstān alliterates with **eorla.** Clearly, then, vocalic alliteration has little in common with assonance. Some scholars believe (as did Sievers) that vocalic alliteration was at least originally a matching of syllable onsets beginning with a glottal stop—the sound heard twice in the expression *Uh-oh,* in the sense 'Something's wrong', produced by closure of the glottis. This is a phenomenon that has been observed locally among Germanic and other speakers, and it would have provided a recognizable consonant.

---

[9] In *Maldon* the velar stop (i.e., *g* pronounced as in Modern English *go*) alliterates in some twenty lines (13, 32, etc.), the palatal continuant alone (ġ pronounced more or less like *y* in *year*) in two (84, 274). In lines 32 and 192 there would be forbidden double alliteration in the off-verse if the two sounds were equated, whereas both lines alliterate regularly if the velar and palatal sounds are assumed not to alliterate with each other. Evidently the poet wished to observe a distinction. Hence in lines 100 and 265, where palatal ġ heads the first stressed syllable of each member of the verse pair, the velar *g* of the second stressed syllable of the on-verse is not to be included in the alliterative scheme. Note that although the preposition **onġēan** (100) precedes its object, in similar verses it requires stress, as it does at *Elene* 43, *Juliana* 628, and *Beowulf* 1034. Possibly *The Wife's Lament* is intended to conform to the same rules as *Maldon,* since ġ alliterates only with ġ (1, 42).

[10] The digraph *sc* alliterates at *Brunanburh* 11, 19, *Rood* 54, and *Maldon* 40, 56, 98, 136; *st* at *Rood* 30, 40, 62, 71, *Maldon* 19, 25, 122, 127, 249, 301, and *The Wife's Lament* 48; *sp* (the rarest) at *Maldon* 34, 137. At *Maldon* 271, **stende** is probably not intended to alliterate with **sealde**; this line most likely has rhyme in place of alliteration, as remarked below.

The number and position of the alliterating syllables is limited by rule. Most verses have two syllables that are more strongly stressed than others. In the off-verse the first of these two must alliterate and the second must not.[11] In the on-verse, one or both may alliterate, but the choice depends upon relative stress. In on-verses containing two stressed syllables, the first regularly alliterates unless it is decidedly weaker than the second. This principle is known as the RULE OF PRECEDENCE.[12] Thus in **ēċe dryhten** (*Cædmon's Hymn* 4a, 8a), **ēċe** takes alliterative precedence of **dryhten** because they are both heavily stressed and **ēċe** comes first. In **nū sculon herian** (1a), on the other hand, the infinitive **herian**, though it comes last, takes alliterative precedence of **nū** and **sculon** because infinitives are more heavily stressed than adverbs and finite verbs (see below).[13] In certain types of rather heavy on-verses DOUBLE ALLITERATION is more or less obligatory—that is, both stressed syllables in the verse must alliterate. Hence, observing only the strongest syllables in the line or verse pair and representing those that alliterate by *a*, those that do not by *x* and *y,* the following patterns will represent the usual practice. Each of the three types is illustrated by a line of *Cædmon's Hymn* with the alliterating unit (or STAVE) underscored:

(1) a a : a x   metodes meahta   and his mōd-ġeþanc

(2) a x : a y   hē ǣrest scōp   ielda bearnum

(3) x a : a y   nū sculon herian   heofon-rīċes weard

---

[11] Exceptions are rare in the metrically stricter poems, and the few that turn up in the manuscripts may be laid to the charge of scribes. Four more or less plausible exceptions appear in *Maldon,* a poem with some notable divergences from the metrical norms of most Old English poetry, at 45b, 75b, and 288b (where the second stressed syllable alliterates instead of the first), and 29b (where both stressed syllables alliterate). Scragg (1981: 69) mistakes the inclusion of 29b in this group for something other than an observation about what is normal in verse. His notion is that *s* and *sn* do not alliterate with each other in *Maldon.* But this is not the case in other poetry; the alliteration in 271 and 282 tells against such a restriction on *s*-clusters; and the point cannot be proved for so short a text, with so few instances of initial *sn.*

[12] The rule is often attributed to Sievers and named after him, though in actuality the principle was first recognized by Rieger (1876: 18–34, esp. 24–25).

[13] At *Maldon* 80a, 242a, and 298a the rule is broken: here it is the second of two words of equal stress that bears the alliteration. The rule is also broken at *Maldon* 7a, where **lēt** illegitimately takes precedence of **handum.**

Rhyme, it should be said, is not a regular feature of traditional Germanic verse. Its consistent use as a means of linking verses appears first in Latin hymns. Yet it occurs as an embellishment, usually in *addition* to alliteration, in some poems. It is used this way in two notable passages in poems by Cynewulf, *Elene* 1236–50 and *Christ II* 591–96, as well as in *The Riming Poem* in the Exeter Book, where the effort to achieve both rhyme and alliteration throughout leads to frequent obscurity of diction. Among the eight poems, only *Maldon* shows persuasive instances of intentional rhyme:

> Byrhtnōþ maðelode,   bord hafenode (42)
> Byrhtwold maðelode,   bord hafenode (309)
> æfre ymbe stunde   hē sealde sume wunde (271)
> Siġebyrhtes brōðor   and swiðe maniġ ōðer (282)

The metrical patterns of the last two of these lines are unusual enough to suggest that the poet has sacrificed meter for the sake of rhyme, as indeed Cynewulf does in some of the lines in *Christ II* mentioned above.

2. Syllables and Stress

In West Germanic verse, a single consonant between vowels belongs to the start of the second syllable rather than to the end of the first. Thus **weras** 'men' is divided **we-ras**. In verse, any stressed syllable that ends in a short vowel or short diphthong is light, like the first syllable in **weras**. On the other hand, uninflected **wer** represents a heavy syllable, since it is closed by a consonant. So also the first syllable in **bindan** is heavy, since it does not end in a short vowel (note that the syllable is closed by the consonant *n,* since the word is syllabified **bin-dan**); and the first syllable of **hieran** is also heavy, since it does not end in a short vowel but in a long diphthong under the syllabification **hie-ran**. But the first syllable of **ġietan** is light, since diphthongs and vowels are treated alike. In sum, then, a stressed syllable is heavy if it contains a long vowel or a long diphthong or if it is closed by a consonant; otherwise it is short. Another way to schematize this is in terms of MORAE. A mora is a unit of phonological length: every consonant and every short vowel or short diphthong comprises one mora, while a long vowel or a long diphthong comprises two. Some linguists in fact represent a short vowel or diphthong by the symbol V and a long one by VV to reflect this difference. A light syllable then ends in a single mora, while a heavy one ends in two or more. Taking C to signify any consonant, we can represent the distinction as follows:

$$\text{Light: we(ras)} = \text{CV} \qquad \text{Heavy:} \quad \begin{array}{l} \text{wer} = \text{CVC} \\ \text{bin(dan)} = \text{CVC} \\ \text{bī(dan)} = \text{CVV} \end{array}$$

It has been said that the reason for the popularity of iambic pentameter as a poetic meter in English is that it approximates the rhythm of everyday speech. So, too, the structure of Old English verses is predicated on stress patterns resembling those that must have prevailed in normal discourse. As in Modern English, sentence stress is related to meaning: words with a significant amount of meaning attached to them are stressed. In the sentence *A new king came to the throne,* the words that receive the most stress are the lexically significant ones, the nouns (*king, throne*) and the adjective (*new*); the function words, on the other hand—the words that serve chiefly a syntactic function (*A, to, the*)—go unstressed, as a result of which their vowels may all be reduced to schwa (the sound of the first vowel in *about*) in rapid speech. The verb (*came*) occupies a middle tier in the hierarchy of stress: it need not receive as much stress as the nouns and the adjective, but it is more heavily stressed than the function words, as shown by the fact that its vowel cannot be reduced to schwa. Stress in Old English seems quite similar, since three comparable categories of words have been identified. Nouns and adjectives are always stressed, and usually there is stress on nonfinite verb forms (participles and infinitives)[14] and on many

---

[14] An exception is to be found at *Maldon* 39b, where the infinitive **niman** is unstressed; also **wesan** at *Wife's Lament* 42b; and probably **weorðan** at *Wanderer* 64a.

adverbs (almost always if the adverb has more than one syllable). These words may be called STRESS-WORDS. Words that generally carry little meaning of their own, but are entirely dependent upon the following word, may be called PROCLITICS. These include prepositions, conjunctions, and, when they are in attributive position, demonstratives (sē, þēs) and possessive adjectives (mīn, ūre, etc.). These are almost never stressed as long as there is nothing out of the ordinary about the syntax of the clause.[15] In a loosely constituted middle tier between these two groups are PARTICLES, which may or may not receive stress, depending on their position in the sentence. These include finite verbs (i.e., those inflected for person, tense, etc.); demonstrative and certain other common adverbs, mostly monosyllabic (þā, þonne, þǽr, oft, ǽr, etc.); personal pronouns (iċ, þē, etc.); and demonstrative pronouns (sē and þēs when used as pronouns).[16]

Even proclitics, however, may be stressed if they come to be displaced from their normal position in the syntax. Occasionally a preposition will not precede its object, as in **siþþan hine Nīþhād on** (*Deor* 5a), and in that case it is stressed. So also when a demonstrative adjective is postposed it is stressed, as in **heofones þisses** (*Meters of Boethius* 24.3b). Similarly for particles, whether or not they are stressed depends entirely on their position. In Modern English, the verb *is* is usually unstressed, but when the syntax places it at the end of the clause it takes on stress, as in the sentence *You know what it is*. So also in Old English, particles displaced from their normal position are stressed. The natural place for particles is in a group (called a DROP or "dip" or "thesis," German

---

[15] An exception is in the verse **ġeond þās weorold** (*Wanderer* 58b, like *Deor* 31b), where the demonstrative bears the alliteration, and thus the primary stress. This exception seems to have a semantic basis: although the demonstrative þēs/þēos/þis is normally unstressed in front of a noun it modifies (as at *Wanderer* 62b, 89a, etc.), in references to "this world" or "this life" (as at *The Phoenix* 151b, *Judith* 66b, *Beowulf* 197, etc.) it is stressed, presumably to indicate a contrast with the next world.

[16] The terms "stress-words," "proclitics," and "particles" correspond roughly to the terms *Satzteile, Satzteilpartikeln,* and *Satzpartikeln* used by Kuhn (1933). Kuhn's conception of these categories is more fluid, though: under his analysis a word may be alternately a *Satzpartikel* and a *Satzteilpartikel,* depending on its position in the clause. For references to the substantial literature on Kuhn's laws, see Momma 1997; also Gade and Fulk 2000: §§II.D.2, III.F.

Senkung) either directly before or directly after the first stress of the clause, but not divided up between these two positions. Particles displaced from this natural position normally take stress. After Hans Kuhn, who first formulated it, this principle is known as KUHN'S FIRST LAW, or the *Satzpartikelgesetz*.[17] Thus, for example, in the verse **sorg biþ ġeniewod** (*Wanderer* 50b) the verb **biþ** is assignable to the first drop of the verse clause, where it may be unstressed, as it is in this case; a few lines later, in **hū gǣstliċ biþ** (73b), the word **hū** occupies the first drop, the first stress falling on **gǣst-**, and so **biþ** must be stressed. Similarly, **oft** is stressed at *Wanderer* 40b (**oft ġebindaþ**), where although it begins a verse it occupies the middle of a clause; but the word is unstressed at *Seafarer* 24b (**full oft þæt earn beġeall**), where it is in the cluster of particles at the beginning of a clause.[18] Kuhn's first law has provoked much discussion in recent years, but the debate is not so much about whether it accurately describes the distribution and stress of particles in verse as about its autonomy as a metricosyntactic principle. It is less a prescription for verse construction than a description of patterns actually found in verse, and when there is little ambiguity in the syntax it is a rather accurate description: see in particular Donoghue 1997: 69–76.

So far the only sort of stress examined has been phrasal stress, determining which words receive prosodic emphasis within syntactic units. Lexical stress, governing which syllables within a word

---

[17] "Particles are stressed unless they appear in the first drop of the verse clause." For the reason explained in the preceding note, Kuhn's actual formulation is somewhat different: "Particles are located in the first drop of the clause, in proclisis to either the first or the second stressed word" (1933: 8).

[18] Note that although particles are required to take stress outside the first drop of the clause, they are not conversely required to remain unstressed in the first drop. If the case were otherwise there would be no stress at all in the verse **swā hē hwīlum ǣr** (*Wanderer* 43b), since it contains only particles and opens a clause. In a string of particles a finite verb is particularly likely to take stress, since verbs have more meaning than other particles. If all this is too confusing, the following rule of thumb may prove useful until the distinctions among stress-words, particles, and proclitics become familiar: if the particle is not at the end of the verse (and so it is not unambiguous), scan the verse without stressing the particle; if that does not produce an acceptable verse type, stress the particle. The alliteration of course is also an aid to identifying stressed syllables.

are stressed, also plays a significant role in scansion. Sievers assumes three degrees of lexical stress. PRIMARY STRESS usually falls on the first syllable of a stressed word. Among nouns the only exceptions are words that begin with one of the three prefixes ġe-, be-, and (inconsistently) for-. Compound adverbs, prepositions, and conjunctions are commonly stressed on the second constituent (to-samne, on-ġēan, on-weġ, for-þām, etc.). With verbs the stress consistently falls on the root, and if the word bears a prefix, that remains unstressed: thus there is stress only after the prefix in to-brecan, for-lǣtan, and ofer-cuman. That is, these three verbs alliterate on *b, l,* and *c,* respectively. The same prefixes when attached to nouns, however, are usually stressed, as with tō-hyht 'hope' and ofer-mōd (with vocalic alliteration at *Maldon* 89b).[19]

A HALF-STRESS falls on most middle syllables of words. It always falls on the root syllable of the second element of a compound. In a true compound the second constituent is recognizable as a word in its own right, and a compound is usually distinguished from a sequence of two words in that the first element is uninflected.[20] Thus ān-haga (*Wanderer* 1), mōd-ċeariġ (2), lagu-lāde (3), hrīm-ċeald (4), and so forth are all compounds. According to Sievers, half-stress also falls on all heavy middle syllables of trisyllabic words even when they are not compounds. Thus there is half-stress on the second syllable of frēondlēasne (*Wanderer* 28a, where -lēas is a derivational suffix rather than a compound element), æðelinga (*Seafarer* 93a), and wealdendes (*Rood* 17b). This type of half-stress is different from that in compounds, however: the half-stress on wealdendes, for example, is lost when the word is uninflected, so that wealdend bears no stress on the final syllable. In hrīm-ċeald, on the other hand, there is half-stress on the second constituent even though no inflectional syllable follows. For this reason a good many metrists distinguish the two kinds of half-stress, referring to that on

---

[19] Linguists explain the differential treatment of prefixes with verbs and nouns (or adjectives) by assuming that at the prehistoric time when patterns of lexical stress were established, prefixes on verbs were still regarded as separate words, while those on nouns and adjectives had become attached to the stem.

[20] Certain combinations of genitive plus noun, however, are treated by editors as compounds, e.g., Hrefna-wudu and Hrefnes-holt in *Beowulf*.

true compounds as SECONDARY STRESS and the other sort as
TERTIARY STRESS.[21] Central to the distinction is the understanding
that derivational suffixes such as **-dōm**, **-ness**, **-fæst**, **-hād**, and **-full**
do not form true compounds but QUASI-COMPOUNDS. They retain no
stress when uninflected, but they gain a half-stress when an inflec-
tional ending is added. Dithematic personal names are treated the
same way: thus **Godrīċ** (*Maldon* 321a) bears no half-stress, while
Þurstānes (298a) does.

All syllables that lack primary stress or half-stress are unstressed.
Inflectional syllables, then, are all unstressed. Generally, in fact, a
final syllable will bear no stress; but there are two sorts of excep-
tions. The second constituent of a compound, again, will bear initial
stress, as with **hrīm-ċeald**. Additionally, word stress frequently is
dependent upon morphology: **reord-berendum** has a pattern of de-
scending stress, with primary stress on the first syllable, secondary
on the second, tertiary on the third, and no stress on the inflectional
ending; but **earfoþlīċe** 'with difficulty' (made up of **earfoþ-** 'diffi-
cult' plus the adverb suffix **-līċe**) has stress on the first and third
syllables and none on the second and fourth. Likewise the adjective
earfoþlīċ bears a degree of stress on the final syllable.

3. Sievers' Basic Verse Types

The three levels of stress outlined above define the three funda-
mental metrical constituents of a verse. These are termed the LIFT,
the HALF-LIFT, and the DROP.[22] A lift (represented $\acute{-}$) is normally a
heavy syllable bearing primary stress, the first stress in a word. A

---

[21] It is debated whether tertiary stress really existed as a degree of stress distin-
guishable from absence of stress or whether syllable weight alone will account for its
effects. Whatever it represents, it remains a useful concept. There is also disagree-
ment about how to define secondary stress: is it the stress found on the second ele-
ments of compounds or should it be defined positionally as a full stress demoted to a
half-stress by its position immediately after another full stress? Sievers' treatment
vacillates between these definitions.

[22] Sievers' terms are *Hebung, Nebenhebung,* and *Senkung.*

half-lift (represented $\smile$) bears half-stress. A drop (represented × or × × or × × ×, etc.) is a group of one or more unstressed syllables. The symbol | marks the foot division, a concept rejected now by most metrists but retained here as a component of Sievers' analysis. If each verse comprises four metrical positions, the allowable combinations of these three constituents produce five basic verse types, designated A through E in their order of frequency:

A: $\acute{} × | \acute{} ×$ ēċe dryhten (C 4a); ōr astealde (C 4b)[23]

B: × $\acute{}$ | × $\acute{}$ hē ǣrest scōp (C 5a); þā middan-ġeard (C7a)[24]

C: × $\acute{}$ | $\acute{}$ ×   on lāst leġdon (B 22a); fram cnēo-māgum (B 8a)

D: $\acute{}$ | $\acute{}$ $\acute{}$ ×   frēa ælmihtiġ (C 9b); heard-sǣliġne (L 19a)

E: $\acute{}$ $\acute{}$ × | $\acute{}$ andlangne dæġ (B 21a); æsc-holt ascōc (M 230b)

In the first foot of the verse a drop may comprise several syllables. In the second foot a drop is usually one syllable, rarely two, almost never three. A drop at the end of the verse (found only in types A, C, and D) may not comprise more than one syllable. The following are verses with expanded drops:

A: mēċa ġemānan (B 40a); fǣġe tō ġefeohte (B 28a)

B: þæt hīe æt campe oft (B 8b); mē sendon tō þē (M 29a)

C: ofer dēop wæter (B 55a); þāra-þe mid Anlāfe (B 26a)

E: wæl-reste ġeċēas (M 113b)

Normally a lift requires a heavy stressed syllable. But when a lift or a half-lift follows immediately upon another it may be a light syllable. Sievers represents these as $\lor$ and $\land$, as in these examples:

---

[23] Now and hereafter, as in the glossary, the eight poems are designated as follows: C = *Cædmon's Hymn*, B = *The Battle of Brunanburh*, R = *The Dream of the Rood*, M = *The Battle of Maldon*, W = *The Wanderer*, S = *The Seafarer*, D = *Deor*, and L = *The Wife's Lament*.

[24] Note that if secondary stress is defined as the stress that falls on the second constituent of a compound (see above, n. 21), then the last syllable of **middan-ġeard** receives secondary stress but nonetheless serves as a full lift. There is a similar mismatch in the examples of type C that follow immediately. These peculiarities are one consequence of Sievers' conception of secondary stress.

C: ofer brād brimu (B71a: × × ‿́ | ⌣ ×)
D: self cunnie (S 35b: ‿́ | ‿́ ⌣ ×)
   reord-berendum (R 89b: ‿́ | ⌣ ‿́ ×)
E: earfoþa dǽl (D 30b: ‿́ ⌣ × | ‿́)

Although a lift is normally a heavy syllable, it may be replaced by a combination of a light syllable and another syllable of any weight—in much the same way that a dactyl (— ⌣ ⌣) in the epic meters of Greek and Latin may be replaced by a spondee (— —) in many positions in the verse. This phenomenon is referred to as RESOLUTION (German *Auflösung*), and the two syllables involved are said to be "resolved." Resolution is compulsory in full lifts except, as noted above, when another lift immediately precedes. In half-lifts resolution is not compulsory, and in fact except in *Beowulf* it is uncommon when a full lift immediately precedes.[25] Unstressed syllables are not resolved. The symbols for resolved lifts and half-lifts are ⌣̣× and ⌣̣×, and the following examples illustrate resolution and non-resolution:

A: cyning and æðeling (B 58a: ⌣̣× × | ⌣̣× ×)
B: þāra þe him biþ eġesa tō mē (R 86b: × × × × × ⌣̣× | × × ‿́)
C: þām-þe þǽr bryne þolodon (R 149b: × × × ⌣̣× | ⌣̣× ×)
   on þām eorþ-scræfe (L 28b: × × ‿́ | ⌣ ×)
D: lucon lagu-strēamas (M 66a: ⌣̣× | ⌣̣× ‿́ ×)
   nearu niht-wacu (S 7a: ⌣̣× | ‿́ ⌣ ×)
E: heofon-rīċes weard (C 1b: ⌣̣× ‿́ × | ‿́)

Some verses may begin with one extrametrical syllable, rarely two. This phenomenon is referred to as ANACRUSIS (German *Auftakt*).[26] Naturally, anacrusis is theoretically possible only in verse types that normally begin with a lift (A, D, and E); but in fact while it is not infrequent in type A, it is not very common in type D, and it probably does not occur in type E. Anacrusis is extremely rare in

[25] There are examples at W 33a and S 23a.
[26] It should be noted that in some German studies of meter, *Auftakt* refers not solely to anacrusis but also to an initial drop.

the off-verse, where it normally occurs only with a particular sub-
type of type A. Examples, in all of which the first syllable is ana-
crustic, are the following:

A: ġebiddaþ him tō þissum bēacne (R 83a: × | ⏑́ × × × × × | ⏑́ ×)
   ġewiton him þā Norð-menn (B 53a: × | ⏑⏑ × × × | ⏑́ ⏑́)
D: behēold hrēow-ċeariġ (R 25a: × | ⏑́ | ⏑́ ⏑ ×)

In words ending in a liquid or a nasal consonant (*l, r, n, m*) that
has become syllabic in the course of the development of Old Eng-
lish (as with **wundor, tācen, bēacen, māðum**, and others, all origi-
nally monosyllabic) the vowel before the final consonant is fre-
quently to be disregarded. Thus **wuldor**, for example, must often be
scanned as a monosyllable, as it probably should be in **weorc wul-
dor-fæder** (C 3a).[27] There is a similar probability of monosyl-
labicity in **ealdor-** (B 3b), **hungor** (S 11b), **māðum-** (W 92b),
morðor- (L 20b) and **wǣpen** (M 130b). Monosyllabic pronuncia-
tion of most of these words is a prehistoric phenomenon, and so
monosyllabic scansion is a sign of an awareness of ancient conven-
tions in the conservative traditions of verse. For that reason it seems
likely that poems with a high incidence of monosyllabism are rela-
tively early compositions; but the phenomenon may occur in poems
of any age, as demonstrated by the examples in *Brunanburh* and
Maldon. Conversely, vowels and diphthongs that result from con-
traction after the loss of intervocalic *h* or *w* must often be scanned
as two syllables: **slēan** 'strike', for example, from **slahan*, must
often be given a disyllabic scansion. The only unambiguous exam-
ple of such disyllabicity in the eight poems is in the word **frēan** (L
33a); but a likely instance is **flēogan** (M 275a), which appears to be
a scribal substitution for **flēon** (like **hēagum**, at *Genesis A* 8b, for
hēam: see Scragg 1981: 82), giving a more usual metrical type.[28]
So, too, some vowels are purely scribal and must be ignored in
scansion: to let one example stand for many, the word **hāliġe** is

---

[27] The reason for classifying this verse as belonging to type C rather than B is that
the poets seem to have avoided compounds with a structure like ***hilde-fruma**, as
demonstrated by Terasawa (1994).

[28] On type B3 see below.

etymologically two syllables, **hāl̇ġe**, with analogical **-i-** imported from the nominative **hāliġ**. Thus, the manuscript reading *halige* (R 11b) is normalized to **hāl̇ġe** in the edited text.

4. Metrical Subtypes

Sievers divided his five types into various subtypes, and it is often useful to be aware of these more particular varieties when scanning verse. The following are the subtypes that Sievers recognized:

Type A: Basic form, *lift, drop, lift, drop*. Subtypes:

A1: All the verses of type A examined so far are of type A1. There is alliteration on the first lift or (in the on-verse only) on both lifts. The first drop is known to have as many as five extra syllables; the second has just one. The minimal form with four syllables to the verse is very common.[29]

A2: A half-lift serves as a drop in either foot, or in both. Because of their relative heaviness, verses of this type usually have double alliteration, and those that do are restricted naturally to the on-verse. Sievers distinguishes three varieties of type A2:

(a) **A2a** has a half-stress in the first drop, as in **ferhþ-loca frēoriġ** (W 33a: $\acute{\ }\smile\times \mid \acute{\ }\times$). The second lift may be short, following, as it does, a heavy or resolved stressed syllable, as in **Bord-weall clufon** (B 5b: $\acute{\ }\grave{\ }\mid \smile\times$). Sievers labels the former type **A2l** and the latter **A2k**, where **l** and **k** stand for *lang* and *kurz* ('long' and 'short').

(b) **A2b** has a half-stress in the second drop, as in **fǣ ġer feorh-bold** (R 73a: $\acute{\ }\times \mid \acute{\ }\grave{\ }$)

(c) **A2ab** has half-stresses in both drops, as in **brēost-hord blōd-rēow** (*Beowulf* 1719a: $\acute{\ }\grave{\ }\mid \acute{\ }\grave{\ }$). There are no examples in the eight poems.

---

[29] The verse **wyrd biþ full arǣdd** (W 5b) would appear to be unclassifiable. In actuality it belongs to type A1: *The Wanderer* is presumably an Anglian composition, and the Anglian form of West Saxon **arǣdd** is **arǣded**. Cf. **onsended** (R 49b) for West Saxon **onsend**.

A3: Sievers describes this type as having alliteration only on the second lift. Most metrists today instead describe it as having just one lift, and that is the analysis adopted in this book. For example, Sievers would stress the first and fourth syllables of **nū sculon herian**, but today most stress only the infinitive: × × × | ‿ ×.[30] Such verses are sometimes referred to as LIGHT VERSES, and naturally because of the requirements of alliteration they can occur only in the on-verse.[31] When the second drop contains a half-stress, Sievers calls the type **A3b**: examples are **ġewiton him þā Norð-menn** (B 53a: × × × × × | ‿ ‿) and **ā scyle ġęong mann** (L 42a: × × × | ‿ ‿).

Type B: Basic form, *drop, lift, drop, lift*. Subtypes:

B1: The second drop contains one syllable, as in **and his sunu forlēt** (B 42b: × × ‿× | × ‿), **þā middan-ġeard** (C7a: × ‿ | × ‿), and **swā hē ǣr on þām bēame dyde** (R 114b: × × × × × ‿ | × ‿×).

B2: The second drop contains two syllables, as in **þāra þe him biþ eġesa tō mē** (R 86b: × × × × × ‿× | × × ‿) and **þe meċ on þissum life beġeat** (L 41b: × × × × × ‿ | × × ‿).[32]

B3: By analogy to type A3 Sievers assumes that in type B as well the first lift may fail to alliterate. An example is **ġesiehþ him beforan** (W 46a: × × × × ‿×), in which the alliteration is on *f*. The type is extremely rare, and many metrists regard it not as a genuine metrical variety but as the result of textual corruption.[33]

---

[30] The ending -**ian** of weak verbs of the *first* class (like **herian**) is generally assumed to have consonantal *i* (*j*), like the Modern English *y* in *year,* and is therefore monosyllabic, whereas in weak verbs of the *second* class (like **clipian**), though the ending is spelt the same way, the *i* forms a separate syllable.

[31] Many verses of this kind contain nonalliterating finite verbs, as in the example given (**sculon**), and as a consequence some metrists assume that even alliterating finite verbs are frequently unstressed; but this view is heavily contested and is not adopted here.

[32] The verse **oþ-þæt Heorrenda nū** (D 39b) is unusual. It is probably best analyzed as belonging to type B2, with rare tertiary stress in the second drop, which usually accommodates only unstressed syllables. The type with three syllables in the second drop occurs rarely, as at S 40b–41b.

[33] Such an explanation is in fact possible in the instance of the manuscript reading **wæron mine fet** (S 9a). For the sake of the meter, some would change **fēt** to **fōtas**, and others would alter the word order (for references see Muir 1994: 2.506). Textual corruption is suggested by the fact that not only is the verse type very rare but the verse violates Kuhn's first law, which demands stress on **wæron**. If we substitute

Type C: Basic form, *drop, lift, lift, drop*. Subtypes:

C1: There is no resolution of the first lift. Examples: **and ġewiss wǣrum** (S 110a: × × $\_\!\_$ | $\_\!\_$ ×) and **þonne hit ǣniġ mǣþ wǣre** (M 195b: × × × × × $\_\!\_$ | $\_\!\_$ ×).

C2: The first lift is resolved, as in **mid ġemete healdan** (S 111b: × × ‿× | $\_\!\_$ ×) and **þām-þe þǣr bryne þolodon** (R 149b: × × × ‿× | ‿× ×).

C3: With a short second lift: **on camp-stede** (B 49a: × $\_\!\_$ | ‿ ×); **ne þurfon mē ymbe Stūrmere** (M 249a: × × × × × × $\_\!\_$ | ‿ ×).

Type D: Basic form, *lift, lift, half-lift, drop*. In all varieties of type D with secondary stress, double alliteration is more or less compulsory, and so verses of this sort are confined to the on-verse. The variety with tertiary stress may appear in either half of the line. The subclassifications are the following:

D1: The half-lift is in third position and is long. Examples: **mǣw singende** (S 22a: $\_\!\_$ | $\_\!\_$ $\_\!\_$ ×); **scadu forþ ēode** (R 54b: ‿× | $\_\!\_$ $\_\!\_$ ×).

D2: The half-lift is in third position and is short. Examples: **nearu niht-wacu** (S 7a: ‿× | $\_\!\_$ ‿ ×), **behēold hrēow-ċeariġ** (R 25a: × | $\_\!\_$ | $\_\!\_$ ‿ ×, with anacrusis), and **bord hafenode** (M42b: $\_\!\_$ | ‿× ‿ ×).

D3: The second lift is short, and the half-lift, in third position, is long. This variety is scarce, and it occurs mostly in seemingly early compositions. There is one example in the eight poems: **reord-berendum** (R 89b: $\_\!\_$ | ‿ $\_\!\_$ ×).

D4: The third and fourth positions are reversed, a drop in the third position and a half-lift in the fourth. Examples: **hrīm hrūsan band** (S 32a: $\_\!\_$ | $\_\!\_$ × $\_\!\_$) and **Bærst bordes lǣriġ** (M 284a: $\_\!\_$ | $\_\!\_$ × ‿×).[34]

D*: This type is referred to as EXPANDED. An extra syllable, rarely two or more, is inserted after the initial lift.[35] The expanded

---

fruron 'froze, were frozen', the syntactic problem is remedied; and even when used attributively, **mīne** is occasionally stressed, as at *Exodus* 262 and *Andreas* 1374, producing a verse of type E: cf. **Dēm minne dōm** (*Psalms* 118.154.1). The scribal change of **fruron** to **wǣron** is not improbable.

[34] Resolution of the half-lift is very rare. It is found just twice in *Beowulf* and once, in the verse cited here, in the eight poems.

[35] These verses would seem to violate the general rule that a verse contains four metrical positions, but Cable (1974: 80–81) explains the expansion as extrametrical

type generally demands double alliteration, because, it is thought, of the verse's relative heaviness. Naturally, because double alliteration is usual, the type is generally restricted to the on-verse. The expanded subtypes correspond in form to the unexpanded subtypes, though D*3 does not occur:

(a) **D*1: sellan sǣ-mannum** (M 38a: ́ × | ́ ́ ×); **eaforan Ēadweardes** (B 7a: ⌣× × | ́ ́ ×); **wōdon þā wæl-wulfas** (M 96a: ́ × × | ́ ́ ×). Highly unusual is the verse **anwealda ælmihtiġ** (R 153a). Perhaps it should be regarded as belonging to this type, with exceptional tertiary stress in the expansion.

(b) **D*2: beorna bēag-ġiefa** (B 2a: ́ × | ́ ⌣ ×); **healde his hordcofan** (W 14a: ́ × × | ́ ⌣ ×); **ieldu him on fareþ** (S 91a: ́ × × | ́ ⌣ ×).[36]

(c) **D*4: wēriġ, wiġes sæd** (B 20a: ́ × | ́ × ́); **bearwas blōstmum nimaþ** (S 48a: ́ × | ́ × ⌣×); **onwendeþ wyrda ġesceaft** (W 107a: × | ́ × | ́ × × ́, with anacrusis).

Type E: Basic form, *lift, half-lift, drop, lift*. Sievers identifies two subtypes; however, the second is now analyzed differently, with the result that type E is generally regarded as having no metrically significant subtypes. Some examples: **mann-cynnes weard** (C 7b: ́ ́ × | ́); **Norð-manna bregu** (B 33a: ́ ́ × | ⌣×); **wæl-reste ġeċēas** (M 113b: ́ ́ × × | ́). It may be unclear whether certain verses comprising three stressed words should be classified as belonging to type D or type E. If there is double alliteration the matter is not usually in doubt: compare **eald enta ġeweorc** (W 86a: ́ | ́ × × ́, D4) and **twelf wintra tīd** (*Beowulf* 147a: ́ ́ × | ́, E). If there is no double alliteration it is safest to rely on the syntax and semantics: normally there is greater syntactic integrity within than across foot boundaries. Hence the verse **hæġl scūrum flēag** (S 17b) is of type D1, since **scūrum** is used adverbially and thus modifies the verb; but **fela ealra ġebād** (R 125b) is of type E, since **ealra** depends on **fela**. But this analysis is controversial, as there are instances in

in the sense that it does not form a metrical position. Rather, it is a device used to relieve the clash of adjacent primary stresses in the first and second positions.

[36] Note that **on** is stressed as an adverb. See the glossary.

which the alliteration and the syntax are at odds, as in **sin-sorgna ġedrēag** (L 45a) and **hrūsan heolstre bewrāh** (W 23a).[37]

5. A Framework for the Five Types

Sievers' system of scansion captures what seem to be some of the most important facts about early Germanic meter. Moreover, by various means it is possible to show that many of his basic assumptions must be fundamentally correct. For example, the existence of resolution as a genuine metrical feature can be demonstrated by reference to the history of Icelandic verse. Just as in English, over the course of time the early Germanic verse form was abandoned and replaced by alternating stress meters—that is, by patterns of stresses occurring at evenly spaced intervals. However, resolution continued for some time to be used in the new verse forms, where its existence cannot be doubted by those who, like speakers of Modern English, are accustomed to counting syllables between stresses in their poetic meters. The reality of resolution can also be proved by statistical means.[38] Resolution in any case is a metrical principle that follows naturally from the phonological structure of Old English: because the language contains no stressed monosyllables ending in a long vowel, other stressed syllables ending in a short vowel are phonologically anomalous, and resolution removes the anomaly by serving to "lengthen" the abnormal syllables.[39] Resolution should be understood as a device that preserves the integrity of Sievers' five-type analysis. Without resolution it would be necessary, for example, to analyze the verses **his ġeworhtne wine**

---

[37] To be classified as belonging to type E this latter verse would demand the assumption of a type E* with expansion after the first lift. Most metrists do not regard this as a normal type, though there are two other examples in the eight poems (W 53b, S 79b).

[38] This point requires too complex a discussion to pursue here. For the evidence see Fulk 1996a: 6–7.

[39] This argument was first advanced by Kuryłowicz (1949); for references to more recent discussion, see Fulk 1995.

(S 115a), **on lufan dryhtnes** (S 121b), and **Norð-manna bregu** (B 33a) as comprising five positions each. The demonstrable reality of resolution as a metrical device implies the correctness of the four-position analysis, since that is the principle it is designed to enable. And the four-position analysis is the framework on which the five-type system is constructed. Thus, although the preceding discussion makes it clear that there is much disagreement about details, in the larger view the reality of resolution as an independently confirmable principle indicates that Sievers' analysis of the verse as containing four positions must be essentially correct.

Yet however useful Sievers' method of scansion may be, it does not constitute a plausible *theory* of Old English meter. That is, it does not adequately explain the patterns it identifies. The metrical system it describes is perplexing to linguists, who find its basis in a combination of syllable weight, syllable count, position count, and three or four levels of stress unparalleled in the world's languages. Whatever metrical rules Anglo-Saxon poets employed when they composed verse, those rules must have been fairly simple and easily intuited by someone to whom the Old English phonological system, with its phonemic length distinctions and lexical and phrasal stress rules, was natural. Much of the scholarly work in this area in the past half century has attempted to explain Sievers' findings in terms that are more congenial to the structure of natural languages and their prosodic systems. This is not the place to review such work, but one study may be mentioned here as an example of an attempt to discern a psychologically plausible framework for the five types.

Thomas Cable (1974) takes as fundamental Sievers' observation that verses for the most part comprise four metrical positions. He assumes that in types with adjacent primary stresses (types C, D, and E), the former of the two adjacent lifts is more prominently stressed, and the letter is therefore subordinated to it. This is a plausible assumption for a variety of reasons. It may explain, for example, why in type C the second lift is frequently short, while the first never is, unless resolved. If each verse is limited to four positions and the second of two adjacent stresses is subordinated,

Sievers' five types are the only stress patterns that can in fact occur. The point may be made graphically if we substitute pitch for stress and represent the possible combinations as follows:

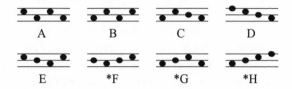

Types F, G, and H do not occur because they violate the condition that the second of two stresses must be subordinated: they would require that three of the four positions in sequence be represented as × ⌣ ⌣ in Sievers' notation, and this sequence does not occur among Sievers' types. Note that Cable's type D here does not include D4, which he groups together with E, assuming there is no metrical difference between them. Cable, it should be said, has since repudiated this analysis under the weight of certain phonological objections (see Cable 1991: 39); but regardless of whether or not the objections can be met, Cable's explanation of the structure of the five-type system remains useful as a mnemonic to those learning to scan, since it brings order to an otherwise sometimes confusing array of metrical types.

6. Hypermetric Verses

The metrical patterns examined so far are those of so-called NORMAL VERSES. A second metrical variety comprises HYPERMETRIC VERSES (German *Schwellverse*), so called because the metrical pattern is somewhat more elaborated than in the normal type. There are fewer than 500 hypermetric lines in the Old English corpus, but they are of some importance in this book because three of the eight poems contain hypermetric passages. Lone pairs of verses in the hypermetric meter (as at R 133 and S 103) do occur in the corpus— even lone verses (as at S 23a), if these are not simply scribal errors or alterations—but for the most part hypermetric verses appear in clusters, as they do at R 8–10, 20–23, 30–34, 39–43, 46–49, 59–69, W 111–15, and S 106–9. The purpose of the alternation between normal and hypermetric forms is not known for certain, but a tendency has been observed for hypermetricity to be associated with an elevated tone. Thus the generalizing lessons of *The Wanderer* and *The Seafarer* are cast in the hypermetric mode, and in *Genesis A,* God tends to speak in hypermetrics.

There is no more agreement about how to analyze hypermetric verses than normal ones; but, once again following the lead of Sievers, as a first approximation it may be useful to think of a hypermetric verse as being like a normal one with an extra foot prefixed to it.[40] In the on-verse this entails alliteration on the added foot. Thus **fǣġre ǣt foldan scēatum** (R 8a) might be analyzed as containing the stress pattern of a normal verse of type A1 (**foldan scēatum**) preceded by an extra foot (**fǣġre ǣt**), yielding a scansion $\acute{\hphantom{x}} \times \times \mid \acute{\hphantom{x}} \times \mid \acute{\hphantom{x}} \times$; similarly **aleġdon hīe þǣr lim-wēriġne** (R 63a) contains a normal D1 pattern (**lim-wēriġne**) with an extra foot preceded by anacrusis (**aleġdon hīe þǣr**), for a scansion $\times \mid \acute{\hphantom{x}} \times \times \times \mid \acute{\hphantom{x}} \mid \acute{\hphantom{x}} \acute{\hphantom{x}} \times$. The alliteration, as in these examples, is shifted leftward from the contained normal verse pattern to occupy the first two lifts. Let us call these two types **HA1** and **HD1**, where **H** indicates a hypermetric on-verse (as opposed to **h**, indicating a hypermetric off-verse).[41]

---

[40] Some Old Icelandic meters similarly resemble the inherited Germanic types with an extra foot appended. But in regard to both hypermetric and skaldic verse this analysis is not a claim about the origin of the type but a synchronic, purely descriptive analysis designed to aid comprehension.

[41] Sievers classifies hypermetric verses differently: in the former example the first two feet resemble a pattern of type A (**fǣġre ǣt foldan**) and the second two feet as well (**foldan scēatum**), and so the classification that he assigns to the type is AA. In the latter example he would not regard the first syllable as anacrustic but would analyze the pattern of **aleġdon hīe þǣr** as belonging to type B; thus the hypermetric type under his method of classification is BD. This is less satisfactory, for a variety of reasons: it makes most off-verses begin with a type C pattern, when there is no apparent reason for this; it creates feet that are compared to normal types but that are unparalleled among those types; and it takes no account of the regularity that feet such as **aleġdon hīe þǣr** are structured like those with anacrusis, generally beginning with a verbal prefix or *ne*.

In the off-verse the alliteration does not shift leftward as it does in the on-verse: the first, extra foot comprises nonalliterating particles and proclitics, followed by a sequence of elements conforming to the metrical pattern of a normal verse with an alliterative pattern such as is usually encountered in the off-verse. Thus **swelċe þǽr fīfe wǽron** (R 8b) alliterates on **f** and contains a normal verse pattern of type Aɪ (**fīfe wǽron**) preceded by a foot made up of unstressed syllables (**swelċe þǽr**), for a scansion × × × | $\acute{-}$ × | $\acute{-}$ × (type hAɪ); and **ġeseah iċ þā frēan mann-cynnes** (R 33b) alliterates on **f** and contains a normal Dɪ type (**frēan mann-cynnes**) preceded by a foot without a lift (**ġeseah iċ þā**), for a scansion × × × × | $\acute{-}$ | $\acute{-}$ $\acute{-}$ × (type hDɪ). Not all hypermetric verses can be analyzed this way, and several other methods of analysis have been proposed. But this method of scansion accounts for nearly all the hypermetric verses in the eight poems.[42] All but a very small number of hypermetric verses, it should be noted, are analyzable as containing a normal verse of type A.

7. Sample Scansions

A. *The Seafarer* 1–57:

> Mæġ iċ be mē selfum   sōð-ġiedd wrecan,
> × × × × | $\acute{-}$ × (A3) $\acute{-}$ $\acute{-}$ | ◡ × (A2k)
>
> sīðas secgan,   hū iċ ġeswinċ-dagum
> $\acute{-}$ × | $\acute{-}$ × (Aɪ)   × × × $\acute{-}$ | ◡ × (C3)
>
> earfoþ-hwīle   oft þrōwode,
> $\acute{-}$ × | $\acute{-}$ × (Aɪ) $\acute{-}$ | $\acute{-}$ ◡ × (D2)
>
> bitre brēost-ċeare   ġebiden hæbbe,
> $\acute{-}$ × | $\acute{-}$ ◡ × (D*2)   × ◡̣ x | $\acute{-}$ × (C2)

---

[42] The one exception is **ġestāg hē on ġealgan hēanne** (R 40b), with alliteration on *st*. However, comparison with the inscription on the Ruthwell Cross reveals that this verse has most likely been altered in the course of transmission, and the Ruthwell version is more original: see the commentary.

5   ġecunnod on ċēole   ċear-selda fela,
    ×│ ⊥ × ×│ ⊥ × (A1)   ⊥ ⊥ ×│ ⌣ × (E)

atol ȳða ġewealc,   þǣr meċ oft beġeat
⌣ ×│ ⊥ × × ⊥ (D4)   × × ⊥│× ⊥ (B1)

nearu niht-wacu   æt nacan stefnan,
⌣ ×│ ⊥ ⌣ × (D2)   × ⌣ ×│ ⊥ × (C2)

þonne hē be clifum cnossaþ.   Ċealde ġeþrungen
× × × × ⌣ ×│ ⊥ × (C2)   ⊥ × ×│ ⊥ × (A1)

fruron mīne fēt,   forste ġebunden
⌣ × ⊥ ×│ ⊥ (E)   ⊥ × ×│ ⊥ × (A1)

10 ċealdum clammum,   þǣr þā ceara seofodon
    ⊥ ×│ ⊥ × (A1)   × × ⌣ ×│ ⌣ × × (C2)

hāt' ymb heortan;   hungor innan slāt[43]
⊥ ×│ ⊥ × (A1)   ⊥│ ⊥ × ⊥ (D4)

mere-wērġes mōd.   Þæt sē mann ne wāt
⌣ × ⊥ ×│ ⊥ (E)   × × ⊥│× ⊥ (B1)

þe him on foldan   fæġrost limpeþ,
× × ×│ ⊥ × (A3)   ⊥ ×│ ⊥ × (A1)

hū iċ earm-ċearig   īs-ċealdne sǣ
× × ⊥│ ⌣ × (C3)   ⊥ ⊥ ×│ ⊥ (E)

15 winter wunode   wreċċan lāstum,
    ⊥ ×│ ⌣ × × (A1)   ⊥ ×│ ⊥ × (A1)

wine-māgum bedroren,
⌣ × ⊥ × ×│ ⌣ × (E)

behangen hrīm-ġiclum;   hæġl scūrum flēag.
×│ ⊥ × │ ⊥ ⊥ × (D*1)   ⊥ ⊥ ×│ ⊥ (E)

Þǣr iċ ne ġehīerde   būtan hlimman sǣ,
× × × ×│ ⊥ × (A3)   × × ⊥│× ⊥ (B1)

īs-ċealdne wǣġ,   hwīlum ielfete sang.
⊥ ⊥ ×│ ⊥ (E)   × × ⊥│× × ⊥ (B2)

---

[43] As noted above (p. 143), **hungor** here probably has monosyllabic value.

20 Dyde iċ mē tō gamene   ganotes hlēoðor,
× × × × × | ⏑ × × (A3)   ⏑ × × | ´ × (A1)

and hwilpan swēġ   fore hleahtor wera,
× ´ | × ´ (B1)   × × ´ | × ⏑ × (B1)

mǣw sinġende   fore medu-drinċe.
´ | ´ ´ × (D1)   × × ⏑ × | ´ × (C2)

Stormas þǣr stān-clifu bēoton,   þǣr him stearn oncwæþ,
´ × × | ´ ⏑ × | ´ × (HA2l)   × × ´ | × ´ (B1)

īsiġ-feðra;   full oft þæt earn beġeall,
´ × | ´ × (A1)   × × × ´ | × ´ (B1)

25 ūriġ-feðra;   nǣniġ hlēo-māga
´ × | ´ × (A1)   × × ´ | ´ × (C1)

fēa-sceaftiġ ferhþ   frēfran meahte.
´ ´ × | ´ (E)   ´ × | ´ × (A1)

For-þon him ġelīefeþ lȳt,   sē-þe āg līfes wynn
× × × × ´ | × ´ (B1)   × × × ´ | × ´ (B1)

ġebiden on burgum,   bealu-sīða hwōn,
× | ⏑ × × | ´ × (A1)   ⏑ × ´ × | ´ (E)

wlanc and wīn-gāl,   hū iċ wēriġ oft
´ × | ´ ´ (A2b)   × × ´ | × ´ (B1)

30 on brim-lāde   bīdan scolde.
× ´ | ´ × (C1)   ´ × | ´ × (A1)

Nāp niht-scua,   norðan snīwde,
´ | ´ ⏑ × (D2)   ´ × | ´ × (A1)

hrīm hrūsan band,   hæġl fēoll on eorðan,
´ | ´ × ´ (D4)   ´ × × | ´ × (A1)

corna ċealdost.   For-þon cnyssaþ nū
´ × | ´ × (A1)   × × ´ | × ´ (B1)

heortan ġeþōhtas   þæt iċ hēan strēamas,
´ × × | ´ × (A1)   × × ´ | ´ × (C1)

35   sealt-ȳða ġelāc   self cunnie;
     ´ ´ × × | ´ (E)   ´ | ´ ⏑ × (D2)

     manaþ mōdes lust   mǣla ġehwelċe
     ⏑ × | ´ × ´ (D4)   ´ × × | ´ × (A1)

     ferhþ to fēran,   þæt iċ feorr heonan
     ´ × | ´ × (A1)   × × ´ | ⏑ × (C3)

     el-þēodiġra   eard ġesēċan.
     ´ | ´ ´ × (D1)   ´ × | ´ × (A1)

     For-ðon nis þæs mōd-wlanc   mann ofer eorðan,
     × × × × | ´ ´ (A3b)   ´ × × | ´ × (A1)

40   nē his ġiefena þæs gōd,   nē on ġeoguþe tō þæs hwæt,
     × × ⏑ × | × × ´ (B2)   × × ⏑ × | × × × ´ (B2)

     nē on his dǣdum tō þæs dēor,   nē him his dryhten tō þæs hold,
     × × × ´ | × × × ´ (B2)   × × × ´ | × × × ´ (B2)

     þæt hē ā his sǣ-fōre   sorge næbbe,
     × × × × ´ | ´ × (C1)   ´ × | ´ × (A1)

     tō hwon hine dryhten   ġedōn wille.
     × × × × | ´ × (A3)   × ´ | ´ × (C1)

     Nē biþ him tō hearpan hyġe   nē tō hrinġ-þeġe—
     × × × × ´ | × ⏑ × (B1)   × × ´ | ⏑ × (C3)

45   nē tō wīfe wynn   nē tō weorolde hyht—
     × × ´ | × ´ (B1)   × × ⏑ × | × ´ (B1)

     nē ymbe āwiht elles⁴⁴   nefne ymb ȳða ġewealc;
     × × × ´ | ´ × (C1)   × × × ´ | × × ´ (B2)

     ac ā hafaþ langunge   sē-þe on lagu fundaþ.
     × × × × ´ | ´ × (C1)   × × × ⏑ × | ´ × (C2)

     Bearwas blōstmum nimaþ,   byriġ fæġriaþ,
     ´ × | ´ × ⏑ × (D*4)   ⏑ × | ´ ⏑ × (D2)

---

44 Here **āwiht** is assumed to stand for the contracted form **āht**: see Fulk 1992: §§131–55.

wangas wlitigiaþ;   weorold ōnetteþ;
⌣× | ⌣x⌣× (D*2)   ⌣×| ⌣⌣× (D1)

50   ealle þā ġemaniaþ   mōdes fūsne
××××| ⌣×× (A3)   ⌣×| ⌣× (A1)

sefan tō sīðe   þām-þe swā þenċeþ
⌣×× | ⌣× (A1)   ××⌣| ⌣× (C1)

on flōd-wegas   feorr ġewītan.
× ⌣ | ⌣× (C3)   ⌣×| ⌣× (A1)

Swelċe ġēac manaþ   ġeōmran reorde;
××⌣| ⌣× (C3)   ⌣×| ⌣× (A1)

sinġeþ sumores weard,   sorge bēodeþ
⌣× | ⌣x×⌣ (D*4)   ⌣×| ⌣× (A1)

55   bitre on brēost-hord.   Þæt sē beorn ne wāt,
⌣×× | ⌣⌣ (A2b)   ××⌣| ×⌣ (B1)

sēft-ēadiġ secg,   hwæt þā sume drēogaþ
⌣⌣× | ⌣ (E)   ××⌣×| ⌣× (C2)

þe þā wræc-lāstas   wīdost lecgaþ.
××⌣| ⌣× (C1)   ⌣×| ⌣× (A1)

B. *The Dream of the Rood* 59–69:

Sāre iċ wæs mid sorgum ġedrēfed,   hnāg iċ hwæðre þām
                                        secgum tō handa,
⌣××××| ⌣×× | ⌣× (HA1)   ×××××| ⌣×× | ⌣× (hA1)

60   ēað-mōd, elne micle.   Ġenāmon hīe þær ælmihtiġne God,[45]
⌣⌣ | ⌣× | ⌣× (HA1)   ×××××| ⌣⌣×× | ⌣ (hE)

ahōfon hine of þām hefigan wīte.   Forlēton mē þā hilde-rincas
× | ⌣××××× | ⌣×× | ⌣× (HA1)   ×××××| ⌣× | ⌣× (hA1)

---

[45] This verse presents an unusual problem: **ælmihtiġne** ought to form a normal verse unto itself of type D, since it comprises four positions. The scansion offered here is provisional.

standan stēame bedrifenne;   eall iċ wæs mid strǣlum
                                              forwundod.

⏑́ × | ⏑́ × × | ⏑̯× × (HA1)   × × × × | ⏑́ × × | ⏑́ × (hA1)

Aleġdon hīe þǣr lim-wēriġne;   ġestōdon him æt his līces
                                                hēafdum;

× | ⏑́ × × × | ⏑́ | ⏑́ ⏑́ × (HD1)   × × × × × × | ⏑́ × | ⏑́ × (hA1)

behēoldon hīe þǣr heofones dryhten,   and hē hine þǣr
                                                 hwīle reste,

× | ⏑́ × × × | ⏑̯× × | ⏑́ × (HA1)   × × × × × | ⏑́ × | ⏑́ × (hA1)

65 mēðe æfter þām miclan ġewinne.   Ongunnon him þā
                                                 mold-ærn wyrċan

⏑́ × × × × | ⏑́ × × | ⏑́ × (HA1)   × × × × × | ⏑́ ⏑́ | ⏑́ × (hA2l)

beornas on banan ġesihþe,   curfon hīe þæt of beorhtan stāne;

⏑́ × × | ⏑̯× × | ⏑́ × (HA1)   × × × × × | ⏑́ × | ⏑́ × (hA1)

ġesetton hīe þǣr-on sigora wealdend.   Ongunnon him þā
                                                  sorg-lēoþ galan,

× | ⏑́ × × × × | ⏑̯× × | ⏑́ × (HA1)   × × × × × | ⏑́ ⏑́ | ⏑ × (hA2k)

earme on þā ǣfen-tīde,   þā hīe woldon eft sīðian,

⏑́ × × × | ⏑́ × | ⏑́ × (HA1)   × × × × | ⏑́ | ⏑́ ⏑ × (hD2)

mēðe fram þām mǣran þēodne;   reste hē þǣr mǣte weorode.

⏑́ × × × | ⏑́ × | ⏑́ × (HA1)   × × × × | ⏑́ × | ⏑̯× × (hA1)

8. For Further Reading

For an abridgment of Sievers' *Altgermanische Metrik,* see Sievers
1905, of which, in turn, the portions most relevant to Old English
are translated into English in Sievers 1968. Cassidy and Ringler
(1971: 274–88) offer a simplified introduction to Sievers' and
Pope's systems of scansion. The widely regarded metrical analysis

of A. J. Bliss is an elaboration of Sievers'. For an elementary but suitably detailed introduction to it, see Bliss 1962; and for the definitive explanation of its guiding principles, see Bliss 1967. Stockwell and Minkova (1997) provide an introduction to a basically Sieversian system on more formal linguistic principles. Another perceptive system of scansion based on Sievers' is that of Hutcheson (1995). For a carefully argued critique of the principles underlying Sieversian approaches, see Hoover 1985. Some studies that shed significant light on analysis of Old English meter from a Sieversian perspective, without proposing any very detailed new system of scansion, are those of Cable (1974, 1991) and Suzuki (1996).

A different and in many respects competing analysis of early Germanic meters sees them as constructed of measures of equal duration, producing metrical ISOCHRONY. The representational systems used in such isochronous approaches therefore tend to resemble musical notation. The most accessible of these, and the one that most earnestly attempts rapprochement with Sievers' analysis, is that of Pope (1942, rev. 1966). Some other significant studies of this variety are by Heusler (1925), Creed (1990), and, in important respects, Obst (1987). Difficult to classify under either heading are the studies of Russom (1987, 1998), aiming to lend psychological plausibility to metrical analysis by basing it upon word structure.

By now the volume of scholarship on the meters of early Germanic poetry is enormous. For a cumulative bibliography of alliterative meters, see Gade and Fulk 2000; for year-to-year additions to scholarship, consult the annual bibliographies listed above, p. 49.

Glossary

The order is alphabetical. Because in some Old English manuscripts the digraph **ae** is equivalent to the ligature **æ** (see, for example, the version of *Cædmon's Hymn* in MS M), it is treated that way in this glossary, and **æ** is alphabetized between **ad** and **af**. The voiceless spirant **þ**, interchanging medially with voiced **ð**, follows **t** as a separate letter. Long vowels and diphthongs are alphabetized interchangeably with their short equivalents, the short ones coming first in homographs. Words beginning with the prefix **ġe-** are listed according to their stems; for example, **ġe-beorg** follows **beorg**.

The treatment of compounds is as follows. All words separated into two constituents by hyphens in the text of the poems (unless the first constituent is merely an unstressed prefix, as with **ġe-** when the stem begins with a vowel, or **oþ-** when the stem begins with **þ**) are registered according to their separate elements and also as compounds. Thus **brim-fuglas** (*Wanderer* 47) is listed according to its constituents, **brim** and **fugol**; but also, under the first constituent, **brim**, the whole compound is listed and defined, and under **fugol** there is a cross-reference to the compound. It is more productive to learn the simple elements than the compounds, since the poets use a comparatively limited group of elements to produce a great variety of compounds, most of which can be interpreted successfully by anyone who knows the meaning of the constituents. At the same time there are often several possible meanings in a constituent, and now and then subtleties in the combinations require careful interpretation. It is therefore safer to define the compound as well as its constituents, making sure that the definition fits the immediate context. Most of the compounds are nominal or adjectival, but even such minor combinations as **for-þon**, **on-weġ**, **sē-þe**, and **þā-ġiet** are treated in the same way for the sake of consistency.

Hyphenation has not been extended in the text to mere prefixes and suffixes, and therefore such words as **forheard** and **fǣrlíċe** are treated like simple words even though it is easy to separate their constituents. Some of the more independent derivational suffixes, however, such as **-fæst** and **-lēas**, have been given separate entries, as if they were constituents of true compounds. In the glossary itself hyphenation has been extended to prefixes for the sake of clarity, and cross-references connect prefixed with unprefixed forms.

Prefixes are ordinarily left undefined, since full definitions would fill a great deal of space. Most of them appear also as separate words and are likewise familiar in modern English. Exception is made on behalf of the very common prefixes ġe- and a-, because they do not appear independently, and their meanings, though sometimes important, are elusive. Those who desire further guidance should consult Bosworth and Toller's *Anglo-Saxon Dictionary* and *Supplement,* and the *Oxford English Dictionary.*

Verbs are cross-referenced with particular care, in order to enable students to keep track of, and compare, the simple verb and its prefixed variations. Throughout, the unprefixed form is used as a guide, by cross-reference, to the prefixed forms. Hence it is always entered even if it does not actually occur in the eight poems.

As a further aid to study, class numbers are assigned to the verbs, and the principal parts of all the strong and preterite-present verbs are spelt out, along with those of a few particularly troublesome weak verbs. Throughout, the principal parts will be found under the unprefixed verb if it actually occurs in the poems; otherwise they may be located under one or more of the prefixed forms.

Nouns that do not belong to the main declensions (the main declensions being masculine and neuter *a*-stems and feminine *ō*-stems) are classified either as weak (wk.) or by stem: *ja*-stem, *i*-stem, *u*-stem, etc. This classification will not always be of practical assistance to students, but often it will guide them (by way of a reference grammar) to the reason for an unusual ending or the presence of front mutation in the stem-vowel. Adjectives are similarly treated, though the useful distinctions are fewer. Among the adjectives in the glossary, the *ja-/jō*-stems are marked simply "ja-stem," the *wa-/wō*-stems simply "wa-stem." All others follow the regular *a-/ō*-declension, except for **cwic(u)**, which is marked "u-stem."

Familiarity with front mutation and the vowel gradation exhibited most obviously in the strong verbs makes it possible to associate a number of words that would otherwise appear to be unrelated. For this reason attention has been called to a good many of the unmutated base-words on which weak verbs of the first class (characterized by the prehistoric ending *-jan* with its regular mutating power) are formed, and to a few of the more conspicuous and helpful gradational correspondences.

In accordance with the convention practiced in most elementary Old English textbooks, the vowels of **sē**, **mē**, **tō**, **þā**, and similar monosyllables are consistently marked long. In actuality, such words are usually unstressed, and unstressed vowels are shortened; but these words may also appear in stressed positions, and our knowledge of the extent to which the long vowels in such positions were extended to unstressed positions is too limited to justify the attempt to distinguish long and short vowels in every instance. To avoid spelling alternations not found in other elementary texts, then, such variable vowel quantities in monosyllables and in syllables with variable stress (as in the second element of the name **Ēadrič**) have for the most part been regularized.

On the other hand, the relative particle þe and verb prefixes such as **a-** and **to-**
are consistently unstressed in the eight poems, and so their vowels are not
marked long.

Abbreviations

The poems are cited according to the order of the texts, by initial and line
number: C (*Cædmon's Hymn*); B (*Brunanburh*); R (*Rood*); M (*Maldon*); W
(*Wanderer*); S (*Seafarer*); D (*Deor*); and L (*Wife's Lament*).

Immediately following the boldface entry of a word is a grammatical nota-
tion. Nouns are classified by gender (*m., f.,* or *n.*) and also, as mentioned
above (p. 160), by the prehistoric stem-endings indicating their declension if
they do not belong to the regular *a-* or *ō*-stem class. The weak declension
(*n*-stems) is marked *wk.* before the specification of gender.

Verbs are classified as follows:

> *v.1* to *v.7* = strong verb, class 1 to class 7 (Arabic numbers).
> *wk.v.I* to *wk.v.III* = weak verb, class I to class III (Roman).
> *pret.-pres.v.* = preterite-present verb.
> *anom.v.* = anomalous verb.
> *contr.v.* = contract verb.

The other parts of speech are designated by easily recognized abbreviations:
pron., adj., adv., prep., conj., interj.; poss. for possessive, *rel.* for relative,
num. for numeral; *comp.* for comparative, *superl.* for superlative. On the des-
ignation of stem-endings for certain adjectives, see above, p. 160.

Declensional forms of nouns are described by case (*n., v., g., d., a., i.,* for
nominative, vocative, genitive, dative, accusative, instrumental) and number
(*s., p.,* for singular, plural) in that order (*ns., gs.,* for nominative singular,
genitive singular, etc., with a point after the second letter only). Adjectives
have a third letter for the gender: *nsm.* for nominative singular masculine, etc.;
but this is omitted for the genitive and dative plural, where there is generally
no distinction of gender in the endings. When there is need to give case alone
or number alone, fuller abbreviations are used (*nom., gen., dat., acc., instr.;
sg., pl.;* and *part. gen.* for partitive genitive). The combinations *dis.* and *dip.*
mean dative or instrumental, singular and plural respectively. This formula is
used for nouns with dative case-endings when they stand alone, without
prepositions, in an apparently instrumental function. Nouns with such endings
following prepositions are said to be dative unless there is clear evidence
(from an adjective or article) that they are instrumental. Occasionally it is
indicated that a word is indeclinable (*indecl.*).

Verb forms are marked *inf.* (infinitive), *pres. part.* (present participle), *pp.*
(past or passive participle), or according to tense (*pres.* or *pret.*), person, and

number (*1s.* for first person singular, *1p.* for first person plural, etc.). The mood is not specified if it is indicative. Imperatives are marked *imper.* (*s.* or *p.*), and subjunctives, *subj.* Occasionally there is reason to indicate that a verb is transitive (*trans.*) or intransitive (*intrans.*) or is used absolutely (*absol.*).

After the main entry, its classification, and a definition, the particular forms occurring in the texts are cited. If the form is the same as the main entry, it is not repeated. If it differs by simple addition of an ending, a dash for the uninflected entry is followed by the letters to be added; if the change is partly internal, the whole form is given. For example, under "**burg**, f. cons.-stem," the notation "as. M 291" means accusative singular **burg** at *Maldon* 291; "dp. –**um**" means dative plural **burgum**; but for "ap." (accusative plural) the internally altered form **byriġ** is given entire.

Occasionally, when a form already indicated is repeated, only its initial is given. Thus, following citation of the form **abrēoðe**, "a. his anġinn" stands for "**abrēoðe his anġinn**."

Among other, commonly received abbreviations are *OE* for Old English, *Gmc.* for Germanic, *cf.* for *confer* (compare), and *q.v.* for *quod vide* (which see). In certain grammatical descriptions, *w.* stands for "with."

Dictionaries and Grammars

For fuller definitions with illustrative quotations from prose and poetry, the most complete dictionary is that of Bosworth and Toller (1898, with supplements to 1972). All three parts of the dictionary should be consulted for a given word; the first volume is especially spotty through the letter G. A more concise but very convenient dictionary is that of J. R. Clark Hall (1960). A comprehensive dictionary published in microfiche form, the *Dictionary of Old English* (Cameron et al. 1986–), is in preparation at the University of Toronto under the current editorship of Antonette diPaolo Healey. As of May, 2000, fascicles through the letter E had appeared. It is based on the *Dictionary of Old English Corpus*—virtually the complete corpus of writings in Old English, minus textual variants and stray glosses—which is available in electronic form, enabling complex searches. For information about current availability of the corpus consult Cathy Ball 1995, an indispensable web site with links to other sites of interest to Anglo-Saxonists, such as those providing digitized facsimiles of Old English manuscripts, including reproductions of some of the eight poems. Based on the corpus is another invaluable lexical tool, the *Microfiche Concordance to Old English* (Healey and Venezky 1980).

Of great value as a lexical aid exclusively to the poetry is the dictionary of Grein (1912–14). For a complete concordance to Krapp and Dobbie's edition of the poetry (1931–53), see Bessinger and Smith 1978.

Useful for derivation is Holthausen's etymological dictionary (1932–34), with the addenda and corrigenda by Bammesberger (1979). For all words that have survived in the language after 1100, the twenty-volume *Oxford English Dictionary,* now in its second edition, is often of great value. Middle English forms of these words, it should be noted, if not the latest on record, are sometimes entered for cross-reference, but the main entry is under the *latest* spelling.

The fullest and most authoritative grammars for phonology and morphology are those of Luick (1914–40), Campbell (1959), Brunner (1965), and Hogg (1992). The most complete syntactic study is that of Mitchell (1985b).

A

ā, adv. *always, ever;* M 315; S 42, 47; L 5, 42.

a- (or **ā-**), unstressed verbal prefix of various origin (Æ-, OR-, AN-, etc.) and various meaning (*up, on, from, away,* etc.), but often modifying only slightly the meaning of the unprefixed verb.

a-bēodan, v.2. *announce, deliver* (*a message*); imper. s. **abēod**, M 49 (absol. use); pret. 3s. **abēad**, M 27. [Cf. **bēodan**.]

a-bīdan, v.1. *await, wait for* (w. gen.); inf. L 53. [Cf. **bīdan**.]

a-brēoðan, v.2. *fail, come to naught;* pres. 3s. subj. **abrēoðe**, M 242 (**a. his anġinn**, *may his conduct have an evil end*—Gordon). [BRĒOÐAN, BRĒAÞ, BRUÐON, BROÐEN, without the usual grammatical change, **ð** to **d**.]

ac, conj. *but;* R 11, 43, 115, 119, 132; M 82, 193, 247, 252, 269, 318; S 47.

āc, f. cons.-stem. *oak.* **āc-trēo**, n. wastem. *oak-tree;* ds. L 28, 36.

a-cweċċan, wk.v.I. *shake, brandish,* pret. 3s. **acweahte**, M 255, 310. [CWEĊĊAN (Gmc. *KWAKJAN), CWEAHTE, CWEAHT; cf. CWACIAN, wk.v.II, *quake*.]

a-cweðan, v.5, trans. *speak, utter;* pres. 3s. **acwiþ**, W 91. [Cf. **cweðan**.]

a-cȳðan, wk.v.I. *make known, manifest;* inf. W 113. [Cf. **ġe-cȳðan**.]

ādl, f. *disease, sickness;* ns. S 70.

æfen(n), n. ja-stem (also m.). *evening.* **æfen-tīd**, f. i-stem. *evening hour;* as **-e**, R 68. (Possibly ap., *in the evening hours,* but **tīd** sometimes has as. **-e** like the ō-stems.)

æfre, adv. *ever;* B 66; D 11; L 39; **æfre ymbe stunde**, *ever and anon, repeatedly,* M 271 [see **ymbe**].

æftan, adv. *from behind;* B 63.

æfter, prep. *after.* (a) w. dat. (temporal), R 65; M 65. (b) w. acc. (marking object of affection), *with longing for,* W 50.

æfter, adv. *after(ward);* C 8; S 77 (i.e., *after death*). **æfter-cweðende**, pres. part., pl., as noun, *those speaking afterward* (*speaking of a man after his death*); gp. **-cweðendra**, S 72.

ǣġhwelċ, pron. and adj. *each, every* (*one*). — as pron. w. part. gen., nsm. M 234 (w. **ūre**, *of us*); asm. **ǣġhwelcne**, R 86 (w. gp. **ānra**, *each one*). — as adj., nsf. R 120. [**ā**, *ever,* plus **ġe-hwelċ**, q.v.]

ǣġðer, pron. *each* (*of two*), *either;* nsm. M 133. — conj. **ǣġðer . . . and**, *both . . . and,* M 224. [Shortened from ǢĠHWÆÐER, **ā** plus **ġe-hwæðer**, *each of two.*]

ælmihtiġ, adj. *almighty;* nsm. C 9; R 39, 93, 98, 106, 153, 156; asm. **-ne**, R 60. [ÆL-, combining form of **eall**, *all,* plus **mihtiġ**, *mighty*.]

æniġ, pron. and adj. *anyone, any.* — pron., nsm. R 110, 117; M 70; dsm. **ænigum**, R 47. — adj., nsf. M 195; gsm. **ænġes**, S 116.

ǣr, adv. *before, formerly, already;* R 118, 137, 145; M 60; W 43, 113; S 102; D 41; — giving pluperf. value to past tense, R 114, 154; M 158, 198, 290. **ǣr-ġewinn**, n. *former struggle, strife of old;* as. R 19. [See **ǣror**, **ǣrest**.]

ǣr, prep. w. dat. (rarely acc.) *before,* S 69. **ǣr-þon**, conj. *before,* R 88.

ǣr, conj. w. subj. *before;* M 61 (correl. w. **ǣr**, adv.), 279, 300; W 64, 69; S 74.

ǣrende, n. ja-stem. *message;* as. M 28.

ǣrest, adv. superl. *earliest, first;* C 5; M 124, 186; R 19 (**þæt hit ǣrest ongann**, *in that it had straightway begun*[?]); L 6; – **þā . . . ǣrest**, *when first, as soon as,* M 5.

ǣrn, n. *dwelling, house.* See **mold-ǣrn**.

ǣrnan, wk.v.I. *cause (a horse) to run; gallop;* pret. 3p. **ǣrndon**, M 191. [Gmc. *RANNJAN, causative based on RANN, second gradation of RINNAN, v.3, *run;* in OE the *r* in these forms was frequently metathesized.]

ǣror, adv. comp. *earlier,* R 108.

ǣr-þon, see **ǣr**, prep.

ǣs, n. *food, carrion;* gs. –**es**, B 63; M 107.

æsc, m. *ash*(-*wood*), *spear* (*of ash*); as. M 43, 310; gp. –**a**, W 99. **æsc-holt**, n. (*ash-wood*) *spear;* as. M 230. **æsc-here**, m. i-stem, *army of ash-spears, viking army;* ns. M 69. (But perhaps, as Gordon suggests, **æsc**- in this last compound is a borrowing of the cognate Old Norse ASKR, designating a viking warship.)

æt, prep. w. dat. *at, in, on, by;* B 4, 8, 42, 44; R 8, 63; M 10, 39 (**æt ūs**, *at our hands, from us*), etc. (16 times); W 111; S 7; L 45 (**æt him selfum ġelang**, *dependent on himself, in his own hands*).

ǣterne, see **ǣtren**.

æt-foran, prep. w. dat. *before, in front of,* M 16. [Cf. **be-foran**.]

æt-gædere, adv. *together, in unison.* **bū-tū æ.**, *both together,* R 48; **samod æ.**, *in joint action together, both together,* W 39. [Cf. **to-gædere**, usually with sense of interaction or interrelation or meeting rather than mere association or simultaneity.]

ǣtren, **ǣterne**, adj. *poisoned, deadly;* nsm. **ǣterne**, M 146; asm. **ǣtrenne**, M 47. [Properly **ǣtren**, later ǢT-TREN, from ĀTER, poison. The odd form **ǣterne** was perhaps influenced

by **norðerne, sūðerne**, etc., or by some old poetic use of a weak form, ǢTRENA, metathesized as ǢTERNA.]

æt-samne, adv. *together;* **bēġen æ.**, *both together,* B 57.

æt-witan, v.1, w. dat. *reproach;* inf., M 220, 250.

æðele, adj. *noble;* nsm. M 280; nsf. wk. B 16; asm.wk. **æðelan**, M 151.

ġe-æðele, adj. *befitting noble descent;* nsn. B 7.

æðeling, m. *nobleman, prince;* (as title) *member of the royal family, prince;* ns. B 3, 58; *Prince,* ds. –**e**, R 58; (broadly) gp. –**a**, S 93.

æðelu, n. ja-stem, pl. *descent,* (*noble*) *origin;* ap. M 216.

ǣwisc, adj. *ashamed.* **ǣwisc-mōd**, adj. *ashamed in spirit;* npm. –**e**, B 56.

a-feallan, v.7. *fall, be laid low* (*in death*); pp. **afeallen**, nsm. M 202. [Cf. **feallan**.]

a-flīeman, wk.v.I. *put to flight;* pret. 3s. **aflīemde**, M 243. [Cf. **ġe-flīeman**.]

a-fȳsan, wk.v.I. (a) *urge forward, impel;* pp. **afȳsed**, nsm. R 125; (b) *drive away;* inf. M 3. [Cf. **fȳsan**.]

āgan, pret.-pres.v. *have, possess;* inf. M 87; pres. 1s. **āg**, M 175; 3s. **āg**, R 107; S 27 (as aux. w. pp.; but cf. Mitchell 1985b: §743); 3s. subj. **āge**, W 64; 1p. subj. **āgen**, S 117; pret. 1s. **āhte**, D 38; L 16; 3s. **āhte**, M 189; D 18, 22. – neg. **nāgan**, *have not;* pres. 1s. **nāg**, R 131. [ĀGAN, ĀG, ĀGON, ĀHTE.]

a-ġiefan, v.5. *give, render;* pret. 3s. **aġeaf**, M 44; pp. **aġiefen**, nsm. M 116. [ĠIEFAN, ĠEAF, ĠEAFON, ĠIEFEN; cf. **for-ġiefan**.]

a-ġietan, wk.v.I. *destroy* (*by shedding blood*); pp. **aġieted**, nsm. B 18. [Base-word ĠEAT, as in pret. s. of **ġēotan**, q.v.]

a-hafen, see **a-hebban**.

a-hēawan, v.7. *cut down;* pp. **a-hēawen**, nsm. R 29 [Cf. **hēawan**.]

a-hebban, v.6. *raise, lift up;* pret. 1s. **ahōf**, R 44; 3s. M 130, 244; 3p. **ahōfon**, R 61; fig. (with ref. to lifting up the voice), *utter loudly;* pret. 1p. **ahōfon**, M 213; pp. **ahafen**, nsm. M 106. [Cf. **hebban**.]

āhte, see **āgan**.

a-lecgan, wk.v.I, *lay;* pret. 3p. **a-leġdon**, R 63. [Cf. **lecgan**.]

a-līefan, wk.v.I. *allow,* inf. M 90. [Base-word **lēaf**, f. *permission;* cf. **ġe-līefan**.]

amen, Lat. (from Hebrew, *verily*); (as closing formula) *may it be so!* S 124.

a-mierran, wk.v.I. *cripple, wound;* pret. 3s. **amierde**, M 165. [Base-word *MEARR; cf. ĠE-MEARR, n. *hindrance.*]

ān, pron. and adj. *one;* – as pron., asm. **–ne**, M 117; gp. **–ra**, w. **ǣġhwelċ, ġehwelċ**, *each one, every-one.* R 86, 108; – as adj., asm. **–ne**, M 226. **ān-floga**, wk.m. *solitary flier;* ns. S 62. **ān-haga**, wk.m. *one who dwells alone; a solitary; a friendless man;* ns. W 1; as. **–n**, W 40. [For the element -HAG- see **haga**.] **ān-hyġdiġ**, adj. *strong-minded;* nsm. D 2. **ān-rǣd**, adj. *resolute;* nsm. M 44, 132. [In **ān-hyġdiġ** and **ān-rǣd** the initial vowel must be long, since it is never spelt *o*, and so the first element of the compound must be **ān**, indicating singleness of purpose.]

āna, adv. *alone,* R 123, 128; M 94; W 8; L 22, 35. [Often used adjectively after noun or pron. as if nsm.wk. of **ān**, but extended to other cases and genders.]

and, conj. *and;* C 2, and frequently in the other poems. [Spelt *and* or *ond* when written out in the MSS, but usu. abbreviated w. a mark like a 7 (=&).]

anda, wk.m. *enmity, spite;* ds. **–n**, W 105.

and-lang, adj. *entire* (with reference to a period of time or a spatial dimension); asm. **–ne**, B 21. [**and-**, *against, corresponding,* plus **lang**, *long;* here the prefix is stressed; the same word with stress on **lang** gave modern "along."]

and-swaru, f. *answer;* as. **–sware**, M 44. [**and-**, *against, counter,* plus SWARU, *asseveration;* cf. SWERIAN, v.6, *swear.*]

an-ġinn, n. *beginning; action, conduct;* as. M 242. [Cf. **on-ġinnan**.]

an-mēdla, wk.m. *pomp, glory;* np. **–n**, S 81. [Base-word **mōd**, q.v.]

an-sīen, f. i-stem. *appearance, face;* ns. S 91. [Cf. **wǣfer-sīen, ġe-sīene**, and **ġe-sēon**.]

an-wealda, wk.m. *ruler, Lord;* ns. R 153. [Cf. **wealdan**.]

ār, m. *messenger;* ns. M 26.

ār, f. *grace, favor, mercy;* ns. S 107; as. **–e**, W 1, 114; *honor, glory,* as. **–e**, D 33. **ār-hwæt**, adj. *abounding in glory, glorious;* npm. **–e**, B 73. (See note in Campbell 1938: 121.)

a-rǣdd, pp. *determined, decided, fixed, settled;* nsf. W 5 (see note). [A syncopated, West Saxon form of A-RǢDED; cf. **rǣdan**.]

a-rǣran, wk.v.I. *rear, erect;* pp. **arǣred**, nsm. R 44.

a-rīsan, v.1. *arise;* pret. 3s. **arās**, R 101. [RĪSAN, RĀS, RISON, RISEN.]

a-sǣġde, see **a-secgan**.

a-scacan, v.6. *shake;* pret. 3s. **ascōc**, M 230. [SCACAN, SCŌC, SCŌCON, SCACEN.]

ġe-āscian, wk.v.II. *learn (by asking);* pret. 1p. **–āscodon**, D 21.

a-secgan, wk.v.III. *say, speak out, tell;* inf. W 11; pret. 3s. **asǣġde**, M 198. [Cf. **secgan**.]

a-settan, wk.v.I. *set, set up, place;*

pres. 3s. subj. **asette**, R 142; pret. 3p. **asetton**, R 32. [Cf. **ġe-settan**.]

a-stāg, see **a-stīgan**.

a-stellan, wk.v.I. *establish;* pret. 3s. **astealde**, C 4. [STELLAN, STEALDE, STEALD; cf. **on-stellan**.]

a-stīgan, v.1. *ascend;* pret. 3s. **astāg**, R 103. [Cf. **ġe-stīgan**.]

a-styrian, wk.v.I. *remove;* pp. **astyred**, nsm. R 30. [STYRIAN, STYREDE, STYRED, *stir, move;* from *STURJAN, related to **storm**, m. *storm*.]

a-swebban, wk.v.I. *put to sleep* (*kill*); pp. **aswefed**, npm. −e, B 30. [SWEBBAN, SWEFEDE, SWEFED; from *SWÆFJAN; cf. SWÆF, pret. of SWEFAN, v.5, *sleep*.]

atol, adj. *terrible;* asn. S 6.

āwa, adv. *always*, S 79.

a-weaxan, v.7. *grow;* pret. 1s. **awēox**, L 3 (MS *weox*). [WEAXAN, WĒOX, WĒOXON, WEAXEN; cf. **weaxan**.]

ā-wiht, n. i-stem. *anything, aught;* ns. L 23; as. S 46.

B

ġe-bād, see **ġe-bīdan**.

bæc, n. *back;* as. in **ofer bæc**, *to the rear, back*, M 276.

bæd, **bædon**, see **biddan**.

ġe-bǣdan, wk.v.I. *constrain;* pp. **ġe-bǣded**, nsm. B 33.

bǣl, n. *fire;* esp. *funeral fire, pyre;* ds. −e, S 114.

bǣren, **bǣron**, see **beran**.

bærnan, wk.v.I, trans. *burn*. See **for-bærnan**.

bærst, see **berstan**.

ġe-bǣru, n. indecl. *demeanor, spirits;* as. L 44; is. L 21.

bana, wk.m. *slayer* (whether a person or a thing: "*bane*"); ns. M 299; gs. −n, R 66 (referring to the Rood, apparently; Cook emended to

BANENA, gp., referring generally to those who crucified Christ).

band, see **bindan**.

baðian, wk.v.II. *bathe;* inf. W 47.

be, stressed form **bī**, prep. w. dat. *by*. − (a) *by, beside, near;* M 319; W 80; S 8, 98; **be healfe**, *by the side* (*of*), M 152, 318; **bī** (postpositive), M 182. − (b) *about, concerning;* S 1; D 35; L 1. − (c) *by, from* (marking agency or source), D 1; **be þām**, *by that* (*this*), M 9.

bēacen, n. *sign, portent;* ns. R 6; as. R 21; ds. **bēacne**, R 83; gp. **bēacna**, R 118.

beadu, f. wō-stem. *battle;* ds. **beadwe**, M 185. **beadu-rǣs**, m. *rush of battle;* ns. M 111. **beadu-weorc**, n. *deed of war;* gp. −a, B 48. [The nominative of **beadu** is not recorded as an independent word.]

bēag, m. *ring, crown, necklace* (any ornament of precious metal bent or looped together; as a plural, in formulas, virtually equivalent to *money* or *wealth*); ap. −as, M 31, 160. [Cf. **būgan**.] **bēag-ġiefa**, wk.m. *ring-giver* (typifying the generous patron); ns. B 2; d. or as. −n, M 290.

bealdlīċe, adv. *boldly;* M 311; superl. **bealdlicost**, M 78.

bealu, n. wa-stem. *evil; malice; pain, hardship;* as. S 112 (*malice*); gp. **bealwa**, R 79 (MS *bealuwara*). **bealu-sīþ**, m. *grievous journey* or *bitter experience;* gp. −a, S 28.

bēam, m. *tree, wooden beam;* spec., *rood-tree, cross;* ns. R 97; ds. −e, R 114, 122; gp. −a, R 6. [Cf. **siġe-bēam**.]

bearn, n. *child, son;* ns. R 83; M 92, 155, 186, 209, 238, 267, 300 (*descendant?*), 320; ap. S 93; − **ielda bearn**, *children of men* (*the human race, people*); np. S 77; dp. −**um**, C 5 (var. **eorðan b.**, *children of earth*).

bearu, m. wa-stem. *grove, wood;* np. **bearwas**, S 48. [Cf. **wudu-bearu**.]

bēatan, v.7. *beat,* pret. 3p. **bēoton**, S 23. [BĒATAN, BĒOT, BĒOTON, BĒATEN.]

bēċ, see **bōc**.

be-cuman, v.4. *come;* pret. 2p. **be-cōmon**, M 58; 3p., B 70. [The prefix indicates arrival but is not usually to be translated. Cf. **cuman**.]

be-dǣlan, wk.v.I, w. dat. or instr. *separate (from), deprive (of);* pp. **bedǣled**, nsm. W 20; D 28. [Cf. **dǣlan**.]

be-delfan, v.3. *bury;* pret. 3s. **bedealf**, R 75. [DELFAN, DEALF, DULFON, DOLFEN, *dig*.]

be-drīfan, v.1. *beat upon; cover over, envelop* (?); pp. **bedrifen**, asm. −**ne**, R 62. [DRĪFAN, DRĀF, DRIFON, DRIFEN.]

be-droren, adj. w. dat. or instr. *deprived, bereft (of);* nsm. S 16; npm. −**e**, W 79. [Pp. of *BE-DRĒOSAN; cf. **drēosan**.]

be-flōwan, v.7. *move by flowing* (?); *surround (by water* ?); pp. **beflōwen**, nsm. L 49 (see note). [Cf. **flōwan**.]

be-foran, prep. w. dat. *before;* B 67 (*earlier than*); W 46 (*in front of*). [Cf. **æt-foran**.]

be-ġeall, see **be-ġiellan**.

be-ġeat, **be-ġēaton**, see **be-ġietan**.

bēġen, m. dual (**bā**, f., **bū**, n.) *both;* nom. B 57; M 182, 183 (by mistake?), 191, 291, 305. [Cf. **bū-tū**.]

be-ġēotan, v.2. *cover* (as with liquid); pp. **begoten**, nsn. R 7; *suffuse, drench;* same form, nsm. R 49. [Cf. **ġēotan**.]

be-ġiellan, v.3. *scream round about* or *cry in answer to* (?); pret. 3s. **be-ġeall**, S 24 (w. acc. **þæt**: see note). [Recorded here only; cf. **ġiellan**.]

be-ġietan, v.5. *get possession of, conquer;* pret. 3p. **beġēaton**, B 73; *keep, hold,* pret. 3s. **beġeat**, S 6; L

32, 41. [ĠIETAN, ĠEAT, ĠĒATON, ĠIETEN; cf. **on-ġietan**.]

be-hangen, see **be-hōn**.

be-healdan, v.7. *behold, gaze at, keep watch over; hold, guard;* pret. 1s. **be-hēold**, R 25, 58; 3s. **behēold on** (*watched* or *watched over*), R 9 (MS *be heoldon*); 3p. **behēoldon**, R 11, 64. [Cf. **healdan**.]

be-hindan, prep. w. dat. *behind,* B 60 (postpos.). [Cf. **hindan**.]

be-hōn, contr.v.7, w. dat. or instr. *hang* (*with*), *cover* (*with*); pp. **be-hangen**, nsm. S 17. [HŌN (from *HANHAN), HĒNG, HĒNGON, HANGEN.]

be-hrīman, wk.v.I. *cover with frost;* pp. **behrimed**, nsm. L 48. [Cf. **hrīm**.]

be-hroren, adj. w. instr. *fallen upon (by), covered (with).* npm. −**e**, W 77. [Pp. of BE-HRĒOSAN, the active verb recorded only as intrans., *fall;* see **hrēosan**.]

be-nam, see **be-niman**.

benċ, f. i-stem. *bench;* ds. −**e**, M 213.

bend, f. jō-stem. *bond;* see **sinu-bend**.

be-niman, v.4, w. acc. of person, instr. of thing. *deprive (of);* pret. 3s. **benam**, D 16. [Cf. **niman**.]

benn, f. jō-stem. *wound;* np. −**a**, W 49.

bēodan, v.2. *announce, forebode;* pres. 3s. **bēodeþ**, S 54. [BĒODAN, BĒAD, BUDON, BODEN; cf. **a-bēodan**.]

bēon-wesan, anom.v. *be;* inf. **bēon**, M 185; **wesan**, R 110, 117; L 42.

(1) ordinary present forms: 1s. **eom**, M 179, 317, L 29; 2s. **eart**, M 36; 3s. **is**, R 80, etc. (8 times); M 31, etc. (4 times); W 106; S 86, 88, 121; L 17, 23, 24, 29; 3p. **sindon**, R 46; W 93; L 30; **sind**, S 64, 80, 86; L 33; 3s. subj. **sīe**, R 112 (see note), 144; M 215; S 122; D 30; **sīe . . . sīe**, *whether (may be)* . . . *or,* L 45-46.

(2) present forms of **bēon**, used in general statements or with future sense: 3s. **biþ**, R 86; W 5, etc. (12

times); S 44, 72 (not in MS), etc. (7 times); L 52; 3p. **bēoþ**, W 49.

(3) preterite forms of **wesan**: 1s. **wæs**, R 20, etc. (9 times); M 217; D 36; 3s. **wæs**, B 7, 40; R 6, etc. (12 times); M 23, etc. (18 times); D 8, 11, 19, 23, 37; 3p. **wǣron**, R 8; M 110; S 9 (emended to *fruron*), 83; 3s. subj. **wǣre**, M 195, 240; W 96; D 26; L 8, 24.

(4) negative forms: pres. 3s. **nis**, *is not*, W 9; S 39; 3p. **nearon**, *are not*, S 82 (MS *næron*); pret. 3s. **næs**, *was not*, M 325.

beorg, m. *hill, mountain; burial mound;* as. R 32; ds. −**e**, R 50.

ġe-**beorg**, n. *defense, protection;* ds. −**e**, M 31, 131, 245.

beorgan, v.3, w. dat. *protect, save;* pret. 3p. **burgon**, M 194. [BEORGAN, BEARG, BURGON, BORGEN.]

beorht, adj. *bright;* nsf. B 15; W 94; dsm.wk. −**an**, R 66; superl. **beorhtost**, asm. (uninflected) R 6.

beorn, m. *warrior, man;* ns. B 45; R 42; W 70, 113; S 55; as. M 270; gs. −**es**, M 131, 160; ds. −**e**, M 154, 245; np. −**as**, R 32, 66; M 92, 111, 182; ap. −**as**, M 17, 62, 277, 305, 311; gp. −**a**, B 2; M 257; dp. −**um**, M 101.

bēot, n. *vow* (typically made before battle; hence) *boast; threat;* as. M 15, 27 (**on bēot**, *threateningly*), 213; W 70. [From *BĪ-HĀT; cf. ġe-**hātan**, and see Gordon's note on M 27.]

bēotian, wk.v.II. *vow, boast;* pret. 3s. **bēotode**, M 290; 3p. **bēotodon**, L 21.

bēoton, see **bēatan**.

bēoþ, see **bēon-wesan**.

beran, v.4. *bear, carry;* inf. M 12, 62; pres. 3s. **bereþ**, R 118; pret. 3p. **bǣron**, R 32; M 99; 3p. subj. **bǣren**, M 67. [BERAN, BÆR, BÆRON, BOREN; cf. **oþ-beran** and ġe-**boren**.]

-**berend**, m. nd-stem. *bearer;* see **gār-**, **reord-berend**.

berstan, v.3. *burst;* inf. R 36; pret. 3s. **bærst**, M 284. [BERSTAN, BÆRST, BURSTON, BORSTEN; orig. BRESTAN, etc. Cf. **to-berstan**.]

be-**slēan**, contr.v.6, w. gen. *bereave of* (*by slaughter*); pp. **beslæġen**, nsm. B 42. [Cf. **slēan**.]

be-**standan**, v.6. *stand around, surround;* pret. 3p. **bestōdon**, M 68. [Cf. **standan**.]

be-**stīeman**, wk.v.I. *make moist, suffuse;* pp. **bestīemed**, nsm. R 48; nsn. R 22. [Base-word **stēam**, m. *vapor, moisture, blood* (?).]

be-**swīcan**, v.1. *betray;* pp. **beswicen**, apm. −**e**, M 238. [SWĪCAN, SWĀC, SWICON, SWICEN.]

be-**swillan**, wk.v.I. *drench;* pp. **beswiled**, nsn. R 23 (MS *beswyled* is best interpreted so, with Dickins and Ross; earlier editors proposed a poorly supported BESYLED, *defiled*).

betera, adj. comp. *better* (declined wk.); nsm. M 276 (as noun); nsn. **betere**, M 31; npm. **beteran**, B 48.

betst, adj. superl. *best;* nsn. S 73 (as noun w. part. gen.).

be-**wāwan**, v.7. *blow against;* pp. **bewāwen**, npm. **bewāwne**, W 76 (**winde b.**, *beaten by the wind*). [WĀWAN, *WĒOW, *WĒOWON, WĀWEN − only pres. stem and pp. on record.]

be-**weaxan**, v.7. *grow over;* pp. **beweaxne**, npm. L 31. [WEAXAN, WĒOX, WĒOXON, WEAXEN; cf. **weaxan**.]

be-**windan**, v.3. *wind* (*about*), *encircle, enwrap;* pp. **bewunden**, asn. R 5. [Cf. **windan**.]

be-**wrēon**, contr.v.1. *put a covering around; cover;* pret. 1s. **bewrāh**, W 23; pp. **bewriġen**, uninfl., R 17, 53. [WRĒON (from *WRĪHAN), WRĀH, WRIGON, WRIĠEN; cf. **on-wrēon**.]

bi, see **be**.

bidan, v.1. *remain;* inf. S 30. [BĪDAN, BĀD, BIDON, BIDEN; cf. **a-bidan**.]

ġe-**bīdan**, v.1. (a) intrans., *wait;* inf. W
70; (b) trans., *obtain by waiting, live
to see; experience, endure;* pres. 3s.
ġe**bīdeþ**, W 1; pret. 1s. ġe**bād**, R
125; M 174; L 3; pp. ġe**biden**,
uninfl. R 50, 79; S 4, 28.

biddan, v.5. *bid, urge, exhort, ask,
pray;* pret. 3s. **bæd**, M 20, 128, 170,
257 (*urged, bade*); pret. 3p. **bædon**,
M 87 (*asked*), 262 (*prayed, be-
sought*), 306 (*exhorted*). [Construed
w. clause or (M 170) inf., and
sometimes acc. of person (M 170,
262). BIDDAN, BÆD, BÆDON, BEDEN.]

ġe-**biddan**, v.5, w. refl. pron. dat. and
prep. **tō**, *pray to;* pres. 3p. ġe-
biddaþ, R 83; pret. 1s. ġe**bæd**,
R 122.

bieldan, wk.v.I. *embolden, encourage;*
bielde, pret. 3s. M 169, 209 (**b. forþ**,
incited to advance), 320; pres. 3s.
subj., M 234. [Base-word BEALD,
bold.]

bierġan, wk.v.I. *taste;* pret. 3s.
bierġde, R 101. [Cf. **on-bierġan**.]

bifian, wk.v.II. *tremble;* inf. R 36;
pret. 1s. **bifode**, R 42.

bill, n. *sword;* as. M 162; dp. **-um**, M
114. **bill-ġeslieht**, m. or n. (*sword-*)
slaughter; gs. **-es**, B 45.

ġe-**bind**, n. *fastening, band; aggre-
gation;* as. in **waðuma ġebind**, W
24, 57 (*congregated waters? con-
finement of the waves? waves' em-
brace?*). [No other occurrence in
poetry; cf. **bindan**.]

bindan, v.3. *bind;* pres. 3s. **bindeþ**, W
102; 3p. **bindaþ**, W 18; 3s. subj.
binde, W 13; pret. 3s. **band**, S 32.
[BINDAN, BAND, BUNDON, BUNDEN.]

ġe-**bindan**, v.3. *bind, hold captive;*
pres. 3p. ġe**bindaþ**, W 40; pp.
ġe**bunden**, uninfl. (for npm. ĠE-
BUNDNE), S 9; nsm. D 24.

bisgu, f. īn-stem. *toil, trouble;* as. S
88. [Cf. **bisiġ**.]

bisiġ, adj. *busy, at work;* npm. **-e**,
M 110.

bismerian, wk.v.II. *mock, revile;* pret.
3p. **bismerodon**, R 48.

biter, adj. *bitter; painful, grievous;*
gsm. **bitres**, R 114; asf. **bitre**, S 4,
55 (MS *bitter*); *grim, fierce*, nsm. M
111; npm. **bitre**, L 31; apm. **bitre**, M
85. [Orig. *BITR; this developed to
BITER, which spread by analogy, but
inconsistently, to inflected forms,
producing the alternation between
biter- and **bitr-** found in the MSS.
The stem **bitr-** also produces gemi-
nation; hence MS *bitter* at S 55.]

biþ, see **bēon-wesan**.

blācian, wk.v.II. *grow pale;* pres. 3s.
blācaþ, S 91.

blǣd, m. (*vital spirit;*) *joy, glory;* ns.
W 33 (**foldan b.**, *earth's glory* – per-
haps also *fruitful abundance;* **blǣd**,
f. *blossom, fruit, growth*); S 79, 88;
as. D 34; dp. **-um**, R 149. [**blǣd**, m.,
is related to BLĀWAN, v.7, *blow,*
blǣd, f., to BLŌWAN, v.7, *bloom.*
The first is more frequent in poetry.]

ġe-**bland**, n. *mixture.* See **ēar-ġebland**.

blanden, pp. adj. *mixed.* [BLANDAN,
v.7.] **blanden-feax**, adj. *grizzle-
haired;* nsm. B 45.

blēo, n. ja-stem. *color;* dip. **blēoum**,
R 22.

bliss, f. *bliss;* ns. R 139, 141; ds. **-e**, R
149, 153. [From *BLĪÞ-S; cf. next
word.]

blīðe, adj. ja-stem. *glad, joyful;* asn. L
44; isn. R 122; L 21; comp. **blīðra**,
nsm. M 146 (*better pleased*).

blōd, n. *blood;* ds. **-e**, R 48.

blōdiġ, adj. *bloody;* asm. **-ne**, M 154.

blōstma, wk.m. *blossom;* dip. **-um**,
S 48.

bōc, f. cons.-stem. *book;* np. **bēċ**,
B 68.

boda, wk.m. *messenger;* vs. M 49.
[Cf. **bēodan**.]

boga, wk.m. *bow; np.* −**n**, M 110. [Cf. **būgan**.]

bold, n. *dwelling.* See **feorh-bold**.

bord, n. *shield; ns.* M 110; *as.* M 15, 42, 62 (or pl.), 131, 245, 270, 283, 309; *gs.* −**es** M 284; *gp.* −**a**, M 295; *dp.* −**um**, M 101. **bord-weall**, m. *shield-wall; as.* B 5; M 277 (or *shield?* see Scragg 1981: 82–83).

ġe-**boren**, adj. (pp., see **beran**), as noun, *one born in the same family; brother; dsm.* −**um**, S 98. [Cf. **beran**.]

bōsm, m. *bosom; ds.* −**e**, B 27.

bōt, f. *remedy; as.* −**e**, W 113.

brād, adj. *broad; asn.* M 15, 163; *apn.* B 71.

bræc, see **brecan**.

ġe-**bræc**, n. *clash; ns.* M 295. [Cf. **brecan**.]

brǣdan, wk.v.I. *spread; inf.* W 47. [Base-word **brād**.]

brægd, see **breġdan**.

brēac, see **brūcan**.

breahtm, m. *noise, clamor, gp.* −**a**, W 86.

brecan, v.4. *break; pret.* 3s. **bræc**, M 277 (*broke through*—see Gordon's note); *pp.* **brocen**, ns. M 1 (the noun modified is missing). [BRECAN, BRÆC, BRÆCON, BROCEN; cf. **to-brecan**.]

breġdan, v.3. *move quickly; draw, pluck out; pret.* 3s. **brægd**, M 154, 162. [BREĠDAN, BRÆĠD, BRUGDON, BROGDEN.]

bregu, m. u-stem. *sovereign, chief; ns.* B 33.

brēost, n. *breast* (usually pl. where Mod. English has sing.); *dp.* −**um**, R 118; M 144; W 113. **brēost-cearu**, f. *breast-care, sorrow of heart; as.* −**ċeare**, S 4; L 44. **brēost-cofa**, wk.m. *the recesses of the breast; ds.* −**n**, W 18. **brēost-hord**, n. (*what is treasured in the breast;*) *inmost feelings; as.* S 55.

brēoðan, v.2. *waste away.* See **a-brēoðan**.

brēr, m. *briar, bramble;* dip. −**um**, L 31.

brim, n. *sea (-surge); ap.* −**u**, B 71. **brim-fugol**, m. *seabird; ap.* −**fuglas**, W 47. **brim-lād**, f. *sea-passage, voyage; ds.* −**e**, S 30. **brim-līðend**, m. nd-stem. *seafarer; gp.* −**ra**, M 27 (*vikings*). **brim-mann**, m. cons.-stem. *seaman; np.* −**menn**, M 295; *gp.* −**manna**, M 49 (*vikings*).

bringan, wk.v.I (pres., strong 3). *bring; pres.* 3s. **brinġeþ**, W 54. [BRINGAN, BRŌHTE, BRŌHT.]

ġe-**bringan**, wk.v.I. *bring; pres.* 3s. subj. ġe**brinġe**, R 139.

brocen, see **brecan**.

brōðor, m. r-stem. *brother; ns.* B 2; M 282; S 98; *np.* **brōðru**, M 191; *gp.* **brōðra**, D 8.

ġe-**brōðor**, m.pl. *brothers* (considered together as children of the same parent); nom. B 57; M 305 (alt. form −**brōðru**).

brūcan, v.2, w. gen. *enjoy, partake of, use; inf.* B 63; R 144; *pres.* 3p. **brūcaþ**, S 88 (b. þurh bisġu, gen. HIRE understood: *gain the use of it by toil*); *pret.* 3s. **brēac**, W 44. [BRŪCAN, BRĒAC, BRUCON, BROCEN.]

brūn, adj. *brown;* (of metals) *gleaming.* **brūn-ecg**, adj. *with gleaming blade; asn.* M 163.

brycg, f. jō-stem. *bridge; ford, causeway; as.* −**e**, M 74, 78. **brycg-weard**, m. *guard of the causeway; ap.* −**as**, M 85.

bryne, m. i-stem. *fire; as.* R 149.

brytta, wk.m. *dispenser, giver* (typically w. gen. of a word for treasure, characterizing a generous lord); sinċes bryttan, as. W 25 (or gs. if sele-drēoriġ is taken as two words).

bryttian, wk.v.II. *divide, distribute;* (hence) *dispose of, enjoy; inf.* B 60.

būgan, v.2. *bow, bend down;* inf. R 36, 42; *turn, retreat;* inf. M 276; pret. 3p. **bugon,** M 185. [BŪGAN, BĒAG, BUGON, BOGEN; cf. **bēag, boga;** also **for-būgan.**]

ġe-bunden, see **ġe-bindan.**

bune, wk.f. *cup, beaker;* ns. W 94 (as symbol of drinking in the hall).

būr, n. *bower, bedchamber.* **būr-þeġn,** m. *servant of the bower; chamberlain;* ds. −e, M 121.

burg, f. cons.-stem. *stronghold, stockaded dwelling or manor; walled town, city;* as. M 291 (probably Byrhtnoþ's manor house; see Gordon's note); D 19; dp. −um, S 28; ap. **byriġ,** S 48 (less probably np.). **burg-tūn,** m. *fortification* (perhaps referring to a hedge) or *fortified place, manor;* np. −as, L 31. **burg-ware,** m.pl. *keepers of the stronghold, citizens;* gp. −wara, W 86. [Cf. **scield-burg.**]

burgon, see **beorgan.**

būtan, conj. (w. subj.) *unless,* M 71; (after negative) *but, except,* S 18.

bū-tū, n. dual. *both;* acc. R 48. [See **bēġen** and **twēġen.**]

-byrd, f. i-stem. *what one bears* (cf. **ġe-byrd,** *birth*) − in compounds, sometimes a social or legal responsibility. See **mund-byrd.** [Cf. **beran.**]

byre, m. i-stem. *opportunity;* as. M 121. [Cf. **beran.**]

byrġan, wk.v.I. *bury;* inf. S 98. [Cf. **beorg.**]

byriġ, see **burg.**

byrne, wk.f. *corselet, coat of mail;* ns. M 144, 284; as. **byrnan,** M 163.

byrn-wiga, wk.m. (*mailed*) *warrior;* ns. W 94.

C

cāf, adj. *quick, vigorous, valiant;* asm. −ne, M 76 (**c. mid his cynne,** *valiant as was his kindred, come of a valiant stock*—Gordon).

cāflīċe, adv. *valiantly;* M 153.

camp, m. *battle;* ds. −e, B 8. **camp-stede,** m. i-stem. *battlefield;* ds. B 29, 49.

ġe-camp, m. *battle;* ds. −e, M 153.

candel, f. *candle;* ns. B 15. [From Lat. CANDĒLA, applied to large candles used in churches; hence the application to heaven's candle, the sun.]

cāsere, m. ja-stem (adapt. of Lat. CAESAR). *emperor;* np. **cāseras,** S 82.

ċeald, n. (*the*) *cold;* dis. −e, S 8.

ċeald, adj. *cold;* asn. M 91; dip. −um, S 10; superl. **ċealdost,** nsn. w. part. gen. S 33. [Cf. **hrīm-, is-, winter-ċeald.**]

ċeallian, wk.v.II. *call, shout;* inf. M 91.

ċeariġ, adj. *troubled, sad, sorrowful.* See **earm-, hrēow-, mōd-, sorg-, winter-ċeariġ.**

cearu, f. *care; sorrow, grief, anxiety;* ns. W 55; as. **ċeare,** W 9; np. **ceara,** S 10. **ċear-seld,** n. *abode of care;* gp. −a, S 5. [Alt. form **caru,** whence mod. "care"; association with Lat. *cura* had already begun in OE. On the diphthong of nom. **cearu,** which probably did not have palatal *c* (*ċ*), see Campbell 1959: §208. Cf. **brēost-, mōd-, ūht-cearu.**]

ġe-ċēas, see **ġe-ċēosan.**

cellod, adj. meaning unknown; asn. M 283, describing a shield.

cempa, wk.m. *warrior;* ns. M 119. [Cf. **camp.**]

cēne, adj. ja-stem. *keen, bold, warlike;* nsm. M 215; npm. M 283 (or adv. *boldly*); comp. **cēnre,** nsf. M 312. [*KŌNJA-.]

ċēol, m. *ship;* ds. −e, S 5.

ċeorfan, v.3. *carve, hew out;* pret. 3p. curfon, R 66. [ĊEORFAN, ĊEARF, CURFON, CORFEN.]

ċeorl, m. *freeman of the lowest rank, yeoman, churl* (but less derogatory than at a later period); ns. M 256; ds. −e, M 132 (a common viking in contrast to the English earl: *the earl to the churl*).

ġe-ċēosan, v.2. *choose;* pret. 3s. ġeċēas, M 113. [ĊĒOSAN, ĊĒAS, CURON, COREN.]

ċierm, m. i-stem. *cry, clamor, uproar;* ns. M 107.

ċierran, wk.v.I. *turn.* See on-ċierran.

clǽne, adj. ja-stem, *clean, pure;* asn. S 110.

clamm, m. *grip, fetter;* dip. −um, S 10.

clēofan, v.2. *cleave, split;* pret. 3p. clufon, B 5; M 283. [CLĒOFAN, CLĒAF, CLUFON, CLOFEN.]

clif, n. *cliff;* dp. −um, S 8. [Cf. stān-clif.]

clipian, wk.v.II. *call out;* pret. 3s. clipode, M 25, 256.

clufon, see clēofan.

clyppan, wk.v.I. *embrace;* pres. 3s. subj. clyppe, W 42. [Cf. ymb-clyppan.]

cnāwan, v.7. *know.* See on-cnāwan.

cnearr, m. *ship;* ns. B 35. [Probably borrowed from, certainly alluding to, Old Norse KNQRR as a specific term for a viking ship (see Sayers 1996); cf. nǽġled-cnearr.]

cnēo, n. wa-stem. *knee;* ds. W 42 (contraction of *CNEOWE); − fig., *a degree of relation in genealogy:* cnēo-mǽġ, m. *a kinsman in one's genealogical line; ancestor;* dp. −māgum, B 8.

cniht, m. *young man, youth;* ns. M 9, 153.

cnossian, wk.v.II. *toss, pitch, drive?* pres. 3s. cnossaþ, S 8. [Recorded only here. The base-word *CNOSS is the same as for cnyssan and implies beating or striking; cf. ĠE-CNOSS, *collision;* but perhaps striking waves rather than rocks.]

cnyssan, wk.v.I. *beat against;* pres. 3p. cnyssaþ, W 101; − fig., *urge insistently, importune,* S 33. [Base-word *CNOSS; see cnossian.]

cofa, wk.m. *coffer, recess, room.* See brēost- and hord-cofa.

cōlian, wk.v.II. *cool;* pret. 3s. cōlode, R 72.

collen-, adj. combining form, pp. of a lost verb *CWELLAN, *swell, spring up, grow big*—which has cognates in Germanic languages. collen-ferhþ adj. *stout-hearted, proud, brave;* nsm. W 71.

cōm, cōmon, see cuman.

corn, n. *kernel, grain;* gp. −a, S 33.

cræftiġ, adj. *skilled.* See lēoþ-cræftiġ.

crēad, see crūdan.

cringan, v.3. *fall in battle, perish;* inf. M 292; pret. 3p. crungon, B 10; M 302. [CRINGAN, CRANG, CRUNGON, CRUNGEN.]

ġe-cringan, v.3. *fall, perish;* pret. 3s. ġecrang, M 250, 324; W 79.

crūdan, v.2. *(crowd,) press on;* pret. 3s. crēad, B 35. [Only pres. and pret. 3s. recorded.]

crungon, see cringan.

cuman, v.4. *come;* pres. 3s. cymeþ, W 103; S 61, 106, 107; 1p. subj. cumen, S 118 (*make our way*); pret. 3s. cōm, B 37 (*made his way*); R 151, 155; M 65; 3p. cōmon, R 57; pp. cumen, nsm. R 80; nsf. M 104; − hwǽr cōm, pret. 3s. *what has become of, where is,* W 92 (three times), 93. [CUMAN, CŌM, CŌMON, CUMEN; cf. be-, ofer-cuman.]

cumbol, n. *banner.* cumbol-ġehnāst, n. *collision of banners* (in battle); gs. −es, B 49.

cunnan, pret.-pres.v. *(can,) know, know how;* pres. 3s. subj. cunne: w.inf., *know how to,* W 113; w. gear(w)e, *know for certain,* W 69 (used absolutely, with the same implication as the next), 71 (w. ind. quest.). [CUNNAN, CANN, CUNNON, CŪÐE.]

cunnian, wk.v.II. *test, find out (by trial); make trial of, experience;* inf. M 215 (**mæġ cunnan**, *one can find out;* see **magan**); pres. 3s. **cunnaþ**, W 29; 1s. subj. **cunnie**, S 35; pret. 3s. **cunnode**, D 1 (w. gen.).

ġe-cunnian, wk.v.II. *explore, make trial of, come to know;* pp. **ġecunnod**, uninfl., S 5.

curfon, see **ċeorfan**.

cūþ, adj. *known, familiar;* nsn. D 19; gp. **cūðra**, W 55. [Cf. **cunnan**.]

cwæþ, see **cweðan**.

cweċċan, wk.v.I. *shake.* See a-**cweċċan**.

cweðan, v.5. *say, speak;* inf. R 116; pres. 3s. **cwiþ**, R 111 (future sense); pret. 3s. **cwæþ**, M 211, 255; W 6, 111. [CWEÐAN, CWÆÞ, CWÆÐON, CWEDEN; cf. a-, on-**cweðan**, and **æfter-cweðende**.]

ġe-cweðan, v.5. *speak;* pret. 3s. **ġecwæþ**, M 168.

cwic(u), adj. u-stem. *alive;* pl. as noun, *the living;* gp. **cwicra**, W 9.

cwide, m. i-stem. *speech, discourse.*
cwide-ġiedd, n. ja-stem. *saying, utterance;* gp. **-a**, W 55 (**cūðra c.**, *familiar utterances*—almost, *familiar accents?*). [Cf. **lār-cwide**.]

cwiþ, see **cweðan**.

cwīðan, wk.v.I. *bewail, lament;* inf. W 9; pret. 3p. **cwīðdon**, R 56.

cymeþ, see **cuman**.

cyne-, adjectival combining form. *royal.* **cyne-rīċe**, n. ja-stem. *kingdom, regime;* gs. **-s**, D 26 (see note on D 7). [From *CUNI-, related to **cyning** and **cynn**.]

cyning, m. *king;* ns. B 1, 35, 58; D 23; gs. **-es**, R 56 (*King*); as. R 44, 133 (*King*); np. **-as**, B 29; S 82.

cynn, n. ja-stem. *kind, race, family,* kindred; as. R 94 (**wīfa c.**, *womankind*); gs. **-es**, M 217, 266; ds. **-e**, M 76. [Cf. **mann-cynn**.]

cyssan, wk.v.I. *kiss;* pres. 3s. subj. **cysse**, W 42. [COSS, m. *kiss, embrace.*]

cyst, f. i-stem. (a) *the best, choicest;* as. R 1. [Cf. **ġe-ċēosan**.] – (b) (*select*) *band;* see **ēorod-cyst**. [But perhaps the word in this second context is unrelated to **ċēosan** and should be normalized as **ċiest**, an i-stem from *CÆSTI-, meaning simply *band, troop, crowd.* Cf. Old Icelandic KOSTR, *pile, heap.*]

ġe-cȳðan, wk.v.I. *make known, declare;* inf. M 216. [Base-word **cūþ**, q.v.; cf. **a-cȳðan**.]

cȳþþ, f. iþō-stem. *known region or people, home;* as. **-e**, B 38, 58. [Base-word **cūþ**; cf. "*kith* and kin.*"]

D

dæd, f. i-stem. *deed;* dp. **-um**, S 41; dip. **-um**, S 76.

dæġ, m. *day;* as. B 21; M 198 (or, more likely, an endingless locative: **on dæġ**, *that day* [Dobbie]); L 37 (used adverbially); np. **dagas**, S 80; gp. **daga**, R 136. **dæġ-weorc**, n. *day's work;* gs. **-es**, M 148. [Cf. **dōm-dæġ**; **ġēar-**, **ġeswinċ-dagas**.]

dæl, m. i-stem. w. gen. *share, portion* (*of*); ns. D 30; *a good share, a deal* (*of*), *many*, as. W 64; D 34.

dælan, wk.v.I. *deal out* or *share;* pres. 1p. subj. **dælen**, M 33 (**hilde d.**, *should join battle*). [Base-word DÂL, n. *division, portion;* cf. be-, to-**dælan**.]

ġe-dælan, wk.v.I. *divide, share; part;* **dēaðe ġedælde**, pret. 3s. *handed over to death*, W 83; 3s. subj. **ġedælde**, *might part*, L 22.

dagas, see **dæġ**.

daroþ, m. *spear;* as. M 149, 255; gp. −**a**, B 54.

dēad, adj. *dead;* nsn.wk. −**e**, S 65 (fig.); ds. −**um**, as noun, *the dead one,* S 98.

dēag, see **dugan**.

dēaþ, m. *death;* ns. S 106; D 8; as. R 101; L 22; gs. **dēaðes**, R 113; ds. **dēaðe**, W 83.

delfan, v.3. *dig.* See **be-delfan**.

dēman, wk.v.I., w. dat., *pass judgment on, judge;* inf. R 107. [Base-word **dōm**, q.v.]

dennian, wk.v.II. *lie flattened?* pret. 3s. **dennode**, B 12. [The only occurrence; meaning unknown. The word is discussed in the note.]

denu, f. *valley;* np. **dena**, L 30.

dēofol, m. and n. *(the) devil;* ds. **dēofle**, S 76.

dēop, adj. *deep;* asn. B 55; dsm.wk. −**an**, R 75.

dēope, adv. *deeply,* W 89.

dēor, n. *animal;* as. B 64.

dēor, adj. *brave, valiant;* nsm. S 41; dip. −**um**, S 76.

deorc, adj. *dark* (with various emotional overtones); asn.wk. −**e**, W 89 (*mysterious and cheerless?*); dp. −**um**, R 46 (*iron-colored and sinister?*).

derian, wk.v.I, w. dat. *injure, harm;* inf. M 70.

dīere, adj. ja-stem. *dear;* nsm. D 37 (w. dat., *dear to*).

dierne, adj. ja-stem. *secret, hidden; deceitful;* asm. (**-rne** for **-rnne**), L 12.

dimm, adj. *gloomy, dark;* npf. −**e**, L 30.

dōgor, n. (or m.) *day;* gp. **dōgra**, W 63.

dol, adj. *foolish;* nsm. S 106.

dolg, n. *wound;* np. R 46.

dōm, m. (a) *doom, judgment;* gs. −**es**, R 107; (b) *stipulation, choice;* as. M 38; (c) *favorable judgment, praise, glory, renown;* as. M 129; ds. −**e**, S 85. **dōm-dæġ**, m. *day of judgment;*

ds. −**e**, R 105. **dōm-ġeorn**, adj. *eager for praise;* npm. −**e**, W 17 (as noun: *men of repute, aspirants to honor*). [Cf. **dēman**.]

dōn, anom.v. *do;* pret. **dyde**, (a) as substitute for a verb previously used: *did,* 3s. R 114; (b) *did, acted* (in a specified manner), 3s. M 280; (c) w. acc. object and **tō**, *made to serve as, took for,* 1s. S 20.

ġe-dōn, anom.v., trans. (a) *do, perform;* pp. **ġedōn**, M 197; (b) w. **tō**, *bring into a condition,* or *put to a purpose;* inf. S 43 (**tō hwon hine dryhten ġedōn wille**, [*as to*] *what the Lord* [or *his lord?*] *will bring him to*—so Gordon, after Whitelock).

dorste, see **durran**.

-drǣdan, v.7. *dread;* only w. prefixes; see **on-drǣdan**.

drēag, see **drēogan**.

ġe-drēag, n. *multitude;* as. L 45. [Rel. to DRYHT f. *army, host;* see **dryhten**.]

drēam, m. *joy, delight, festivity; music, musical entertainment;* ns. R 140; S 80; gs. −**es**, R 144; dis. −**e**, W 79; np. −**as**, S 65, 86; dp. −**um**, R 133. [Mod. "dream" is a sense not recorded in OE. Cf. **sele-drēam**.]

ġe-drēfan, wk.v.I. *trouble, afflict;* pp. **ġedrēfed**, nsm. R 20, 59. [Base-word DRŌF, adj. *turbid, troubled.*]

dreng, m. (*viking*) *warrior;* gp. −**a**, M 149. [The vikings' own term for their warriors; see Gordon's note. As it is a Norse borrowing, the **g** is velar.]

drēogan, v.2. *undergo, endure;* inf. L 26; pres. 3s. **drēogeþ**, L 50; 3p. **drēogaþ**, S 56; pret. 3s. **drēag**, D 2. [DRĒOGAN, DRĒAG, DRUGON, DROGEN.]

drēor, m. *blood.* **drēor-sele**, m. i-stem. *blood-hall, desolate lodgings;* asm. L 50.

drēoriġ, adj. (*bloody;*) *sad, dejected;* nsf. B 54 (*dejected—and bloody?*); asm. −**ne**, W 17 (modifying **hyġe**

understood). **drēoriġ-hlēor,** adj. *sad-faced;* nsm. W 83. [Cf. **drēor** and **sele-drēoriġ.**]

drēosan, v.2. *fall, droop, fail;* pres. 3s. **drēoseþ,** W 63. [DRĒOSAN, DRĒAS, DRURON, DROREN; cf. **be-droren.**]

ġe-drēosan, v.2. *fail, come to an end;* pret. 3s. **ġedrēas,** W 36; pp. **ġe-droren,** *fallen;* nsf. S 86.

drīfan, v.1. *drive.* See **be-, þurh-drīfan.**

drinċ, m. *drink;* see **medu-drinċ.**

ġe-droren, see **ġe-drēosan.**

dryhten, m. (a) *lord (leader of a* DRYHT f. *army, host);* ns. B 1; S 41 (and 43?); ds. **dryhtne,** D 37; – – (b) *the Lord* (used attributively or as a proper name); ns. C 4, 8; R 101, 105, 144; M 148; S 43 (or in sense [a]?), 124; D 32; as. R 64; S 106; gs. **dryhtnes,** B 16; R 9, 35, 75, 113, 136, 140; S 65, 121. [Cf. **mann-, wine-dryhten,** sense (a).]

dryhtlicost, adj. superl. *most lordly;* dsm. –**um,** S 85.

dugan, pret.-pres.v. *avail;* pres. 3s. **dēag,** M 48 (future sense). [DUGAN, DĒAG, DUGON, DOHTE.]

duguþ, f. (a) *that which avails, benefit, advantage;* ds. –**e,** M 197 (**him to d.,** *for their benefit*). – (b) *seasoned retainers;* (less specifically) *military band, company of warriors, host;* ns. W 79; S 86; ds. –**e,** W 97; *(heavenly) host,* dp. –**um,** S 80. [Cf. **dugan.**]

dūn, f. *hill;* np. –**a,** L 30.

durran, pret.-pres.v. *dare;* pres. subj. 1s. **durre,** W 10; pret. 1s. **dorste,** R 35, 42, 45, 47. [DURRAN, DEARR, DURRON, DORSTE.]

dyde, see **dōn.**

E

ēa, f. cons.-stem. *river.* **ēa-stæþ,** n. *riverbank;* ds. –**e,** M 63.

ēa, interj. *O!* or *Oh!* **ēa-lā,** interj. *O, oh;* W 94 (twice), 95.

ēac, adv. *also,* B 2; R 92; S 119. **swelċe . . . ēac,** *and likewise, also;* B 19, 30, 37.

ēac, prep. w. dat. or instr. *in addition to,* M 11; L 44 (instr.).

ēacen, adj. *increased, great; pregnant;* nsf. D 11. [Pp. of obsolescent ĒACAN, v.7, *increase.*]

ēadiġ, adj. *blessed;* nsm. S 107; *prosperous, fortunate;* see **sēft-ēadiġ.**

ēadiġnes, f. jō-stem. *beatitude, happiness;* as. –**e,** S 120.

eafora, wk.m. *son, heir, descendant;* np. –**n,** B 7; ap. –**n,** B 52.

eald, adj. *old;* nsm. B 46; M 310; L 29; wk. –**a,** M 218 (**e. fæder,** *grandfather*); gsn. –**es** L 4 (as adv. *of old, long ago*); npn. **eald,** W 87; apn. –**e** (the generalized form, or asn.wk.), M 47; npm. –**e,** B 69. **eald-ġewyrht,** f. i-stem (or n.). *deed of old, former action;* dp. –**um,** R 100.

ealdian, wk.v.II. *grow old;* pres. 3s. **ealdaþ,** S 89.

ealdor, m. *lord;* ns. M 202, 222, 314; gs. **ealdres,** M 53; ds. **ealdre,** M 11; – w. limiting gen., *the Lord:* **wuldres ealdor,** ns. R 90; S 123. **ealdor-mann,** m. *nobleman of the highest rank, "ealdorman";* ns. M 219.

ealdor, n. *life; age, eternity;* ds. **ealdre,** S 79 (**āwa tō ealdre,** *ever for life, for ever and ever*). **ealdor-lang,** adj. *age-long, eternal;* asm. –**ne,** B 3.

ealgian, wk.v.II. *defend;* inf. M 52 (MS *gealgean;* see Gordon's note); pret. 3p. subj. **ealgoden,** B 9.

eall, adj. *all;* nsm. W 74; nsn. R 6 (or adv.); W 106, 110; nsf. R 12, 55, 82; W 36, 79, 115; S 86; L 46; asn. R 58, 94; W 60; gsm. –**es,** L 41; asf. –**e,** M 304; S 124; ism. –**e,** D 16; npm. –**e,** R 9 (MS – deleted), 128; M 63, 203, 207; S 81; np.(n.?) –**e,** S 50 (**ealle**

þā, indef. antecedent); apm. −e, R 37, 74, 93; M 231, 238, 320; apf. −e, M 196; gp. **ealra**, R 125; M 174; W 63; dp. **eallum**, R 154; M 233. − as pron., asn. M 256 (**ofer eall**, see **ofer**); dp. **eallum**, *to all men*, M 216. [Cf. **ælmihtiġ**.]

eall, adv. *entirely;* R 6 (or adj., nsn.), 20, 48, 62; M 314; L 29.

ēar, m. *sea*. **ēar-ġebland**, n. *concourse of waters, sea-surge;* as. B 26.

eard, m. *land, homeland, country;* as. B 73; M 53, 58, 222; S 38. **eard-ġeard**, m. *(enclosed) plot of ground, dwelling place, region;* as. W 85. **eard-stapa**, wk.m. *land-treader, wanderer;* ns. W 6.

earfoþe, n. ja-stem (also **earfeþe**). *hardship, tribulation, trouble;* ap. −u, D 2 (MS −a); gp. −a, W 6; D 30; L 39. **earfoþ-hwīl**, f. *time of hardship;* as. −e, S 3.

earfoþlīċ, adj. *full of trouble, distressful;* nsn. W 106.

earg, adj. *slack, cowardly;* nsn. M 238. [Cf. **un-earg, ierġþu**.]

earm, m. *arm;* as. M 165.

earm, adj. *poor, destitute, wretched, miserable;* asm. −ne, W 40; npm. −e, R 68; gp. −ra, R 19 (as noun). **earm-ċeariġ**, adj. *wretched and sorrowful, miserably sad;* nsm. W 20; S 14.

earn, m. *eagle;* ns. M 107; S 24; as. B 63.

ġe-earnian, wk.v.II. *earn, deserve;* pres. 3s. **ġe-earnaþ**, R 109.

ġe-earnung, f. *act deserving gratitude (or other recompense); favor;* ap. −a, M 196.

eart, see **bēon-wesan**.

ēastan, adv., *from the east;* B 69.

ēað-, combining form of **ēaðe**, adj. and adv. *easy, easily; gentle, gently.* **ēað-mōd**, adj. *humble, meek, submissive;* nsm. R 60; S 107.

eaxl, f. *shoulder;* dp. −um, R 32. **eaxl-ġespann**, n. *shoulder-beam or shoulder-joint, intersection;* ds. −e, R 9.

ebba, wk.m. *ebb tide;* ds. −n, M 65.

ēċe, adj. ja-stem. *eternal;* nsm. C 4, 8; S 124; gsm. −s, B 16; gsn.wk. **ēċan**, S 79; asf.wk. **ēċan**, S 120. [From *ŌKJA-.]

ēċe, adv. *eternally, for ever;* S 67.

ecg, f. jō-stem. *edge, (sword-) blade;* ns. M 60; dip. −um, B 4, 68. **ecg-hete**, m. i-stem. *sword-hate, deadly violence;* ns. S 70. [Cf. **brūn-ecg**.]

efstan, wk.v.I. *hasten;* inf. R 34; pret. 3p. **efston**, M 206. [Also spelt EFESTAN; base-word OFOST, f. *haste;* cf. **ofostlīċe**.]

eft, adv. *again, back, afterward;* B 56; R 68, 101, 103; M 201; W 45; S 61; L 23; **eft onġēan**, *back again, in reply*, M 49, 156.

eġesa, wk.m. *awe, terror; awful power;* ns. R 86; S 103; ds. −n, S 101.

eġeslīċ, adj. *fearful, dreadful;* nsf. R 74.

el-, combining form (from prehist. *ALJA-, *ALI-), *other, alien, foreign.* [Cf. **elles**.] **el-þēodiġ**, adj. *of a foreign country;* gp. −ra, S 38 (as noun: *of foreigners, strangers—* possibly, *strangers on earth*, PEREGRINI).

ellen, n. (rarely m.), *courage, valor, zeal, fortitude;* as. **on ellen**, *valiantly*, M 211; ds. **mid elne**, *valiantly*, W 114; is. **elne micle**, *with great zeal*, R 34, 60, 123.

elles, adv. *of another sort; else;* S 46; L 23. [Gs. of unrecorded adj. *ELL (from *ALJA-), *other, alien;* cf. **el-**.]

ende, m. ja-stem. *end, outermost part;* ds. R 29 (*edge*).

endelēas, adj. *endless;* nsm. D 30.

enġel, m. *angel;* ns. R 9; np. **englas**, R 106; gp. **engla**, M 178; dp. **englum**, R 153; S 78. [Lat. ANGELUS, vulg.

ANGILUS; the word should have g in oblique cases, otherwise ǵ.].

ent, m. *giant;* gp. **−a**, W 87 (**enta ǵeweorc**, *work(s) of giants*—a recurrent poetic expression for ancient ruins, presumably occasioned by wonder at the remains of Roman building in Britain).

ēode, ēoden, ēodon, see **gān**.

eodor, m. *enclosure, dwelling;* np. **−as**, W 77.

eoh, m. *war horse, charger;* as. M 189.

eom, see **bēon-wesan**.

eorl, m. (a) *man, warrior;* ns. W 84, 114; D 2; ds. **−e**, W 12; D 33; ap. **−as**, W 99; gp. **−a**, B 1; W 60; S 72; D 41. (b) *earl* (a title corresponding to Old Norse JARL and substituted in late Old English times for the earlier, native rank of **ealdormann**; in M it is applied exclusively to Byrhtnoþ); ns. M 6, 51 (partly sense [a]?), 89, 132, 146, 203, 233; gs. **−es**, M 165; ds. **−e**, M 28, 159; − referring to Norse JARLS, np. **−as**, B 31.

eornoste, adv. *resolutely,* M 281.

ēorod, n. *troop* (orig. *of horsemen:* **eoh**, *horse*, plus RĀD, *group of riders*). **ēorod-cyst**, f. i-stem. *picked company*, or **-ċiest**, f. i-stem. *band of horsemen;* dip. **−um**, B 21. [See **cyst**.]

eorðe (comb. form **eorþ-, eorð-**) wk.f. *earth, the earth;* **eorðan**, gs. C 5 (var.); R 37; W 106, 110; S 61, 81, 89, 105; ds. R 42, 74, 137, 145; M 107, 126, 157, 233, 286, 303; S 32 (or as.), 93; L 33; as. S 39. **eorþ-scræf**, n. *earth-pit, subterranean space; cavern; grave, barrow;* ds. **−e**, W 84; L 28; ap. **−scrafu**, L 36. **eorþ-sele**, m. i-stem. *underground dwelling, cavern, barrow;* ns. L 29. **eorð-weġ**, m. *earthly way;* ds. **−e**, R 120. **eorð-wela**, wk.m. *earthly wealth;* in pl., *earthly riches, worldly goods;* np. **−n**, S 67.

ēow, see **ġē**.

ēðel, m. *home, native land;* ns. R 156; as. M 52; S 60 (fig., **hwæles e.**) dis. **ēðle**, W 20. [*ŌÐIL-.]

F

fæder, m. r-stem. *father;* ds. W 115 (*Father*); **ealda fæder**, *grandfather,* ns. M 218. [Cf. **hēah-, wuldor-fæder**.]

fǣġe, adj. ja-stem. *fated to die (fey);* nsm. M 119; npm. B 12, 28; M 105; gsm. **−s**, M 297 (as noun); dsm. **fæġum**, S 71 (as noun); dsm.wk. **fæġan**, M 125.

fæġen, adj. *glad, cheerful;* nsm. W 68.

fæġer or **fǣġer**, adj. *beautiful, fair;* nsn. **fæġer**, R 73; dsf. wk. **fæġran**, R 21; **fæġre**, npm. R 8, 10 (or possibly an adverb; see next word). [Orig. FÆĠR; developed like **biter**, q.v. The origin of the long vowel required by the meter in some poems is obscure.]

fæġre or **fǣġre**, adv. *fairly, well;* M 22 (w. æ); possibly R 10 (w. ǣ).

fæġrian, wk.v.II. *make beautiful, adorn;* pres. 3p. **fæġriaþ**, S 48. (Less probably, *become beautiful;* see Gordon's note.)

fæġrost, adv. superl. *most pleasantly,* S 13.

fǣhþ(u), f. iþō-stem. *hostility, feud;* gs. or as. **fæhþe**, M 225; as. **fæhþu**, L 26. [Base-word **fāh**, q.v.]

fǣr, m. *sudden attack.* **fǣr-scaða**, wk.m. *sudden raider (viking);* ds. **−n**, M 142.

fǣrlīċe, adv. *suddenly, with terrible swiftness;* W 61.

fæst, adj. *firm, fixed.* As suffix; used with **sigor-, stede-**, and **þrym-**.]

fæste, adv. *firmly, fast;* (a) *so as not to be moved or shaken,* w. **standan**, R 38, 43; M 171, 301; (b) *so as not to* *be overcome: securely,* M 103; (c) *with firm grasp or restraint,* M 21; W 13, 18.

fæsten, n. ja-stem. *fastness, place of safety;* as. M 194.

fæstlīċe, adv. *stoutly, resolutely;* M 82, 254.

fæstnian, wk.v.II. *make fast, confirm;* inf. M 35.

ġe-fæstnian, wk.v.II. *fasten;* pret. 3p. **ġefæstnodon,** R 33.

fæstnung, f. *firmness, stability, permanence;* ns. W 115.

-fæt, m. uncertain meaning, perhaps related to **fōt;** not the same as FÆT, n. *container, vat;* appears only as second element of **sīþ-fæt,** q.v.

fāg, adj. *colored, stained* (hence *guilty*); *decorated;* nsm. R 13 (*stained*); W 98 (*decorated*). [In both instances there may be overtones of **fāh** (next word): the MSS spell the two words alike, either *fag* or *fah,* though *fag* for **fāh** is rare.]

fāh, adj. *outlawed; hostile;* nsm. L 46.

faran, v.6. *go, pass;* inf. M 88, 156; w. **on,** adv., and dat. of person, *advance* (relative to someone), *gain upon, overtake:* pres. 3s. **him on fareþ,** *overtakes him,* S 91. [FARAN, FŌR, FŌRON, FAREN.]

faru, f. *expedition, passage.* See **hæġl-faru.**

fēa, adv. (apn. of **fēawe,** adj. npm. *few*), (*few things*), *little, but little;* R 115. **fēa-sceaftiġ,** adj. *wretched, desolate;* asn. S 26. (The usual adj. is FĒA-SCEAFT, *having few things, destitute;* perhaps it is here modified for figurative application to spiritual poverty.)

feaht, see **feohtan.**

feallan, v.7. *fall;* inf. R 43; M 54, 105; pres. 3s. **fealleþ,** W 63; pret. 3s. **fēoll,** M 119, 126, 166, 286, 303; S 32; 3p. **fēollon,** B 12; M 111.

[FEALLAN, FĒOLL, FĒOLLON, FEALLEN; cf. **a-feallan.**]

fealu, adj. wa-stem. *fallow; yellow;* (a) describing the sea or its waves: *fallow* (i.e., *desolate*) or perhaps *glossy* (see Barley 1974: 24–25); asm. **fealone,** B 36; apm. **fealwe,** W 46. (b) **fealu-hilte,** adj. ja-stem. *having a yellow* (*golden*) *hilt;* nsn. M 166.

feax, n. *hair* (*of the head*); as adjectival suffix, *-haired.* See **blanden-, gamol-feax.**

ġe-feċċan (earlier **-fetian**), wk.v.II (orig. III). *carry off, take, fetch;* inf. M 160 (MS *gefecgan*); pres. 3s. subj. **ġefeċċe,** R 138 (MS *gefetige*).

fela, n., indecl. pron. *much, many* (w. part. gen.); nom. M 73; acc. R 50, 125, 131; M 90; W 54; S 5; (indicating extent of time) D 38; L 39. **fela-lēof,** adj. *dearly loved;* **-an** gsm.wk. as noun, L 26.

ġe-fēlan, wk.v.I. *feel;* inf. S 95. [From *FŌLJAN.]

feld, m. u-stem. *field;* ns. B 12; ds. **-a,** M 241. [Cf. **wæl-feld.**]

fēng, see **fōn.**

feoh, n. *property; money; wealth;* ns. W 108; as. M 39. **feoh-ġifre,** adj. *greedy for wealth;* nsm. W 68.

ġe-feoht, n. *fight;* ds. **-e,** B 28; M 12.

feohtan, v.3. *fight;* inf. M 16, 261; pret. 3s. **feaht,** M 254, 277, 281, 298. [FEOHTAN, FEAHT, FUHTON, FOHTEN; cf. **un-befohten.**]

ġe-feohtan, v.3, trans. *acquire by fighting, win;* inf. M 129.

feohte, wk.f. *battle;* ns. M 103.

fēol, f. *file.* **fēol-heard,** adj. *hard as a file;* apn. **-e** (generalized form), M 108. ("The file was used to test the temper of the blade" – Gordon.)

fēoll, fēollon, see **feallan.**

fēond, m. nd-stem. *enemy;* np. **-as,** R 30, 33; ap. **-as,** R 38; gp. **-a,** S 75 (either secular enemies or devils); dp. −um, M 103, 264; ap. **fiend**, M 82. [**fiend** is standard West Saxon for nap., but **fēondas** occurs in poetic texts, esp. those thought to be of Anglian origin.]

feorh, n. (rarely m.) *life, soul, spirit;* ns. S 94; as. B 36; M 125, 142, 184; S 71; gs. **feores**, M 260, 317; ds. **feore**, M 194, 259. **feorh-bold**, n. *dwelling of the soul, body;* ns. R 73. **feorh-hūs**, n. *house of the soul, body;* as. M 297. [Cf. **firas**.]

feorr, adj. *far;* gs. −es, L 47.

feorr, adv. *far, afar, far away;* M 3, 57; W 26; S 37, 52; L 25; w. dat., *far from*, W 21; *at a distance in time, long ago*, W 90.

feorran, adv. *from afar*, R 57.

ġe-**fēra**, wk.m. *companion, comrade; member of a lord's comitatus, retainer;* ns. M 280; ap. −n, M 170, 229; in figurative use, ds. −n, W 30. [Base-word **fōr**, f. *journey*, corresponding to pret. 1s. of **faran**; cf. also **fēran**.]

fēran, wk.v.I. *go, journey;* inf. M 41, 221; S 37; L 9. [Base-word **fōr**; see preceding word.]

ferhþ, m. or n. *spirit, soul, heart;* ns. W 54; as. S 26 (here neuter), 37; ds. −e, W 90. **ferhþ-loca**, wk.m. *enclosure of the spirit, breast; thoughts; feelings* (conceived as locked in the breast); ns. W 33; as. −n, W 13. [Cf. **collen-ferhþ**.]

ferian, wk.v.I. *carry, transport;* pret. 3s. **ferede**, W 81; rare meaning, *go;* inf. M 179 (mistake for **fēran**?). [Base-word FÆR, n. *a going, passage.*]

fēt, see **fōt**.

feter, f. *fetter;* dip. −um, W 21.

fēða, wk.m. *troop* (*on foot*); as. −n, M 88. [Not related to **fōt**.]

feðer, f. *feather;* ap. **feðra**, W 47.

-**feðra**, wk.m. *feathered one* (formed from adjectival -**feðer**). See **isiġ-**, **ūriġ-feðra**. [These compounds have the same form as wk. adjectives but their position in the verse suggests that they are nouns.]

fiell, m. i-stem. *fall, death;* as. R 56; M 71, 264.

fiellan, wk.v.I. *fell, cut down;* inf. R 73. [Cf. **feallan**.]

ġe-**fiellan**, wk.v.I. (a) *fell, kill;* inf. R 38; pp. **ġefielled**, nsn. B 67; (b) *deprive of* (*by killing*), w. gen., pp. **ġefielled**, nsm. B 41 (perhaps a mistake for BEFIELLED, since BE-normally lends this sense with verbs of killing).

fiend, see **fēond**.

fierd, f. i-stem. *army* (on the march); spec., the local levy organized for the defense of the realm; ds. −e, M 221. **fierd-rinċ**, m. *warrior* (of the English levy); ns. M 140.

fīf, num. adj. *five;* npm. **fīfe**, B 28; R 8.

findan, v.3. *find;* inf. W 26; pret. 1s. **funde**, L 18; 3p. **fundon**, M 85. [FINDAN, FAND or FUNDE, FUNDON, FUNDEN; cf. **on-findan**.]

firas, m.pl. *men, human beings;* dp. **firum**, C 9. [Related to **feorh**, q.v.]

flǣsc, n. i-stem. *flesh.* **flǣsc-hama**, wk.m. *fleshly covering, body;* ns. S 94.

flān, m. *arrow, dart;* as. M 269 (generic); gs. −es, M 71.

flēag, see **flēogan**.

flēam, m. *flight* (of a fugitive); as. M 81, 254; ds. −e, B 37; M 186.

flēogan, v.2. (a) *fly;* inf. M 7, 109, 150; pret. 3s. **flēag**, S 17; (b) *flee;* inf. M 275 (probably a scribal substitution for **flēon**: see p. 143). [FLĒOGAN, FLĒAG, FLUGON, FLOGEN.]

flēon, contr.v.2. *flee;* inf. M 247; pret. 3p. **flugon**, M 194. [FLĒON (from *FLĒOHAN), FLĒAH, FLUGON, FLOGEN.]

flēotan, v.2. *float; fleet;* pres. part. **flēotende**, as noun, *floating* or *fleeting one;* gp. **flēotendra**, W 54. (Both senses may be operative if the actual seabirds are confused with the visionary companions.) [FLĒOTAN, FLĒAT, FLUTON, FLOTEN.]

flett, n. ja-stem. *floor* (typically of a hall; hence metaphorical for the life of a noble retainer and also for life on the floor of this earth); as. W 61.

flīema, wk.m. *fugitive.* See **here-flīema**.

ġe-flīeman, wk.v.I, *put to flight;* pp. **ġeflīemed**, nsm. B 32. [Cf. **flēam** and **a-flīeman**.]

flōd, m. or n. *flood;* (a) *current, stream, sea;* as. B 36 (m.); (b) *flood tide;* ns. M 65, 72 (m.). **flōd-weġ**, m. *sea-way;* ap. −**as**, S 52 (*paths of ocean*). [Cf. **mere-flōd**.]

-floga, wk.m. *flier.* See **ān-floga**.

flot, n. *water?* (occurs only in prep. phrases, **tō flote**, **on flot**, *afloat;* might mean the act or state of floating, or water deep enough to float a ship); as. in **on flot**, B 35, M 41. [Cf. **flēotan**.]

flota, wk.m. *floater: sailor, viking;* as. −**n**, M 227; np. −**n**, M 72; gp. **flotena**, B 32. [Cf. **scip-flota**.]

flōwan, v.7. *flow;* pres. part. **flōwende**, nsm. M 65. [FLŌWAN, FLĒOW, FLĒOWON, FLŌWEN; cf. **be-flōwan**.]

flugon (*fled*), see **flēon**.

flyht, m. i-stem. *flight;* as. M 71.

folc, n. (a) *people;* ns. R 140; M 45; as. M 54; D 22; gs. −**es**, B 67; M 202; (b) *army, host;* ns. M 241; as. M 22; ds. −**e**, M 227, 259 (**on folce**, *on an* [*enemy*] *host?*), 323. **folc-land**, n. *country;* gs. −**es**, L 47. **folc-stede**, m. i-stem, *place of assembly, battlefield;* ds. B 41.

folde, wk.f. *earth, ground, land;* **foldan**, gs. R 8, 43; W 33; ds. R 132; M 166, 227; S 13, 75; as. C 9; M 54.

folgoþ, m. (*position of*) *service; office; condition of life;* as. D 38; L 9. [The term regularly refers to a retainer's position in his lord's retinue.]

folme, wk.f. *hand;* ds. **folman**, M 150; dp. **folmum**, M 21, 108. [FOLM, f., is the commoner form, but M 150, confirmed as ds. by **handa**, 149, points to wk. **folme**.]

fōn, contr.v.7. *take, seize;* pret. 3s. **fēng**, M 10 (**tō wǣpnum f.**, *took up arms*). [FŌN, (from *FANHAN), FĒNG, FĒNGON, FANGEN; cf. **on-fōn**.]

for, prep. w. dat., instr., or acc. *for;* − (a) w. dat. or instr., *in the presence of, before,* R 112; S 101, 103 (**for þon**, *before which,* or *because of which*); *because of,* R 21, 111 (**unforht for**, *unafraid of*); M 64, 89; L 10; *for the sake of,* R 113; *in expiation of,* R 99, 146; *for* (*fear* or *dislike of*), M 96; *for* (*fear of losing*), M 259. − (b) w. acc., *for the sake of; before* R 93 (both meanings are possible: see note). **for-þon**, adv. and conj. (a) adv. *therefore, wherefore,* R 84; M 241; W 17, 64; L 17; *indeed,* W 37, 58; S 27, 33 (*as for that? but yet?*), 39 (*for indeed?*), 58, 72. − (b) conj. *for, because,* S 64, 108; L 39. [In S 103, **þon** is probably a relative pronoun: see above, **for** (a). The interpretation of **for-þon**, in S and elsewhere, has been much disputed. The suggestions above are offered without conviction.] **for-hwon**, interrogative adv. and conj. *for what reason, why, wherefore;* as conj., W 59.

fōr, f. *journey.* See **sǣ-fōr**.

for-bærnan, wk.v.I. *burn up, consume* (in fire); pp. **forbærned**, asm. −**ne**, S 114.

for-būgan, v.2, w. acc. *turn away from, flee from;* pret. 3s. **forbēag**, M 325. [Cf. **būgan**.]

for-cūþ, adj. *infamous;* see **un-forcūþ**, and cf. **fracuþ**, with stress on first syllable.

ford, m. u-stem. *ford;* as. M 88; ds. **-a**, M 81.

fore, prep. *for, in place of;* w. acc., S 21; w. dat., S 22. (Possibly we should read **hleahtre**, dat., for **hleahtor**, acc. in S 21.)

for-ġiefan, v.5. *give (away), grant;* pret. 3s. **forġeaf**, R 147; M 139, 148; pp. **forġiefen**, ap. (m. or n.) **-e**, S 93 *(given up, consigned).* [Cf. **a-ġiefan**.]

for-ġieldan, v.3, w. acc. *buy off;* pres. 2p. subj. **forġielden**, M 32. [ĠIELDAN, ĠEALD, GULDON, GOLDEN, *yield, give, pay.*]

for-grindan, v.3. *grind to pieces, destroy;* pp. **for-grunden**, asm. uninfl. B 43. [Cf. **ġe-grindan**.]

for-heard, adj. *very hard;* asm. **-ne**, M 156 (**gār** understood; stressed on first syllable).

for-hēawan, v.7. *hew down, cut down;* pp. **forhēawen**, nsm. M 115, 223, 288, 314. [Cf. **hēawan**.]

for-hogode, see **for-hycgan**.

forht, adj. *afraid, fearful;* nsm. R 21; W 68. [Cf. **un-forht**.]

forhtian, wk.v.II. *be afraid;* pres. 3p. **forhtiaþ**, R 115 (future sense); pret. 3p. subj. **forhtoden**, M 21.

for-hwon, see **for**.

for-hycgan, wk.v.III (and II). *despise, scorn;* pret. 3s. **forhogode**, M 254. [Cf. **hycgan**.]

for-lǣtan, v.7. (a) *leave, abandon;* inf. M 2, 208; pret. 3s. **forlēt** B 42; M 187; 3p. **forlēton**, R 61; (b) w. inf., *let, cause to;* pret. 3s. **forlēt**, M 149, 156, 321. [Cf. **lǣtan**.]

forma, wk.adj. *earliest, first;* asm. **-n**, M 77.

for-maniġ, adj. *very many;* nsm. M 239 (prob. stressed on second syllable).

for-niman, v.4. *carry off, destroy;* pret. 3s. **fornam**, W 80; 3p. **fornāmon**, W 99. [Cf. **niman**.]

forst, m. *frost;* dis. **-e**, S 9.

for-swelgan, v.3. *swallow (up);* inf. S 95. [SWELGAN, SWEALG, SWULGON. SWOLGEN.]

forþ, adv. *forth, away, onward;* B 20; R 54, 132; M 3, 12, 170, 205, 209, 225, 229, 260, 269, 297; **- tō forþ**, *too successfully, too deeply,* M 150. **forð-ġeorn**, adj. *eager to advance;* nsm. M 281. **forð-ġesceaft**, f. *preordained condition;* as. R 10 (see note). **forð-weġ**, m. *the way forth* (into the hereafter); ds. **-e** R 125 (see note); W 81.

ġe-forðian, wk.v.II. *carry out, accomplish;* pp. **ġeforðod**, uninfl. M 289.

for-þolian, wk.v.II. *endure the absence of, do without, forgo;* inf. W 38. [Cf. **þolian**.]

for-þon, see **for**.

for-wegan, v.5. *carry off, destroy, kill;* pp. **for-weġen**, nsm. M 228. [Cf. **wegan**.]

for-wundian, wk.v.II. *wound (sorely);* pp. **forwundod**, nsm. R 14, 62. [Cf. **ġe-wundian**.]

fōt, m. cons.-stem. *foot;* gs. **-es**, M 247; dp. **-um**, M 119, 171; np. **fēt**, S 9. **fōt-mǣl**, n. *foot's length;* as. as adv. M 275.

fracuþ, adj. *wicked, shameful, proscribed;* gsm. **fracuðes**, R 10 (as noun, *a criminal's*). [The second constituent presumably was stressed when medial fricatives were voiced; hence **ð** in inflected forms.]

fram, adv. *away;* M 317. **fram-sīþ**, m. *departure;* ns. L 33. **fram-weard**, adj. *on the way out, passing away;* dsm. **-um**, S 71.

fram, prep. w. dat. or instr. *from;* B 8; R 69; M 185, 187, 193, 252, 316 (the last clearly w. instr.).

franca, wk.m. *spear;* as. –n, M 140; ds. –n, M 77. [Originally a spear favored by the Franks, but in poetry equated with **gār**; see Gordon's note on M 77.]

frēa, wk.m. (a) *lord;* as. –n, M 259; ds. –n, M 12, 16, 184, 289; gs. –n, L 33 (*husband*). (b) *the Lord;* ns. C 9; as. –n, R 33.

frēfran, wk.v.I. *comfort;* inf. W 28; S 26 (MS *feran*). [Base-word **frōfor**, q.v.]

ġe-fremman, wk.v.I. *perform, bring about, accomplish;* inf. W 16, 114; pret. 3p. **gefremedon**, S 84.

fremu, f. *beneficial action; good deed;* dip. –m, S 75 (MS *fremman*).

frēo, adj. ja-stem. *free, noble.* **frēo-mǣġ**, m. (*noble*) *kinsman;* dip. –māgum, W 21.

frēod, f. *peace;* ds. –e, M 39.

frēond, m. nd-stem. *friend, loved one, kinsman;* ns. R 144; W 108; L 47; np. –as, R 76; gp. –a, B 41, R 132; L 17; np. **friend**, L 33; ap. **friend**, M 229. [Standard West Saxon has nap. **friend**, but the analogical –as occurs in some poems, esp. those thought to be of Anglian origin.]

frēondlēas, adj. *friendless;* asm. –ne, W 28.

frēondscipe, m. *intimacy,* (*conjugal*) *love, friendship;* ns. L 25.

frēoriġ, adj. *cold, frozen;* nsm. W 33. [Cf. **frēosan**.]

frēosan, v.3. *freeze;* pret. 3p. **fruron** (MS *wæron*), S 9. [FRĒOSAN, FRĒAS, FRURON, FROREN.]

friend, see **frēond**.

frige, f.pl. *love;* np. D 14.

friġnan, v.3. *ask;* pres. 3s. **friġneþ**, R 112 (future sense). [FRIĠNAN, FRÆĠN, FRUGNON, FRUGNEN; parts 1, 3, and 4 are often spelt without G, indicating the pronunciation FRĪN- and FRŪN-.]

ġe-friġnan, v.3. *learn* (by asking); pret. 1p. **ġefrugnon**, D 14; 3p. R 76.

friþ, m. *peace;* as. M 39; gs. **friðes**, M 41 (instr. force, *at peace*—see **healdan**); ds. **friðe**, M 179.

frōd, adj. *old, wise, experienced;* nsm. M 140, 317 (**frōd feores**, *advanced in years*); W 90; nsm.wk. as noun, **sē frōda**, *the old campaigner*, B 37.

frōfor, f. *comfort, help, support;* as. **frōfre**, W 115.

ġe-frugnon, see **ġe-friġnan**.

fruma, wk.m. *origin; ruler;* see **lēod-fruma**.

fruron, see **frēosan**.

frymdiġ, adj. *asking, desirous;* nsm. M 179 (**iċ eom f. tō þē**, *I beseech you*).

fugol, m. *bird;* ns. W 81. [Cf. **brim-fugol**.]

full, adj. w. gen. *full* (*of*); nsf. S 100; asm. **fulne**, S 113 (w. gen. **fȳres**).

full, adv. *wholly, very;* M 153, 253, 311; W 5; S 24; L 1, 18, 21, 32, 46.

fundian, wk.v.II, w. prep. or adv. (indicating the goal), *direct one's course* (*to*); pres. 3s. **fundaþ**, S 47 (**sē-þe on lagu fundaþ**, *he who will go to sea*); and w. inf. (indicating purpose), R 103 (**hider eft fundaþ ... mann-cynn sēċan**, *he will come hither again to seek humankind*).

fundon, see **findan**.

furðor, adv. comp. *further;* **f. gān**, *advance*, M 247.

fūs, adj. (a) *eager* (*to set out, to press on*); nsm. M 281; asm. –ne, S 50; (b) *hastening;* npm. –e, R 57 (as noun); (c) *brilliant, shining;* asn.wk. –e, R 21 (the meaning *mobile, quickly shifting*, suggested by Cook, lacks confirmation from other passages—see note in Dickins and Ross). [Related to **fundian**; the base of **fȳsan**.]

fylstan, wk.v.I. w. dat., *help;* inf. M 265.

fȳr, n. *fire;* gs. **–es**, S 113.

fyrmest, adj. superl. *foremost, first;* nsm. M 323.

fȳsan, wk.v.I, trans. *send forth rapidly; speed, shoot;* pret. 3s. **fȳsde**, M 269. [May also be intransitive, *hasten;* base-word **fūs**, q.v.; cf. **a-fȳsan**.]

G

gǣstlič, adj. *ghostly, spectral;* nsm. W 73. [The meaning *ghastly, terrifying* is tempting here and may be correct, but see *OED* s.v. "ghastly"—the word cannot with certainty be connected with OE **gǣstlič**.]

gafol, n. *tribute;* as. M 61; ds. **–e**, M 32, 46.

gāl, adj. *libidinous, licentious, giddy.* See **win-gāl**.

galan, v.6. *sing;* inf. R 67. [GALAN, GŌL, GŌLON, GALEN.]

gamen, n. *entertainment;* ds. **–e**, S 20.

gamol, adj. *old, aged.* **gamol-feax**, adj. *hoary-haired, grey-headed;* nsm. S 92 (as noun).

gān, anom.v. *go;* inf. M 247; imper. pl. **gāþ**, M 93 (*=come*); pret. 3s. **ēode**, R 54; M 132, 159, 225, 297, 323; 3p. **ēodon**, M 260; 3p. subj. **ēoden**, M 229. [Cf. **ofer-gān**.]

gang, m. *going, passage; flow* (of blood), ds. **–e**, R 23. [Cf. **upp-ganga**, and next two words.]

ġe-gang, m. *going, passage, lapse,* as. S 69 (MS *ge:* see note).

gangan, v.7. *go, move along, proceed;* inf. M 62; **gangan forþ**, *advance;* inf. M 3, 170; **tō scipe gangan**, *embark;* inf. M 40 (w. refl. dat. **ūs**, *take to our ships*); pres. 1s. **gange**, L 35; 2p. subj. **gangen**, *should embark,* M 56. [GANGAN, ĠEONG, ĠEONGON, GANGEN.]

ġe-gangan, v.7. (*go and*) *get, obtain;* inf. M 59.

ganot, m. *gannet;* gs. **–es**, S 20.

gār, m. *spear;* ns. M 296; as. M 13, 134, 154, 237, 321; ds. **–e**, M 138; ap. **–as**, M 46, 67, 109; dip. **–um**, B 18. **gār-berend**, m. nd-stem. *spear-bearer, spearman;* np. M 262. **gār-mittung**, f. *encounter of spears;* gs. **–e**, B 50. **gār-rǣs**, m. *rush of spears, battle;* as. M 32.

gāst, m. *soul, spirit;* as. R 49; ds. **–e**, M 176; np. **–as**, R 11; gp. **–a**, R 152.

gāþ, see **gān**.

ġe, conj. *and,* L 25.

ġe-, prefix, sometimes signifying *together.* With verbs a sign of completed action, often untranslatable but sometimes distinctive. All words beginning with this prefix are listed according to the first letter of their stems.

ġē, pron. 2nd pers. pl. *you;* nom. M 32, 34, 56, 57, 59; dat. **ēow**, M 31, 46, 48, 93; acc. **ēow**, M 41. [Early Mod.E. *ye*.]

ġēac, m. *cuckoo;* ns. S 53.

ġealga, wk.m. *gallows, cross;* ns. R 10; as. **–n**, R 40. **ġealg-trēo**, n. wa-stem. *gallows-tree, cross;* ds. **–we**, R 146. [Mod. pronunciation from Anglian GALGA.]

ġēara, adv. *formerly;* **ġēara ġēo**, *in years gone by, long ago,* R 28; W 22. **ġēar-dagas**, m.pl. *former times, days of yore;* dp. **–dagum**, W 44. [The origin of **ġēara** is obscure, though presumably it is related to ĠEAR (Anglian ĠĒR), n. *year.* The initial constituent of **ġēar-dagas** may actually be ĠEAR, as the poem's editors have generally assumed; but derivation from **ġēara** seems semantically more satisfactory, and adverbial elements in noun compounds are by no means unparalleled. See **ġēo**.]

ġeard, m. *yard; enclosed field or plot of ground* (which may sometimes be of great extent). See **eard-, middan-ġeard**.

ġearu, adj. wa-stem. *ready;* nsm. M 274; npm. **ġearwe**, M 72, 100.

ġearulīċe, adv. *readily;* (with verb of perceiving) *clearly;* D 10.

ġearwe, or ġeare, adv. *readily;* (with verb of knowing) *clearly, for certain, well;* W 69, 71. [The two spellings represent a heavy and a light stressed syllable respectively, and their alternate use here accords with metrical requirements.]

ġeatu, f. wō-stem. *equipment, gear.* See **here-ġeatu**.

ġēo, adv. *of old, formerly;* R 87; S 83; **ġeāra ġēo**, *in years gone by, long ago*, R 28; W 22. **ġēo-wine**, m. i-stem. *friend* (or *lord*) *of former days;* ap. S 92. [Often spelt *iu* in the MSS.]

ġēoc, f. *help;* ds. −e, S 101.

ġeoguþ, f. *youth* (as a period of life); ds. −e, W 35; S 40.

ġeōmor, adj. *sad, mournful;* nsm. L 17; dsf. −re, L 1; disf.wk. **ġeōmran**, S 53. **ġeōmor-mōd**, adj. *gloomy* (*of spirit*), *sober-minded;* nsm. L 42. [Cf. **hyġe-ġeōmor**.]

ġeond, prep. w. acc. *through, throughout, over;* W 3, 58, 75; S 90; D 31 (**wendeþ ġeond**, *goes about through*); L 36.

ġeond-hweorfan, v.3. *pass through, rove through;* pres. 3s. −hweorfeþ, W 51. [Cf. **hweorfan**.]

ġeond-sċēawian, wk.v.II, *survey;* pres. 3s. −sċēawaþ, W 52. [Cf. **sċēawian**.]

ġeond-þenċan, wk.v.I. *consider thoroughly, contemplate;* pres. 1s. −þenċe, W 60; 3s. −þenċeþ, W 89. [Cf. **þenċan**.]

ġeong, adj. *young;* nsm. R 39; M 210; L 42; nsm.wk. **sē ġeonga**, as epithet, M 155; asm. −ne, B 44; npm. −e, B 29.

ġeorn, adj., w. gen. *eager (for);* nsm. M 107; W 69; npm. −e, M 73. [Cf. **dōm-, forð-ġeorn**.]

ġeorne, adv. *eagerly,* M 123, 206; W 52; (with a verb of seeing, implying careful observation) *well, clearly;* M 84.

ġeornfull, adj. *eager;* nsm. M 274.

ġeornlīċe, adv. *eagerly,* M 265.

ġēotan, v.2. *pour out, shed* (blood); pres. part. **ġēotende**, *dripping* (with blood), np. R 70 (the emendation adopted by Cook for MS *reotende;* see **grēotan** for the alternative here preferred). [ĠĒOTAN, ĠĒAT, GUTON, GOTEN; cf. **be-ġēotan** and **a-ġīetan**.]

ġiċel, m. *piece of ice, icicle.* [To be derived from *JEKIL- > *JIKIL-, and therefore OE **c** should stand for **ċ**; a ME form spelt with **ch** is in fact attested. The much commoner spelling with ME **k** reflects either the unattested OE syncopated stem **ġicl-** (the spelling adopted at S 17, which also produces a more usual metrical type) or a stem with **c** produced by the suffix ablaut seen in ON JQKULL, *glacier*.] See **hrim-ġiċel**.

ġiedd, n. ja-stem. *saying; song, poem;* as. L 1. [Cf. **cwide-, sōð-ġiedd**.]

ġiefa, wk.m. *giver.* See **bēag-, gold-, māðum-, sinċ-ġiefa**.

ġiefan, v.5. *give.* See **a-, for-, of-ġiefan**. [ĠIEFAN, ĠEAF, ĠĒAFON, ĠIEFEN.]

ġiefu, f. *gift;* gp. **ġiefena**, S 40 (with **gōd**, *generous of gifts?* or *well-endowed with natural abilities, generously gifted?* − Gordon recommends the first, but the other seems more appropriate). **ġief-stōl**, m. *gift-seat* (the high seat or throne, from which gifts were dispensed); the *ceremony of gift-giving;* gs. −es, W 44.

ġieldan, v.3. *yield, give, pay.* See for-ġieldan.

ġiellan, v.3. *(yell,)* cry out loudly; pres. 3s. ġielleþ, S 62. [ĠIELLAN, ĠEALL, GULLON, *GOLLEN; cf. be-ġiellan.]

ġielp, m. or n. *boasting; a boast;* gs. −es, W 69. ġielp-word, n. *vaunting word;* dip. M 274.

ġielpan, v.3. *boast;* inf. B 44 (w. gen.). [ĠIELPAN, ĠEALP, GULPON, GOLPEN.]

ġieman, wk.v.I, w. gen. *heed, care for;* pret. 3p. ġiemdon, M 192.

ġierwan, wk.v.I. *prepare, dress, adorn;* pret. 3p. ġieredon, R 77. [Base-word ġearu; cf. ġe-, on-gierwan.]

ġe-ġierwan, wk.v.I. *adorn;* pp. ġe-ġiered, asn. R 16; ġeġierwed, the same, R 23. [The form without *w* is historically correct, the other analogical, and the alternation confirmed by the meter.]

ġiest, m. i-stem. *stranger;* np. −as, M 86.

ġiet, adv. *yet.* See þā-ġiet.

ġieta, adv. *yet;* B 66; R 28.

ġietan, v.5. *get.* See be-, on-ġietan. [ĠIETAN, ĠEAT, ĠĒATON, ĠIETEN.]

ġīetan, wk.v.I. *destroy.* See a-ġīetan.

ġif, conj. *if,* M 34, 36, 196.

ġīfre, adj. ja-stem. *greedy, ravenous;* nsm. S 62. [Cf. feoh-, wæl-ġifre.]

ġimm, m. *jewel;* np. −as, R 7, 16. [From Lat. GEMMA.]

-ġinnan, v.3. *begin.* Never without prefix. See on-ġinnan.

ġisel, m. *hostage;* ns. M 265.

glēaw, adj. *sagacious, sharp-sighted, wise, prudent;* nsm. W 73.

glēo, n. *joy, high spirits; music.* glēo-stafas, m.pl. *signs of joy, joyful salutations, songs?* dp. −stafum, W 52. [See stæf.]

glidan, v.1. *glide;* pret. 3s. glād, B 15. [GLĪDAN, GLĀD, GLIDON, GLIDEN.]

gnornian, wk.v.II. *mourn, feel sorrow,* lament; inf. M 315; pres. 3s. gnornaþ, S 92.

gōd, adj. *good;* nsm. M 315; S 40 (*well-endowed, excellent? generous?*); asn. M 13, 237; asm.wk. −an, M 187 (as noun); dsm. −um, M 4; apm. −e, M 170; asf. in gōde hwīle, *a good while,* R 70. [Cf. betera, betst, sēlest.]

gōd, n. *(that which is) good;* gs. −es, M 176.

gold, n. *gold;* ns. W 32 (see wunden); S 101; as. R 18; ds. −e, R 7, 16; M 35; dis. −e, R 77; S 97. gold-ġiefa, wk.m. *gold-giver;* np. −n, S 83.

gold-wine, m. *friendly patron, bountiful friend* (since the lord typically gives gold to his loyal retainers); ns. W 35; as. W 22.

grǣdiġ, adj. *greedy;* nsm. S 62; asm. −ne, B 64.

grǣf, n. *grave;* as. S 97

grǣġ, adj. *grey;* asn.wk. grǣġe, B 64.

gram, adj. *fierce;* npm. −e, M 262; dp. −um, M 100 (as noun, *foes*).

ġe-gremian or -gremman, wk.v.I. *enrage;* pp. ġegremed, nsm. M 138; up. −e, M 296. [Base-word gram.]

grēot, n. *sand, dust;* ds. −e, M 315.

grēotan, v.2. *weep;* pres. part. grēotende, np. R 70 (MS *reotende,* from RĒOTAN, v.2, *weep,* lacks alliteration; see ġēotan for alternative emendation). [Only the present stem of this verb is on record.]

grētan, wk.v.I. *approach; speak to, hail, greet;* pres. 3s. grēteþ, W 52. [The base-word *GRŌT has not survived.]

grimm, adj. *grim, fierce, savage;* nsm. M 61; D 23.

ġe-grindan, v.3. *grind, sharpen;* pp. ġegrunden, ap. ġegrundene, M 109 (normalized ġegrundne: see note). [GRINDAN, GRAND, GRUNDON, GRUNDEN; cf. for-grindan.]

griþ, n. *truce, peace;* as. M 35. [A Scandinavian term for a truce based on definite conditions; less general than **friþ**; see Gordon's note.]

grund, m. *ground; land, surface of the earth; bottom, foundation;* as. M 287 (*the ground*); ap. **–as**, B 15 (*surfaces of earth; the land*); S 104 (**stiðe grundas**, *the rocky foundations*).

ġe-grundene, see **ġe-grindan**.

grundlēas, adj. *bottomless; boundless;* npf. **–e**, D 15.

gryre, m. i-stem. *terror.* **gryre-lēoþ**, n. *terrible song;* gp. **–a**, M 285.

guma, wk.m. *man;* ns. B 18; W 45; gs. **–n**, R 49, 146 (generic sing. or late form of pl. **gumena?**); np. **–n**, M 94; gp. **gumena**, B 50.

gūþ, f. *battle;* as. **gūðe**, M 325; gs. **gūðe**, M 192; ds. **gūðe**, B 44; M 13, 94, 187, 285, 296 (or instr.), 321. **gūþ-hafoc**, m. *war-hawk;* as. B 64. **gūþ-plega**, wk.m. *battle-play;* ns. M 61. **gūð-rinċ**, m. *warrior;* ns. M 138.

H

habban, wk.v.III. *have.* (a) as independent v.; inf. M 236; S 113 (*cause to be;* not in MS); L 43; pres. 3s. **hafaþ**, W 31; S 47; pret. 1s. **hæfde**, L 7; 3s. **hæfde**, M 13, 121, 199 (*held*); D 3. – neg. **næbbe** (**ne hæbbe**), pres. 3s. subj. S 42. (b) as aux. w. pp.; pres. 1s. **hæbbe**, R 50, 79; S 4; 2s. **hafast**, M 231; 3s. **hafaþ**, M 237 (the transcript reads *hæfð;* see below); pret. 3s. **hæfde**, R 49; M 22, 197, 289; D 10; 3p. **hæfdon**, R 16, 52. [West Saxon normally has HÆFST, HÆFÞ, but it has seemed best to adopt the commoner poetic forms.]

hæġl, m. *hail;* ns. S 17, 32; dis. **–e**, W 48. **hæġl-faru**, f. *shower of hail, hailstorm* (perhaps with analogy to

an army on the march; see **faru**); as. **–fære**, W 105.

hǣlan, wk.v.I. *heal, save;* inf. R 85. [Base-word **hāl**, q.v.]

hæle, or **hæleþ**, m. þ-stem. *man, warrior, hero;* ns. **hæle**, W 73; **hæleþ**, R 39; vs. **hæleþ**, R 78, 95; np. **hæleþ**, M 214, 249; gp. **hæleþa**, B 25; M 74; dp. **hæleþum**, W 105. [Originally ns. **hæle**, np. **hæleþ**.]

hǣlend, m. nd-stem. *Healer, Savior* (translation of "Jesus"); gs. **–es**, R 25. [Cf. **hǣlan** and **hāl**.]

hǣðen, adj. *heathen;* npm. **hǣðne**, M 55, 181.

hafaþ, see **habban**.

hafenian, wk.v.II. *raise aloft;* pret. 3s. **hafenode**, M 42, 309.

hafoc, m. *hawk;* as. M 8. [Cf. **gūþ-hafoc**.]

haga, wk.m. *hedge, enclosure,* as in **wiġ-haga**, q.v.; in **ān-haga** the wk. ending **-a** signifies an agent and **hag-** may signify a hedged dwelling (hence "lone-dweller"), but the sense of narrow confinement is appropriate.

hāl, adj. *whole, safe and sound, unhurt;* npm. **–e**, M 292.

hāliġ, adj. *holy;* nsm. C 6; npm. **hālġe**, R 11; – declined wk. as m. noun, **hālga**, *holy one;* ds. **–n**, S 122 (*God*); dp. **hālgum**, R 143, 154 (*saints*—see note).

hām, m. *home, dwelling;* as. R 148; S 117; ds. **–e**, M 292; ap. **–as**, B 10; **–as.** as adv. w. verb of motion, *home*(*ward*), M 251.

hama, wk.m. *covering.* See **flǣsc-hama**.

hamor, m. *hammer;* gp. **–a**, B 6.

hand, f. u-stem. *hand;* ns. M 141; as. M 112; S 96; ds. **–a**, R 59; M 149; ap. **–a**, W 43; dp. **–um**, M 4 (see note), 7, 14; W 4. **hand-plega**, wk.m. *hand-to-hand combat;* gs. **–n**, B 25.

hār, adj. *grey; hoary, old;* nsm. B 39; M 169; nsm.wk. **−a**, W 82.

hasu, adj. wa-stem. *dark, dusky.* **hasupāda**, wk.m. *dusky-coated one;* as. **−n**, B 62. (The same in form as a wk. adj. corresponding to strong HASU-PĀD, *dusky-coated.*)

hāt, adj. *hot;* npf. **hāt'** (for **hāte**), S 11; comp. **hātra**, npm. **−n**, S 64 (fig.). **hāt-heort** adj. *hot-tempered;* nsm. W 66.

hātan, v.7. (a) *command;* pres. 1s. **hāte**, R 95; pret. 3s. **hēt**, M 2, 62, 74, 101; L 15, 27 (MS *heht*); 3p. **hēton**, R 31; M 30; − (b) *call, name;* pp. **hāten**, nsm. M 75, 218. [MS *heht,* which is Anglian and poetic, reflects the ancient reduplicated preterite, while **hēt** reflects the newer variety of preterites of this class that arose in Northwest Germanic: for a survey of explanations see Fulk 1987; HĀTAN, HĒT, HĒTON, HĀTEN.]

ġe-hātan, v.7. *promise, vow;* pres. 1s. **ġehāte**, M 246; pret. 3s. **ġehēt**, M 289.

hē, hēo, hit, pron. 3rd pers. *he, she, it,* pl. *they.* **hē**, nsm. C 3, 5; B 40; R 34, etc. (15 times); M 7, etc. (56 times); W 2, etc. (10 times); S 8 (*it*), 42, etc. (9 times); L 51. **his**, gsm. or n. C 2; B 2, 38, 40, 42; R 49, 63, 92, 102, 106, 156; M 11, etc. (20 times); W 13, etc. (8 times); S 40, etc. (11 times); L 46. **him**, dsm. or n. R 65, 67, 108, 118; M 7, etc. (15 times; refl. in 300); W 1, 10 (w. *þe, to whom*), etc. (7 times); S 13 (w. *þe, to whom*), etc. (11 times); D 1, 3; L 45. **hine**, asm. R 11, 39, 61, 64; M 164, 181; W 32, 35; S 43, 77, 99; D 5. **hēo**, nsf. W 96; D 10, 11. **hire**, gsf. D 8, 9. **hīe**, asf. M 180; S 103 (refl., *itself*); D 16 (or neut. pl.?). **hit**, nsn. R 19, 22, 26, 97; M 66, 137, 190, 195, 240; L 24; asn. S 102. **hīe**, np.

B 8, 48, 51; R 32, 46, 48, 60, 63, 64, 66, 67, 68, 115, 116, 132; M 19, etc. (19 times); W 61; S 84; L 12. **hīe**, ap. M 82, 127, 209, 283, 320. **hira**, gp. B 47; R 31, 47, 155; M 20, etc. (11 times); W 18. **him**, dp. B 7, 60; R 86, 88; M 66, 197, 198 (poss. sg. in ref. to Byrhtnoþ, as Scragg thinks), 265; S 23; refl., B 53; R 31, 63 (see note), 83, 133; S 67, 84 (**mid him**, *among themselves*).

hēafod, n. *head;* as. W 43; ds. **hēafdum**, R 63. [This is most likely a locative dative singlar, perhaps instrumental in origin: see Campbell 1959: §574.4 and Grant 1991. The few recorded instances are all datives with **æt**; otherwise we find ds. **hēafde**.]

hēah, adj. *high;* nsm. W 98; asm. **hēanne**, R 40; W 82; apm. wk. **hēan**, S. 34 (*high* or *deep*). **hēahfæder**, m. r-stem. *God the Father;* ds. **−e**, R 134. [Cf. **upp-hēah**.]

healdan, v.7. *hold, grasp, possess; keep, guard, maintain, control;* inf. M 14, 19, 74, 102, 236; S 109, 111; pres. 3 p. **healdaþ**, S 87; 3s. subj. **healde**, W 14 (*hold in, keep to himself*); pret. 3p. subj. **hēolden**, M 20; − w. instrumental genitive, **ēow friðes healdan** (inf.), *keep you at peace, remain at peace with you?* M 41. [HEALDAN, HĒOLD, HĒOLDON, HEALDEN; cf. **be-healdan**.]

ġe-healdan, v.7. *keep hold of;* inf. M 167; *keep* (*unbroken*), pres. 3s. **ġe-healdeþ**, W 112.

healf, f. *side;* ds. **−e**, M 152, 318; as. **−e**, R 20.

heall, f. *hall;* ds. **−e**, M 214. [Cf. **medu-heall**.]

heals, m. *neck;* as. M 141.

hēan, adj. *lowly, abject, downcast;* nsm. W 23.

hēan, hēanne, infl. forms, see **hēah**.

hēanliċ, adj. *humiliating;* nsn. M 55.

heard, adj. *hard; severe, bitter; hard-fighting, fierce, unyielding;* nsm. M 130 (**wiġes heard,** *fierce in battle*); L 43; asn. M 214; gsm. −es, B 25; gsn. −es, M 266; asm. −ne, M 167, 236; asf. −e, M 33. − comp. **heardra,** *harder, more resolute,* nsm. M 312; superl. **heardost,** *bitterest, most severe;* nsn. R 87. **heard-sæliġ,** adj. *luckless, ill-fortuned;* asm. −ne, L 19. [Cf. **fēol-, for-, wiġ-heard.**]

heardliċe, adv. *fiercely;* M 261.

hearm, m. *grief, sorrow;* gp. −a, M 223.

hearpe, wk.f. *harp, lyre;* ds. **hearpan,** S 44.

hearra, wk.m. *lord;* ns. M 204. [Cf. German HERR. The OE word may derive from Old Saxon.]

heaðu-, *battle, war* (a word occurring only as the first constituent of compounds). **heaðu-lind,** f. *battle-shield (of linden);* ap. −a, B 6.

hēawan, v.7. *hew;* pret. 3s. **hēow,** M 324; 3p. **hēowon,** B 6, 23; M 181. [HĒAWAN, HĒOW, HĒOWON, HĒAWEN; cf. **a-, for-hēawan.**]

hebban, v.6. *lift, raise;* inf. R 31. [HEBBAN, HŌF, HŌFON, HAFEN; cf. **a-hebban.**]

hefiġ, adj. *heavy, oppressive;* dsn.wk. **hefigan,** R 61; *sad, depressed;* comp. **hefiġran,** npf. W 49.

hell, f. *hell.* **hell-scaða,** wk.m. *fiend of hell;* np. −n, M 180.

helm, m. *covering, helmet,* etc. See **niht-helm.** [Cf. HELAN, v.4, *conceal, hide.*]

help, f. *help;* as. −e, W 16; ds. −e, R 102.

ġe-hende, prep. w. dat. *near,* M 294 (postpos.). [Base-word **hand.**]

hēo, see **hē.**

heofon, m. *heaven;* as. C 6; gs. −es, R 64; ap. −as, R 103; gp. −a, R 45; dp.

−um, R 85, 134, 140, 154; M 172; W 107, 115; S 107, 122. **heofon-rīċe,** n. ja-stem. *kingdom of heaven;* gs. −s, C 1; R 91.

heofonliċ, adj. *heavenly;* asm. −ne, R 148.

hēolden, see **healdan.**

heolstor, m. *concealment, darkness;* dis. **heolstre,** W 23. [Cf. HELAN, v.4, *conceal, hide.*]

heonan, adv. *hence, from here;* R 132; M 246; S 37; L 6.

-heort, adjectival combining form of **heorte,** *heart.* See **hāt-heort.**

heorte, wk.f. *heart;* ns. M 312; **heortan,** gs. W 49; L 43; ds. M 145; as. S 11, 34 (obj. of **cnyssaþ;** or gs. with **ġeþōhtas**).

heorþ, m. *hearth.* **heorð-ġenēat,** m. *sharer of the hearth, member of the chief's household troops, his closest followers;* np. −as, M 204. **heorð-weorod,** n. *the body of household retainers;* as. M 24.

hēow, hēowon, see **hēawan.**

hēr, adv. *here,* M 36, 51, 241, 243, 314; L 15, 32; *in this world,* R 108, 137, 145; W 108 (twice), 109 (twice); S 102; *in this year,* B 1 (the typical introduction to an entry in the Chronicle).

here, m. ja-stem. *army;* ds. M 292 (West Saxon variant of **herġe,** the usual dative); gs. **herġes,** B 31. **here-fliema,** wk.m. *fugitive* (from a pursuing host); ap. −n, B 23. **here-ġeatu,** f. *war-equipment;* in law a "heriot," "a feudal service originally consisting of weapons, horses and other military equipments, restored to a lord on the death of his tenant" (see Gordon's note, taking up a suggestion of Brett [1927]); as. −ġeatwe, M 48. **here-lāf,** f. *remnant of an army after a battle; group of survivors;* dp. −um. B 47. [Cf. **æsc-here.**]

herian, wk.v.I. *praise, extol;* inf. C 1; pres. 3p. subj. **herien,** S 77. [HERIAN (from *HÆRJAN), HEREDE, HERED.]

hēt, hēton, ġe-hēt, see **hātan,** ġe-**hātan.**

hete, m. i-stem. *hate, hostility.* See **ecg-hete.**

hettend, m. nd-stem. *enemy;* np. B 10. [Cf. HATIAN, *hate,* and HETTAN, *persecute.*]

hider, adv. *hither;* B 69; R 103; M 57.

hīe, see **hē.**

hīeldan, wk.v.I. *bend;* inf. R 45 (w. refl. pron.). [Base-word HEALD, adj. *bent, inclined.*]

hīenan, wk.v.I. *bring low, lay low, afflict;* inf. M 180; pret. 3s. **hīende,** M 324 (used absolutely: *laid low*). [Base-word **hēan,** adj., q.v.]

ġe-**hīeran,** wk.v.I. *hear, perceive, understand;* inf. R 78; pres. 2s. **ġehīerst,** M 45; pret. 1s. **gehīerde,** R 26; M 117; S 18.

hild, f. jō-stem. *battle, war;* as. −e M 33; ds. −e, M 8, 48, 55, 123, 223, 288, 324. **hilde-rinċ,** m. *warrior;* ns. B 39; M 169; np. −as, R 61; gp. −a, R 72.

-**hilte,** adjectival combining form, *hilted,* corresponding to ĠE-HILTE, n. ja-stem, *sword-hilt.* See **fealu-hilte.**

him, see **hē.**

hindan, adv. *from behind;* B 23. [Cf. **be-hindan.**]

hine, hira, see **hē.**

hīred, m. *household, family, court, body of retainers;* as. L 15 (MS *heard* for *heord:* see note). **hīred-mann,** m. *household retainer;* np. −menn, M 261.

his, hit, see **hē.**

hlāford, m. *lord;* ns. M 135, 189, 224, 240; L 6, 15 (both *husband*); as. D 39; ds. −e, M 318; *the Lord,* as. R 45.

hlāfordlēas, adj. *lordless;* nsm. M 251.

hleahtor, m. *laughter;* as. S 21 (perhaps for ds. **hleahtre;** see **fore**).

ġe-**hlēapan,** v.7. *leap upon, mount;* pret. 3s. **ġehlēop,** M 189. [HLĒAPAN, HLĒOP, HLĒOPON, HLĒAPEN.]

hlemm, m. ja-stem. *noise (of a blow);* but in **inwitt-hlemm** (q.v.) the meaning appears to be *wound.*

hlēo, n. wa-stem. *shelter; protector, lord;* ns. M 74; D 41. **hlēo-mǣġ,** m. *protecting kinsman;* gp. −māga, S 25.

ġe-**hlēop,** see ġe-**hlēapan.**

hlēor, n. *check, face;* as adjectival combining form, -**hlēor,** *faced.* See **drēoriġ-hlēor.**

hlēoðor, n. *cry, (bird-) call;* as. S 20. [Cf. next word.]

hlēoðrian, wk.v.II. *call out, speak;* pret. 3s. **hlēoðrode,** R 26.

hliehhan, v.6. *laugh;* inf. B 47; pret. 3s. **hlōg,** M 147. [HLIEHHAN, HLŌG, HLŌGON, —; cf. **hleahtor.**]

hlīfian, wk.v.II. *tower, rise up;* pres. 1s. **hlīfie,** R 85.

hlimman, v.3. *roar, resound;* inf. S 18. [HLIMMAN, *HLAMM, HLUMMON, —.]

hliþ, n. *cliff, slope.* See **stān-hliþ.**

hlōg, see **hliehhan.**

ġe-**hlystan,** wk.v.I. *listen;* pret. 3p. **ġehlyston,** M 92.

ġe-**hnǣġan,** wk.v.I. *bring low, abase, humble;* pp. **ġehnǣġed,** nsm. S 88. [Base-word HNĀG, adj. *low;* cf. **hnīgan.**]

hnāg, see **hnīgan.**

ġe-**hnǣst,** n. *collision* (in battle). See **cumbol-ġehnāst.**

hnīgan, v.1. *bow down;* pret. 1s. **hnāg,** R 59. [HNĪGAN, HNĀG, HNIGON, HNIĠEN; cf. ġe-**hnǣġan.**]

hogode, hogodon, see **hycgan.**

ġe-**hola,** wk.m. *confidant, friend;* gp. **ġeholena,** W 31.

hold, adj. *kind, friendly, gracious,* nsm. S 41; asm. −ne, D 39; gp. −ra, L 17; superl. **holdost,** *most loyal, devoted;* asn. M 24. [Describes a lord's regard for his followers and also theirs for him; hence the two shades of meaning.]

holm, m. *wave, (high) sea;* pl. *seas, ocean;* as. W 82; gp. **−a,** S 64.

holt, n. *forest, wood; wooden shaft;* gs. **−es,** R 29; M 8. **holt-wudu,** m. u-stem, *trees of the forest;* as. R 91 (MS *holm wudu*). [Cf. **æsc-holt.**]

hōn, contr.v.7. *hang.* See **be-hōn.**

hord, n. *treasure, hoard;* as. or ap. B 10. **hord-cofa,** wk.m. *treasure-chest* (i.e., the breast as container of thoughts); as. **−n,** W 14. [Cf. **brēost-hord.**]

hors, n. *horse;* as. M 2.

hræd, adj. *quick, swift, sudden, hasty.* **hræd-wyrde,** adj. ja-stem. *hasty of speech;* nsm. W 66.

hræfn, m. *raven;* as. B 61; np. **−as,** M 106.

hræðe, adv. *quickly, soon;* M 30, 164, 288.

hrǽw, n. *corpse;* ns. R 72; as. R 53; ap. B 60.

hrēam, m. *outcry, clamor;* ns. M 106.

hrēman, wk.v.I. *exult;* inf. B 39 (w. gen.). [Cf. Old Saxon HRŌM, *glory;* German RUHM.]

hrēmiġ, adj. *exultant;* npm. **hrēmġe,** B 59 (w. gen.).

hrēoh, adj. *rough, fierce, angry, troubled;* nsm.wk. **hrēo,** (=*HRĒOHA), W 16; asf. **hrēo** (=*HRĒOHE), W 105.

hrēosan, v.2. *fall;* inf. W 48; pres. part. **hrēosende,** nsf. W 102. [HRĒOSAN, HRĒAS, HRURON, HROREN; cf. **be-hroren.**]

hrēow, f. wō-stem. *sorrow, (rue).* **hrēow-ċeariġ,** adj. *sorrowful, troubled;* nsm. R 25.

hrēran, wk.v.I. *stir (up), move;* inf. W 4. [Base-word HRŌR, adj. *vigorous, active;* cf. **on-hrēran.**]

hreðer, m. or n. *breast, bosom* (esp. as the seat of feelings); *heart;* as. S 63;

gp. **hreðra,** W 72. **hreðer-loca,** wk.m. *enclosure of the breast or heart: the breast;* as. **−n,** S 58.

hrīm, m. *rime, (hoar-) frost;* ns. S 32; as. W 48; dis. **−e,** W 77. **hrīm-ċeald,** adj. *frost-cold;* **−e,** W 4. **hrīm-ġiċel,** m. *icicle;* dip. **−ġiclum,** S 17 (on which see **ġiċel**).

hring, m. *ring;* ap. **hringas,** M 161 (*gold rings, ornaments*). **hring-loca,** wk.m. *linked ring* (of corselet); ap. **−n,** M 145. **hring-þegu,** f. *receiving of (gold) rings* (by a liegeman from his lord); ds. **−þeġe,** S 44.

hrīþ, f. *snowstorm;* ns. W 102. [The only occurrence of the word in OE; the meaning inferred from the context and from Old Norse HRĪÐ, f. *tempest.*]

hrīðiġ, adj. *snow-covered? storm-beaten?* npm. **hrīðġe,** W 77. [Only occurrence; see preceding word.]

hrōf, m. *roof;* ds. **−e,** C 6.

hrūse, wk.f. *earth, ground;* gs. **hrūsan,** W 23; as. W 102 (MS has nom. *hruse*); S 32.

hryre, m. i-stem. *fall, ruin;* gs. **hryres** (MS *hryre*), W 7. [Cf. HROREN, pp. of **hrēosan.**]

hū, interr. adv. and conj. *how;* (a) introducing subord. clause, M 19; W 30, 35, 61, 73; S 2, 14, 29, 118; D 12; (b) introducing an exclamation, W 95.

hungor, m. *hunger;* ns. S 11.

hūru, adv. *certainly,* R 10.

hūs, n. *building, house.* See **feorh-hūs.**

hwā, hwæt, pron. (1) interr. *who, what;* (a) in indirect questions, nsm. **hwā,** M 95, 124, 215; asn. **hwæt,** R 116; isn. **hwon,** S 43 (**tō hwon,** *to what:* scil. *what end, what service, what fate*); (b) as a relative containing its antecedent, *what, that which;* asn. **hwæt,** R 2 (MS *hæt*); M

45; S 56; L 2. (2) indef. pron. *some-one, something;* nsm. **hwā**, M 71. (3) indef. pron. *each* (normally **ġe-hwā**); asm. **hwone**, M 2.

ġe-hwā, **ġe-hwæt**, pron. w. part. gen. *each;* gsn. **ġehwæs**, C 3; dsm. **ġe-hwǣm**, W 63; S 72; asm. **ġehwone**, B 9.

hwæl, m. *whale;* gs. **-es**, S 60. **hwæl-weġ**, m. *whale's way, ocean;* as. S 63 (MS *wæl weg*).

hwǣr, adv. and conj. *where;* (a) interr. adv. R 112; W 92, 93 (five times); S 117; L 8 (**h. landes**, *in what country, where in the world*); (b) rel. conj. containing its antecedent: (*a place*) *where*, W 26.

hwæt, adj. *quick, vigorous, active;* nsm. S 40; in certain compounds, *quick at producing, abounding in.* See **ār-hwæt**.

hwæt, interj. *well; now;* R 1 (see note), 90; M 231.

hwæt, pron., see **hwā**.

ġe-hwæðer, adj. *either;* asf. **-e**, M 112.

hwæð(e)re, adv. conj. *nevertheless, but;* R 18, 24, 38, 42, 57, 59, 70, 75, 101.

ġe-hwelċ, pron. w. part. gen. *each;* nsm. M 128, 257; S 90, 111; dsm. **-um**, R 108 (**ānra ġ.** *each one*); ism. **-e**, R 136; W 8; S 36; isn. **-e**, S 68. [Fusion of **ġe-hwā** and **līċ**; cf. **ǣġhwelċ**.]

hweorfan, v.3. *turn, go, take* (or *change*) *one's course;* inf. W 72; pres. 3s. **hweorfeþ**, S 58, 60 (w. comparison to a bird: *flies, takes its flight*). HWEORFAN, HWEARF, HWUR-FON, HWORFEN; cf. **ġeond-**, **on-hweorfan**.]

hwettan, wk.v.I. *whet, incite;* pres. 3s. **hweteþ**, S 63. [Base-word **hwæt**, adj., q.v.]

hwider, interr. conj. *whither,* W 72.

hwīl, f. (*an indefinite period of*) *time,*

while. (a) as. **-e** as adv. *for a time,* R 64, 84; D 36; **ealle h.** *all the time, continually,* M 304; **gōde h.** *for a good while,* R 70; **lange h.** *for a long time,* R 24. (b) dp. **-um** as adv. *at times, sometimes;* W 43; S 19; correl. *at one time . . . at another time; now . . . now,* R 22, 23; M 270. (c) **þā hwīle þe**, conj. *while, for as long as;* M 14, 83, 235, 272. [Cf. **earfoþ-**, **langung-hwīl**.]

hwilpe, wk.f. *whaup* (English and Scottish dialect), *curlew;* gs. **-n**, S 21. (See Gordon's note.)

hwīlum, adv., see **hwīl**.

hwīt, adj. *white;* asm. uninflected (because parenthetical?), B 63. [On the grammar, see Campbell 1938: 119. He says **earn æftan hwīt** is parenthetical and therefore ns.]

hwon, instr. of **hwæt**, see **hwā** and **for-hwon** under **for**.

hwōn, pron. w. gen. *little, few;* as. S 28.

hwone, see **hwā**.

hwonne, interr. adv. *when;* as rel. conj. containing its antecedent, w. subj. (*the time*) *when,* R 136; M 66 (w. **tō lang**, *too long until the time when*).

hycgan, wk.v.III. (and II). *think, con-sider, be intent* (*on*), *intend, purpose;* inf. M 4; S 117; L 11; pres. 3s. subj. **hycge**, W 14; pret. 3s. **hogode**, M 133 (w. gen., *was intent on, purposed*); 3s. subj., M 128; 3p. **hogodon**, M 123. [HYCGAN, HOGDE or HOGODE, HOGD or HOGOD; cf. **for-hycgan**; **morðor-**, **stīþ-hycgende**.]

hȳdan, wk.v.I. *hide, hoard;* pres. 3s. **hȳdeþ**, S 102.

ġe-hȳdan, wk.v.I. *hide, bury;* pret. 3s. **gehȳdde**, W 84.

ġe-hȳġd, f. and n. i-stem. *thought, in-tention; conception;* ns. W 72; S 116.

hyġdiġ, adj. *mindful;* in composition,

minded, disposed. See **an-**, **wan-hyġdiġ**.

hyġe, m. i-stem. *mind, thought; soul, spirit; purpose, courage;* ns. M 312; W 16; S 44, 58; L 17; ds. M 4; S 96.

hyġe-ġeōmor, adj. *melancholic, humorless;* asm. **−ne**, L 19.

hyht, m. i-stem. *joyous expectation, pleasure, bliss;* ns. R 126, 148; S 45, 122.

hyrned, pp. adj. *horned.* **hyrned-nebba**, wk.m. *horny-beaked one,* as. **−n**, B 62. [The same in form as a wk. adj., corresponding to strong HYRNED-NEBB, *horny-beaked;* cf. **isiġ-**, **ūriġ-feðra**.]

hyse, m. i-stem, inflected according to ja-stems (with gemination), **hyss-**, *young man, young warrior;* ns. M 152; gs. **hysses**, M 141; np. **hyssas**, M 112, 123; ap. **hyssas**, M 169; gp. **hyssa**, M 2, 128.

I

iċ, pron. 1st pers. sg. *I;* ns. R 1, etc. (43 times); M 117, etc. (14 times); W 8, etc. (8 times); S 1, 2, etc. (9 times); D 35, 36, 38; L 1, 2, etc. (15 times). **min**, gs., only in the rejected emendation **min myne wisse**, W 27 (but see **min**, poss. adj.). **mē**, ds. R 2, 4, 46, 83, 86, 126, 129, 135, 144; M 55, 220, 223, 249, 318 (refl.); S 1, 20 (refl.), 61, 64; D 35, 37, 41; L 1, 9 (refl.), 18. **mē**, as. R 30, 31, 32 (twice), 33, 34, 42, 45, 46, 61, 75, 77, 81, 90, 122, 136, 139, 142; M 29, 252. **meċ**, as. W 28; S 6; L 14, 15, 27, 32, 41. (The form **meċ** is Anglian and is also found in poetic and other elevated discourse.) [See **wē**, **wit**.]

idel, adj. *empty, vain;* nsn. W 110; npn. **idlu**, W 87.

ielde, m. i-stem, pl. *men* (conceived as the successive generations, or men of old); gp. **ielda**, C 5; W 85; S 77. [Base-word **eald**, *old*]

ieldu, f. īn-stem. *age, old age;* ns. S 70, 91.

ielfetu, f. (*wild*) *swan;* gs. **ielfete**, S 19.

iergþu, f. iþō-stem. *slackness;* as. **iergþe**, M 6. [Base-word **earg**, q.v.; **g** is not palatal (cf. Campbell 1959: §589.6), since it is usually written *h*.]

iermþu, f. iþō-stem. *misery, distress, hardship;* gp. **iermþa**, L 3. [Base-word **earm**, q.v.]

ierre, adj. ja-stem. *angry, wrathful;* nsm. M 44, 253.

ieðan, wk.v.I. *lay waste, depopulate, destroy;* pret. 3s. **ieðde**, W 85. [Cf. the rare adj. ĪEÐE, *empty, waste,* cognate w. German ÖDE.]

iġ, f. jō-stem (alt. sp. **ieġ**, from *AUJŌ-; see **ēa**,), *watery place, island.* **iġ-land**, n. *island;* is. **−e**, B 66. [Mod. "island" from this word, influenced by OF ILE from Lat. INSULA, respelt ISLE by early modern scholars.]

in-dryhten, adj. *noble, excellent;* nsm. W 12. [This adj. is probably formed from **in-dryhtu**, the prefix indicating a quality inherent in a noble **dryht**, though it is sometimes regarded as an intensive.]

in-dryhtu, f. īn-stem. *nobility;* ns. S 89. [Cf. preceding word.]

inn, adv. *in,* M 58, 157.

innan, adv. (*from*) *within,* S 11.

inwitt, n. *malice, fraud.* **inwitt-hlemm**, m. *malicious wound;* np. **−as**, R 47. [It is uncertain whether **inwitt** is borrowed from Lat. INVIDIA or of Gmc. origin; on the odd meaning of the second element see **hlemm**.]

inwitta, wk.m. *malicious or deceitful one;* ns. B 46. [Cf. preceding word.]

iren, n. ja-stem, *iron, iron blade;* ns. M 253 (**ord and iren** as variation of **wǣpen**: *point* [*of spear*] *and iron* *blade;* or, as hendiadys, *iron point or pointed iron?*).

is, see **bēon-wesan.**

īs, n. *ice.* **īs-ċeald,** adj. *ice-cold;* asm. **−ne,** S 14, 19.

isiġ, adj. *icy.* **isiġ-feðra,** wk.m. *icy-feathered one;* ns. S 24. [Usually regarded as a wk. adj., but like **ūriġ-feðra,** q.v., it is placed as if in apposition and can be taken as a characterizing noun like **hyrned-nebba,** q.v. The corresponding strong adj. would be **ĪSIĠ-FEÐER.]**

L

lā, interj. *look* (Mod.E. *lo*); see **ēa-lā.**

ġe-lāc, n. *tossing, play; tumult;* as. S 35; L 7.

lād, f. *way, course.* See **brim-, lagu-lād.** [Cf. **lid, lida, līðend.**]

lǣdan, wk.v.I. *lead; extend upward, grow;* inf. R 5 (*extend*); M 88 (*lead*). [Base-word **lād.**]

lǣġ, lǣġe, see **licgan.**

lǣne, adj. ja-stem. *transitory, brief, fleeting;* ns. W 108 (n. and m.), 109 (m. and f.); nsn. S 66; dsn.wk. **lǣnan,** R 109 (MS *−um*), 138. [Lit. *on loan:* LÆN, f. *a loan.*]

lǣran, wk.v.I. *instruct;* pret. 3s. **lǣrde,** M 311. [Base-word **lār,** f., q.v.]

lǣriġ, m. *rim* (*of shield*); ns. M 284. [Etymology unknown.]

ġe-lǣstan, wk.v.I, w. dat. *support, help; follow;* inf. M 11; w. acc., *fulfill;* pret. 3s. **ġelǣste,** M 15. [Base-word **lāst,** m., q.v.]

lǣtan, v.7, w. inf. *let, cause to;* pret. 3s. **lēt,** M 7, 140; 3p. **lēton,** B 60; M 108. [LÆTAN, LĒT, LĒTON, LÆTEN; cf. **for-lǣtan.**]

lāf, f. *remnant;* **hamora lāf,** *what is left by the hammers of the smith: a*

sword; dip. **−um,** B 6; **daroþa lāf,** *what is left by the spears: the remnant that survives after a battle;* ns. B 54. [Cf. **here-lāf.**]

lāgon, see **licgan.**

lagu, m. u-stem. *sea, water;* as. S 47 (**on l.,** *to sea*). **lagu-lād** f. *waterway, sea;* as. **−e,** W 3. **lagu-strēam,** m. *sea-stream;* np. **−as,** M 66 (tidal streams, coming up the river).

ġe-lagu, n.pl. (uniquely recorded, apparently an inflected form of *ĠE-LÆĠ, n. *lay, layer, material spread out*), *stretches, expanse;* ap. in **holma ġelagu,** *expanse of the seas,* S 64. [Etymologically distinct from **lagu,** m.; cf. **licgan.**]

land, n. *land;* as. B 9, 27, 56, 59; gs. **−es,** M 90, 275; L 8 (**hwǣr l.,** *in what country, where in the world*); ds. **−e,** M 99; S 66. **land-riht,** n. *land-right* (the rights and privileges of an estate); as. D 40. **land-stede,** m. i-stem. *place on the land, plot of ground;* ds. L 16. [Cf. **folc-, īġ-land.**]

lang, adj. *long;* (*in duration*) nsn. M 66; asf. **−e,** R 24; (*in stature*) nsm. wk. **sē langa** (as distinguishing epithet), *the tall,* M 273. [Cf. **ealdor-, sumor-lang;** also **leng.**]

ġe-lang, adj. (a) w. prep. **on** (Anglian IN), *comprehended in, inseparable from;* nsn. S 121; (b) w. prep. **æt,** *dependent on;* nsf. L 45 (**æt him selfum ġelang,** *dependent on himself, in his own hands*).

lange, adv. *for a long time;* W 3, 38.

langian, wkv.II. *yearn, suffer longing* (impers. with acc. of person); pret. 3s. **langode,** L 14. [Base-word **lang,** q.v.; cf. **of-langian.**]

langoþ, m. *longing;* as. D 3; gs. **−es,** L 41; ds. **−e,** L 53.

langung, f. *longing, restless desire, anxiety;* as. **−e,** S 47. **langung-hwīl,**

f. *time of longing;* gp. −a, R 126 (according to Dickins and Ross, times of weariness of spirit, *accidia;* but the dreamer seems hardly to be blaming himself here).

lār, f. *lore, instruction, knowledge.* **lār-cwide,** m. i-stem, *speech of instruction, counsel;* dip. −**cwidum,** W 38. [Cf. **lǣran.**]

lāst, m. *footstep, track, path;* as. B 22; ds. −**e,** W 97 (**on** l., w. dat. *on the track of, behind, after*); dip. −**um,** S 15 (**wreċċan** l., *in the paths of an exile*). **lāst-word,** n. *reputation left behind* (after death); gp. −**a,** S 73 (Gordon's definition). [Cf. **wrǣc-lāst.**]

lāþ, adj. *hostile, hateful, hated;* asm. **lāðne,** S 112 (as noun); dsf. **lāðre,** M 90; npm. **lāðe,** M 86; gp. **lāðra,** B 9 (as noun, *enemies*); dp. **lāðum,** B 22; comp. **lāðre,** asn. M 50; superl. **lāðost,** nsm. R 88.

lāðlīċe, adv. *wretchedly, horribly;* superl. **lāðlicost,** L 14. [Cf. **lāþ.**]

lēan, n. *recompense.* See **wiðer-lēan.**

lēas, adj. *lacking, deprived of;* nsn. L 32; npn. −**e,** W 86 (analogical -*e,* generalized from the npm.; the npm. of long monosyllables usually has no ending, having lost its original -*u;* but the extra syllable is metrically necessary); − as suffix, -*less;* see **ende-, frēond-, grund-, hlāford-, wine-lēas.**

lecgan, wk.v.I. *lay;* pres. 3p. **lecgaþ,** S 57; 3s. subj. **lecge,** W 42; pret. 3s. **leġde,** D 5; 3p. **leġdon,** B 22 (elliptically w. **on last,** *pursued*). [LECGAN, LEĠDE, LEĠ(E)D; baseword LǢĠ; cf. **licgan;** also **a-lecgan.**]

leġer, n. *bed;* as. L 34.

lenġ, comp. adv. *longer;* M 171. [Cf. **lang.**]

lēode (comb. form **lēod-**), m. i-stem, pl. *people;* np. B 11; ap. M 37; dp. **lēodum,** R 88; M 23, 50; L 6.

lēod-fruma, wk.m. *lord, leader of a people;* ns. L 8. [Cf. **LĒOD,** m. *man, leader;* **LĒOD,** f. *people, nation.* The plural **lēode** is usually assigned to the former.]

lēof, adj. *dear, beloved;* gsm. −**es,** W 38; L 53 (as noun); dsm. −**um,** M 319; asm. −**ne,** M 7, 208 (as noun); S 112 (as noun); dsf. −**re,** W 97; vsm.wk. −**a,** R 78, 95; npm. −**e,** L 34 (as noun, *lovers*); gp. −**ra,** W 31; L 16 (as noun); superl. **lēofost,** nsn. M 23 (see note). [Cf. **fela-lēof.**]

leofaþ, see **libban.**

lēoht, n. *light;* dis. −**e,** R 5.

lēoþ, n. *song.* **lēoþ-cræftiġ,** adj. *skilled in song;* nsm. D 40. [Cf. **gryre-, sorg-lēoþ.**]

lēt, lēton, see **lǣtan.**

ġe-lettan, wk.v.I. *hinder;* pret. 3s. **ġelette,** M 164.

libban, wk.v.III. *live;* pres. 3s. **leofaþ,** S 102, 107; 3p. **libbaþ,** R 134; 3s. subj. **libbe,** S 78; pret. 1p. **lifdon,** L 14; 3p. **lifdon,** S 85; − pres. part. **libbende,** m.pl. L 34; gp. **libbendra,** S 73 (as noun, *the living*). [Spellings of the stem such as **lifi-** and **lifg-** (see the apparatus for R 134, S 78, etc.) are chiefly Anglian.]

-liċ or **−līċ,** suffix used to form many adjectives. The vowel is short when it follows a stressed syll. (cf. **gǣstliċ**) or a resolvable pair of sylls. (cf. **heofonliċ**) and thus is unstressed; otherwise it is long (cf. **earfoþlīċ**).

līċ, n. *body;* gs. −**es,** R 63.

-lica, wk.m. *image, likeness.* See **wyrm-lica.**

-līċe, suffix used to form adverbs. The vowel is usually long, but it is shortened before comp. and superl. endings (cf. **dryhtlicost**) unless the suffix follows an unstressed syllable that is metrically unresolvable (cf. EARFOÞLĪCOST, *with most difficulty*).

licgan, v.5. *lie, lie dead;* pres. part. **licgende**, nsm. R 24; pres. 3s. **liġeþ**, M 222, 232, 314; 3p. **licgaþ**, W 78; pret. 3s. **læġ**, B 17; M 157, 204, 227, 276, 294; 3p. **lāgon**, B 28; M 112, 183; pret. 3s. subj. **læġe**, M 279; w. refl. dat., *lie down;* inf. M 319; pret. 3s. subj. **læġe**, M 300 (see note). [LICGAN, LÆĠ, LĀGON, LEĠEN.]

lid, n. *ship;* gs. **-es**, B 27, 34. **lidmann**, m. *shipman, sailor (viking);* np. **-menn**, M 99; gp. **-manna**, M 164. [Cf. LĪDAN, v.1, *sail;* and **lida**.]

lida, wk.m. *sailor.* See **sǣ-lida**.

lïefan, wk.v.I, *allow, permit.* See **a-lïefan**.

ġe-lïefan, wk.v.I. *believe;* (a) w. subordinate clause as object, pres. 1s. **ġeliefe**, S 66; 3s. **ġeliefeþ**, S 27 (w. refl. **him**, *admits to himself*); (b) w. **on** and dat. (or acc.), *believe in, trust in;* pres. 3s. **ġeliefeþ**, S 108. [Base-word LÊAF, f. *leave, permission;* cf. **a-lïefan**; also ĠELÊAFA, wk.m. *belief.*]

lïehtan, wk.v.I. *alight;* pret. 3s. **liehte**, M 23. [Cf. LĪOHT, later LÊOHT, adj. *light in weight.*]

lïesan, wk.v.I. *liberate, redeem, ransom;* inf. R 41; M 37. [Cf. **lêas**, adj.; also **on-lïesan**.]

lïf, n. *life;* ns. S 65, 121; as. R 147; M 208; W 60, 89; gs. **-es**, R 88, 126; S 27, 79; ds. **-e**, R 109, 138; L 41.

lifdon, see **libban**.

liġeþ, see **licgan**.

lim, n. *limb.* **lim-wêriġ**, adj. *weary of limb;* asm. **-ne**, R 63.

limpan, v.3. impers. w. dat. *befall;* pres. 3s. **limpeþ**, S 13. [LIMPAN, LAMP, LUMPON, LUMPEN.]

lind, f. *linden wood; shield (of linden wood);* as. **-e**, M 244; ap. **-a**, M 99. [Cf. **heaðu-lind**.]

lïðend, m. nd-stem. *sailor, seaman.* See **brim-lïðend**.

loca, wk.m. *lock, link;* see **hring-loca**; *enclosure, locker, stronghold;* see **ferhþ-, hreðer-loca**. [Cf. **lūcan**.]

lof, n. and m. *praise;* ns. S 73, 78.

losian, wk.v.II. *be lost, fail;* pres. 3s. **losaþ**, S 94.

lūcan, v.2. *lock, unite, join;* pret. 3p. **lucon**, M 66. [LŪCAN, LÊAC, LUCON, LOCEN.]

lufu, f. *love* (often inflected, as here, according to the wk. decl., as if from the rare nom. LUFE); ds. **lufan**, S 121; as. **lufan**, S 112 (not in MS). [Cf. **sorg-lufu**.]

lust, m. *desire;* ns. S 36.

lyft, f. i-stem (also m. and n.) *air;* as. R 5 (**on lyft**, *aloft, on high*).

lȳt, indecl. subst., adj. and adv. *little, few;* as subst., w. part. gen., as. W 31; L 16; as adv., S 27.

lȳtel, adj. *little;* isn. **lȳtle**, B 34.

lytigian, wk.v.II. *use guile;* inf. M 86. [Derivation from Lat. LĪTIGĀRE, *quarrel,* as proposed by Earl 1992, seems unlikely, since one would expect OE *LĪDGIAN or *LĪÐGIAN, on the pattern of SCRŪDNIAN from Lat. SCRŪTINĀRE. And so the word is best derived, as it usually has been, from LYTIĠ *deceitful,* base-word LOT *deceit.*]

lȳtlian, wk.v.II. *grow less, dwindle, diminish;* pres. 3s. **lȳtlaþ**, M 313.

M

mā, n., w. part. gen. *more;* ns. M 195; as. L 4; as adv. *more,* B 46. [Cf. **mǣst**.]

ġe-mǣc, adj. *appropriate, well-suited, similar;* asm. **-ne**, L 18. [Akin to MACIAN, *make.*]

mæcg, m. ja-stem. *man;* gp. **-a**, B 40 (alt. reading for **mêċa**).

mæġ, mæġe, see **magan**.

mǣġ, m. *kinsman;* ns. M 5, 114, 224, 287; W 109; np. **māgas**, L 11; gp. **māga**, B 40; W 51. [Cf. **cnēo-, frēo-, hlēo-, wine-mǣġ**.]

mæġen, n. *strength;* ns. M 313.

mǣl, f. *speech?* gp. **-a**, M 212 (see note).

mǣl, n. (a) *measure;* see **fōt-mǣl**; (b) *time, occasion;* gp. **-a**, S 36.

mǣlan, wk.v.I. *speak;* pret. 3s. **mǣlde**, M 26, 43, 210. [Cf. **maðelian**.]

ġe-mǣlan, wk.v.I. *speak;* pret. 3s. **ġemǣlde**, M 230, 244.

mǣre, adj. ja-stem. *glorious, famous;* nsf. wk. R 12, 82; W 100 (*Wyrd the mighty?*); nsn. (or m.), B 14 (**tungol** is usually neuter in the poetry but once masc.); dsm.wk. **mǣran**, R 69.

mǣrþu, f. iþō-stem. *glorious deed;* gp. **-a**, S 84.

mǣst, adj. superl. *most, greatest;* asf. **-e**, M 175; **-as** noun, n., w. part. gen. *the greatest (of);* ns. M 223; *the greatest number (of);* as. S 84. [Cf. **miċel, mā, māra**.]

ġe-mǣtan, wk.v.I, impers. w. dat. of person. *dream;* pret. 3s. **ġemǣtte**, R 2.

mǣte, adj. ja-stem. *small, limited;* isn. R 69, 124. [Cf. METAN, v.5, *measure*.]

mǣþ, f. *proper measure, fitness;* ns. M 195.

mæðel, n. *assembly; speech.* **mæðel-stede**, m. i-stem. *meeting-place;* ds. M 199.

mǣw, m. i-stem. *mew; seagull;* as. S 22.

māg-, see **mǣġ**.

magan, pret.-pres.v. *be able, can.* – (a) w. inf., pres. 1s. **mæġ**, R 85; W 58; S 1; L 2, 38, 39; 2s. **meaht**, R 78; 3s. **mæġ**, R 110; M 215 (subjectless **mǣġ cunnian**, *one can find out, it can be tested*), 258, 315 (see note); W 15, 64; S 94; D 31; impers. w. **ofergān** understood, *it*

can pass over, D 7, 13, 17, 20, 27, 42; 3s. subj. **mǣġe**, M 235; pret. 1s. **meahte**, R 18, 37; 3s. **meahte**, M 9, 14, 70, 124 (subj.?), 167, 171; S 26; D 11; 1s. subj. (?) **meahte**, W 26. (b) w. prep. phrase implying an inf. of being or of motion, pres. 3s. **mæġ** (*can be*), S 100; pret. 3s. **meahte** (*could go*), M 64. [MAGAN, MǢĠ, MAGON, MEAHTE.]

magu, m. (*son;*) *young man, warrior;* ns. W 92. **magu-þeġn**, m. (*young*) *retainer;* np. **-as**, W 62.

man, m. (weakly stressed form of **mann**), indef. pron. *one* (used in ns. only), R 73, 75; M 9; S 109; L 27. [Normally spelt with single *n* in the MSS, but the same spelling sometimes serves for the stressed form. Constructions with **man** are usually best translated in the passive voice.]

ġe-man, see **ġe-munan**.

ġe-māna, wk.m. *fellowship, meeting;* gs. (or dis.?) **-n**, depending on **hrēman**, B 40. [ĠEMǢNE, adj. *common;* German GEMEIN.]

manian, wk.v.II. *exhort, remind, urge;* inf. M 228; pres. 3s. **manaþ**, S 36 (w. clause), 53 (used absolutely).

ġe-manian, wk.v.II. *exhort, admonish, remind;* pres. 3p. **gemaniaþ**, S 50 (w. **tō** and dat.); pp. **ġemanod**, apm. **-e** (agreeing w. **þeġnas**, obj. of **hafast**), M 231.

maniġ, adj. and pron. *many* (*a*); – as adj., nsm. B 17; M 282; D 24; dsm. **manigum**, D 33; asm. **-ne**, M 188, 243; np. **-e**, D 14; dp. **manigum**, R 99; – as pron., npm. **-e**, M 200; gp. **-ra**, R 41; dp. **manigum**, D 19. [Cf. **formaniġ**.]

mann, m. cons.-stem. *person, man, woman;* ns. R 112; M 147, 239; W 109; S 12, 39; D 40; L 42; as. M 77, 243; D 6; gs. **-es**, S 116; L 11; ds. **menn**, M 125, 319; np. **menn**, R 12,

82, 128; M 105, 206; ap. **menn**, R 93; gp. **manna**, M 195; S 90, 111; dp. **mannum**, R 96, 102. **mann-cynn**, n. ja-stem. *humankind;* as. R 41, 104; gs. −es, C 7; R 33, 99. **mann-dryhten**, m. (*liege*) *lord;* as. W 41. (For this meaning see Klaeber's glossary to *Beowulf* [1950].) [Cf. **brim-, ealdor-, hired-, lid-, sǽ-mann**; and **Norð-mann**, pr. n.; also **man**, pron.]

manna, wk.m. *man;* as. −n, L 18.

mára, comp. adj. *more, greater;* nsn. **máre**, B 65; M 313. [Cf. **micel, má**, and **mǽst**.]

maðelian, wk.v.II. *make a speech, speak;* pret. 3s. **maðelode**, M 42, 309.

máðum, m. *gift, treasure, precious object;* dip. **máðmum**, S 99. **máð-um-ġiefa**, m. *giver of treasure;* ns. W 92.

mé, see **iċ**.

meaht, f. i-stem. *might, power;* dis. **meahte**, R 102; ds. S 108 (less probably as., which should have no ending; possibly ap. *powers,* since **ġelíefan on** takes acc. more often than dat.); ap. −a, C 2 (Northumbrian -*i;* the West Saxon -*e* may be as.). [The mutated form **miht** gives mod. "might"; cf. **magan**.]

meaht, meahte, verbs, see **magan**.

mearh, m. *horse, steed;* ns. W 92; as. M 188; ds. **méare**, M 239.

meċ, see **iċ**.

méċe, m. ja-stem. *sword;* as. M 167, 236; gp. **méċa**, B 40 (alt. reading MÆCGA, see **mæcg**); dip. **méċum**, B 24. [A poetic word appearing almost exclusively in this Anglian form; but MS A has the equivalent West Saxon root vowel in *mæcan* at B 40.]

medu, m. u-stem. *mead;* ds. M 212. **medu-drinċ**, m. (*mead-drink,*) *mead;* ds. −e, S 22. **medu-heall**, f. *mead-hall;* ds. −e, W 27.

ġe-menġan, wk.v.I. *mingle;* pp. **ġe-menġed**, W 48 (uninflected; one might expect apm. ĠEMENGDE). [Base-word ĠE-MANG, n. *mixture, throng.*]

meniġu, f. ín-stem. *multitude;* ds. **meniġe**, R 112, 151.

menn, see **mann**.

mere, m. i-stem. *sea* (elsewhere also *lake*); as. B 54. **mere-flód**, m. *ocean-stream;* ds. −e, S 59. **mere-wériġ**, adj. *sea-weary;* gs. −werġes, S 12 (as noun).

ġe-met, n. *measure;* ds. S 111 (**mid ġemete**, with moderation).

metod, m. *the measurer,* perhaps originally referring to fate, but in these and other poems almost consistently *God* (as ordainer of fate or creator); ns. S 108, 116; vs. M 175; gs. −es, C 2; W 2; S 103; ds. −e, M 147. [Cf. METAN, v. 5, *mete, measure.*]

méðe, adj. ja-stem. *weary;* nsm. R 65; npm. R 69. [From *MÓÐJA-.]

micel, adj. *much, great;* nsm. R 130; S 103; nsf. R 139; gsn. **micles**, M 217; ds.wk. **miclan**, R 65, 102; ism. **micle**, R 34, 60, 123 (w. **elne**); asf. **micle**, L 51. [Cf. **má, mára, mǽst**.]

micle, isn. of **micel**, n., adv. w. comp., *much;* M 50.

mid, prep. *with, amid, by,* etc. (1) w. dat. (instr.); (a) of persons acting, moving, or being together: (*in company*) *with, together with, accompanied by;* B 26, 47; R 121, 134, 143, 151; M 51, 79, 101a, 191; and with latent personification, S 59 (**mid mere-flóde**). (b) of associated abstractions: (*in conjunction*) *with,* R 149 (twice). (c) *having in hold, taking;* M 40, 56. (d) *amid, among;* M 23, 76; S 78, 80, 84 (**mid him**, *among themselves*). (e) of instrumentality: *with, by means of;* R 7, 14, 16,

20, 22, 23 (twice), 46, 48, 53, 59, 62, 102; M 14, 21, 32, 77, 101b, 114, 118, 124, 126, 136, 138, 226, 228; W 4, 29 (or manner); S 96. (f) of manner: *with, in;* B 37; M 68, 179; W 114; S 111. (2) w. acc., *along with,* S 99 (postpos.). [The acc. w. **mid** reflects Anglian usage.]

mid, adv. *in attendance, at the same time* (an extension of the preposition), R 106.

midd, adj. *middle, mid;* dsf. **midre,** R 2.

middan-ġeard, m. (*this*) *world, the earth;* ns. W 62; as. C 7; R 104; W 75; S 90. [Gothic MIDJUN-GARDS, OHG MITTIN-GART; the first element related to **midd,** adj.; cf. Old Icel. MIÐ-GARÐR.]

mierran, wk.v.I. *hinder.* See **a-mierran.**

mihtiġ, adj. *mighty;* nsm. R 151; comp. **mihtiġra,** nsm. S 116. [Cf. **ælmihtiġ.**]

milde, adj. ja-stem. *merciful;* vsm. M 175.

milds, f. jō-stem. *mildness, mercy, favor;* as. **-e,** W 2.

min, poss. adj. *my, mine;* nsm. M 218, 222, 224 (twice), 250; W 59; S 58, 59; L 6, 8, 15, 17, 47, 50; vsm. R 78, 95; nsf. R 130; M 177; gsm. **-es,** M 53; L 26; dsm. **-um,** R 30; M 176, 318; asm. **-ne,** M 248; W 10, 19, 22; gsf. **-re,** L 2, 40; dsf. **-re,** L 10; asf. **-e,** W 9; npm. **-e,** S 9; apm. **-e,** W 27 (*my* [*people*]); L 38; apn. **-e,** M 216; gp. **-ra,** L 5. [Cf. **iċ.**]

misliċ, adj. *various, diverse;* dip. **-licum,** S 99.

missenliċe, adv. *variously,* W 75 (*in various places or forms*); or **missen-liċ,** adj. *various,* npm. **-e.** [If the word is taken as an adv., its relation to the following phrase is closer and the syntax simpler. The alternate

form MISLĪĊE would be metrically more regular.]

mittung, f. *encounter.* See **ġār-mittung.**

mīðan, v.1. *hide.* See **mōd-mīðende.**

mōd, n. *mind, heart, spirit, mood;* ns. M 313; W 15; as. W 51; S 12, 108; L 20; gs. **-es,** S 36, 50; ds. **-e,** R 130; W 41, 111; S 109; is. **-e,** R 122. **mōd-ċeariġ,** adj. *sad, troubled in spirit;* nsm. W 2. **mōd-cearu,** f. *affliction of the spirit, grief;* gs. **-ċeare,** L 40; as. **-ċeare,** L 51. **mōd-ġeþanc,** m. or n. (*mind's*) *purpose, counsel;* as. C 2. **mōd-mīðende,** pres. part. adj. ja-stem. *secretive, concealing one's thoughts;* asm. **-ne,** L 20. [Cf. **mīðan.**] **mōd-sefa,** wk.m. *heart, soul, mind, inmost thoughts;* ns. R 124; W 59; S 59; as. **-n,** W 10, 19. **mōd-wlanc,** adj. *proud in spirit;* nsm. S 39. [Cf. **ǣwisc-, ēað-, ġeōmor-, ofer-, stīð-, wēriġ-mōd.**]

mōdiġ, adj. *bold, courageous, spirited;* nsm. R 41; M 147; npm. **mōdġe,** M 80; W 62.

mōdiġlīċe, adv. *boldly, with a show of courage;* M 200.

mōdor, f. r-stem. *mother;* as. R 92.

molde, wk.f. *earth;* ns. S 103; as. **moldan,** R 12, 82. **mold-ærn,** n. *earth-hall, sepulchre;* as. R 65.

morgen, m. *morning.* **morgen-tīd,** f. i-stem, *morningtide;* as. B 14.

morðor, n. *homicide, crime.* **morðor-hycgende,** pres. part. adj. ja-stem. *intent on violence, bloody-minded;* asm. **-ne,** L 20. [Cf. **hycgan.**]

mōst, mōste, mōston, see **mōtan.**

ġe-mōt, n. *meeting, encounter;* ns. M 301; as. M 199; gs. **-es,** B 50.

mōtan, pret.-pres.v. *be permitted, may, must;* pres. 1s. **mōt,** R 142; L 37; 2s. **mōst,** M 30; 1s. subj. **mōte,** R 127; 3s. subj. **mōte,** M 95, 177; 1p. subj. **mōten,** S 119 (**tō mōten,** *may go* *there*); 3p. subj. **mōten**, M 180; pret. 3s. **mōste**, M 272; 3p. **mōston**, M 83; 3p. subj. **mōsten**, M 87, 263. [MŌTAN, MŌT, MŌTON, MŌSTE.]

ġe-**munan**, pret.-pres.v. *remember, be mindful of;* – w. acc., pres. 1s. **ġeman**, R 28; 3s. **ġeman**, W 34, 90; L 51; pret. 3s. **gemunde**, M 225 (acc. or gen.); 3p. subj. **ġemunden**, M 196; – imper.pl. **ġemunaþ**, M 212 (emended: see note). [MUNAN, MAN, MUNON, MUNDE.]

mund, f. *hand, protection.* **mund-byrd**, f. i-stem, *protection* (as a social or legal obligation, such as a king owes to his subjects); ns. R 130 (*hope of protection*).

murnan, v.3. *mourn;* w. **for**, *trouble about, care for;* inf. M 259; pret. 3p. **murnon**, M 96. [MURNAN, MEARN, MURNON, —.]

mylen, m. *mill; honing place? grind-stone?* **mylen-scearp**, adj. *sharp from the grinding?* dip. **-um**, B 24. [A unique extention of the meaning of **mylen** (from Lat. MOLĪNA, a mill for grinding grain); on the interpretive possibilities see Campbell 1938: 105.]

ġe-**mynd**, f. i-stem (or n.). *memory;* as. W 51. [Cf. ġe-**munan**.]

ġe-**myndiġ**, adj. *mindful;* nsm. W 6.

myne, m. *thought, intention; remem-brance, favor, affection;* as. W 27 (often emended to [**mīn**] **myne wisse**, *might show me favor, feel affection for me*—an adaptation of *Beowulf* 169, itself of doubtful meaning; here the MS reading is taken as **mine wisse**; see **mīn** and **witan**).

N

nā (**ne ā**), adv. *never, not* (*at all*); M 21, 258, 268, 325; W 54, 66, 96; S 66; L 4, 24.

naca, wk.m. *boat, ship;* gs. **-n**, S 7.

næbbe (**ne hæbbe**), see **habban**.

næfre (**ne æfre**), adv. *never;* W 69, 112.

nægl or **næġel**, m. *nail;* dip. **næġlum**, R 46. [Orig. NÆĠL; cf. **biter**.]

næġled, pp. adj. *nailed, studded.* **næġled-cnearr**, m. *nailed ship;* dip. **-um**, B 53.

næniġ (**ne æniġ**), pron. and adj. *not any, none;* as pron. w. part. gen., nsm. S 25.

næs (**ne wæs**), see **bēon-wesan**.

nāg (**ne āg**), see **āgan**.

nama, wk.m. *name;* ns. M 267; D 37; ds. **-n**, R 113 (in a phrase imitative of the Bible, **for dryhtnes naman**, *for the Lord's* [*name's*] *sake*).

ġe-**nāme**, ġe-**nāmon**, see ġe-**niman**.

nān (**ne ān**), pron. (and adj.). *not one, none;* as pron. w. part. gen., nsm. W 9; dp. **-um**, B 25.

nāp, ġe-**nāp**, see **nīpan**, ġe-**nīpan**.

ne, negative particle. *not;* B 24, etc. (5 times); R 10, etc. (7 times); M 21, etc. (18 times); W 15, etc. (4 times); S 12, etc. (6 times); D 8, 11; L 22, 39. [Negative affix in **nā**, **næbbe**, **næfre**, etc. See also next word.]

nē, conj. *neither; nor;* B 46; M 259; W 16, 66 (twice), etc. (9 times all told); S 40 (twice), 41 (twice), etc. (15 times all told); L 41. [The distinc-tion between **ne** and **nē** is of long standing in editions, but it is purely editorial, drawn for the benefit of modern readers. There is no evidence to prove that the words were actually differentiated in Old English.]

nēah, adv. *near;* M 103; W 26; L 25.

ġe-**neahhe**, adv. *frequently;* M 269; W 56; D 25, 32.

nealles (**ne ealles**), adv. *not at all;* W 32, 33.

nearon (**ne earon**), see **bēon-wesan**.

nearu, adj. wa-stem. *narrow, close;* (fig.) *anxious;* nsf. S 7.

ġe-nēat, m. *follower, retainer;* ns. M 310. [Cf. **heorð-ġenēat**.]

nēawest, f. *presence (together), closeness, companionship;* ns. L 24 (not in MS). [**nēah** (q.v.); WIST, *state of being,* der. from **wesan**.]

-nebba, wk.m. *beaked one,* from adjectival -NEBB, *beaked,* corresponding to NEBB, n. ja-stem. *bill, beak, nose, face.* See **hyrned-nebba**.

nefne (**ne efne**), conj. (following a negative) and prep. (with acc.). *except, but;* S 46 (conj.); L 22 (prep). [A Mercian word; cf. the next.]

nemþe, conj. (following a negative) *unless,* W 113. [An Anglian word, interchangeable with the preceding one; prob. from *NE-EFNE-ÞE.]

nēotan, v.2, w. gen. *make use of;* inf. M 308. [NĒOTAN, NĒAT, NUTON, NOTEN.]

ġe-nerian, wk.v.I. *save;* pret. 3s. **ġenerede**, B 36.

nied, f. i-stem. *need, (dire) necessity;* dis. −e, B 33; pl., *constraints, fetters;* ap. −a, D 5.

niewe, adj. ja-stem. *new;* gsn. **niewes** as adv. *of new, recently;* L 4.

ġe-niewian, wk.v.II. *renew;* pp. **ġeniewod**, nsm. R 148; nsf. W 50, 55.

niht, f. (orig. a cons.-stem). *night;* ds. −e, R 2. **niht-helm**, m. *cover of night;* as. W 96. **niht-scua**, wk.m. *shadow of night;* ns. W 104; S 31. **niht-wacu**, f. *night-watch;* ns. S 7.

niman, v.4. *take; receive;* inf. M 39; L 15; *take off, kill,* inf. M 252; w. dat. or instr. *take on, assume,* pres. 3p. **nimaþ**, S 48 (**bearwas blostmum nimaþ**, *the groves take on blossoms, burst into bloom*—for the idiom, Gordon compares **fōn** w. dat.; see her note). [NIMAN, NAM, NŌMON, NUMEN; cf. **be-, for-niman**.]

ġe-niman, v.4. *take; lay hold of;* pret. 3p. **ġenāmon**, R 30, 60; *receive,* pret. 3s. subj. **ġenāme**, M 71.

nīpan, v.1. *grow dark, darken;* pres. 3s. **nīpeþ**, W 104; pret. 3s. **nāp**, S 31. [NĪPAN, NĀP, NIPON, NIPEN.]

ġe-nīpan, v.1, *become dark, vanish;* pret. 3s. **ġenāp**, W 96.

nis (**ne is**), see **bēon-wesan**.

nīþ, m. *violence, enmity, malice;* as. S 75.

ġe-nōg, adj. *enough;* npm. −e, R 33; (by understatement, *many*).

nolde, noldon, nolden, see **nyllan**.

norþ, adv. (*in, to the*) *north;* B 38.

norðan, adv. *from the north;* W 104; S 31.

norðerne, adj. ja-stem. *northern;* nsm.wk. **norðerna**, B 18.

nū, adv. *now,* C 1; R 78, 80, 84, 95, 126, 134; M 93, 175, 215, 316; W 9, 75, 97; S 33, 58, 82, 90; D 39; L 4, 24; − conj. *now that,* M 57, 222, 232, 250.

nyllan (**ne willan**), anom.v. *will not;* pres. 1s. **nylle**, M 246; pret. 3s. **nolde**, M 6, 9, 275; 3p. **noldon**, M 81, 185; 3p. subj. **nolden**, M 201.

O

of, prep. w. dat. *from, of, out of;* R 30, 49, 61, 66, 120, 133; M 7, 108, 149, 150, 154, 162, 221; W 113; S 107; L 6, 53.

ofer, prep. w. acc. *over.* (a) of motion: *over, across, through;* B 15, 19, 26, 55, 71; M 88, 91, 97, 98; W 24, 57, 82; S 60, 64; *over, beyond,* S 58; L 7; **ofer bæc**, *to the rear, back,* M 276. (b) of distribution or extent: *throughout,* R 12, 82; S 39. (c) of intensity and extent: **ofer eall**, *over all* (louder than all else and to all parts: so all could hear), M 256. (d) of degree: *above, more than,* R 91, 94. (e) of crossing someone's will or command: *contrary to, in disregard of,* R 35.

ōfer, m. *bank, shore;* ds. **ōfre,** M 28.

ofer-cuman, v.4. *overcome, overthrow;* pret. 3p. **ofercōmon,** B 72; − pass. w. gen. subject, *pass over;* pp. **ofercumen,** nsn. D 26 (þæt þæs **cyneriċes o. wǣre,** *that that regime would be overthrown*). [Cf. **cuman.**]

ofer-gān, anom.v., impers. w. gen. *pass over, go by;* pret. 3s. **oferēode,** D 7 (see note), 13, 17, 20, 27, 42. [Cf. **gān.**]

ofer-mōd, n. *pride, overconfidence;* ds. **−e,** M 89 (see note). [Cf. **mōd.**]

of-ġiefan, v.5. *give up, relinquish, leave;* pret. 3p. **ofġēafon,** W 61. [Cf. **a-, for-ġiefan.**]

of-langian, wk.v.II. *give over to longing, possess with longing;* pp. **oflangod,** nsf. L 29. [Cf. **langian.**]

ofostliċe, adv. *speedily,* M 143. [Also spelt OFSTLIĊE; cf. **efstan.**]

of-scēotan, v.2. *kill by shooting or hurling a weapon;* pret. 3s. **ofscēat,** M 77, *struck dead* (with a cast of his spear). [Cf. **scēotan.**]

oft, adv. *often;* B 8; M 188, 212, 296, 321; W 1, 8, 17, 20, 40, 53, 90; S 3, 6, 24, 29, 53; D 4; L 21, 32, 51; − comp. **oftor,** R 128.

on, prep. *in, on,* etc.

(1) w. dat. or instr. (a) of position: *in, on;* B 27, etc. (8 times); R 9, etc. (30 times; postpos. at 98; at 125 prob. should be acc.); M 25, etc. (37 times); W 12, etc. (12 times—either dat. or acc. at 42; at 81 prob. should be acc.); S 5, etc. (9 times); D 9, 29; L 13, etc. (7 times); *in* (transl. *from*), M 125; *in* (transl. *of*), M 142; *in* (transl. *among*), M 217, 266. − (b) of condition, state: *in,* S 85; D 25. − (c) of respect: *in,* S 41. − (d) of hostile

action: *on, at the expense of,* M 129, 259. − (e) of an inclusive source: **gelang on,** *comprehended in, inseparable from,* S 121. − (f) of trust: *in,* S 108 (or acc. − see **meaht**). − (g) of controlling mood: *in, with,* W 105. − (h) of time: *in,* W 35, 44; S 40; *on,* R 105.

(2) w. acc. (a) of motion: *into, to, on, onto, upon, toward;* B 36, 38, 54; R 5, 32b, 34 (postpos.), 40, 103, 104, 152; M 58, 78, 163, 178, 194, 270, 291, 322; S 32, 47, 52, 63, 120; D 5, 6; L 50. − (b) of time: *in,* B 14; R 68; **on ealle tīd,** *during (for) all time,* S 124; **on dæġ,** *that day* (Dobbie), M 198. − (c) in various phrases where motion is sometimes but not always clearly implicit: **on bēot,** *threateningly,* M 27 (see Gordon's note); **on ellen,** *valiantly,* M 211; **on flot,** *afloat, into (deep) water, to sea,* B 35; M 41; **on . . . hand,** *on . . . hand,* M 112; **on . . . healfe,** *on . . . side,* R 20; **on lāst,** *on the track, in pursuit,* B 22; **on hira selfra dōm,** *as they themselves shall decide,* M 38. − (d) **bēodeþ sorge on brēost-hord,** *forebodes sorrow in the heart* (implying that sorrow will enter into the heart?), S 55. [In West Saxon the preferred form of the preposition is almost always *on,* while in the Anglian dialects both forms are regularly employed, *on* and *in.* The latter appears in MS 8 times in W, 11 in S, and twice in L: see the textual apparatus.]

on-weġ, prep. phrase as adv. *away;* W 53; S 74.

on, adv. *on, onward;* S 91 (**ieldu him on fareþ,** *old age catches up to him, overtakes him*—Gordon points out that if **on** were the postpos. prep. it ought to be preceded by acc. **hine**).

on-bierġan, wk.v.I, w. gen. *taste (of)*,

partake (of); inf. R 114. [Cf. **bier-ġan.**]

on-ċierran, wk.v.I. *turn, change;* refl., *turn aside or be changed;* pres. 3s. **onċierreþ,** S 103 (for þon hie seo molde onċierreþ, *before which* [the terrible power of God] *the earth will turn aside;* see note).

on-cnāwan, v.7. *perceive;* inf. M 9. [CNĀWAN, CNEOW, CNEOWON, CNĀWEN.]

on-cweðan, v.5. w. dat. of person, *reply to, answer;* pret. 3s. **oncwæþ,** M 245; S 23. [Cf. **cweðan.**]

on-drædan, v.7, w. refl. dat. and acc. *dread;* pres. 3s. **ondrædeþ,** S 106. [-DRÆDAN, DRED (DREORD), DREDON, DRÆDEN.]

on-efen, prep. w. dat. *close by, beside,* M 184.

ōnettan, wk.v.I. *hasten on;* pres. 3s. **ōnetteþ,** S 49. [From Gmc. *ON-HAITJAN; stress on first syll. early obscured the compound.]

on-fand, see **on-findan.**

on-fēng, see **on-fōn.**

on-findan, v.3. *find, find out, perceive;* pret. 3s. **onfunde,** M 5; *experience, come to know;* pret. 3s. **onfand,** D 4. [Cf. **findan.**]

on-fōn, contr.v.7. *receive;* pret. 3s. **onfēng,** M 110 (w. acc.). [Cf. **fōn.**]

on-funde, see **on-findan.**

on-gann, see **on-ġinnan.**

on-ġēan adv. *again; in return,* M 49; *back, out again,* M 137; **eft o.,** *back again,* M 156.

on-ġēan, prep. w. dat. *against,* M 100.

on-ġēaton, see **on-ġietan.**

on-ġierwan, wk.v.I. *unclothe, strip;* pret. 3s. (refl.), **onġierede,** R 39. [The prefix here is negative; cf. **ġierwan.**]

on-ġietan, v.5. *perceive, apprehend, realize;* inf. R 18; W 73; pret. 3p. **onġēaton,** M 84; pp. **onġieten,** un-infl., D 10. [ĠIETAN, ĠEAT, ĠEATON, ĠIETEN; cf. **be-ġietan.**]

on-ġinnan, v. 3. *begin, undertake;* pres. 3p. subj. **onġinnen,** R 116; pret. 3s. **ongann,** R 19, 27, 73; M 12, 17, 89, 91, 228, 265; pret. 3p. **ongunnon,** R 65, 67; M 86, 261; L 11. [-ĠINNAN, GANN, GUNNON, GUNNEN; recorded only with be- or on-.]

on-hrēran, wk.v.I. *stir, move;* inf. S 96. [Cf. **hrēran.**]

on-hweorfan, v.3. *change, reverse.* pp. **onhworfen,** nsn. L 23. [Cf. **hweorfan.**]

on-līesan, wk.v.I. *liberate, redeem;* pret. 3s. **onlīesde,** R 147. [Cf. **līesan.**]

on-sendan, wk.v.I. *send on, send forth;* pres. 3s. **onsendeþ,** W 104; pp. **onsended,** uninfl., R 49 (*yielded up*). [In West Saxon the pp. is commonly syncopated to **onsend;** cf. **sendan.**]

on-stellan, wk.v.I. *establish;* pret. 3s. **onstealde,** C 4 (var.). Cf. **a-stellan.**

on-wæcnan, v.6 (irreg.). *wake up;* pres. 3s. **onwæcneþ,** W 45. [WÆCNAN, WŌC, WŌCON, WÆCNED.]

on-weġ, adv., see **on.**

on-wendan, wk.v.I, trans. *change, turn;* pres. 3s. **on-wendeþ,** W 107. [Cf. **wendan.**]

on-wrēon, contr.v.1. *uncover, disclose;* imper. sg. **onwrēoh,** R 97. [The prefix here is negative; cf. **be-wrēon.**]

open, adj. *open;* npm. **opene,** R 47.

ōr, n. *beginning;* as. C 4.

ord, m. *point; point of origin, beginning,* as. C 4 (var.); *point of a weapon* (usually a spear), ns. M 60, 146, 157, 253 (**ord and īren**—see **īren**); as. M 47, 110; ds. **-e,** M 124, 226; *battle-line,* ns. M 69; *forefront of the battle,* ds. **-e,** M 273.

orne, adj. ja-stem. *not mean; excessive.* See **un-orne.**

oþ, conj. *until;* B 16.

oþ, prep. *to, up to, till*. **oþ-þæt**, conj. *until,* R 26, 32; M 278, 324; W 71, 86; D 39.

oþ-beran, v.4. *carry off;* pret. 3s. **oþbær**, W 81. [**oþ**- here has the sense of *away;* cf. **beran**.]

ōðer, adj. and pron. *other, another.* (a) adj., asm. **−ne**, M 234; dsn. **ōðrum**, M 64. (b) pron., nsm. M 282; asm. **−ne**, M 143; dsm. **ōðrum**, M 70, 133; **ōðer** (asn.) **twēġa**, *one of two things,* M 207.

oþþe, conj. *or,* R 36; M 208, 292; W 26, 28; S 70 (twice), 114; L 4.

oþ-þringan, v.3. *wrest away;* pres. 3s. **oþ-þringeþ**, S 71. [Cf. **ġe-þringan**.]

P

-pāda, wk.m. *coated one,* formed from adjectival -PĀD, *coated,* corresponding to PĀD, f. *coat.* See **hasu-, sealwiġ-pāda**; also **hyrned-nebba, īsiġ-feðra, ūriġ-feðra**.

plega, wk.m. *play, sport, fight.* See **gūþ-, hand-, wiġ-plega**.

plegian, wk.v.II. *play;* pret. 3p. **plegodon**, B 52.

prass, m. *military array;* ds. **−e**, M 68. [See Scragg's note.]

R

rād, see **rīdan**.

ġe-ræċan, wk.v.I. *reach;* pret. 3s. **ġe-ræhte**, *reached with a weapon, pierced,* M 158, 226; **feorh ġ.**, *reached the life, pierced fatally,* M 142.

rædan, wk.v.I. *give counsel, instruct;* pret. 3s. **rædde**, M 18. [Cf. ĠE-RĀD, adj. *wise, skillful;* also RÆD, n. *counsel, advice;* and RÆDAN, v.7 (pret. RĒD or REORD), *advise,* etc.]

ġe-rædan, wk.v.I. *decide;* pres. 2s. **ġerædest**, M 36.

ġe-rædu, n. ja-stem pl. *trappings;* dp. **−m**, M 190. [Cf. RĀD, f. *riding; harness;* and **rīdan**, v.1.]

ræran, wk.v.I. *rear, raise.* See **a- ræran**.

ræs, m. *rush, onset, attack.* See **beadu-, gār-ræs**.

rand, m. *boss of a shield* (the metal center); *shield;* ap. **−as**, M 20.

rēaf, n. *raiment;* as. M 161 (*coat of mail?*). [Another meaning, *spoil, booty,* seems less appropriate.]

rēċan (later **reċċan**), wk.v.I, w. gen. *care about;* pret. 3p. **rōhton**, M 260. [RĒĊAN (from *RŌKJAN), RŌHTE, RŌHT.]

recene, adv. *quickly,* M 93; W 112.

ġe-reġnian, wk.v.II. *adorn, ornament;* pp. **ġereġnod**, asn. M 161.

reord, f. (or n.) *voice, speech;* dis. **−e**, S 53 (of a bird). **reord-berend**, m. nd-stem. *speech-bearer* (a periphrasis for a human being as one endowed with speech; it appears in several of the religious poems, sometimes, as here, with point); np. R 3; dp. **−um**, R 89.

rest, f. jō-stem. *resting place, bed;* as. **−e**, R 3 (obj. of **wunodon**: *were in bed*). [Cf. **wæl-rest**.]

restan, wk.v.I. *rest, lie, remain;* pret. 3s. **reste**, R 64 (refl.), 69 (intrans.).

ġe-restan, wk.v.I. *rest (oneself),* gain *rest (from,* with gen.); inf. L 40.

rīċe, n. ja-stem. *realm, kingdom;* ns. W 106; as. R 119, 152; gs. **−s**, S 81; D 23. [Cf. **cyne-, heofon-, weorold- rīċe**.]

rīċe, adj. ja-stem. *powerful;* as. **rīcne**, R 44; gp. **rīcra**, R 131; **rīċost**, superl., nsm. M 36.

rīdan, v.1. *ride;* inf. M 291; pret. 3s. **rād**, M 18, 239. [RĪDAN, RĀD, RIDON, RIDEN.]

riht, adj. *right, proper, true;* nsn. M 190; asm. **–ne**, R 89.

riht, n. *right, privilege, just title.* See **land-riht.**

ġe-rihtan, wk.v.I. *direct;* pp. **ġeriht**, nsf. R 131.

rihte, adv. *rightly, correctly*, M 20.

rinċ, m. *warrior, man;* dp. **rincum**, M 18. [Cf. **fierd-, gūð-, hilde-, sǣrinċ.**]

rīsan, v.1. *rise.* See **a-rīsan.**

rōd, f. *rood, cross;* ns. R 44, 136; ds. **–e**, R 56, 131; as. **–e**, R 119. [The original sense was *twig, branch, pole.*]

rodor, m. *the heavens, sky.* See **upprodor.**

rōhton, see **rēċan.**

rūn, f. *(private) counsel;* ds. in **sundor æt rūne** *(apart in private meditation)*, W 111.

ġe-rȳman, wk.v.I. *open* (a way); pret. 1s. **ġerȳmde**, R 89; pp. **ġerȳmed**, nsn. M 93. [Base-word RŪM, adj. *spacious.*]

S

sǣ, m. or f. i-stem. *sea* (applied to large bodies of water, usually salt but occasionally fresh); as. (f.) W 4; (m.) S 14, 18. **sǣ-fōr**, f. *sea-voyage;* gs. or ds. **–e**, S 42. **sǣ-lida**, wk.m. *seafarer;* vs. M 45; as. **–n**, M 286. **sǣ-mann**, m. *seaman;* dp. **–um**, M 38, 278; np. **–menn**, M 29. **sǣ-rinċ**, m. *sea-warrior, viking;* ns. M 134. [**sǣ** is almost exclusively masc. in Anglian prose texts.]

sæċċ, f. jō-stem. *strife, battle;* ds. **–e**, B 4, 42.

sæd, adj. *sated;* nsm. B 20 (w. gen., *sated with*). [Cognate w. Lat. SATIS; mod. "sad" has shifted its meaning.]

sæġde, ġe-sæġde, sæġe, sæġeþ, see **secgan, ġe-secgan.**

sæl, n. *hall.* See **win-sæl.**

sǣl, m. i-stem (or f.). *time, occasion;* ns. R 80; *(happy time,) joy, pleasure,* dip. **–um**, D 28.

sǣlan, wk.v.I. *fasten, bind, tie;* inf. W 21. [From SĀL, m. or f. *rope.*]

sǣliġ, adj. *fortunate; disposed by fortune;* see **heard-sǣliġ.**

ġe-sǣliġ, adj. *prosperous; fortunate;* see **weorold-ġesǣliġ.**

sæt, see **sittan.**

ġe-sæt, see **ġe-sittan.**

sāg, see **sigan.**

samod, adv. *together, jointly, in unison;* W 39.

sang, m. *song;* as. S 19.

sang, v., see **singan.**

sār, n. *pain;* as. S 95.

sār, adj. *sore, painful, grievous;* nsm. D 9; npf. **–e**, W 50 (**sāre æfter**, *sore with longing for*); gp. **–ra**, R 80.

sāre, adv. *sorely*, R 59.

ġe-sāwe, see **ġe-sēon.**

sāwol, f. *soul;* ns. R 120; M 177; ds. **sāwle**, S 100.

ġe-sāwon, see **ġe-sēon.**

scacan, v.6. *shake;* see **a-scacan.**

scadu, f. wō-stem. *shadow, darkness;* ns. R 54.

scaða, wk.m. *one who does harm; ravager, enemy, warrior.* See **fǣr-, hell-scaða.**

scēaf, see **scūfan.**

sceaft, m. *shaft (of spear);* ns. M 136.

ġe-sceaft, f. i-stem. *creature, creation;* ns. B 16; R 12, 55, 82; **wyrda ġesceaft**, *the operation of the fates* (?); *course of events*, ns. W 107. [Cf. **forð-ġesceaft**; related to SCEAP-, base of **scieppan**, q.v.]

-sceaftiġ, adjectival component, *fortuned, possessed of such a fortune* (?). See **fēa-sceaftiġ.**

sceal, see **sculan.**

scealc, m. *retainer, warrior;* np. **–as**, M 181.

sceard, adj., w. gen. *bereft (of)*; nsm. B 40.

scearp, adj. *sharp*. See **mylen-scearp**.

sceat, m. *surface, region, expanse;* ap. **-as**, R 37; S 61, 105; dp. **-um**, R 8, 43. [The meaning in R is sometimes taken to be *corner*, but *surface* is appropriate at all three places.]

scēat, v., see **scēotan**.

sceatt, m. *coin; tax;* dp. **-um**, M 40, 56 (*tribute money*).

scēaþ, f. *sheath;* ds. **scēaðe**, M 162.

scēawian, wk.v.II. *see, behold; look at;* pret. 1s. **scēawode**, R 137. [Cf. **ġeond-scēawian**.]

ġe-scēawian, wk.v.II. *show, display;* pres. 3s. **ġescēawaþ**, D 33.

scēotan, v.2. *shoot, hurl; hit with a missile;* pret. 3s. **scēat**, M 143 (*pierced* with a spear), 270 (*shot* an arrow); pp. **scoten**, nsm. B 19 (*shot* by an arrow or *pierced* by a dart). [SCĒOTAN, SCĒAT, SCUTON, SCOTEN; cf. **of-scēotan**.]

scield, m. *shield;* as. B 19; ds. **-e**, M 136; ap. **-as**, M 98. **scield-burg**, f. cons.-stem. *wall of shields;* ns. M 242.

scieppan, v. 6. *create;* pret. 3s. **scōp**, C 5 (var. **ġescōp**). [SCIEPPAN, SCŌP, SCŌPON, SCEAPEN.]

scieppend, m. nd-stem. (*the*) *Creator;* ns. C 6; W 85.

scieþþan, v.6. w.dat. *injure;* inf. R 47. [SCIEÞÞAN, SCŌD, SCŌDON, SCEAÐEN. The present stem is recorded only as SCEÞ- (seemingly an Anglian spelling) and, once, LWS SCYÞ- (corresponding to EWS *SCIEÞ-). The passive participle is recorded once, at *Genesis A* 869, where it is *sceaþen* instead of the expected SCEADEN.]

scīma, wk.m. *light, radiance;* as. **-n**, R 54.

scīnan, v.1. *shine;* inf. R 15. [SCĪNAN, SCĀN, SCINON, SCINEN.]

scip, n. *ship;* ds. **-e**, M 40, 56. **scip-flota**, wk.m. *sailor, seaman;* np. **-n**, B 11.

scir, adj. *bright, clear;* asn. M 98; asm. **-ne**, R 54.

scolde, scolden, scoldon, see **sculan**.

scop, m. *court poet and singer;* ns. D 36.

scōp, see **scieppan**.

scoten, see **scēotan**.

scræf, n. *pit, cavern, grave*. See **eorþ-scræf**.

scua, wk.m. *shade, shadow*. See **niht-scua**.

scūfan, v.2. *shove, thrust;* pret. 3s. **scēaf**, M 136. [SCŪFAN, SCĒAF, SCUFON, SCOFEN.]

sculan, pret.-pres.v. *shall, must, have to, be destined to;* w. inf. except as indicated; pres. 1s. **sceal**, L 25; 3s. **sceal**, R 119; M 60, 252; W 37, 56, 70, 73, 112; S 109; L 43, 52; − w. **bēon** understood, *must be*, M 312, 313; W 65, 66; − 1p. **sculon**, C 1; 2p. **scule (ġē)**, M 59; 3p. **sculon**, M 54, 220; 3s. subj. **scyle**, S 74 (v. of motion understood: *must go*), 111 (*should, ought to*); L 42 (see note); pret. 1s. **scolde**, *had to*, R 43; W 8, 19; S 30; 3s. **scolde**, M 16 (*had occasion to, was called upon to*), 3s. subj. **scolde**, W 3 (*may have had to*); D 12 (v. of action understood: *ought to act*); pret. 3p. **scoldon**, M 19 (*should, ought to*), 105 (*were to, were destined to*); 3p. subj. **scolden**, M 291, 307 (*should*). [SCULAN, SCEAL, SCULON, SCOLDE.]

scūr, m. *shower;* dip. **-um**, S 17.

scyle, see **sculan**.

sē, sēo, þæt, dem. adj. and pron., often translatable as a def. art., though that is not its actual function in OE. *that, the, that one.* (a) as adj., **sē**, nsm. B 37; R 13, etc. (7 times); M 6, etc. (15 times); W 16, 82; S 12, etc. (5 times); L 50 (sē mīn wine, *that friend of mine*); – sēo, nsf. B 16; M 104, 144, 284; W 95, 100, 115; S 103, 107; D 16; L 24 (not in MS); – þæt, nsn. R 6; S 94; asn. B 64; R 18, 21; M 22, 102, 137, 168, 194; S 108; – þæs, gsm. R 49; M 131, 141, 160, 165; L 11, 41; gsn. M 8, 148, 202; D 26; – þǣre, gsf. M 95; L 40; dsf. R 21, 112, 131; M 8, 220; S 100; – þām, dsm. or dsn. B 29; R 9, etc. (11 times); M 10, etc. (19 times); S 122; dp. R 11, 59, 143, 154; M 40, 190, 278; L 28; – þone, asm. B 61, 62; R 127; M 19, etc. (10 times) ; – þā, asf. R 20, 68, 119; M 48, 72,74, 78, 139, 163, 325; W 113; S 120; in þā hwīle þe, M 14, 83, 235, 272 (see hwīl); np. B 53, 57; R 46, 61; M 96, 182, 261, 305; S 10, 56, 87; ap. M 82, 145, 196, 212, 277, 322; S 57; – þāra, gp. M 174. (b) as dem. pron. *that (one), those, (he, she, it, they)* etc., sē, nsm. M 75, 150, 157, 227, 310; S 104; – þæt, nsn. R 28a, 39, 74; M 76, 223, 325; S 72; D 19, 23 (pointing to a person); L 23; asn. R 28b, 58, 66; M 5, 36, 84, 246; S 12, 24, 55, 109; D 12, 35; L 2, 11; – þæs, gsn. M 120 (w. þanc, *for that*), 239; S 122 (w. þanc); D 7 (see note), 13, 17, 20, 27, 42; tō þæs, *to that extent*, S 40b, 41 (twice); alone as adv., *to that extent*, S 39, 40a; – þām, dsm. R 129; dsn. M 9, 34; dpm. R 9 (MS þær); – þā, np. M 81; S 50; – þȳ, isn. as adv. w. comp., *by that, the*, B 46; M 146; W 49; correlatively, M 312, 313 (3 times w. comp., once as conj., *the . . . as*). (c) as rel. pron., *who, which*, etc., sē, nsm. R 107; M 27, 153; – þæt, asn. M 289 and S 99 (in both cases þæt = þætte < þæt-þe, *that which*); D 41; – þæs, gsn. B 51 (possibly, but see note and cf. [f] below); – þā, np. M

184; – þon, isn. S 103 (w. for, *before which, for which*); L 44 (w. ēac, *in addition to which*). (d) as indef. pron. *he who, whoever*, sē, nsm. W 88. (e) w. þe, as compound rel. pron. *he who*, etc., sē-þe, nsm. R 98, 113, 145; M 258, 316; W 29, 37, 112; S 27, 47, 106a, 107; – sēo-þe, nsf. R 121; – þām-þe, dsm. W 31, 56, 114; S 51; L 52: dp. R 149, 154; – þone-þe, asm. W 27; – þāra-þe, gp. B 26; R 86. (f) þæs-þe, gsn. as conj., B 68 (*according to what, as*); þæs (=þæs-þe; see note), B 51 (*after, when; because*).

ġe-seah, see ġe-sēon.

sealde, ġe-sealde, ġe-sealdon, see sellan, ġe-sellan.

sealt, n. *salt*. sealt-ȳþ, f. jō-stem. *salt seawave;* gp. –a, S 35.

sealwiġ, adj. *dark-colored.* sealwiġ-pāda, wk.m. *dark-coated one;* ap. –n, B 61 (referring to the raven, the eagle, and the wolf; stylistically less satisfactory if treated as as., referring only to the raven). [On the form, see -pāda.]

sēarian, wk.v.II. *grow sere, wither, fade;* pres. 3s. sēaraþ, S 89.

sēaþ, m. *pit;* ds. sēaðe, R 75.

sēċan, wk.v.I. *seek;* – (a) *set out for, seek out, go to, come to;* inf. B 55; R 104, 127 (*resort to*); L 9; pret. 3p. sōhton, B 58, 71 (*invaded*); R 133; M 193; – (b) *search for, try to find;* pret. 1s. sōhte, W 25; – (c) *try to obtain;* pres. 3s. sēċeþ, W 114. [SĒCAN (from *SŌKJAN), SŌHTE, SŌHT.]

ġe-sēċan, wk.v.I. *seek, go to, come to;* inf. R 119; M 222; pres. 1s. subj. ġesēċe, S 38; pret. 3s. ġesōhte, M 287 (*sank to*); 3p. ġesōhton, B 27.

secg, m. ja-stem. *retainer, man, warrior;* ns. B 17; M 159; S 56; D 24; ap. –as, M 298; gp. –a, B 13; W 53; dp. –um, R 59. [From *SAGJA-, cognate w. Lat. SOCIUS. Cf. **sele-secg**.]

secgan, wk.v.III. *say, tell, relate;* inf. R 1; M 30; S 2; D 35; L 2; imper. sg. **sǣġe**, M 50; pres. 3s. **sǣġeþ**, M 45; 3p. **secgaþ**, B 68; 2s. subj. **secge**, R 96; pret. 3s. **sǣġde**, M 147. [SECGAN, SÆĠDE, SÆĠD; cf. **a-secgan**.]

ġe-secgan, wk.v.III. *say;* pret. 3s. **ġe-sǣġde**, M 120 (w. **þanc**, *gave thanks*).

sefa, wk.m. *mind, spirit, heart;* as. −**n**, W 57; S 51; ds. −**n**, D 9, 29. [Cf. **mōd-sefa**.]

sēft-, combining form corresponding to SĒFTE, adj. *soft.* **sēft-ēadiġ**, adj. *blessed with comfort;* nsm. S 56 (Grein's emendation, for MS *eft eadig*). [Cf. **sōfte**.]

seld, n. *hall.* See **cear-seld**.

ġe-selda, wk.m. *companion, fellow-retainer;* np. −**n**, W 53. [Lit. *one of the same dwelling*.]

seldliċ, adj. *rare, wonderful;* nsm. R 13; comp. **seldlicre**, asn. R 4 (*exceedingly rare?*).

sele, m. i-stem. *hall;* perhaps as separate word, as. W 25; but see **sele-drēoriġ** below. **sele-drēam**, m. *hall-joy, festivity in the hall;* np. −**as**, W 93. **sele-drēoriġ**, adj. *sad for want of a hall, homesick;* nsm. W 25 (see note). **sele-secg**, m. *hall-warrior, retainer;* ap. −**as**, W 34. [Cf. **drēor-**, **eorþ-sele**.]

sēlest, adj. superl. *best;* asn. (with partitive genitive), R 118; nsm.wk. −**a**, R 27. [Comp. SĒL, adv., **sēlra**, adj.; the positive is lacking; from *SŌLI-*.]

self, dem. adj. and pron. (*him-, her-, it-*) *self.* (a) as adj., nsm. S 35; nsm.wk. −**a**, R 105; asf. −**e**, R 92; gsf. −**re**, D 9; dsm. −**um**, S 1; D 35; L 45; gp. −**ra**, M 38. − (b) as pron., dsm. −**um**, D 29; gsf. −**re**, L 2.

sellan, wk.v.I. *give;* inf. M 38, 46 (*hand over, pay*); pres. 1p. subj. **sellen**, M 61 (*pay*); pret. 3s. **sealde**, M 271 (*gave, inflicted*). [SELLAN, SEALDE, SEALD.]

ġe-sellan, wk.v.I. *give;* pret. 3s. **ġe-sealde**, M 188 (*gave, presented*); D 41 (the same); pret. 3p. **ġe-sealdon**, M 184 (*gave, yielded up*).

sēlra, adj. comp. *better;* asm. −**n**, D 6. [Cf. **sēlest**.]

ġe-sēman, wk.v.I. *reconcile, decide the terms between;* inf. M 60. [Base-word SŌM, f. *agreement.*]

sendan, wk.v.I. *send;* inf. M 30; W 56; pret. 3s. **sende**, M 134; 3p. **sendon**, M 29. [SENDAN, SENDE, SENDED; base-word SAND, f. *a sending, message;* cf. **on-sendan**.]

sēo, see **sē**.

seofian, wk.v.II. *lament, sigh;* pret. 3p. **seofodon**, S 10.

seofon, num. adj. *seven;* npm. −**e**, B 30.

seolfor, n. *silver;* dis. **seolfre**, R 77.

ġe-sēon, contr.v.5. *see;* pres. 3s. **ġe-siehþ**, W 46; pret. 1s. **ġeseah**, R 14, 21, 33, 36, 51; 3p. **ġesāwon**, M 84, 203; 1s. subj. **ġesāwe**, R 4. [SĒON (from *SEHWAN*), SEAH, SĀWON, SEWEN.]

ġe-set, n. *seat;* np. **ġesetu**, W 93.

setl, n. *seat;* ds. −**e**, B 17.

ġe-settan, wk.v.I. *set, seat, place;* pret. 3p. **ġesetton**, R 67; pp. **ġeseted**, nsn. R 141. [SETTAN, SETTE, SETED; cf. **a-settan**, **sittan**.]

sē-þe, see **sē**.

sīde, wk.f. *side;* ds. **sīdan**, R 49.

sīde, adv. *widely;* **wīde and sīde**, *far and wide*, R 81.

sie, see **bēon-wesan**.

ġe-siehþ, v., see **ġe-sēon**.

sīen, f. i-stem. *sight, spectacle.* See **wǣfer-sīen**, and cf. **an-sīen**.

ġe-sīene, adj. ja-stem, *visible;* npn. R 46. [Cf. **ġe-sēon**.]

ġe-sierwed, pp. adj. *armed;* nsm. M
159. [As from ĠE-SIERWAN, wk.v.I,
unrecorded in other forms; base-
word SEARU, f. wō-stem, *equipment.*]

sigan, v.1. *sink;* pret. 3s. sāg, B 17.
[SĪGAN, SĀG, SIGON, SIĠEN.]

siġe, m. i-stem. *victory.* siġe-bēam, m.
tree of victory (the cross); ns. R 13;
as. R 127.

sigor, m. *victory;* gp. −a, R 67.

sigorfæst, adj. *victorious;* nsm. R 150.

ġe-sihþ, f. jō-stem. *sight, vision;* ds.
−e, R 21, 41, 66; as. −e, R 96.

simle, adv. *ever, always;* S 68. [Less
commonly spelt SIMBLE; the B is
epenthetic.]

sinċ, n. *treasure;* as. M 59; gs. −es, W
25; ds. −e, R 23. sinċ-ġiefa, wk.m.
giver of treasure, bountiful lord; as.
−n, M 278. sinċ-þegu, f. *receiving of
treasure;* as. −þeġe, W 34.

sind, sindon, see bēon-wesan.

singal, adj. *ever-living, perpetual;* nsf.
R 141. [SIN-, *always* (Lat. SEMPER,
OE sim-le); second element obscure.]

singan, v.3. *sing;* pres. part. singende,
asm. uninfl., S 22; pres. 3s. singeþ, S
54; pret. 3s. sang, M 284. [SINGAN,
SANG, SUNGON, SUNGEN.]

sin-sorg, f. *perpetual sorrow;* gp. −na,
L 45. [Gp. −na is late WS rather
than evidence of a weak noun (see
Campbell 1959: §§586, 617); for
sin- see singal.]

sinu, f. wō-stem. *sinew.* sinu-bend, f.
jō-stem. *sinew-bond* (a bond made
by cutting a sinew, by ham-
stringing); ap. −a, D 6.

sittan, v.5. *sit;* inf. L 37; pres. 3s.
siteþ, D 28; L 47; pret. 3s. sæt, D
24. [SITTAN, SÆT, SǢTON, SETEN.]

ġe-sittan, v.5. *sit;* pret. 3s. ġesæt,
W 111.

sīþ, m. (a) *journey, voyage, venture;*
ds. sīðe, S 51; − (b) *experience, trial,*
as. L 2; ap. sīðas, S 2. sīþ-fæt, m.

expedition; ds. −e, R 150. [Cf.
bealu-, fram-, wræc-sīþ.]

sīðian, wk.v.II. *travel, journey, pass;*
inf. R 68; M 177; pres. 1s. subj.
sīðie, M 251.

ġe-sīþþ, n. *companionship, company;*
ds. −e, D 3.

siþþan, adv. *afterward,* R 142; S 78; −
conj. *after,* B 13, 69; R 3, 49, 71
(MS; emended to stefn, q.v.); W 22;
D 5; L 3.

slǣp, m. *sleep;* ns. W 39; is. slǣp' (for
slǣpe), D 16.

slāt, see slītan.

sleaht, m. or n. (var. of slieht, i-stem),
slaughter. See wæl-sleaht, and cf.
bill-ġeslieht.

slēan, contr.v.6, *strike;* pret. 3s. slōg,
M 163, 285; 3s. subj. slōge, M 117.
[SLĒAN (from *SLEAHAN), SLŌG,
SLŌGON, SLÆĠEN; cf. be-slēan.]

ġe-slēan, contr.v.6. *obtain by striking,
win;* pret. 3p. ġeslōgon, B 4.

ġe-slieht, m. or n. i-stem. *slaughter.*
See bill-ġeslieht, and cf. sleaht and
slēan.

slītan, v.1. *lacerate, tear, lend;* pret.
3s. slāt, S 11. [SLĪTAN, SLĀT, SLITON,
SLITEN.]

slīðen, adj. *cruel, dire, fierce;* nsf.
W 30.

slōg, slōge, ġe-slōgon, see slēan,
ġe-slēan.

smiþ, m. *smith.* See wiġ-smiþ.

snāw, m. *snow;* as. W 48.

snell, adj. *keen, bold;* np. −e, M 29.

snīwan, v.1, with wk. pret. *snow;* pret.
3s. snīwde, S 31.

snottor, adj. *wise, discerning;* nsm. W
111 (as noun). [Geminate -tt- has
been extended analogically from the
oblique cases. Both snotor and
snottor appear to be metrically
substantiated in different poems.]

sōfte, adv. *easily;* M 59. [Cf. the
mutated sēft-.]

sōht-, ġe-**sōht-**, see **sēċan**, ġe-**sēċan**.

sorg, f. *sorrow;* ns. W 30, 39, 50; as. −e, S 42 (*anxiety?*), 54; D 3; gp. −a, R 80; dip. −um, R 20, 59; D 24.

sorg-ċeariġ, adj. *troubled by sorrow, sorrowful;* nsm. D 28 (as noun, or modifying an indefinite "someone" that is understood). **sorg-lēoþ**, n. *song of sorrow, dirge;* as. R 67. **sorg-lufu**, f. *sorrowful love;* ns. D 16. [Cf. **sin-sorg**.]

sōþ, n. *truth;* ds. **sōð**, W 11 (**tō s.**, *for a truth, indeed*). **sōð-ġiedd**, n. ja-stem. *lay of truth* (as opposed to legendary matter); as. S 1.

ġe-**spann**, n. *fastening, joint.* See **eaxl-ġespann**.

spēdan, wk.v.I. *be prosperous, be wealthy;* pres. 2p. **spēdaþ**, M 34 (**ġif ġē s. tō þām**, *if you have that much wealth, if you are good for the necessary amount*—see Gordon's note). [Base-word SPĒD, f. i-stem (from *SPŌDI-), *success, wealth.*]

spēdiġ, adj. *successful;* nsm. R 151.

spell, n. *message;* as. M 50.

spere, n. i-stem. *spear;* as. M 137 (*spearhead*); ap. **speru**, M 108. [Cf. **wæl-spere**.]

spillan, wk.v.I. *destroy;* inf. M 34 (**ūs spillan**, *slaughter each other*).

sprang, see **springan**.

sprecan, v.5, intrans. or trans. *speak;* with a clause, *say;* inf. R 27; pres. 3s. **spriċeþ**, W 70; pret. 3s. **spræc**, M 211, 274; 1p. **sprǣcon**, M 212; 3p. M 200. [SPRECAN, SPRÆC, SPRǢCON, SPRECEN.]

sprenġan, wk.v.I. *cause to spring or quiver;* pret. 3s. **sprengde**, M 137 (the subject may be **sē sceaft** rather than Byrhtnoþ). [Based on SPRANG, 2nd grade of **springan**.]

springan, v.3. *spring;* pret. 3s. **sprang**, M 137. [SPRINGAN, SPRANG, SPRUNGON, SPRUNGEN.]

stæf, m. *sign, letter of the alphabet; verbal formula.* See **glēo-stafas**.

stæþ, n. *bank, shore;* ds. **stæðe**, M 25. [Cf. **ēa-stæþ**.]

ġe-**stæg**, see ġe-**stigan**.

stān, m. *stone;* ds. −e, R 66. **stān-clif**, n. *rocky cliff, crag;* ap. −u, S 23. **stān-hliþ**, n. *rocky slope, stone declivity;* ds. −hliðe, L 48 ap. −hliðu, W 101 (fig. for high stone walls, or transition from image of a ruined citadel to weatherbeaten cliffs of the earth itself?).

standan, v.6. *stand, remain, endure;* inf. R 43, 62; M 19; pres. 3s. **stent**, M 51; **standeþ**, W 74, 97, 115; 3p. **standaþ**, W 76; S 67; pret. 1s. **stōd**, R 38; 3s. **stōd**, M 25, 28, 145, 152, 273; 1p. **stōdon**, R 71; 3p. **stōdon**, R 7; M 72, 79, 100, 127, 182, 301; W 87; 3p. subj. **stōden**, M 63. [STANDAN, STŌD, STŌDON, STANDEN; cf. **be-**, **wiþ-standan**.]

ġe-**standan**, v.6. *stand, stand up;* inf. M 171; pret. 3p. ġe**stōdon**, R 63 (w. refl. dat., *took their stand?*—see note).

stang, see **stingan**.

-stapa, wk.m. *stepper, treader.* See **eard-stapa**.

staðol, m. *(fixed) position; foundation;* ds. −e, R 71; dp. −um, S 109 (**healdan on s.**, *keep in place, control*—Gordon).

ġe-**staðolian**, wk.v.II. *establish, confirm, make steadfast;* pres. 3s. ġe**staðolaþ**, S 108; pret. 3s. ġe**staðolode**, S 104.

steall, m. *standing place.* See **weall-steall**.

ġe-**steall**, n. *foundation, resting place?* ns. W 110 (**eorðan ġ.**, *earthly resting place, habitation?*)

stēam, m. *vapor, moisture* (in droplets?); dis. −e, R 62 (uniquely here referring to blood: see note).

stearn, m. *tern* (perhaps not the modern tern or sea swallow but a small species of seagull—see Gordon's note); ns. S 23.

stede, m. i-stem. *place, position;* as. M 19. [Cf. **camp-, folc-, land-, mæðel-stede.**]

stedefæst, adj. *steadfast, unyielding;* npm. −e, M 127, 249.

stefn, m. i-stem. *stem.* (a) *prow or stern of a ship;* ds. −e, B 34; (b) *trunk of a tree;* ds. −e, R 30.

stefn, f. *voice;* ns. R 71 (not in MS, which has *sippan*).

stefna, wk.m. *stem of ship, prow or stern;* ds. −n, S 7 (prow, as the place for a lookout, or stern, where one steers?).

stefnettan, wk.v.I, *stand firm?* pret. 3p. **stefnetton**, M 122. [From STEFNAN *fix, institute,* base-word **stefn** *tree trunk,* plus Gmc. suffix *-ATJAN. Possibly the OE word has the meaning *stop* (*talking*)—see Harris 1976—but this meaning in the ME reflex may be a development of *stand firm*.]

stellan, wk.v.I. *place.* See **a-** and **on-stellan.**

stent, see **standan.**

steppan, v.6. *step, go, advance;* pret. 3s. **stōp**, M 8, 78, 131. [STEPPAN, or STÆPPAN, STŌP, STŌPON, STAPEN.]

stieran, wk.v.I, w. dat. *steer, control,* inf. S 109.

ġe-**stigan**, v.1. *climb up, mount, ascend;* inf. R 34; pret. 3s. ġe**stāg**, R 40. [STĪGAN, STĀG, STIGON, STIĠEN; cf. **a-stigan.**]

stihtan, wk.v.I. *direct;* pret. 3s. **stihte**, M 127.

stingan, v.3. *stab, pierce;* pret. 3s. **stang**, M 138. [STINGAN, STANG, STUNGON, STUNGEN.]

stiþ, adj. *hard, firm, stubborn, severe;* nsn. M 301; apm. **stīðe**, S 104.

stīþ-hycgende, pres. part. adj. ja-stem. *firm of purpose, resolute;* npm. M 122. [Cf. **hycgan.**] **stīð-mōd**, adj. *brave, unflinching;* nsm. R 40.

stīðlīċe, adv. *sternly, harshly;* M 25.

stōd, stōden, stōdon, see **standan.**

ġe-**stōdon**, see ġe-**standan.**

stōl, m. *seat, high-seat, throne.* See **ġief-stōl.**

stōp, see **steppan.**

storm, m. *storm;* dis. −e, L 48; np. −as, W 101; S 23.

stōw, f. *place.* See **wæl-stōw.**

stræl, m. or f. *arrow;* dip. −um, R 62.

strang, adj. *strong;* nsm. R 40; dsn. −um, S 109 (*headstrong*); npm. −e, R 30.

strēam, m. *stream;* as. M 68; in pl., *seas, ocean;* ap. −as, S 34. [Cf. **lagu-strēam.**]

strēġan, wk.v.I. *strew, spread;* inf. S 97. [A form (not West Saxon) occurring only here. Related WS forms are STREWIAN and STRĒAWIAN, wk.II.]

stund, f. *a time,* (*short*) *while;* as. −e, M 271. See **ymb.**

styrian, wk.v.I. *stir, move.* See **a-styrian.**

sum, pron. and adj. (a) pron., *one, a certain one;* w. part. gen., nsm. M 149, 164; nsn. S 68; asn. M 285; − without gen., in a series of singulars, *one . . . another,* etc.; asm. −ne, W 81, 82, 83; − in pl., *some, a number;* apm. −e, W 80 (preceding the series of singulars; understatement for "many"?); dp. −um, D 34; *certain ones,* npm. −e, S 56 (þā *sume, those particular ones*—not *some of those;* see Gordon's note). (b) adj. *some, a;* asf. −e, M 271.

sumor, m. (here a-stem; sometimes u-stem). *summer;* gs. −es, S 54.

sumor-lang, adj. *summer-long, long as in summer;* asm. −ne, L 37.

sundor, adv. *separately, apart;* **him sundor**, *by himself,* W 111.

sunne, wk.f. *sun;* ns. B 13.

sunu, m. u-stem. *son;* ns. R 150; M 76, 115, 298; as. B 42.

sūðerne, adj. ja-stem. *southern;* asm. (**-rne** for **-rnne**), M 134 (*of southern make*).

swā, adv. *so; in such manner; in like manner; accordingly;* M 33, 59, 122, 132, 198, 209, 243, 280, 319, 320, 323; W 6, 19, 62, 85, 111; S 51; D 7, 13, 17, 20, 27, 42; correl. w. the conj., *so, as,* D 9a; – conj. *as,* C 3; B 7; R 92, 108, 114; M 290; W 14, 43, 75; S 90; correl. w. the adv., D 9b; w. subj., *as if,* W 96; L 24.

swǣs, adj. *dear, beloved;* asm. **-ne**, W 50 (as noun, *loved one*).

swǣtan, wk.v.I. *bleed;* inf. R 20. [Base-word **swāt**, m. *blood.*]

swancor, adj. *supple;* apf. **swancre**, D 6.

swāt, m. *blood;* gs. **-es**, R 23; dis. **-e**, B 13.

sweart, adj. *dark, black;* asm.wk. **-an**, B 61.

swebban, wk.v.I. *put to sleep; kill.* See **a-swebban**.

swefn, n. (*sleep,*) *dream, vision;* gp. **-a**, R 1.

swēġ, m. i-stem. *sound;* (*bird's*) *song* or *cry;* as. S 21.

swelċ, rel. pron. *such as;* np. **-e**, S 83. [**swā** plus **lïċ**.]

swelċe, conj. adv. *likewise, and also;* B 19, 30, 37, 57; R 8; S 53; L 43. **swelċe swā**, conj. *just as,* R 92.

swelgan, v.3. *swallow.* See **for-swelgan**.

sweltan, v.3. *die, perish;* inf. M 293. [SWELTAN, SWEALT, SWULTON, SWOLTEN.]

swenġ, m. i-stem. *blow, stroke;* gs. **-es**, M 118.

sweorcan, v.3. *become gloomy;* pres. 3s. **sweorceþ**, D 29. [SWEORCAN, SWEARC, SWURCON, SWORCEN.]

ġe-sweorcan, v.3. *grow dark, gloomy;* pres. 3s. subj. **ġesweorce**, W 59.

sweord, n. *sword;* ns. M 166; as. M 15, 161, 237; gs. **-es**, B 68; ds. **-e**, M 118; ap. **sweord**, M 47; gp. **-a**, B 4; dip. **-um**, B 30.

sweostor, f. r-stem. *sister;* gs. M 115.

sweotule, adv. *clearly,* W 11.

swēte, adj. ja-stem. *sweet;* asn. S 95 (as noun). [Cf. unmutated SWŌT, *sweet.*]

swīcan, v.1. *deceive, fail, desert.* See **be-swīcan**.

swillan, wk.v.I. *wash.* See **be-swillan**.

swimman, v.3. *swim;* pres. 3p. **swimmaþ**, W 53 (fig.?—or partly literal, the spirits of the vision fading into sea birds?). [SWIMMAN, SWAMM, SWUMMON, SWUMMMEN.]

ġe-swinċ, n. i-stem. *toil.* **ġeswinċdagas**, m.pl. *days of toil or hardship;* dip. **-dagum**, S 2.

swïþ, adj. *strong;* comp. **swïðre**, nsf. S 115; asf. in **on þā swïðran healfe**, *on the right* (*the stronger*) *side,* R 20.

swïðe, adv. *greatly, very; fiercely, severely;* M 115, 118, 282; W 56.

symbel, n. *feast, banquet;* ds. **symble**, R 141; gp. **symbla**, W 93.

synn, f. jō-stem. *sin;* gp. **-a**, S 100; dp. **-um**, R 99, 146; dip. **-um**, R 13.

T

tǣċan, wk.v.I. *show, direct, teach;* pret. 3s. **tǣhte**, M 18. [TǢĊAN, TǢHTE, TǢHT; cf. TĀCN, n. *token, sign.*]

tǣsan, wk.v.I. *lacerate, rive;* pret. 3s. **tǣsde**, M 270.

tēoġan, wk.v.II (contr.). *adorn, prepare, create;* pret. 3s. **tēode**, C 8. [The inf. is from *TEOHOJAN, w. breaking, contr. to TĒOJAN; pret. TĒODE, pp. TĒOD.]

tīd, f. i-stem. *time, hour, period of time;* ns. M 104; as. S 124; gs. −e, S 69. [Cf. **ǣfen-, morgen-tīd.**]

til, adj. *good;* asm. −ne, D 38; *praiseworthy, commendable*, nsm. W 112.

til, prep. w. dat. *for,* C 6 (Moore MS— the rest have **tō**).

tilian, wk.v.II. *strive, endeavor;* pres. 1p. subj. **tilien**, S 119.

tīr, m. *glory;* ns. M 104; as. B 3.

tō, adv. *too* (w. adj. or adv., denoting excess); M 55, 66, 90, 150, 164; W 66 (twice), 67 (twice), 68 (3 times), 69, 112; L 51.

tō, prep. as adv. *thither, to that place;* S 119.

tō, prep. w. dat., instr., rarely gen., *to, for, at*, etc.

(1) w. dat. or instr. (a) where the meaning is still expressed by "to" (in various senses), B 17, 28, 34; R 42, etc. (9 times); M 8, etc. (20 times); W 36; S 51, 61; **tō þām**, *to that extent,* M 34; **tō hwon** (instr.), *to what* (*end, service, fate*), S 43; − (b) marking purpose, function, service, value, effect: *for, as,* C 6; R 31, 102, 153; M 46, 131, 197, 245; W 11, 30; S 20, 69 (**tō twēon**, *as an occasion for uncertainty*), 101; D 3; − (c) marking proximity to and expected participation in: *at,* R 141; − (d) marking object of thought: *on, of,* M 4 (twice), 128; (*thought*) *for,* (*delight*) *in,* S 44 (twice), 45 (twice); − (e) marking object inspiring awe or desire: *toward, of, for,* R 86, 129; − (f) marking source of help: *from,* W 115; − (g) marking time: *at, toward,* R 2; **tō ealdre**, *for ever,* S 79; − (h) **fōn tō** (*take to,*) *seize upon, take up,* M 10.

(2) w. uninflected inf. (often dat.), *to,* S 37.

(3) w. gen., **tō þæs**, *to that extent,* S 40, 41 (twice).

to-berstan, v.3. *burst asunder, be shattered;* pret. 3s. **tobærst**, M 136, 144. [Cf. **berstan.**]

to-brecan, v.4. *break apart, break through;* pp. **tobrocen**, nsf. M 242. [Cf. **brecan.**]

to-dǣlan, wk.v.I. *separate;* pret. 3p. subj. **todǣlden**, L 12. [Cf. **dǣlan.**]

to-gædere, adv. *together,* M 67. [Cf. **æt-gædere.**]

to-ġēanes, prep. w. dat. *against;* S 76 (postpos.)

ġe-toht, n. *battle;* ds. −e, M 104.

torn, n. *passion, anger;* as. W 112.

to-twǣman, wk.v.I. *divide, split in two;* pp. **totwǣmed**, nsn. M 241. [Base-word TWĀM, dat. of **twēġen**, q.v.]

trēo, n. wa-stem. *tree, cross;* as. R 4, 14, 17, 25. [Cf. **āc-, ġealg-trēo.**]

trēow, f. wō-stem. *good faith, pledge, agreement;* as. −e, W 112.

trym, m. or n. *step, space;* as. M 247 (adverbial acc., marking extent).

trymian or **trymman**, wk.v.I. *make firm, encourage; put in order, marshal, array;* inf. **trymian**, M 17; pret. 3p. **trymedon**, M 305. [Base-word TRUM, adj. *firm, strong.* On the alternation between **trymian** and **trymman**, see Brunner 1965: §400 Anm. 2.]

ġe-trymian or **ġe-trymman**, wk.v.I. same as preceding; pp. **ġetrymmed**, M 22 (perhaps both *drawn up in order* and *encouraged: arrayed for battle*). [MS getrymmed is irreg. but seems required by the meter; the normalized spelling would be **ġetrymed**.]

tū, see **bū-tū** and **twēġen**.

tūn m. *enclosed area,* hence *field, estate; homestead, manor; village;* see **burg-tūn**.

tungol, n. *star;* ns. B 14.

twǣman, wk.v.I. *divide;* see **totwǣman**.

twēġen, m., **twā**, f., **tū**, n. *two;* nom. **twēġen**, M 80; gen. **twēġa**, M 207. [Cf. **bū-tū**.]

twēo, wk.m. *doubt, uncertainty;* ds. **-n**. S 69 (**tō twēon weorðeþ**, *becomes uncertain* or *leads to uncertainty*). [From *TWEOHA.]

þ

þā, adv. and conj. − (a) as adv., *then, after that, next;* C 7; R 27, etc. (10 times); M 2, etc. (35 times); − (b) as rel. conj., *when,* R 36, 41, 42, 68, 151, 155; M 5, 10, 16, 22, 84, 121, 165, 199, 239, 276; L 9 (or adv.?), 18. **þā-ġiet**, adv. *still,* M 168, 273.

þā, dem. adj. and pron., see **sē**.

þær, adv. and conj.− (a) as adv., *there,* B 17, 32, 37; R 8, etc. (15 times; *þær* in the MS is emended at R 9); M 17, etc. (19 times); W 54; S 18, 23a; L 37; (perhaps) *thereupon, then,* R 30, 31, 32, 57, 60; − (b) as rel. conj., *where,* R 123, 139, 140, 141, 142, 156; M 23, 24, 28; W 115; S 6, 23b, 121; L 38; − (vaguely logical) *whereas, while,* S 10. **þær-on**, adv. *therein,* R 67.

þære, **þæs**, **þæs-þe**, see **sē**.

þæt, conj. *that.* − (a) in substantive clauses (subject, object, appositive), B 8; R 4, etc. (8 times; on 34 see note); M 6, etc. (20 times); W 12, 13, 41; S 67, 74, 77, 123 (explaining **þæs**, pron.); D 10, 11, 14 (introducing clause as obj. of **ġefrugnon**), 26, 30, 31, 36; L 12, 22; − (b) in apposition to a noun signifying a time: *that, when* R 81; M 105; − (c) in causal clauses: *in that, for, because;* B 48; R 19, 107; M 221, 243, 251; L 47; − (d) the clausal equivalent to a noun in the gen. case governed by a noun or adj. in the

main clause: *that,* M 176, 180; − (e) the clause stating what is urged or asked; *that,* M 229, 257, 263, 307; − (f) in a clause of purpose: *that, in order that,* M 177; S 34, 37, 119; − (g) in clauses of result or manner: *that, so that,* M 63, 119, 135, 136, 137, 142, 144, 150, 157, 226, 227, 286; S 42; D 16; L 13.

þæt, dem. adj. and pron., see **sē**.

þām, **þām-þe**, see **sē**.

þanc, m. and n., w. gen. *thanks (for);* ns. S 122; as. M 120, 147.

ġe-þanc, m. or n. *thought;* as. M 13 (**gōd ġ.**, *an unflinching spirit*). [Cf. **mōd-ġeþanc**.]

ġe-þancian, wk.v.II, w. dat. of person and gen. of thing. *thank, give thanks to;* pres. 1s. **ġeþancie**, M 173.

þāra, see **sē**.

þās, see **þēs**.

þe, indecl. particle, serving as rel. pron., any case, number, or gender. *who, which, that,* etc.; R 111, 118, 137; M 36, etc. (19 times; at 190, obj. of **on** understood or with **hit** *which:* see note); S 57, 100; L 41; **þe ... him**, dsm. *to whom,* W 10; S 13; in **þā hwīle þe**, conj. *while* (lit. *the time in which*), M 14, 83, 235, 272. [Also in combination with **þēah**, q.v., and with the dem. pron.: see **sē**. In the MSS also isn. of the dem. pron., here normalized as **þȳ**; see **sē**.]

þē, pers. pron., see **þū**.

þēah, adv. *though,* however, M 289. **þēah-þe**, conj. *though,* W 2; S 97, 113.

ġe-þeah, see **ġe-þicgan**.

þearf, f. (a) *need;* ns. M 233; as. **-e**, M 175; − (b) (*time of*) *need, distress;* ds. **-e**, M 201, 307; − (c) *what is needful, morally requisite, or desirable;* ds. **-e**, M 232 (*our good, what we must do*). [Cf. **wēa-þearf**.]

þearf, v., see **þurfan**.

þearle, adv. *severely, sorely, grievously;* B 23; R 52; M 158.

þēaw, m. *custom, habit;* ns. W 12.

þeġn, m. *servant, minister;* esp. *a (noble) retainer;* as. M 151; np. —as, R 75 (*the Lord's servants*); M 205, 220; ap. —as, M 232. [Cf. būr-, magu-þeġn.]

þeġnlīċe, adv. *as befitting a* þeġn; *loyally, nobly,* M 294.

-þegu, f. *receipt, receiving.* See hring-, sinċ-þegu, and cf. ġe-þicgan.

þenċan, wk.v.I. *think;* inf. S 96; pres. 3p. þenċaþ, R 115; — w. inf., *purpose, intend, desire (to);* pres. 1s. þenċe, M 319; 3s. þenċeþ, R 121; M 258, 316; S 51. [ÞENĊAN, ÞŌHTE, ÞŌHT; base-word þanc, *thought;* cf. ġeond-þenċan.]

ġe-þenċan, wk.v.I. *think, determine, reflect, consider;* — w. indirect question, *think why* or *how,* inf. W 58; S 118; D 12; w. subst. clause, *reflect that,* inf. D 31.

þenden, conj. *while,* S 102.

þenian or þennan, wk.v.I. *stretch out;* inf. þenian, R 52 (w. **God** as object and unstated subject; equivalent to passive, *stretched out,* w. **God** as subject). [On the alternation between þenian and þennan, see Brunner 1965: §400 Anm. 2.]

þēod, f. *people;* ds. —e, M 90, 220; gp. —a, M 173; dp. —um, B 22.

þēoden, m. *prince, lord;* ns. M 120, 232; vs. M 178; as. M 158; ds. þēodne, R 69; M 294; gs. þēodnes, W 95.

-þēodiġ, adj. combining form. *of a people or country.* See el-þēodiġ.

þēs, þēos, þis, dem. adj. and pron. *this;* — (a) as adj., þēs, nsm. W 62, L 29; þēos, nsf. R 12, 82; S 86; þis, nsn. M 45; W 110; S 65; asn. W 89; L 1; þisne, asm. R 104; M 32, 52; W 75,

85, 88; þās, asf. R 96; W 58; S 87; D 31; ap. M 298; W 91, 101; apn. L 36; þisse, gsf. W 74; dsf. M 221; þissum, dsm. L 16; þissum, dsn. R 83, 109, 138; L 41; þȳs, ism. M 316; isn. B 66. (b) as pron., þisses, gsn., D 7 (see note), 13, 17, 20, 27, 42; þissum, dsn. B 67 (*this, the present time*).

ġe-þicgan, v.5. *receive;* pret. 3s. ġe-þeah, D 40 (MS geþah, as if to a verb of class 1: see Brunner 1965: §391 Anm. 9). [ÞICGAN, ÞEAH (occas. ÞĀH), ÞǢGON, ÞEĠEN.]

þider, adv. *thither, to there,* S 118.

þīestre, n. ja-stem. *darkness;* often pl., *shades of night;* np. þīestru, R 52. [An alternate ÞĪESTRU, f. īn-stem, is also found and cannot always be distinguished from the neuter.]

þīn, poss. adj. *your, yours* (sg.); asn. M 178; apm. —e, M 37; dp. —um M 50.

þing, n. (*thing,*) *state, condition; affair, trouble;* ns. D 9; gp. þinga (*circumstances*), S 68.

þingan, wk.v.I. *determine.* See un-þinged.

þis, þisne, þisse, þisses, þissum, see þēs.

ġe-þōht, m. *thought, will;* ns. L 43; as. D 22; L 12; is. —e, W 88; np. —as, S 34.

þolian, wk.v.II. (a) trans., *suffer, undergo, endure;* pret. 3p. þolodon, R 149; (b) intrans. *endure, hold out;* inf. M 201, 307. [Cf. for-þolian.]

ġe-þolian, wk.v.II, trans. *endure, put up with;* inf. M 6.

þon, pron., ism. and isn., see sē, pron., for, ǣr.

þonan, adv. *thence, from there,* W 23.

þone, þone-þe, see sē.

þonne, adv. and conj. — (a) as adv., *then* (temporal), R 107, 115, 117, 139, 142; W 45, 49; S 94a, 118, 119;

D 31; *then* (consequential), *therefore,* W 88; – (b) as rel. conj., *when, while* M 213; W 39, 51, 60, 70, 74, 103; S 8, 84, 94b (correl.), 102; L 35; – (c) conj. w. comp., *than,* R 128; M 33, 195; S 65, 116; L 4.

þorfte, þorfton, see **þurfan.**

þrāg, f. (*period of*) *time;* ns. W 95.

ġe-þrang, n. *throng, press;* ds. –e, M 299.

þrie, m., **þrēo,** f. and n. pl. *three;* gen. **þrēora,** M 299; S 68 (w. **sum,** *one of three things*).

ġe-þringan, v.3. *press, constrict;* pp. **ġeþrungen,** npm. uninflected (for **ġeþrungne**), S 8 (*pinched*). [ÞRIN-GAN, ÞRANG, ÞRUNGON, ÞRUNGEN; cf. **oþ-þringan.**]

þriste, adv. *resolutely, unflinchingly,* D 12.

þritiġ, num. *thirty;* as subst. w. part. gen., acc. (extent of time), D 18.

þrōwian, wk.v.II. *suffer;* intrans., pret. 3s. **þrōwode,** R 84, 98, 145; trans., *suffer, endure,* pret. 1s. **þrōwode,** S 3.

ġe-þrungen, see **ġe-þringan.**

þrymm, m. ja-stem. *glory, majesty;* ns. W 95.

þrymfæst, adj. *glorious;* nsm. R 84. [**þrymm** (q.v.); **fæst** (q.v.).]

þrȳþ, f. i-stem. *strength, power;* often in plural w. reference to the powers of inanimate things, as here of spears: np. **þrȳðe,** W 99.

þū, pron. 2nd pers. sg. *you;* ns. R 78, 96; M 30, 36, 37, 45, 176, 231; **þē,** ds. M 29, 30, 177, 179; as. R 95; M 173. [See **þin,** poss. adj., and **ġē.**]

þūhte, see **þynċan.**

þurfan, pret.-pres.v. *need, have reason to* (w. inf.); pres. 3s **þearf,** R 117; 1 p. **þurfe (wē),** M 34; 3p. **þurfon,** M 249; pret. 3s. **þorfte,** B 39, 44; 3p. **þorfton,** B 47. [ÞURFAN, ÞEARF, ÞURFON, ÞORFTE.]

þurh, prep. w. acc. *through;* – (a) of motion: *through,* R 18; M 141, 145, 151; – (b) expressing cause or agency: *through, by, by reason of, by means of;* R 10, 119; M 71; S 88; L 12.

þurh-drīfan, v.1. *drive through, pierce;* pret. 3p. **þurhdrifon,** R 46. [DRĪFAN, DRĀF, DRIFON, DRIFEN.]

þurh-wadan, v.6. *pass through, pierce;* pret. 3s. **þurhwōd,** M 296. [Cf. **wadan.**]

þus, adv. *thus,* M 57.

þȳ, see **sē.**

ġe-þyldiġ, adj. *patient;* nsm. W 65.

þynċan, wk.v.I, impers. w. dat. of person. *seem;* pres. 3s. **þynċeþ,** M 55; W 41; D 29; pret. 3s. **þūhte,** R 4; M 66. [ÞYNĊAN, ÞŪHTE, ÞŪHT; based on *ÞUNK-* of the ablaut series *ÞINK-, *ÞANK-, *ÞUNK-. Cf. **þenċan.**]

þȳs, see **þēs.**

U

ūhta (comb. form **ūht-**), wk.m. *period before daybreak, early morning;* ds. –n, L 35; gp. **ūhtna,** W 8. **ūht-cearu,** f. *anxiety before dawn, insomnia;* as. –ċeare, L 7.

un-befohten, adj. *unopposed, without a fight;* npm. **unbefohtne,** M 57. [C has *unbefohtene,* here normalized; but see the note on **ġegrundene,** M 109. The normalized form is not required by the meter. Cf. **feohtan.**]

unc, see **wit.**

uncer, poss. adj., dual. *of us two, our;* ns. L 25.

under, prep. *beneath, under;* w. dat., R 55, 85; W 107; L 28, 36, 48; w. acc. (after a verb implying motion), W 96.

un-earg, adj. *undaunted, unflinching;* npm. –e, M 206.

un-forcŭþ, adj. *undisgraced, reputable;* nsm. M 51.

un-forht, adj. (a) *unafraid, undaunted;* nsm. R 110; npm. −e, M 79; (b) (*very*) *frightened, terrified;* nsm. R 117 (often em. to **anforht**; but **an-** is hardly more secure than **un-** as an intensive prefix: for both the evidence is slender. The meaning of the word, however, is clear). [Cf. **forht**.]

ġe-unnan, pret.-pres.v., w. gen. *grant,* pres. subj. 2s. **ġeunne**, M 176. [UNNAN, ANN, UNNON, ŪÐE.]

un-orne, adj. ja-stem. *unpretentious, simple, humble;* nsm. M 256. [Cf. **orne**.]

un-rim, n. *countless number;* ns. B 31 (w. part. gen.). [RĪM, n. *number.*]

un-þinġed, adj. *unprepared for, unexpected;* nsm. S 106. [Cf. ÞINGAN, wk.v.I, *invite, determine upon.*]

un-wāclïċe, adv. *without weakening;* M 308. [Cf. **wāc, wācian.**]

un-wearnum, adv. *irresistibly;* S 63. [WEARN, f. *hindrance.*]

un-weaxen, adj. *not fully grown;* nsm. M 152. [Der. from pp. of **weaxan**, v.7, *grow.*]

upp, adv. *up;* B 13, 70; R 71; M 130; L 3. **upp-ganga**, wk.m. *passage up on land, passage to shore;* as. −n, M 87 (see Wollmann 1996: 232–33). **upp-hēah**, adj. *steep;* npf. −hēa, L 30. **upp-rodor**, m. *high heaven, the heavens above;* as. S 105.

uppe, adv. *up,* R 9.

ūre, poss. adj. *our;* nsm. M 232, 240, 314; nsn. M 313; **ūrne**, asm. M 58; **ūrum**, dp. M 56. [Cf. the pron. **wē**.]

ūriġ, adj. *dewy.* **ūriġ-feðra**, wk.m. *dewy-feathered one;* ns. S 25. [A valid word though in a seemingly corrupt passage; a wk. noun or wk. adj. with subst. function, from strong adj. *ŪRIĠ-FEÐER*, *dewy-feathered;* see **-feðra**.]

ūs, ūsiċ, see **wē**.

ūt, adv. *out;* B 35; M 72.

ūð-wita, wk.m. *wise man;* np. −n, B 69. [The stressed prefix is intensive; it may once have meant *beyond.* Cf. **wita**.]

W

wā, m. *misery, woe;* ns. L 52.

wāc, adj. *weak, lacking firmness* (psychically or physically); nsm. W 67 (**wāc wiga**, *weak in battles*); asm. −ne, M 43 (of a spear shaft vigorously shaken: *pliant, slender*); comp. **wācra**, npm. −n, as noun, *the inferior, degenerate,* S 87. [Implies lack of resolve in **un-wāclïċe**, q.v.]

wācian, wk.v.II. *weaken, prove pliant;* inf. M 10.

wacu, f. *watch.* See **niht-wacu**.

wadan, v.6. (a) intrans., *pass, proceed, advance;* inf. M 140; pret. 1s. **wōd**, W 24; 3s. M 130, 253; 3p. **wōdon**, M 96, 295; − (b) trans., *tread, traverse;* inf. W 5. [WADAN, WŌD, WŌDON, WADEN; cf. **þurh-wadan**.]

ġe-wadan, v.6. *go, pass* (*all the way*); pret. 3s. **ġewōd**, M 157.

wæcnan, v.6 (irreg.). *awake.* See **on-wæcnan**.

wǣd, f. (or **wǣde**, n. ja-stem). *clothing, an article of clothing, covering;* dp. −um, R 15, 22 (the alternating vesture of the cross, now precious ornaments, now blood).

wǣfer-sïen, f. i-stem. *spectacle, show;* ds. −e, R 31. [**wǣfer** does not occur alone, but it is used in several compounds referring to theatrical exhibitions and is probably related to WĀFIAN, wk.v.II, *marvel at, gaze at.* Cf. **ġe-sïene, an-sïen**, and **ġe-sēon**.]

wǣġ, m. i-stem. *wave, surf;* as. S 19; ap. **wǣgas**, W 46.

wǣgon, see **wegan**.

wæl, n. *slaughter; the slain collectively, number of slain;* in compounds often translatable by *battle,* ns. B 65; M 126, 303; ds. −e, M 279, 300. **wæl-feld**, m. u-stem. *battlefield;* ds. −a, B 51. **wæl-ġīfre**, adj. *greedy for slaughter;* npn. -ġifru, W 100. **wæl-rest**, f. *a resting place among the slain;* as. −e, M 113. **wæl-sleaht**, n. (or m.) *deadly combat;* gp. −a, W 7, 91. **wæl-spere**, n. i-stem. *deadly spear;* as. M 322. **wæl-stōw**, f. *place of slaughter, battlefield;* gs. −e, M 95; ds. −e, B 43; M 293. **wæl-wulf**, m. *death-dealing wolf;* np. −as, M 96 (epithet for the vikings).

wǣpen, n. *weapon;* ns. M 252; as. M 130, 235; np. W 100; gs. **wǣpnes**, M 168; ds. **wǣpne**, M 228; gp. **wǣpna**, M 83, 272, 308; dp. **wǣpnum**, M 10, 126. **wǣpen-ġewrixl**, n. *weapon-exchange, trading of blows;* gs. −es, B 51.

wǣr, f. *covenant, pledge;* dip. −um, S 110 (**ġewiss wǣrum**, *unfailing in its* [the mind's] *pledges;* MS **werum** can also be taken as dp. of **wer**: *constant toward men;* but see note).

wǣre, wǣron, wǣs, see **bēon-wesan**.

wǣta, wk.m. *moisture, blood;* ds. −n, R 22.

wæter, n. *water;* as. B 55; M 91, 98; ds. −e, M 64, 96; L 49.

wamm, m. *blemish, iniquity;* dp. −um, R 14.

wan, adj. *lacking, wanting* (generally as first member of a compound). **wan-hyġdiġ**, adj. *heedless, reckless, imprudent;* nsm. W 67.

wand, see **windan**.

wandian, wk.v.II. *turn aside, waver, flinch;* inf. M 258; pret. 3s. **wandode**, M 268. [Cf. **windan**.]

wang, m. *field, meadow;* ap. −as, S 49 (less probably np.).

wann, adj. *dark;* nsm. W 103; nsf. R 55.

-ware, m.pl. suffix (orig. f.pl. of WARU, *people*), *inhabitants, people.* See **burg-ware**.

warian, wk.v.II. *guard, take charge of; attend* (as a guardian or ruling spirit); pres. 3s. **waraþ**, W 32.

wāt, see **witan**.

ġe-wāt, see **ġe-wītan**.

waðum, m. *wave, stream, sea;* gp. −a. W 24, 57. (MS **waðena, waþema**.)

wāwan, v.7. *blow, be blown about in the wind.* See **be-wāwan**.

wē, pron. 1st pers. pl. *we;* nom. C 1 (var.); R 70; M 33, 34, 35, 40, 61, 212, 213; S 117 (twice), 118, 119 (twice); D 14, 21; **ūre**, gen. M 234 (w. **ǣġhwelċ**); **ūs**, dat. B 68; R 147b; M 39, 40, 93, 233; W 115; acc. R 73, 75, 147a; M 34 (refl., *each other*), 60, 237. **ūsiċ**, acc. S 123. [See **iċ**, **wit**, and **ūre**, poss. adj.]

wēa, wk.m. *woe, misery;* as. −n, D 4; gs. −n, D 25; gp. −na, D 34. **wēa-þearf**, f. *grievous need;* ds. −e, L 10.

ġe-wealc, n. *rolling, tossing;* as. S 6, 46.

weald, m. u-stem. *forest, woodland;* ds. −a, B 65.

ġe-weald, n. *control, prerogative, power;* as. R 107; M 178.

wealdan, v.7., w. gen. *wield;* inf. M 83, 168, 272; *hold, be master of,* inf. M 95. [WEALDAN, WĒOLD, WĒOLDON, WEALDEN.]

wealdend, m. nd-stem. *ruler;* esp. *the Lord;* ns. R 111, 155; vs. M 173 (w. gen.); as. R 67 (w. gen.); gs. −es, R 17, 53; ds. −e, R 121; in the secular sense, np. W 78.

weall, m. *wall;* ns. W 98; ds. −e, W 80; np. −as, W 76. **weall-steall**, m. *site of a wall, wall-stead, foundation;* as. W 88. [Cf. **bord-weall**.]

weard, m. *guardian, lord;* w. defining

gen., (a) *God:* **heofon-rīċes** w., as. C 1; **mann-cynnes** w., ns. C 7; (b) *the cuckoo:* **sumeres** w., ns. S 54. [Cf. **brycg-weard.**]

weardian, wk.v.II. *guard, occupy, inhabit;* pres. 3p. **weardiaþ**, L 34.

wearg, m. *criminal;* ap. **−as**, R 31.

wearþ, see **weorðan.**

weaxan, v.7. *grow, increase.* See **a-**, **be-weaxan; unweaxen.** [WEAXAN, WĒOX, WĒOXON, WEAXEN.]

weġ, m. *way, path, road;* as. R 88. [Cf. **eorð-**, **flōd-**, **forð-**, **hwael-weġ**, and **on-weġ**, adv. under **on.**]

wegan, v.5. *carry, bear;* pret. 3p. **wǣgon**, M 98. [WEGAN, WǢĠ, WǢGON, WEĠEN; cf. **for-wegan.**]

wēl, adv. *well, fully;* R 129, 143; as quasi-adj., **wēl biþ**, *it will be well, turn out well,* W 114.

wela, wk.m. *wealth;* ns. W 74. [Cf. **eorð-wela.**]

wēman, wk.v.I. *allure, entertain;* inf. W 29.

wēn, f. i-stem. *expectation;* dp. **−um**, D 25.

wēnan, wk.v.I. (a) *believe, suppose;* **wēnde**, pret. 3s. M 239 (w. gen. **þæs**, and explanatory clause); (b) *expect, hope, look forward to;* pres. 1s. **wēne**, R 135 (w. refl. pron. dat. and clause).

wendan, wk.v.I. *turn;* (a) *change;* inf. R 22; (b) *go (away); go about;* inf. M 316; pres. 3s. **wendeþ**, D 32; 1s. subj. **wende**, M 252; pret. 3p. **wendon**, M 193; (c) **w. forþ**, *go forth, advance;* pret. 3p. **wendon**, M 205. [WENDAN, WENDE, WENDED; base-word WAND, corresponding to pret. of **windan**, q.v.; cf. **on-wendan.**]

wennan or **wenian**, wk.v.I. *accustom* (mod. "wean" with wider application); pret. 3s. **wenede**, W 36 (**w. tō wiste**, *accustomed him to the feast,*

was ever feasting him). [Related to **wunian**, q.v.]

wēop, see **wēpan.**

weorc, n. *work; pain;* as. R 79 (*pain* or *work*); ap. C 3 (*works;* or as. *work*). [The meaning *pain* is due to scribal substitution of **weorc** for Anglian WÆRC: see the note on R 79. Cf. **beadu-**, **dæġ-weorc.**]

ġe-weorc, n. *a piece of construction, a work;* np. W 87.

weornian, wk.v.II. *decay;* 3p. **weorniaþ**, W 78 (MS *w oriað;* see note.)

weorod, n. *band of men, host, company;* ns. M 64, 97; as. M 102; ds. **−e**, R 152; M 51; is. **−e**, B 34; R 69, 124; gp. **−a**, R 51. [Cf. **heorð-weorod.**]

weorold, f. i-stem. *world;* ns. S 49; as. W 58, 107; S 87; D 31; gs. **−e**, R 133; W 74; L 46; ds. **−e**, M 174; S 45. **weorold-ġesǣliġ**, adj. *blessed with this world's goods, prosperous;* nsm. M 219. **weorold-rīċe**, n. *kingdom of the world;* ds. W 65; L 13. [**wer**, *man;* Gmc. *ALD, *age, lifetime* (cf. OE **ealdor**, *life*), reduced to **-old.**]

weorðan, v.3. *become, be;* − (a) as independent verb: inf. W 64; pres. 3s. **weorðeþ**, W 110; S 69; pret. 3s. **wearþ**, M 113, 186 (**w. on flēame**, *took to flight;* C's transcript has pl. **wurdon**), 295 (*came to pass, there was*); 3p. **wurdon**, B 48 (**beteran w.**, *were the better, had the better of it*); D 15; − (b) as auxiliary w. pass. part., forming passive, pret. 3s. **wearþ**, B 32, 65; M 106, 114, 116, 135, 138, 241, 288; 3s. subj. **wurde**, M 1; forming pluperfect, pret. 3s. **wearþ**, M 202. [WEORÐAN, WEARÞ, WURDON, WORDEN.]

ġe-weorðan, v.3. *become;* pp. **ġe-worden**, nsm. R 87.

weorðian, wk.v.II. *honor, adore;* inf. R 129; pres. 3p. **weorðiaþ**, R 81.

ġe-weorðian, wk.v.II. *honor, exalt;* pret. 3s. ġeweorðode, R 90, 94; S 123; *adorn,* pp. ġeweorðod, asm. R 15.

weorðlīċe, adv. *splendidly, worthily, honorably;* R 17; M 279.

wēpan, v.7. *weep;* inf. L 38 (trans. *weep over, lament*); pret. 3s. wēop, R 55. [WĒPAN, WĒOP, WĒOPON, WŌPEN.]

wer, m. *man;* ns. W 64; gp. -a, S 21; dp. -um, S 110 (alt. reading: see wǣr).

werian, wk.v.I. *defend;* pret. 3p. weredon (w. refl. pron.), M 82, 283.

wēriġ, adj. *weary, exhausted, afflicted;* nsm. B 20; W 15; S 29; asm. -ne, W 57; npm. wērġe, M 303. wēriġ-mōd, adj. *weary at heart;* nsm. L 49. (wēriġ mōd, W 15, is taken by some editors as an example of this compound used as a substantive; see note.) [Cf. lim-, mere-wēriġ.]

wesan, see bēon-wesan.

west, adv. *west*(*ward*), M 97.

wēste, adj. ja-stem. *waste;* nsm. W 74.

wīċ, n. *habitation, settlement, place;* ns. L 32; as. L 52.

wicg, n. ja-stem. *horse, steed;* ds. -e, M 240.

wīċing, m. *pirate, viking;* as. M 139; ap. -as, M 322; gp. -a, M 26, 73, 97; dp. -um, M 116.

wide, adv. *widely, far;* S 60; D 22; L 46; wide and side, *far and wide,* R 81; superl. widost, *farthest, most widely,* S 57.

ge-widost, adv. superl. *as far apart as possible;* L 13. [Cf. wide.]

wiernan, wk.v.I., w. gen. of thing. *refuse, deny, withhold;* pret. 3s. wiernde, M 118; 3p. wierndon, B 24 (w. dat. of pers.). [Base-word WEARN, f. *hindrance.*]

wīf, n. *woman;* ds. -e, S 45; gp. -a, R 94.

wīġ, n. *war, battle;* ns. W 80; gs. -es, B 20, 59; M 73, 130; ds. -e, M 10, 128, 193, 235, 252; gp. wīga, W 67. wīġ-haga, wk.m. *battle-hedge* (shield-wall); as. -n, M 102. wīġ-heard, adj. *hardy in battle;* asm. -ne, M 75. wīġ-plega, wk.m. *play of battle;* ds. -n, M 268; is. -n, M 316. wīġ-smiþ, m. *war-smith* (kenning for *warrior*); np. -smiðas, B 72.

wiga, wk.m. *warrior;* ns. M 210; as. -n, M 75, 235; ds. -n, M 126; np. -n, M 79, 302; gp. wigena, M 135. [Cf. byrn-wiga.]

wiġend, m. nd-stem. *warrior;* np. M 302.

willa, wk.m. *desire;* ns. R 129.

willan, anom.v. *be willing, desire, will* (w. inf. except as noted); pres. 1s. R 1; M 216, 247, 317 (fram ne w., *will not go away*); D 35; 3s. wile, R 107; M 52; 1p. willaþ, M 35, 40; 3p. willaþ, M 46; 1s. subj. wille, M 221; 2s. subj. wille, M 37; 3s. subj. wille, W 14 (hycgan understood), 72; S 43, 97, 99, 113; pret. 3s. wolde, R 34, 41, 113 (or subj.); M 11, 129, 160; 3s. subj. wolde, W 28; pret. 3p. woldon, R 68; M 207.

win, n. *wine.* win-gāl, adj. *flushed, or made careless, with wine;* nsm. S 29.

win-sæl, n. *wine-hall;* np. -salu, W 78.

wind, m. *wind;* dis. -e, W 76.

windan, v.3. *wind;* - (a) intrans., *fly, speed; circle round;* inf. M 322; pret. 3p. wundon, M 106; - (b) trans., *wave, brandish;* pret. 3s. wand, M 43. [WINDAN, WAND, WUNDON, WUNDEN; cf. be-windan and wunden.]

wine, m. i-stem (treated as a-stem). *friend, loved one, comrade, patron;* ns. M 250; L 49, 50; as. S 115; ap. winas, M 228. wine-dryhten, m. *lord and friend, patron;* as. M 248, 263; gs. -dryhtnes, W 37. wine-mǣġ, m.

GLOSSARY

beloved kinsman; ap. −**magas,** M 306; gp. −**māga,** W 7; dip. −**māgum,** S 16. [Cf. **ġeō-, gold-wine.**]

winelēas, adj. *friendless, lordless;* nsm. W 45; L 10.

ġe-winn, n. *battle, struggle, agony;* as. M 214; ds. −**e,** R 65; M 248; 302. [Cf. **ǣr-ġewinn.**]

winnan, v.3, *endure, suffer; resist;* pret. 3s. **wann,** L 5. [WINNAN, WANN, WUNNON, WUNNEN.]

ġe-winnan, v.3, trans. *win* (by fighting), *conquer;* inf. M 125.

winter, m. (elsewhere with u-stem forms), *winter;* as. S 15 (as adv., *in winter*); gs. −**es,** W 103; pl., in reckoning age, *years;* gp. **wintra,** W 64; D 18, 38; dip. **wintrum,** M 210.

winter-ċeald, adj. *winter-cold;* asf. −**e,** D 4. **winter-ċeariġ,** adj. *winter-sad;* nsm. W 24.

wīs, adj. *wise;* nsm. M 219; W 64; ism. −**e,** W 88.

wīse, wk.f. *manner, way* (*of behaving*); dip. **wīsum,** S 110.

wīsian, wk.v.II. *guide, direct;* pret. 3s. **wīsode,** M 141.

wīsliċ, adj. *certain, assured;* asm. **wislicne,** D 34. [Cf. next word.]

ġe-wiss, adj. *trustworthy, unfailing;* asn. S 110.

wisse, see **witan.**

wist, f. *means of subsistence, food, feast;* ds. −**e,** W 36.

wit, pron. 1st pers. dual, *we two;* nom., L 13, 21; acc. **unc,** R 48; L 12, 22. [See **iċ, wē.**]

wita, wk.m. *wise man, counselor;* ns. W 65.

witan, pret.-pres.v. *know, have knowledge of;* pres. 1s. **wāt,** W 11; 3s. **wāt,** M 94; W 29, 37 (*understands:* see note); S 12, 55, 92; pret. 3s. **wisse,** M 24; subj. W 27 (**mine wisse,** *might know about my people;* for the traditional emendation, see

myne). [WITAN, WĀT, WITON, WISSE or WISTE.]

ġe-wītan, v.1. *go, depart;* − (a) w. limiting adv. or prep. (**forþ, upp, ūt, þurh,** etc.); inf. S 52; pret. 3s. **ġe-wāt,** B 35; R 71; M 72, 150; W 95; L 6; 3p. **ġewiton,** R 133; − (b) w. inf. specifying the manner of going or attendant action; pret. 1s. **ġewāt,** L 9; 3p. **ġewiton,** B 53 (w. refl. dat.); − (c) unmodified: pp. **ġewiten,** *departed;* npm. −**e,** S 80, 86. [WĪTAN, WĀT, WITON, WITEN.]

wīte, n. ja-stem. *punishment, torment, torture;* as. L 5; ds. R 61; gp. **wita,** R 87.

witiġ, adj. *wise;* nsm. D 32 (**w. dryhten,** *God in his wisdom—* Malone).

wiþ, prep. *with, against, toward,* etc. − (a) w. gen., *toward,* M 8, 131; − (b) w. dat. *against,* M 103; *in exchange for,* M 31, 35, 39; − (c) w. acc. *against,* B 9, 52; M 82, 277, 298; S 75; *toward,* S 112 (twice); − (d) w. acc. or dat. (*in friendly rivalry*) *with,* M 290.

wiðer-lēan, n. *requital;* ns. M 116.

wiþ-standan, v.6. w. dat. *withstand;* inf. W 15. [Cf. **standan.**]

wlanc, adj. *proud, high-spirited, bold, lusty;* nsm. S 29; nsf. W 80; asm. −**ne,** M 139; dsn.wk. −**an,** M 240 (of a horse: *spirited,* or *proud, splendid?*); npm. −**e** B 72; M 205. [Cf. **mōd-wlanc.**]

wlītan, v.1. *look;* pret. 3s. **wlāt,** M 172. [WLĪTAN, WLĀT, WLITON, WLITEN.]

wlitigian, wk.v.II. *make beautiful, brighten;* pres. 3p. **wlitigiaþ,** S 49. (Less probably, *become beautiful.*) [From WLITIĠ, adj., *beautiful.*]

wōd, wōdon, ġe-wōd, see **wadan, ġe-wadan.**

wolcen, m. or n. *cloud, sky;* dp. **wolcnum,** R 53, 55.

wolde, woldon, see **willan.**

wōma, wk.m. *noise, tumult* (or *proclaimer, herald?*); ns. W 103.

word, n. *word, speech, command;* as. R 35; M 168; ap. R 27; W 91; ds. **-e,** R 111; dip. **-um** (as formal indication of speech: *with, in words*), R 97; M 26, 43, 210, 250, 306. [Cf. **ġielp-, lāst-word.**]

ġe-worden, see **ġe-weorðan.**

ġe-worhtne, ġe-worhton, see **ġe-wyrċan.**

worn, m. *a great number, multitude;* – as., w. part. gen., W 91.

wracu, f. *misery;* as. **wrǣce,** D 4.

wrǣc, n. *persecution, exile;* gs. **-es,** D 1. **wrǣc-lāst,** m. *path or track of exile;* ns. W 32; ap. **-as,** W 5; S 57 (**w.** lecgaþ, *lay tracks of exile: direct their exiled steps, travel*—Gordon). **wrǣc-sīþ,** m. *hardship, experience of exile;* ap. **-sīðas,** L 38; gp. **-sīða,** L 5.

wrǣc, wrǣce, verb-forms, see **wrecan.**

wrāþ, adj. *hostile, cruel, angry;* gp. **wrāðra,** R 51; W 7.

wrāðe, adv. *fiercely, cruelly;* L 32.

wrecan, v.5. (a) w. acc. of person, *avenge* (someone); inf. M 248, 258; pret. 3s. **wrǣc,** M 279; 3s. subj. **wrǣce,** M 257; – (b) *utter, recite;* inf. S 1; pres. 1s. **wrece,** L 1 (fut. sense). [WRECAN, WRÆC, WRÆCON, WRECEN.]

ġe-wrecan, v.5, w. acc. of person. *avenge* (someone); inf. M 208, 263.

wreċċa, wk.m. *an exile;* ns. L 10; gs. **-n,** S 15.

wrēon, contr.v.1. *cover.* See **be-, on-wrēon.**

ġe-wrixl, n. *exchange.* See **wǣpen-ġewrixl.**

wudu, m. u-stem. *wood, forest;* ns. R 27; as. M 193. **wudu-bearu,** m. *forest, grove;* ds. **-bearwe,** L 27 (MS *wuda bearwa*). [Cf. **holt-wudu.**]

wuldor, n. *glory; the realm of glory, heaven;* gs. **wuldres,** R 14, 90, 97, 133; S 123; ds. **wuldre,** R 135, 143, 155. **wuldor-fæder,** m. r-stem. *glorious or heavenly Father,* gs. C 3.

wulf, m. *wolf;* ns. W 82; as. B 65. [Cf. **wæl-wulf.**]

wund, f. *wound;* as. **-e,** M 139, 271; dip. **-um,** B 43; M 293, 303.

wund, adj. *wounded;* nsm. M 113, 144.

wunden, pp. adj. *wound, twisted;* **wunden gold,** *twisted gold* (i.e., gold rings, ornamental gold, the traditional gift of the lord to his retainers); nsn. W 32. [Cf. **windan,** v.3.]

ġe-wundian, wk.v.II. *wound;* pp. **ġe-wundod,** nsm. M 135. [Cf. **for-wundian.**]

wundon, see **windan.**

wundor, n. *wonder;* gp. **wundra,** C 3; dip. **wundrum,** as adv. *wondrously,* W 98.

wunian, wk.v.II. (a) intrans., *dwell, live, remain;* inf. R 121, 143; L 27; pres. 3p. **wuniaþ,** R 135; S 87 (*remain*); pret. 3p. **wunodon,** R 155; – (b) trans., *remain on, dwell in;* pret. 1s. **wunode,** S 15; *occupy, be in,* pret. 3p. **wunodon,** R 3 (**reste w.,** *were in bed*). [Related to **wennan,** q.v.]

wurde, wurdon, see **weorðan.**

wurma, wk.m., or **wurme,** wk.f., meaning unknown. ds. **-n,** D 1. [See **wyrm.**]

wuton or **uton,** hortatory auxiliary. *let us* (pres. 1p. subj., originally of **witan**); S 117.

wylfen, adj. *wolfish;* asm. **-ne,** D 22.

wynn, f. i-stem. *joy, delight, pleasure;* ns. W 36; S 45; L 46; as. S 27; dip. **-um,** R 15 (as adv., *beautifully*); W 29; gp. **-a,** M 174; L 32.

wynliċ, adj. *pleasant, agreeable;* comp. **wynlicran,** asn. L 52. [Cf. **wynn.**]

wyrċan, wk.v.I. *make, form;* inf. R 65; M 102.

ġe-wyrċan, wk.v.I. (a) *make, form;* pret. 3p. **ġeworhton**, R 31 (acc. **mē** understood); pp. **ġeworht**, asm. **−ne**, S 115 (**his ġ. wine**, *the friend he has made* or *his fast friend*); − (b) *bring about, work, accomplish;* inf. M 264; pres. 3s. subj. **ġewyrċe**, S 74 (*let him bring it about*); − (c) **flēam ġewyrċan**, lit. *make flight, take to flight;* inf. M 81.

wyrd, f. i-stem. *events; fate, destiny;* ns. R 74; W 5, 100 (personified, **wyrd sēo mǣre**, *Wyrd the renowned, Wyrd the mighty*); S 115; ds. **−e**, W 15; gp. **−a**, R 51; W 107. [Related to *WURD-, reduced grade of **weorðan**, *become;* hence, *that which comes to pass.* On the meaning see the note to W 107.]

-wyrde, adjectival combining form, ja-stem. *-worded, -spoken;* see **hrædwyrde**. [Based on **word**, n., prehist. *WURD-.]

ġe-wyrht, f. i-stem (or n.). *deed.* See **eald-ġewyrht**, and cf. **wyrċan**.

wyrm, m. i-stem. *serpent, snake;* dp. **−um**, D 1 (usual normalization of MS *wurman*). [Malone suggests that be **wurman** may refer to snake rings, gold rings made by Weland and coveted by Niþhad, or to swords with serpentine markings, instruments of the hamstringing.] **wyrmlīca**, wk.m. *likeness of a serpent;* dip. **−līcum**, W 98 (probably alluding to serpentine ornamentation such as was practiced by Roman builders).

wȳscan, wk.v.I. *wish;* pret. 3s. **wȳscte**, D 25. [Gmc. *WUNSKJAN; cf. Germ. WUNSCH, WÜNSCHEN.]

Y

yfel, n. *evil, harm;* gs. **−es**, M 133 (dep. on **hogode**).

ymb, or **ymbe**, prep. w. acc. − (a) *about, near, round about;* **ymbe**, B 5; M 249; **ymb**, S 11. (b) *about, concerning;* **ymbe**, M 214; S 46a; **ymb**, S 46b; D 12. (c) governing words for periods of time: *after;* **ǣfre ymbe stunde**, *ever after a while, ever and anon,* M 271.

ymb-clyppan, wk.v.I. *embrace;* pret. 3s. **ymbclypte**, R 42. [Cf. **clyppan**.]

ȳþ, f. jō-stem. *sea wave;* gp. **ȳða**, S 6, 46; L 7. [Cf. **sealt-ȳþ**.]

Proper Names

Most personal names among the early Germanic peoples were compounds made of elements of the language for which it is possible to trace the etymology. Such names in the list below are separated into their elements by hyphens, but no systematic effort has been made to expound the meaning of the individual elements. Spellings in the manuscripts show that the weakly stressed second elements of names were subject to vowel reduction, with the consequence that their meaning was obscured. The etymological values of these vowels, however, are for the most part retained in this book.

The historical and legendary names in *Brunanburh, Maldon,* and *Deor* are summarily treated here. For several of them much fuller discussion is provided by the editions of Campbell, Gordon, Scragg, and Malone. For *Deor* Malone's later articles (collected in Malone 1959) should also be consulted.

Ādam, Adam; gs. **−es**, R 100.

Ælf-here, one of the three defenders of the ford at Maldon; ns. M 80.

Ælf-nōþ, one of two retainers who fell beside Byrhtnoþ when he died; ns. M 183.

Ælf-riċ, father of Ælfwine, probably the ealdorman of Mercia who was banished in 985 or 986; gs. **−es**, M 209. See Gordon's ed.

Ælf-wine, scion of a distinguished Mercian family: kinsman of Byrhtnoþ, son of Ælfric, grandson of Ealhhelm. See Gordon's ed. He sets the pattern of sacrifice after Byrhtnoþ's death. ns. M 211; vs. M 231.

Æsc-ferþ, son of Ecglaf, a Northumbrian of noble family, a hostage in Byrhtnoþ's household; ns. M 267.

Æðel-gār, father of the virtuous Godric; gs. **−es**, M 320.

Æðel-rēd, Ethelred II, king of England 978–1016 (Æ. UNRÆD, E. the "Unready," i.e., shiftless or ill-advised); gs. **−es**, M 53, 151, 203. [The second element of the name is RÆD, *advice, counsel,* which figures also in the traditional epithet.]

Æðel-riċ, retainer of Byrhtnoþ and brother of Sigebyrht, cited for valiant conduct in the last phase of the battle; ns. M 280. [On the possibility that he survived the battle, see Gordon's ed.]

Æðel-stān, Athelstan, king of England 924–39; ns. B 1.

Anlāf, leader of the vikings from Dublin at Brunanburh; ns. B 46; gs. **−es**, B 31; ds. **−e**, B 26. [Early form of Old Norse ÓLÁFR (Olaf); on his identity see Campbell's edition.]

Beadu-hild, daughter of Niþhad, mother of the famous Widia by Weland; ds. **−e**, D 8.

Briten, f. Britain; as. **−e**, B 71. [The

spelling of this name, ultimately from Brythonic *PRITAN(N)JA, perhaps via Lat. BRITANNIA, varies greatly: e.g., also BRYTEN, BRITON, BREOTON.]

Brūnan-burg, unidentified site of the battle of A.D. 937; as. B 5. [The second element is certainly **burg** (q.v); the first may be gs. of BRŪNA, wk.m., pr. name, *Brown*. The sources are in disagreement, however, about the correct form of the name, and the first element may in actuality be BRUNNAN-, though the derivation of this is obscure.]

Byrht-helm, father of Byrhtnoþ; gs. −es, M 92.

Byrht-nōþ, earl or "ealdorman" of Essex 956–91. Gordon thinks he was born about 926, so that he was about 65 when he was killed at Maldon. See Scragg's introduction. ns. M 17, 42, 101, 127, 162; as. M 257; gs. **Byrht-nōðes**, M 114. [Place-names show that **þ** is voiced to **ð** before inflections, the second element having received stress at the time that fricatives were voiced. BYRHT, late WS form of BEORHT, adj. *bright* (see Campbell 1959: §305 n. 1); NŌÞ, f. *daring*.]

Byrht-wold, the old retainer of Byrht-noþ whose prescription for courage in defeat opens the last speech of the incomplete poem, 312 ff.; ns. M 309. [WOLD, unstressed form of WEALD, WALD, *power*.]

Ċēola, father of the Wulfstan who led the defense of the ford at Maldon; gs. −n, M 76.

Constantinus, Constantine III, king of the united Picts and Scots at Brunanburh; ns. B 38.

Crist, Christ; ns. R 56; ds. −e, R 116.

Dene, m. i-stem pl. Danes (a name often applied to Scandinavians in general); dp. **Denum**, M 129 (chiefly Norwegians).

Dēor, known only as speaker of the poem of that name, who says he was formerly the scop of the Hedenings; ns. D 37.

Dinġes mere, the otherwise unknown name of some part of the sea off the coast of Britain, probably an estuary between northern England and Ireland; as. (less probably ds.), B 54. [See **mere** in the main glossary.]

Dun-here, a simple freeman at Maldon; ns. M 255. [The first element is DUNN, attested as a separate name.]

Dyflin, Dublin, where Anlaf ruled a Norse kingdom at the time of the battle of Brunanburh; as. B 55.

Ēad-mund, Prince Edmund, younger half-brother of Athelstan, ruling after him, 939–46; ns. B 3.

Ēad-riċ, a retainer of Byrhtnoþ's; ns. M 11.

Ēad-weard, (1) Edward the Elder, king of Wessex 899–924, son of Alfred and father of Athelstan; gs. −es, B 7, 52. (2) a retainer of Byrhtnoþ's; ns. M 117. (3) **Ēadweard sē langa**, E. the Tall, a retainer of Byrhtnoþ's, perhaps the same as (2); ns. M 273.

Ēad-wold, a retainer of Byrhtnoþ's, brother of Oswold; ns. M 304.

Ealh-helm, grandfather of Ælfwine, father-in-law of Ælfric; "ealdorman" of Mercia ca. 940–50; ns. M 218. [EALH, m. *temple*.]

East-Seaxe, m. i-stem pl. the East Saxons, centered in Essex; gp. **Ēast-Seaxna**, M 69.

Ecg-lāf, a Northumbrian nobleman, father of Æscferþ; gs. −es, M 267.

Engle, m. i-stem pl. the Angli, Angles as contrasted with Saxons; np. B 70.

Eorman-riċ, the Ermanaric of history, ruler of the Goths in the third quarter of the fourth century, who died ca. 375 when the Huns invaded his empire, centered near the mouth of the

Danube. Known in legend as a violent man, and eventually as a tyrant who meted out savage punishment for imagined crimes; gs. −es, D 21.

Gadd, kinsman of Offa; gs. −es, M 287.

Ġēat, legendary hero, perhaps originally a god, lover of Mæþhild; gs. −es, D 15.

God, God; ns. R 39, 93, 98, 106, 156; M 94; as. R 51, 60; M 262; gs. −es, B 15; R 83, 152; S 101. [GOD, n. (*heathen*) *god*.]

God-rīċ, (1) son of Odda; leader of the flight from the battle of Maldon; ns. M 187, 237, 325. (2) son of Æðelgar; a retainer of Byrhtnoþ's who, unlike the preceding, fought to the last; ns. M 321.

God-wiġ, son of Odda; a fugitive with his brothers Godric (1) and Godwine; ns. M 192.

God-wine, son of Odda; a fugitive with his brothers Godric (1) and Godwig; ns. M 192. (C's transcript calls him *Godrine*.)

Gotan, wk.m.pl. the Goths; at the time of Ermanaric's death the Ostrogoths and Visigoths were separated; gp. **Gotena**, D 23.

Hedeningas, m.pl. the people ruled by Heden, a legendary Germanic king, wooer of Hagen's daughter Hild, and once the lord of Deor; gp. −a, D 36.

Heorrenda, a scop of Heden, celebrated in one of the versions of the Hild saga; according to Deor, his successful rival; ns. D 39.

Īras, m.pl. the Irish; gp. **Īra**, B 56.

Lēof-sunu, retainer of Byrhtnoþ, probably from Sturmer in Essex; the third to speak after Byrhtnoþ's death; ns. M 244.

Maccus, one of the three defenders of the ford at Maldon; ns. M 80. [Prob. from Old Norse MAGNÚS.]

Mǣringas, m.pl. a people ruled by Þeodric; prob. Ostrogoths; gp. **Mǣringa**, D 19.

Mǣþ-hild, a legendary woman, beloved by Geat; gs. −e, D 14 (see note).

Māria, the Virgin Mary; as. −n, R 92.

Mierċe, m. i-stem pl. the Mercians; np. B 24; dp. **Mierċum**, M 217.

Nīþ-hād, legendary king, persecutor of Weland; ns. D 5.

Norþ-Hymbre, m. i-stem pl. the Northumbrians; dp. **-Hymbrum**, M 266.

Norð-mann, m. cons.-stem, Norseman; np. **Norð-menn**, B 53; gp. **-manna**, B 33.

Odda, father of the fugitives Godric (1), Godwig, and Godwine; gs. −n, M 186, 238. [See Gordon's glossary for the possible origin of the name, Scandinavian or English.]

Offa, an officer of Byrhtnoþ's, apparently second in command under him; his speech after B's death, M 231 ff., seems to indicate that he is now the leader; ns. M 198, 230, 286, 288; gs. −n, M 5.

Ōs-wold, a retainer of Byrhtnoþ's, brother of Eadwold; ns. M 304.

Pante, wk.f. the river near Maldon in Essex, now called Blackwater, though the old name Pant (pron. Pont) is still applied to part of the river. See Gordon's glossary. gs. **Pantan**, M 68; as. **Pantan**, M 97.

Scottas, m.pl. Scots here, though the term in Old English is applied indiscriminately to Scots and Irishmen, since the Gaelic speakers of Scotland came from Ireland beginning in the sixth century; gp. **Scotta**, B 11, 32. [The spelling *Sceotta* in MS A shows that at least in the South the *sc* was palatalized.]

Scyttisc, pr. adj. Scottish (or, elsewhere, Irish: see **Scottas**); nsm. B 19.

Seaxe, m. i-stem pl. the Saxons, as distinguished from the Angles; np. B

70. [The reference is to the invasion of the fifth century recounted by Bede and the Anglo-Saxon Chronicle.]

Siġe-byrht, brother of Æðelric, one of Byrhtnoþ's retainers. It is not definitely stated that Sigebyrht was present at the battle; gs. −es, M 282.

Stūr-mere, a pool (**mere**) in the river Stour in Essex, from which the village of Sturmer takes its name (see Gordon's glossary); as. M 249.

Þēod-riċ, a ruler of disputed identity; most likely Theodoric the Ostrogoth, in later legend Dietrich von Bern; ns. D 18 (see note).

Þur-stān, father of Wistan; gs. −es, M 298. [The name is adapted, according to Gordon, from OE Scand. ÞUR-STÆIN (corresponding to Old Icelandic ÞORSTEINN); the first el. is ÞŪR, OE variant of Old Norse ÞÓRR (cognate with OE ÞUNOR), the god.]

Wealh, m. a Welshman (originally a foreigner), Briton; ap. **Wēalas**, B 72.

Wēland, legendary smith; ns. D 1.

West-Seaxe, m. i-stem pl. West Saxons; np. B 20; gp. **West-Seaxna**, B 59.

Wiġ-helm, father or ancestor (?) of Wigstan; gs. −es, M 300 (see note).

Wī-stān, one of Byrhtnoþ's retainers, son of Þurstan; ns. M 297. [The first element is most likely WĪH, WĒOH *idol, shrine,* making this an anglicization of Old Norse WĪSTÆINN (VÉ-STEINN) and equivalent to WĪHSTĀN, WĒOHSTĀN in *Beowulf;* cf. WĪĠ-WEORÐUNG, *honor to idols,* also in *Beowulf.* But especially if the man was named for Wighelm, the first element may be **wiġ,** *war,* q.v. See Gordon's glossary.]

Wulf-mǣr, (1) son of Byrhtnoþ's sister; ns. M 113. (2) **Wulfmǣr sē ġeonga**, W. the Young, a retainer of Byrhtnoþ's, son of Wulfstan; ns. M 155, 183.

Wulf-stān, chief defender of the ford at Maldon, son of Ceola, father of Wulfmær (2); ns. M 75; gs. −es, M 155; ds. −e, M 79.

Works Cited

The titles of journals and series are abbreviated as follows:

AN&Q	American Notes & Queries	OEN	Old English Newsletter
ASE	Anglo-Saxon England	PBA	Proceedings of the British
CL	Comparative Literature		Academy
EETS	Early English Text Society	PBB	Beiträge zur Geschichte der
EHR	English Historical Review		deutschen Sprache und
ELN	English Language Notes		Literatur [Paul-Braunes
ES	English Studies		Beiträge]
EStn	Englische Studien	PMLA	Publications of the Modern
JEGP	Journal of English and		Language Association
	Germanic Philology	PQ	Philological Quarterly
LSE	Leeds Studies in English	RES	Review of English Studies
MÆ	Medium Ævum	SN	Studia Neophilologica
MLR	Modern Language Review	SP	Studies in Philology
MP	Modern Philology	SS	Scandinavian Studies
N&Q	Notes and Queries	YES	Yearbook of English Studies
NM	Neuphilologische Mitteil-	ZfdPh	Zeitschrift für deutsche
	ungen		Philologie

Abels, Richard. 1991. "English Tactics, Strategy, and Military Organization in the Late Tenth Century." In Scragg 1991a: 143–55.

Adriaen, M., ed. 1957. *Expositio evangelii secundum Lucam. Fragmenta in Esaiam.* Corpus Christianorum Series Latina 14. Turnhout: Brepols.

Aðalbjarnarson, Bjarni. See Bjarni Aðalbjarnarson.

Aertsen, Henk, and Rolf H. Bremmer, Jr., eds. 1994. *Companion to Old English Poetry.* Amsterdam: VU Univ. Press.

Alfred, William. 1982. "The Drama of *The Wanderer.*" In *The Wisdom of Poetry: Essays in Early English Literature in Honor of Morton W. Bloomfield,* ed. Larry D. Benson and Siegfried Wenzel, 31–44. Kalamazoo: Medieval Institute Publications, Western Michigan Univ.

Andersen, Hans Erik. 1991. *The Battle of Maldon: The Meaning, Dating and Historicity of an Old English Poem.* Copenhagen: Dept. of English, Univ. of Copenhagen.

Anderson, James E. 1986. *Two Literary Riddles in the Exeter Book.* Norman: Univ. of Oklahoma Press.

Anderson, O. S. [later named Arngart]. 1937–38. *The Seafarer: An Interpretation.* Humanistiska Vetenskapssamfundets i Lund Årsberättelse 1. Lund: Gleerup.

Arngart, O. S. [earlier named Anderson]. 1952. *The Leningrad Bede.* Early English Manuscripts in Facsimile 2. Copenhagen: Rosenkilde & Bagger.

Backhouse, Janet, et al. 1984. *The Golden Age of Anglo-Saxon Art, 966–1066.* Bloomington: Indiana Univ. Press.

Ball, Cathy. 1995. *Old English Pages.* ‹http://www.georgetown.edu/cball/oe/ old_english.html#reference›. [Updated continually.]

Ball, C[hristopher] J. E. 1985. "Homonymy and Polysemy in Old English: A Problem for Lexicographers." In *Problems of Old English Lexicography: Studies in Memory of Angus Cameron,* ed. Alfred Bammesberger, 39–46. Eichstätter Beiträge 15. Regensburg: F. Pustet.

Bammesberger, Alfred. 1979. *Beiträge zu einem etymologischen Wörterbuch des Altenglischen: Berichtigung und Nachträge zum Altenglischen etymologischen Wörterbuch von Ferdinand Holthausen.* Heidelberg: C. Winter.

Barley, Nigel F. 1974. "Old English Colour Classification: Where Do Matters Stand?" *ASE* 3.15–28.

Bately, Janet M. 1966. "The Old English Orosius: The Question of Dictation." *Anglia* 84.255–304.

————, ed. 1980. *The Old English Orosius.* EETS s.s. 6. London: Oxford Univ. Press.

Battles, Paul. 1994. "Of Graves, Caves, and Subterranean Dwellings: *eorð-scræf* and *eorðsele* in *The Wife's Lament.*" *PQ* 73.267–86.

Becker, Alfred. 1973. *Franks Casket: Zu den Bildern und Inschriften des Runenkästchens von Auzon.* Regensburg: H. Carl.

Behaghel, Otto, ed. 1984. *Heliand und Genesis.* 9th ed. rev. by Burkhard Taeger. Tübingen: M. Niemeyer.

Bennett, J. A. W. 1982. *Poetry of the Passion: Studies in Twelve Centuries of English Verse.* Oxford: Clarendon.

Bessinger, J. B., Jr. 1962. "*Maldon* and the *Óláfsdrápa:* An Historical Caveat." *CL* 14.23–35. Rpt. in Greenfield 1963: 23–35; and Stevens and Mandel 1968: 237–52.

Bessinger, J. B., Jr., and Stanley J. Kahrl, eds. 1968. *Essential Articles for the Study of Old English Poetry.* Hamden, CT: Archon.

Bessinger, J. B., Jr., and Philip H. Smith, Jr. 1978. *A Concordance to the Anglo-Saxon Poetic Records.* Ithaca: Cornell Univ. Press.

Biggs, Frederick M. 1997. "Deor's Threatened 'Blame Poem'." *SP* 94.289–320.

Bjarni Aðalbjarnarson, ed. 1941. *Snorri Sturluson, Heimskringla.* Vol. 1. Íslenzk fornrit 26. Reykjavík: Hið íslenzka fornritafélag.

Bjork, Robert E. 1989. "*Sundor æt rune:* The Voluntary Exile of *The Wanderer.*" *Neophilologus* 73.119–29.

Blair, Peter Hunter. 1959. *The Moore Bede.* Early English Manuscripts in Facsimile 9. Copenhagen: Rosenkilde & Bagger.

Bliss, A. J. 1962. *Introduction to Old English Metre.* Oxford: B. Blackwell. Rpt. 1993, Old English Newsletter Subsidia 20, ed. Daniel Donoghue. Binghamton, NY: Center for Medieval and Early Renaissance Studies.

————. 1967. *The Metre of 'Beowulf'.* Oxford: B. Blackwell.

Blockley, Mary. 1998. "Cædmon's Conjunction: *Cædmon's Hymn* 7a Revisited." *Speculum* 73.1–31.

Bloomfield, Morton W. 1964. "The Form of 'Deor'." *PMLA* 79.534–41.

Bode, Wilhelm. 1886. *Die Kenningar in der angelsächsischen Dichtung.* Darmstadt: E. Zernin.

Boenig, Robert. 1996. "The Anglo-Saxon Harp." *Speculum* 71.290–320.

Bolton, W. F. 1968. "'The Dream of the Rood' 9b: 'Engel' = Nuntius?" *N&Q* 213 (n.s. 15), 165–66.

Bosworth, Joseph, and T. Northcote Toller. 1898. *An Anglo-Saxon Dictionary.* Oxford: Oxford Univ. Press. *Supplement* by Toller, 1921. *Enlarged Addenda and Corrigenda* by Alistair Campbell, 1972.

Bracher, Frederick. 1937. "Understatement in Old English Poetry." *PMLA* 52.915–34. Rpt. in Bessinger and Kahrl 1968: 228–54.

Brett, Cyril. 1927. "Notes on Old and Middle English." *MLR* 22.257–64.

Bright, James W. 1891. *An Anglo-Saxon Reader.* New York: H. Holt.

Britton, G. C. 1967. "*Bealuwara weorc* in the *Dream of the Rood*." *NM* 68. 273–76.

Brodeur, Arthur Gilchrist. 1959. *The Art of 'Beowulf'.* Berkeley: Univ. of California Press.

Brown, George Hardin. 1978. "An Iconographic Explanation of 'The Wanderer', Lines 81b–82a." *Viator* 9.31–38.

Brunner, Karl. 1965. *Altenglische Grammatik, nach der Angelsächsische Grammatik von Eduard Sievers.* Tübingen: M. Niemeyer.

Cable, Thomas. 1974. *The Meter and Melody of 'Beowulf'.* Illinois Studies in Language and Literature 64. Urbana: Univ. of Illinois Press.

————. 1991. *The English Alliterative Tradition.* Philadelphia: Univ. of Pennsylvania Press.

Caie, Graham. 1979. *Bibliography of Junius XI Manuscript, with Appendix on 'Cædmon's Hymn'.* Anglica et Americana 6. Copenhagen: Dept. of English, Univ. of Copenhagen.

Cain, Christopher M. 1997. "The 'Fearful Symmetry' of *Maldon:* The Apocalypse, the Poet, and the Millennium." *Comitatus* 28.1–16.

Cameron, Angus, et al. 1986–. *Dictionary of Old English.* Fascicles A–F to date. Toronto: Pontifical Institute of Mediaeval Studies, Univ. of Toronto.

Campbell, A., ed. 1938. *The Battle of Brunanburh.* London: W. Heinemann.

————. 1959. *Old English Grammar.* Oxford: Clarendon.

Carr, Charles T. 1939. *Nominal Compounds in Germanic.* St. Andrews Univ. Publications 41. London: Oxford Univ. Press.

Cassidy, Brendan, ed. 1992. *The Ruthwell Cross: Papers from a Colloquium.* Princeton: Princeton Univ. Press.

Cassidy, F. G., and Richard N. Ringler. 1971. *Bright's Old English Grammar and Reader.* 3rd ed. New York: Holt, Rinehart.

Cavill, Paul. 1992. "'Engel dryhtnes' in *The Dream of the Rood*." *NM* 93.287–92.

————. 1995. "Interpretation of *The Battle of Maldon,* Lines 84–90: A Review and Reassessment." *SN* 67.149–64.

Chambers, R. W. 1912. *Widsith: A Study in Old English Heroic Legend.* Cambridge: Cambridge Univ. Press.

Chambers, R. W., Max Förster, and Robin Flower, eds. 1933. *The Exeter Book of Old English Poetry*. London: Humphries.

Clark, Cecily. 1983. "On Dating *The Battle of Maldon:* Certain Evidence Reviewed." *Nottingham Mediaeval Studies* 27.1–22.

Clark, George. 1979. "The Hero of *Maldon:* Vir pius et strenuus." *Speculum* 54.257–82.

———. 1992. "Maldon: History, Poetry, and Truth." In *De Gustibus: Essays for Alain Renoir,* ed. John Miles Foley, 66–84. New York: Garland.

Clemoes, Peter. 1969. "*Mens absentia cogitans* in *The Seafarer* and *The Wanderer.*" In *Medieval Literature and Civilization: Studies in Memory of G. N. Garmonsway,* ed. D. A. Pearsall and R. A. Waldron, 62–77. London: Athlone.

Colgrave, Bertram, and R. A. B. Mynors, eds. 1969. *Bede's Ecclesiastical History of the English People*. Oxford: Clarendon.

Collier, Wendy E. J. 1991. "A Bibliography of the Battle of Maldon." In Scragg 1991a: 294–301. There is an updated electronic version on the World Wide Web at ‹http://www.wmich.edu/medieval/rawl/maldon/index.html›.

Collins, Douglas C. 1959. "Kenning in Anglo-Saxon Poetry." *Essays and Studies* 12.1–17.

Conde Silvestre, Juan C. 1992. "*The Wanderer* and *The Seafarer:* A Bibliography 1971–91." *SELIM: Journal of the Spanish Society for Mediaeval English Language and Literature* 2.170–86.

Conner, Patrick W. 1993. *Anglo-Saxon Exeter: A Tenth-Century Cultural History*. Woodbridge: Boydell.

Cook, Albert S., ed. 1905. *The Dream of the Rood: An Old English Poem Attributed to Cynewulf*. Oxford: Clarendon.

Cooper, Janet, ed. 1993. *The Battle of Maldon: Fiction and Fact*. London: Hambledon.

Craigie, W. A. 1926. *Specimens of Anglo-Saxon Poetry*. Vol. 2. Edinburgh: I. Hutchen.

Creed, Robert P. 1990. *Reconstructing the Rhythm of 'Beowulf'*. Columbia: Univ. of Missouri Press.

Cross, James E. 1956. "'Ubi Sunt' Passages in Old English." *Vetenskaps-Societetens i Lund Årsbok 1956,* 23–44.

———. 1958–59. "On *The Wanderer,* Lines 80–84: A Study of a Figure and a Theme." *Vetenskaps-Societetens i Lund Årsbok* 1.75–110.

———. 1959. "On the Allegory of *The Seafarer:* Illustrative Notes." *MÆ* 28.104–106.

———. 1961. "On the Genre of *The Wanderer.*" *Neophilologus* 45.63–72. Rpt. in Bessinger and Kahrl 1968: 515–32.

———. 1962. "Aspects of Microcosm and Macrocosm in Old English Literature." In Greenfield 1963: 1–22.

Dahl, Ivar. 1938. *Substantival Inflexion in Early Old English: Vocalic Stems*. Lund Studies in English 7. Lund: Gleerup.

Damico, Helen, and John Leyerle, eds. 1993. *Heroic Poetry in the Anglo-Saxon Period: Studies in Honor of Jess B. Bessinger, Jr.* Studies in

Medieval Culture 32. Kalamazoo: Medieval Institute Publications, Western Michigan Univ.

Dickins, Bruce, and Alan S. C. Ross, eds. 1966. *The Dream of the Rood*. Corrected [4th] ed. London: Methuen.

Dobbie, Elliott Van Kirk. 1937. *The Manuscripts of Cædmon's Hymn and Bede's Death Song*. New York: Columbia Univ. Press.

Dodgson, John McN. 1991. "The Site of the Battle of Maldon." In Scragg 1991a: 170–79.

Donoghue, Daniel. 1987. *Style in Old English: The Test of the Auxiliary*. New Haven: Yale Univ. Press.

————. 1997. "Language Matters." In O'Brien O'Keeffe 1997: 59–78.

Dumville, David. 1981. "*Beowulf* and the Celtic World: The Uses of Evidence." *Traditio* 37.109–60.

Dumville, David, and Simon Keynes, gen. eds. 1983–. *The Anglo-Saxon Chronicle: A Collaborative Edition*. 6 vols. to date. Cambridge: D. S. Brewer. The relevant volumes are III (MS A, ed. Janet Bately, 1986), IV (MS B, ed. Simon Taylor, 1983), and VI (MS D, ed. G. P. Cubbin, 1996).

Dunning, T. P., and A. J. Bliss, eds. 1969. *The Wanderer*. London: Methuen.

Earl, James W. 1992. "The Battle of Maldon, Line 86: OE *lytegian* = Lat. *litigare?*" In *Old English and New: Studies in Language and Linguistics in Honor of Frederic G. Cassidy*, ed. Joan H. Hall et al., 76–82. New York: Garland.

————. 1994. *Thinking about 'Beowulf'*. Stanford: Stanford Univ. Press.

Ekwall, Eilert. 1934. Review of Smith 1933 and Malone 1933. *MLR* 29.78–82.

Erickson, Jon. 1975. "The *Deor* Genitives." *Archivum Linguisticum* 6.77–84.

Erzgräber, W. 1961. "*Der Wanderer:* Eine Interpretation von Aufbau und Gehalt." In Viebrock and Erzgräber 1961: 57–85.

Faulkes, Anthony, trans. 1987. *Snorri Sturluson, Edda*. London: Dent.

Finnegan, Robert Emmett. 1983. "The Gospel of Nicodemus and *The Dream of the Rood*, 148b–56." *NM* 84.338–43.

Fischer, Walther. 1935. "*Wanderer* v. 25 und v. 6–7. *Anglia* 59.299–302.

Flower, Robin, and Hugh Smith, eds. 1941. *The Parker Chronicle and Laws (Corpus Christi College, Cambridge, MS. 173)*. EETS o.s. 208 (for 1937). London: Oxford Univ. Press. Rpt. 1973.

Foley, John Miles. 1991. "Texts That Speak to Readers Who Hear: Old English Poetry and the Languages of Oral Tradition." In *Speaking Two Languages: Traditional Disciplines and Contemporary Theory in Medieval Studies*, ed. Allen J. Frantzen, 141–56. Albany: State Univ. of New York Press.

Fowler, Roger. 1966. *Old English Prose and Verse*. London: Routledge.

Frank, Roberta. 1991. "*The Battle of Maldon* and Heroic Literature." In Scragg 1991a: 196–207.

Frankis, P. J. 1962. "*Deor* and *Wulf and Eadwacer:* Some Conjectures." *MÆ* 31.161–75.

Frantzen, Allen J. 1990. *Desire for Origins: New Language, Old English, and Teaching the Tradition*. New Brunswick, NJ: Rutgers Univ. Press.

Fritz, Donald W. 1969. "Cædmon: A Traditional Christian Poet." *Mediaeval Studies* 31.334–37.

Fulk, R. D. 1987. "The Reduplicating Verbs and Their Development in Northwest Germanic." *PBB* 109.159–79.

————, ed. 1991. *Interpretations of 'Beowulf': A Critical Anthology.* Bloomington: Indiana Univ. Press.

————. 1992. *A History of Old English Meter.* Philadelphia: Univ. of Pennsylvania Press.

————. 1995. "Kuryłowicz on Resolution in Old English." In *Kuryłowicz Memorial Volume I,* ed. W. Smoczyński, 491–97. Cracow: Universitas.

————. 1996a. "Inductive Methods in the Textual Criticism of Old English Verse." *Medievalia et Humanistica* n.s. 23.1–24.

————. 1996b. "Rhetoric, Form, and Linguistic Structure in Early Germanic Verse: Toward a Synthesis." *Interdisciplinary Journal of Germanic Linguistics and Semiotic Analysis* 1.63–88.

Gade, Kari Ellen, and R. D. Fulk. 2000. *A Bibliography of Germanic Alliterative Meters.* Old English Newsletter Subsidia 28. Kalamazoo: Medieval Institute, Western Michigan Univ.

Galloway, Andrew. 1994. "Dream-Theory in *The Dream of the Rood* and *The Wanderer.*" *RES* n.s. 45.475–85.

Gardner, Thomas. 1969. "The Old English Kenning: A Characteristic Feature of Germanic Poetical Diction?" *MP* 67.109–17.

————. 1972. "The Application of the Term 'Kenning'." *Neophilologus* 56.464–68.

Gendre, Renato. 1988–89. "La *Battaglia di Brunanburh* v. 54a: *drēorig daraða lāf.*" In *Studi sulla cultura germanica,* ed. M. A. D'Aronco et al., 161–77. *Romanobarbarica* 10 (special issue). Rome: Herder.

Glanz, Elaine. 1997. "*Standan steame bedrifenne* in *The Dream of the Rood.*" *Mediaevalia* 21.189–208.

Gneuss, Helmut. 1976a. "*The Battle of Maldon* 89: Byrhtnoð's *ofermod* Once Again." *SP* 73.117–37. Rpt. in O'Brien O'Keeffe 1994: 149–72.

————. 1976b. *Die Battle of Maldon als historisches und literarisches Zeugnis.* Munich: Bayerische Akademie der Wissenschaften.

Godden, Malcolm. 1985. "Anglo-Saxons on the Mind." In *Learning and Literature in Anglo-Saxon England,* ed. M. Lapidge and H. Gneuss, 271–98. Cambridge: Cambridge Univ. Press.

Godden, Malcolm, and Michael Lapidge, eds. 1991. *The Cambridge Companion to Old English Literature.* Cambridge: Cambridge Univ. Press.

Gollancz, Israel, ed. 1895. *The Exeter Book, Part I: Poems I–VIII.* EETS o.s. 194. London: Oxford Univ. Press.

Gordon, E. V., ed. 1937. *The Battle of Maldon.* London: Methuen. Rpt. 1976, with a supplement by D. G. Scragg. Manchester: Univ. of Manchester Press; New York: Barnes & Noble.

Gordon, I. L. 1960. *The Seafarer.* London: Methuen. Rpt. 1996 with a bibliography by Mary Clayton. Exeter: Univ. of Exeter Press.

Grant, Raymond J. S. 1991. *"The Dream of the Rood,* Line 63b: A Part-Time Idiom?" *NM* 92.289–95.

Grasso, Anthony R. 1991. "Theology and Structure in 'The Dream of the Rood'." *Religion and Literature* 23 (2), 23–38.

Green, Martin. 1983. Introduction to his *Old English Elegies: New Essays in Criticism and Research,* 11–28. Rutherford, NJ: Fairleigh Dickinson Univ. Press.

Greenfield, Stanley B., ed. 1963. *Studies in Old English Literature in Honor of Arthur G. Brodeur.* Eugene: Univ. of Oregon Books.

Greenfield, Stanley B., and Daniel G. Calder, eds. 1986. *A New Critical History of Old English Literature.* New York: New York Univ. Press.

Greenfield, Stanley B., and Fred C. Robinson. 1980. *A Bibliography of Publications on Old English Literature to the End of 1972.* Toronto: Univ. of Toronto Press.

Grein, C. W. M., ed. 1857. *Bibliothek der angelsächsischen Poesie, I.* Göttingen: G. Wigand.

————. 1865. "Zur Textkritik der angelsächsischen Dichter." *Germania* 10.416–29.

————. 1912–14. *Sprachschatz der angelsächsischen Dichter.* Ed. F. Holthausen and J. J. Köhler. Heidelberg: C. Winter.

Griffith, Mark S. 1993. "Convention and Originality in the Old English 'Beasts of Battle' Typescene." *ASE* 22.179–99.

————. 1996. "Does *wyrd bið ful aræd* Mean 'Fate Is Wholly Inexorable'?" In Toswell and Tyler 1996: 133–56.

————. 1998. "Dialect and Literary Dialect in *The Battle of Maldon.*" *N&Q* n.s. 45.272–73.

Hall, J[ames] R. 1986. "'Angels . . . and All the Holy Ones': *The Dream of the Rood* 153b–54a." *AN&Q* 24.65–68.

————. 1992. Review of Kiernan 1990. "The Year's Work in Old English Studies." *OEN* 25 (2), 36.

Hall, J[ohn] R. Clark. 1960. *A Concise Anglo-Saxon Dictionary.* 4th ed., with a supplement by Herbert D. Meritt. Cambridge: Cambridge Univ. Press. Rpt. 1984, Toronto: Univ. of Toronto Press.

Hamer, R. 1992. *"The Seafarer,* Line 99b." *N&Q* n.s. 39.13–15.

Harris, Joseph. 1976. *"Stemnettan: Battle of Maldon,* Line 122a." *PQ* 55.113–17.

————. 1986. "'Brunanburh' 12b–13a and Some Skaldic Passages." In *Magister Regis: Studies in Honor of Robert Earl Kaske,* ed. Arthur Groos, with Emerson Brown et al., 61–68. New York: Fordham Univ. Press.

————. 1987. *"Deor* and Its Refrain: Preliminaries to an Interpretation." *Traditio* 43.23–53.

————. 1993. "Love and Death in the *Männerbund:* An Essay with Special Reference to the *Bjarkamál* and *The Battle of Maldon.*" In Damico and Leyerle 1993: 77–114.

Healey, Antonette diPaolo, and Richard Venezky. 1980. *A Microfiche Concordance to Old English.* Publications of the Dictionary of Old English 1. Toronto: Pontifical Institute of Medieval Studies, Univ. of Toronto.

Heaney, Seamus, trans. 1999. *Beowulf*. London: Faber & Faber.

Hecht, Hans, ed. 1900–1907. *Bischofs Wærferth von Worcester Übersetzung der Dialoge Gregors des Grossen*. 2 vols. Bibliothek der angelsächsischen Prosa, ed. C. W. M. Grein. Vol. 5. Leipzig: G. Wigand.

Hermann, John P. 1978. *"The Dream of the Rood* 19a: *earmra ærgewinn."* *ELN* 15.241–44.

Heusler, Andreas. 1925. *Deutsche Versgeschichte, mit Einschluß des altenglischen und altnordischen Stabreimverses*. Grundriß der germanischen Philologie 8, no. 1, gen. ed. Hermann Paul. Berlin: W. de Gruyter.

Hill, John M. 1991. "Transcendental Loyalty in *The Battle of Maldon*." In Niles 1991: 67–88.

Hill, Joyce, ed. 1994. *Old English Minor Heroic Poems*. Rev. ed. Durham Medieval Texts 4. New Elvet, Durham, U.K.: Dept. of English Studies.

Hill, Thomas D. 1997. "The *Liber Eliensis* 'Historical Selections' and the Old English *Battle of Maldon*." *JEGP* 96.1–12.

Hoad, Terry. 1994. "Old English Weak Genitive Plural *-an*: Towards Establishing the Evidence." In *From Anglo-Saxon to Early Middle English: Studies Presented to E. G. Stanley*, ed. Malcolm Godden et al., 108–29. Oxford: Clarendon.

Hofmann, Dietrich. 1955. *Nordisch-englische Lehnbeziehungen der Wikingerzeit*. Biblioteca Arnamagnæana 14. Copenhagen: Munksgaard.

Hofstetter, Walter. 1987. *Winchester und der spätaltenglische Sprachgebrauch: Untersuchungen zur geographischen und zeitlichen Verbreitung altenglischer Synonyme*. Munich: W. Fink.

Hogg, Richard M. 1992. *A Grammar of Old English*. Vol. I, *Phonology*. Oxford: B. Blackwell.

Holthausen, F. 1932–34. *Altenglisches etymologisches Wörterbuch*. 3rd, unrev. ed. 1974. Heidelberg: C. Winter.

Honegger, Thomas. 1998. "Form and Function: The Beasts of Battle Revisited." *ES* 79.289–98.

Hoover, David L. 1985. *A New Theory of Old English Meter*. New York: Lang.

Horgan, A. D. 1987. *"The Wanderer:* A Boethian Poem?" *RES* n.s. 38.40–46.

Hough, Carole. 1998. *"The Battle of Maldon* Line 33." *RES* n.s. 49.322–26.

Howe, Nicholas. 1989. *Migration and Mythmaking in Anglo-Saxon England*. New Haven: Yale Univ. Press.

Howlett, David. 1992. "Inscriptions and Design of the Ruthwell Cross." In Cassidy 1992: 71–93.

Huppé, Bernard F. 1970. *The Web of Words*. Albany: State Univ. of New York Press.

Hurst, D., ed. 1969. *Bedae Venerabilis opera*. Vol. 2, *Opera exegetica*. Corpus Christianorum Series Latina 119A. Turnhout: Brepols.

Hutcheson, B. R. 1995. *Old English Poetic Metre*. Cambridge: D. S. Brewer.

Irving, Edward B., Jr. 1986. "Crucifixion Witnessed, or Dramatic Interaction in *The Dream of the Rood*." In *Modes of Interpretation in Old English*

Literature: Essays in Honour of Stanley B. Greenfield, ed. Phyllis Rugg Brown et al., 101–13. Toronto: Univ. of Toronto Press.

Isaac, G. R. 1997. "The Date and Origin of *Cædmon's Hymn.*" *NM* 98. 217–28.

Jacobs, Nicholas. 1989. "Syntactical Connection and Logical Disconnection: The Case of *The Seafarer.*" *MÆ* 58.105–13.

Jensen, Emily. 1990. "'The Wife's Lament's' *eorðscræf:* Literal or Figural Sign?" *NM* 91.449–57.

Jost, Karl. 1961. "Welund und Sampson: Ein Beitrag zur Erklärung der 1. *Deor*-Strophe." In Viebrock and Erzgräber 1961: 86–87.

Kershaw, N. 1922. *Anglo-Saxon and Norse Poems.* Cambridge: Cambridge Univ. Press.

Kiernan, Kevin S. 1990. "Reading Cædmon's 'Hymn' with Someone Else's Glosses." *Representations,* no. 32.157–74.

Klaeber, Fr. 1950. *'Beowulf' and 'The Fight at Finnsburg'.* 3rd ed. with 1st and 2nd supplements. Lexington, MA: D. C. Heath.

Klinck, Anne L. 1992. *The Old English Elegies: A Critical Edition and Genre Study.* Montreal: McGill-Queen's Univ. Press.

Kluge, F. 1883. "Zu altenglischen Dichtungen: I. Der Seefahrer." *EStn* 6.322–27.

————. 1888. *Angelsächsisches Lesebuch.* Halle: M. Niemeyer.

Kock, E. A. 1918. "Jubilee Jaunts and Jottings." *Lunds Universitets Årsskrift* n.s. 1, 14 (26), 1–82.

Krapp, George Philip, and Elliott Van Kirk Dobbie, eds. 1931–53. *The Anglo-Saxon Poetic Records.* 6 vols. New York: Columbia Univ. Press. Contents of the individual volumes: I, *The Junius Manuscript* (Krapp, 1931); II, *The Vercelli Book* (Krapp, 1932); III, *The Exeter Book* (Krapp and Dobbie, 1936); IV, *Beowulf and Judith* (Dobbie, 1953); V, *The Paris Psalter and the Meters of Boethius* (Krapp, 1932); VI, *The Anglo-Saxon Minor Poems* (Dobbie, 1942).

Krause, Wolfgang. 1930. *Die Kenning als typische Stilfigur der germanischen und keltischen Dichtersprache.* Halle: Niemeyer.

Kuhn, Hans. 1933. "Zur Wortstellung und -betonung im Altgermanischen." *PBB* 57.1–109. Rpt. with an addendum in his *Kleine Schriften,* 1.18–103. Berlin: W. de Gruyter, 1969–72.

————. 1963. "Dietrichs dreissig Jahre." *Märchen, Mythos, Dichtung: Festschrift zum 90. Geburtstag Friedrich von der Leyens,* ed. Hugo Kuhn and Kurt Schier, 117–20. Munich: C. Beck. Rpt. in Kuhn's *Kleine Schriften,* 2.135–37. Berlin: W. de Gruyter, 1969–72.

Kuryłowicz, Jerzy. 1949. "Latin and Germanic Metre." *English and Germanic Studies* 2.34–38.

Laborde, E. D. 1925. "The Site of the Battle of Maldon." *EHR* 40.161–73.

Lawrence, W. W. 1902. "*The Wanderer* and *The Seafarer.*" *Journal of Germanic Philology* 4.460–80.

Lees, Clare A., and Gillian R. Overing. 1994. "Birthing Bishops and Fathering Poets: Bede, Hild, and the Relations of Cultural Production." *Exemplaria* 6.35–65.

Lerer, Seth. 1991. *Literacy and Power in Anglo-Saxon Literature*. Lincoln: Univ. of Nebraska Press.

Leslie, R. F. 1959. "Analysis of Stylistic Devices and Effects in Anglo-Saxon Literature." In *Stil- und Formprobleme in der Literatur: Vorträge des VII. Kongresses der Internationalen Vereinigung für moderne Sprachen und Literaturen in Heidelberg*, 129–36. Heidelberg: C. Winter. Rpt. in Bessinger and Kahrl 1968: 255–63; and Stevens and Mandel 1968: 76–81.

————, ed. 1961. *Three Old English Elegies*. Manchester: Manchester Univ. Press. Rpt. 1988, Exeter: Exeter Univ. Press.

————, ed. 1966. *The Wanderer*. Manchester: Manchester Univ. Press. Rpt. 1985 with updated bibliography. Exeter: Univ. of Exeter Press.

Luick, Karl. 1914–40. *Historische Grammatik der englischen Sprache*. Leipzig: C. Tauchniz. Rpt. 1964 Oxford: B. Blackwell; Cambridge, MA: Harvard Univ. Press.

Lumiansky, R. M. 1950. "The Dramatic Structure of the Old English *Wanderer*." *Neophilologus* 34.104–12.

Lutz, Angelika. 1981. *Die Version G der angelsächsischen Chronik: Rekonstruktion und Edition*. Munich: W. Fink.

Magennis, Hugh. 1992. "Images of Laughter in Old English Poetry, with Particular Reference to the 'hleahtor wera' of *The Seafarer*." *ES* 73.193–204.

Magoun, F. P., Jr. 1955. "Bede's Story of Cædman: The Case History of an Anglo-Saxon Oral Singer." *Speculum* 30.49–63.

Malone, Kemp. 1933. *Deor*. London: Methuen. Rev. ed. 1977, Exeter: Univ. of Exeter Press.

————. 1939. "Becca and Seafola." *EStn* 73.180–84. Rpt. in Malone 1959: 164–67.

————. 1959. *Studies in Heroic Legend and in Current Speech*. Ed. Stefán Einarsson and Norman E. Eliason. Copenhagen: Rosenkilde & Bagger.

————. 1961. "Cædmon and English Poetry." *MLN* 76.193–95.

Mandel, Jerome. 1971. "Contrast in Old English Poetry." *Chaucer Review* 6.1–13.

————. 1977. "Exemplum and Refrain: The Meaning of *Deor*." *YES* 7.1–9.

————. 1987. *Alternative Readings in Old English Poetry*. New York: Lang.

Marquardt, Hertha. 1938. *Die altenglische Kenningar*. Halle: M. Niemeyer.

McEntire, Sandra. 1986. "The Devotional Context of the Cross before A.D. 1000." In *Sources of Anglo-Saxon Culture*, ed. Paul E. Szarmach, 345–56. Studies in Medieval Culture 20. Kalamazoo: Medieval Institute Publications, Western Michigan Univ.

Miller, Thomas, ed. 1890–99. *The Old English Version of Bede's Ecclesiastical History of the English People*. EETS o.s. 95, 96, 110, 111. London: N. Trübner. Rpt. 1959 (Part I, text and translation) and 1963 (Part II, collation of the MSS). London: Oxford Univ. Press.

Millns, Tony. 1977. "*The Wanderer* 98: 'Weal wundrum heah wyrmlicum fah'." *RES* n.s. 28.431–38.

Mitchell, Bruce. 1968. "Some Syntactical Problems in *The Wanderer*." *NM* 69.172–98. Rpt. in Mitchell 1988: 99–117.

————. 1969. "Postscript on Bede's *Mihi Cantare Habes.*" *NM* 70. 369–80. Rpt. in Mitchell 1988: 73–81.

————. 1980. "The Dangers of Disguise: Old English Texts in Modern Punctuation." *RES* n.s. 31.385–413. Rpt. in Mitchell 1988: 172–202.

————. 1985a. "*Cædmon's Hymn,* Line 1: What Is the Subject of *scylun* or Its Variants?" *LSE* n.s. 16.190–97. Rpt. in Mitchell 1988: 88–95.

————. 1985b. *Old English Syntax.* 2 vols. Oxford: Clarendon.

————. 1985c. "The Syntax of *The Seafarer,* Lines 50–52." *RES* n.s. 36. 535–37. Rpt. in Mitchell 1988: 203–6.

————. 1988. *On Old English: Selected Papers.* Oxford: B. Blackwell.

Mitchell, Bruce, and Fred C. Robinson. 1992. *A Guide to Old English.* 5th ed. Oxford: B. Blackwell.

Mohr, Wolfgang. 1933. *Kenningstudien: Beiträge zur Stilgeschichte der altgermanischen Dichtung.* Stuttgart: V. Kohlhammer.

Momma, H. 1997. *The Composition of Old English Poetry.* Cambridge Studies in Anglo-Saxon England 20. Cambridge: Cambridge Univ. Press.

Morris, R., ed. 1874–80. *The Blickling Homilies.* EETS o.s. 58, 63, 73. Rpt. 1967 as one volume, London: Oxford Univ. Press.

Muir, Bernard J., ed. 1994. *The Exeter Anthology of Old English Poetry.* 2 vols. Exeter: Univ. of Exeter Press.

Neckel, Gustav, and Hans Kuhn, eds. 1983. *Edda: Die Lieder des Codex Regius.* Heidelberg: C. Winter.

Niles, John D. 1987. "Skaldic Technique in *Brunanburh.*" *SS* 59.356–66.

————, ed. 1991. "Part One: History into Literature." *Mediaevalia* 17.1–176.

Norman, F. 1937. "'Deor': A Criticism and an Interpretation." *MLR* 32.374–81.

————. 1937–38. "*Deor* and Modern Scandinavian Ballads." *London Mediaeval Studies* 1.165–78.

North, Richard. 1991. "Getting to Know the General in *The Battle of Maldon.*" *MÆ* 60.1–15.

O'Brien O'Keeffe, Katherine. 1990. *Visible Song: Transitional Literacy in Old English Verse.* Cambridge Studies in Anglo-Saxon England 4. Cambridge: Cambridge Univ. Press.

————. 1991. "Heroic Values and Christian Ethics." In Godden and Lapidge 1991: 107–25.

————, ed. 1994. *Old English Shorter Poems: Basic Readings.* New York: Garland.

————, ed. 1997. *Reading Old English Texts.* Cambridge: Cambridge Univ. Press.

Obst, Wolfgang. 1987. *Der Rhythmus des 'Beowulf': Eine Akzent- und Takttheorie.* Anglistische Forschungen 187. Heidelberg: C. Winter.

Ogawa, Hiroshi. 1989. *Old English Modal Verbs: A Syntactical Study.* Anglistica 26. Copenhagen: Rosenkilde & Bagger.

Orchard, Andy. 1996. "Poetic Inspiration and Prosaic Translation: The Making of *Cædmon's Hymn.*" In Toswell and Tyler 1996: 402–22.

Orton, Peter R. 1980. "The Technique of Object Personification in *The Dream of the Rood* and Comparison with the Old English *Riddles*." *LSE* n.s. 11 (1980 for 1979), 1–18.

————. 1982a. "*The Seafarer* 58–64a." *Neophilologus* 66.450–59.

————. 1982b. "*The Seafarer* 6b–10a and 18–22." *NM* 83.255–59.

Paetzel, Walther. 1913. *Die Variationen in der altgermanischen Alliterationspoesie*. Palaestra 48. Berlin: Mayer & Müller.

Pasternack, Carol Braun. 1984. "Stylistic Disjunctions in *The Dream of the Rood*." *ASE* 13.167–86.

Patch, Howard R. 1919. "Liturgical Influence in *The Dream of the Rood*." *PMLA* 34.233–57.

Pheifer, J. D. 1965. "*The Seafarer* 53–55." *RES* n.s. 16.282–84.

Plummer, Charles, and John Earle, eds. 1892–99. *Two of the Saxon Chronicles Parallel*. 2 vols. Oxford: Clarendon. Rpt. 1952 with two notes by Dorothy Whitelock.

Pokorny, Julius. 1959. *Indogermanisches etymologisches Wörterbuch*. 2 vols. Bern: A. Francke.

Pope, John C. 1942. *The Rhythm of 'Beowulf'*. [2nd ed. 1966.] New Haven: Yale Univ. Press.

————. 1965. "Dramatic Voices in *The Wanderer* and *The Seafarer*." In *Franciplegius: Medieval and Linguistic Studies in Honor of Francis Peabody Magoun, Jr.,* ed. Jess B. Bessinger, Jr., and Robert P. Creed, 164–93. Rpt. in Bessinger and Kahrl 1968: 533–70; and Stevens and Mandel 1968: 163–97.

————. 1974. "Second Thoughts on the Interpretation of *The Seafarer*." *ASE* 3.75–86. Rpt. in O'Brien O'Keeffe 1994: 213–29.

————. 1978. "Palaeography and Poetry: Some Solved and Unsolved Problems of the Exeter Book." In *Medieval Scribes, Manuscripts, and Libraries: Essays Presented to N. R. Ker,* ed. M. B. Parkes and Andrew G. Watson, 25–65. London: Scolar.

————. 1993. "Offa in *The Battle of Maldon*." In Damico and Leyerle 1993: 1–27.

————. 1995. "A Supposed Crux: Old English *apolwarum* in *Maxims I*." *MP* 93.204–13.

Pulsiano, Phillip. 1997. "'Danish Men's Words Are Worse than Murder': Viking Guile and *The Battle of Maldon*." *JEGP* 96.13–25.

Raby, F. J. E., ed. 1959. *Oxford Book of Medieval Latin Verse*. Oxford: Clarendon.

Richman, Gerald. 1982. "Speaker and Speech Boundaries in *The Wanderer*." *JEGP* 81.469–79.

Rieger, Max. 1869. "Der *Seefahrer* als Dialog hergestellt." *ZfdPh* 1.334–39.

————. 1876. "Die alt- und angelsächsische Verskunst." *ZfdPh* 7.1–64. Also pub. in a separate volume as an offprint, Halle: Waisenhaus.

Ringler, Richard N. 1966. "*Him sēo wēn gelēah:* The Design for Irony in Grendel's Last Visit to Heorot." *Speculum* 41.49–67. Rpt. in Fulk 1991: 127–45.

Robinson, Fred C. 1976. "Some Aspects of the *Maldon* Poet's Artistry." *JEGP* 75.25–40. Rpt. in Robinson 1993c: 122–37.

————. 1985. *'Beowulf' and the Appositive Style.* Knoxville: Univ. of Tennessee Press.

————. 1991. "A Metronymic in *The Battle of Maldon*?" In *Essays in Honor of Edward B. King,* ed. Robert G. Benson and Eric W. Naylor, 239–43. Sewanee, TN: Univ. of the South. Rpt. in Robinson 1993c: 170–74.

————. 1993a. "The Accentuation of *Nū* in *Cædmon's Hymn.*" In Damico and Leyerle 1993: 115–20.

————. 1993b. "Another Eighteenth-Century Transcription of *Maldon*?" In *The Centre and Its Compass: Studies in Medieval Literature in Honor of Professor John Leyerle,* ed. Robert A. Taylor et al., 407–15. Studies in Medieval Culture 33. Kalamazoo: Medieval Institute Publications, Western Michigan Univ.

————. 1993c. *'The Tomb of Beowulf' and Other Essays on Old English.* Oxford: B. Blackwell.

Robinson, Fred C., and E. G. Stanley, eds. 1991. *Old English Verse Texts from Many Sources.* Early English Manuscripts in Facsimile 23. Copenhagen: Rosenkilde & Bagger.

Rogers, H. L. 1985. "*The Battle of Maldon:* David Casley's Transcript." *N&Q* 230 (n.s. 32), 147–55.

Russom, Geoffrey. 1987. *Old English Meter and Linguistic Theory.* Cambridge: Cambridge Univ. Press.

————. 1998. *'Beowulf' and Old Germanic Metre.* Cambridge: Cambridge Univ. Press.

Rypins, Stanley, ed. 1924. *Three Old English Prose Texts in MS. Cotton Vitellius A xv.* EETS o.s. 161. London: Oxford Univ. Press.

Samouce, Warren A. 1963. "General Byrhtnoth." *JEGP* 62.129–35.

Sawyer, P. H. 1968. *Anglo-Saxon Charters: An Annotated List and Bibliography.* London: Royal Historical Society.

Sayers, William. 1996. "The Etymology and Semantics of Old Norse *knǫrr* 'cargo ship': The Irish and English Evidence." *SS* 68.279–90.

Schabram, Hans. 1965. *Superbia: Studien zum altenglischen Wortschatz, I.* Munich: W. Fink.

Schlauch, Margaret. 1940. "The 'Dream of the Rood' as Prosopopoeia." In *Essays and Studies in Honor of Carleton Brown,* 23–34. London: Oxford Univ. Press; New York: New York Univ. Press. Rpt. in Bessinger and Kahrl 1968: 428–41.

Schröer, Arnold. 1882. "The Grave." *Anglia* 5.289–90.

Schücking, Levin L. 1906. "Das angelsächische Gedicht von der 'Klage der Frau'." *Zeitschrift für deutsches Altertum und deutsche Literatur* 48.436–49.

Scragg, Donald G., ed. 1981. *The Battle of Maldon.* Manchester: Manchester Univ. Press.

————, ed. 1991a. *The Battle of Maldon, AD 991.* Oxford: B. Blackwell.

—————. 1991b. *"The Battle of Maldon."* In Scragg 1991a: 1–36.

—————. 1991c. "The Nature of Old English Verse." In Godden and Lapidge 1991: 55–70.

—————. 1993. *"The Battle of Maldon:* Fact or Fiction?" In Cooper 1993: 19–31.

Sedgefield, Walter John, ed. 1899. *King Alfred's Old English Version of Boethius 'De consolatio philosophiae'.* Oxford: Clarendon. Rpt. 1968, Darmstadt: Wissenschaftliche Buchgesellschaft.

—————. 1922. *An Anglo-Saxon Verse Book.* Manchester: Manchester Univ. Press.

Shepherd, Geoffrey. 1954. "The Prophetic Cædmon." *RES* n.s. 5.113–22.

Shippey, T. A. 1972. *Old English Verse.* London: Hutchinson.

—————. 1994. *"The Wanderer* and *The Seafarer* as Wisdom Poetry." In Aertsen and Bremmer 1994: 145–58.

Sievers, Eduard. 1885–87. "Zur Rhythmik des germanischen Alliterationsverses." *PBB* 10.209–314, 451–545; 12.454–82.

—————. 1893. *Altgermanische Metrik.* Halle: M. Niemeyer.

—————. 1905. "Altgermanische Metrik." In *Grundriß der germanischen Philologie,* ed. Hermann Paul. Vol. 2, pt. 2, 1–38. 2nd ed. Strassburg: K. Trübner.

—————. 1968. "Old Germanic Metrics and Old English Metrics." Trans. Gawaina D. Luster. In Bessinger and Kahrl 1968: 267–88. [A translation of parts of Sievers 1905.]

Sisam, Celia, ed. 1976. *The Vercelli Book.* Early English Manuscripts in Facsimile 19. Copenhagen: Rosenkilde & Bagger.

Sisam, Kenneth. 1912–13. "To *Seafarer* ll. 72 ff." *EStn* 46.336.

—————. 1945. *"Seafarer,* Lines 97–102." *RES* 21.316–17.

Smith, A. H., ed. 1933. *Three Northumbrian Poems: Cædmon's Hymn, Bede's Death Song, and the Leiden Riddle.* Rev. rpt. 1978 with a bibliography compiled by M. J. Swanton. Exeter: Univ. of Exeter.

Smithers, G. V. 1957–59. "The Meaning of *The Seafarer* and *The Wanderer."* *MÆ* 26.137–53; 28.1–22, 99–104.

Smol, Anna. 1994. "Things Speaking and Speech 'Thinging': Riddlic Voices and *The Seafarer." English Studies in Canada* 20.249–65.

Stanley, Eric Gerald. 1993. "Ἀπὸ κοινοῦ, Chiefly in *Beowulf."* In *Anglo-Saxonica: Beiträge zur Vor- und Frühgeschichte der englischen Sprache,* ed. Klaus R. Grinda and Claus-Dieter Wetzel, 181–207. Munich: W. Fink.

Stenton, F. M. 1971. *Anglo-Saxon England.* 3rd ed. Oxford: Clarendon.

Stephens, George. 1866. *The Old-Northern Runic Monuments of Scandinavia and England.* Vol. 1. London: J. Smith; Copenhagen: Michaelsen & Tillge.

Stevens, Martin, and Jerome Mandel, eds. 1968. *Old English Literature: Twenty-Two Analytical Essays.* Lincoln: Univ. of Nebraska Press.

Stockwell, Robert P., and Donka Minkova. 1997. "Prosody." In *A 'Beowulf' Handbook,* ed. Robert E. Bjork and John D. Niles, 55–83. Lincoln: Univ. of Nebraska Press.

Storch, Theodor. 1886. *Angelsächsische Nominalcomposita.* Strassburg: K. Trübner.

Suzuki, Seiichi. 1996. *The Metrical Organization of 'Beowulf': Prototype and Isomophism.* Berlin: Mouton de Gruyter.

Swanton, Michael, ed. 1970. *The Dream of the Rood.* Manchester: Manchester Univ. Press; New York: Barnes & Noble. New ed. 1996, Exeter: Univ. of Exeter Press.

Sweet, Henry, ed. 1871. *King Alfred's West-Saxon Version of Gregory's Pastoral Care.* 2 vols. EETS o.s. 45, 50. London: Oxford Univ. Press. Rpt. 1988, Millwood, NY: Kraus Rpt.

Szarmach, Paul E. 1993. "The (Sub-) Genre of *The Battle of Maldon.*" In Cooper 1993: 43–61.

Terasawa, Jun. 1994. *Nominal Compounds in Old English: A Metrical Approach.* Anglistica 27. Copenhagen: Rosenkilde & Bagger.

Thorpe, Benjamin, ed. 1842. *Codex Exoniensis.* London: Society of Antiquaries.

————, ed. 1861. *The Anglo-Saxon Chronicle.* Rerum Britannicarum medii aevi scriptores 23. London: Longman.

Timmer, Benno J. 1942. "Irony in Old English Poetry." *ES* 24.171–75.

Tolkien, J. R. R. 1953. "The Homecoming of Beorhtnoth, Beorhthelm's Son." *Essays and Studies* n.s. 6.1–18.

Toswell, M. J. 1996. "Tacitus, Old English Heroic Poetry, and Ethnographic Preconceptions." In Toswell and Tyler 1996: 493–507.

Toswell, M. J., and E. M. Tyler, eds. 1996. *Studies in English Language and Literature: 'Doubt Wisely': Papers in Honour of E. G. Stanley.* London: Routledge.

Viebrock, H., and W. Erzgräber, eds. 1961. *Festschrift zum 75. Geburtstag von Theodor Spira.* Heidelberg: C. Winter.

Vogüé, Adalbert de, ed. 1979. *Gregoire le grand, Dialogues.* Vol. 2 (Books I–III). Sources chrétiennes 260. Paris: Cerf.

Wanley, Humphrey. 1705. *Antiquæ literaturæ Septentrionalis liber alter.* Oxford. [Vol. 2 of George Hickes's *Linguarum veterum Septentrionalium thesaurus.* Rpt. 1970, Menston: Scolar.]

Whitbread, Leslie. 1942. "The Cædmon Story: Bibliography." *N&Q* 183.224.

Whitelock, Dorothy. 1950. "The Interpretation of *The Seafarer.*" In *The Early Cultures of North-West Europe* (*H. M. Chadwick Memorial Studies*), ed. Cyril Fox and Bruce Dickins, 261–72. Rpt. in Bessinger and Kahrl 1968: 442–57; and Stevens and Mandel 1969: 198–211.

————, trans. and ed. 1961. *The Anglo-Saxon Chronicle, A Revised Translation.* With David C. Douglas and Susie I. Tucker. London: Eyre & Spottiswoode; New Brunswick, NJ: Rutgers Univ. Press.

————, ed. 1967. *Sweet's Anglo-Saxon Reader in Prose and Verse.* Rev. ed. Oxford: Clarendon.

————, ed. 1979. *English Historical Documents c. 500–1042.* 2nd ed. London: Eyre Methuen.

Wollmann, Alfred. 1996. "Scandinavian Loanwords in Old English." In *The Origins and Development of Emigrant Languages,* ed. Hans F. Nielsen and Lene Schøsler, 215–42. RASK Suppl. Vol. 6, NOWELE Suppl. Vol. 17. Odense: Odense Univ. Press.

Woolf, Rosemary. 1958. "Doctrinal Influences on *The Dream of the Rood.*" *MÆ* 27.137–53.

————. 1976. "The Ideal of Men Dying with Their Lord in the *Germania* and in *The Battle of Maldon.*" *ASE* 5.63–81.

Wrenn, C. L. 1936. Review of the first edition (1934) of Dickins and Ross 1966. *RES* 12.105–8.

————. 1946. "The Poetry of Cædmon." *PBA* 32.277–95.

Wülfing, J. Ernst. 1894–1901. *Die Syntax in den Werken Alfreds des Grossen.* 2 vols. Bonn: P. Hanstein.

Wyld, Henry Cecil. 1925. "Diction and Imagery in Anglo-Saxon Poetry." *Essays and Studies* 11.49–91.